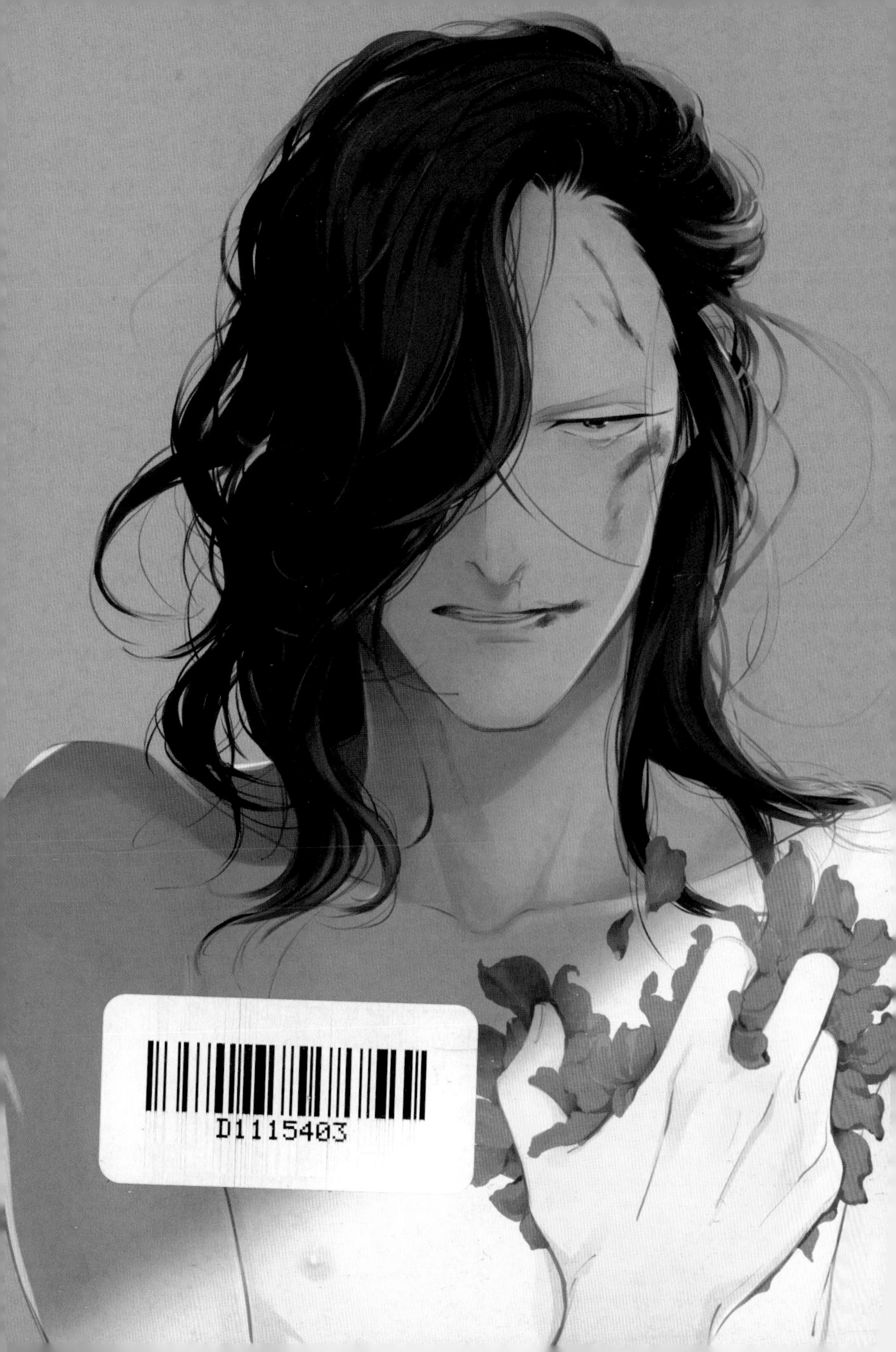

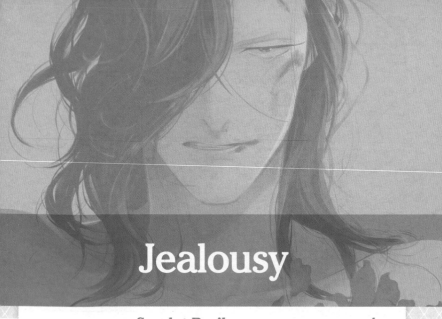

Jealousy

Story and Art by **Scarlet Beriko**
volume **4**

CONTENTS

Chapter 16 005

Chapter 17 045

Chapter 18 081

Chapter 19 123

Chapter 20 163

Chapter 21 197

Cover Behind the Scenes 223

Afterword 224

SUBLIME
SuBLime **Manga Edition**

jealousy

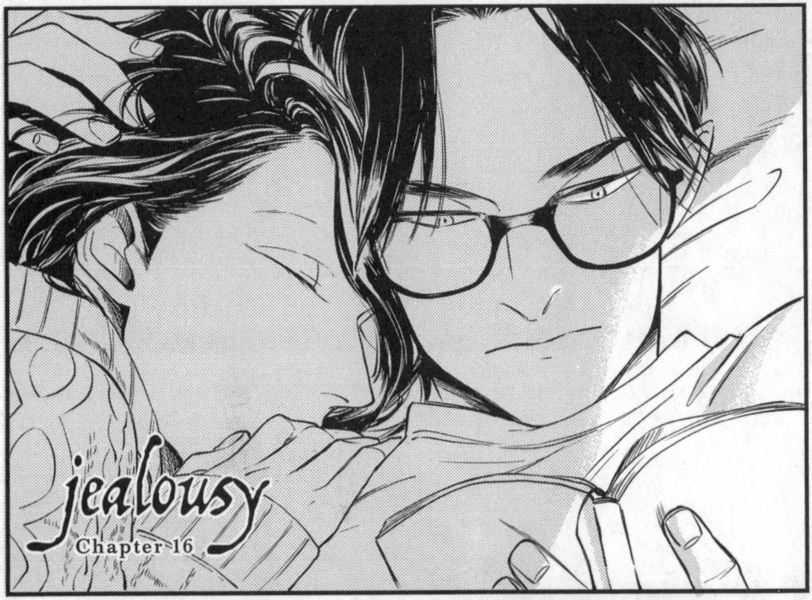
jealousy
Chapter 16
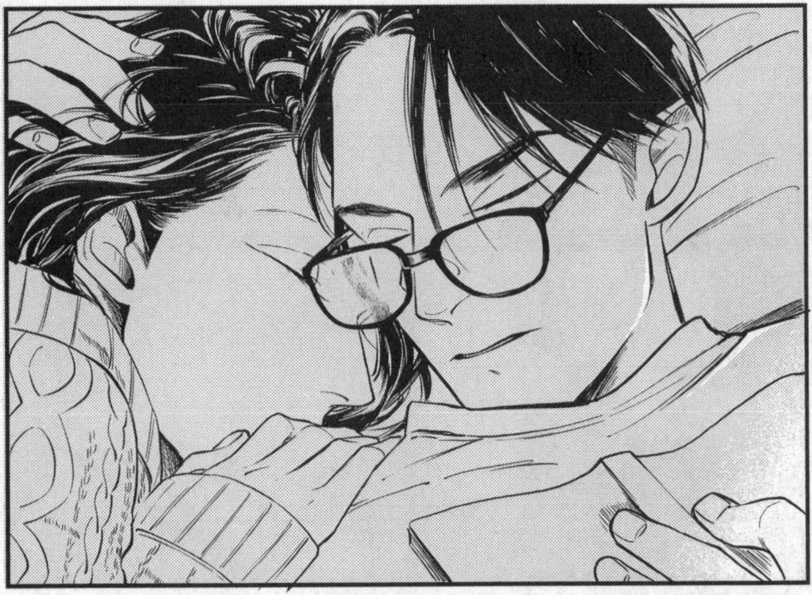

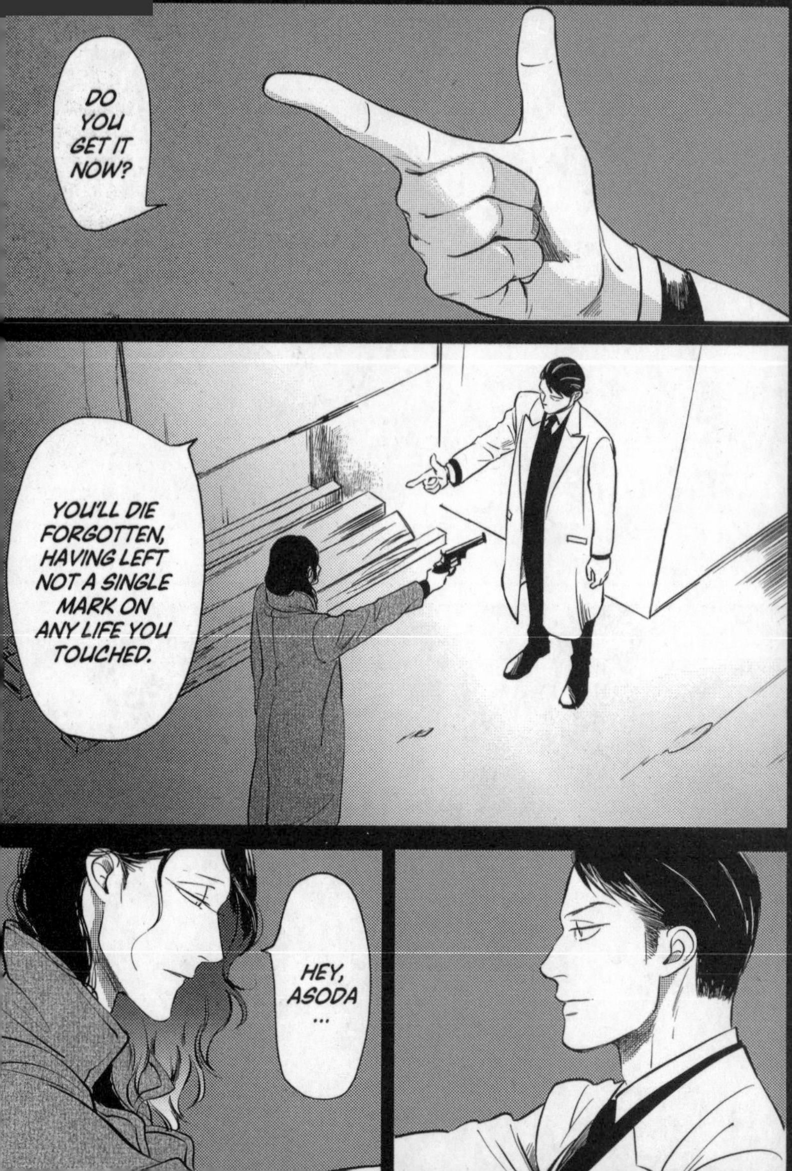
DO YOU GET IT NOW?
YOU'LL DIE FORGOTTEN, HAVING LEFT NOT A SINGLE MARK ON ANY LIFE YOU TOUCHED.
HEY, ASODA...

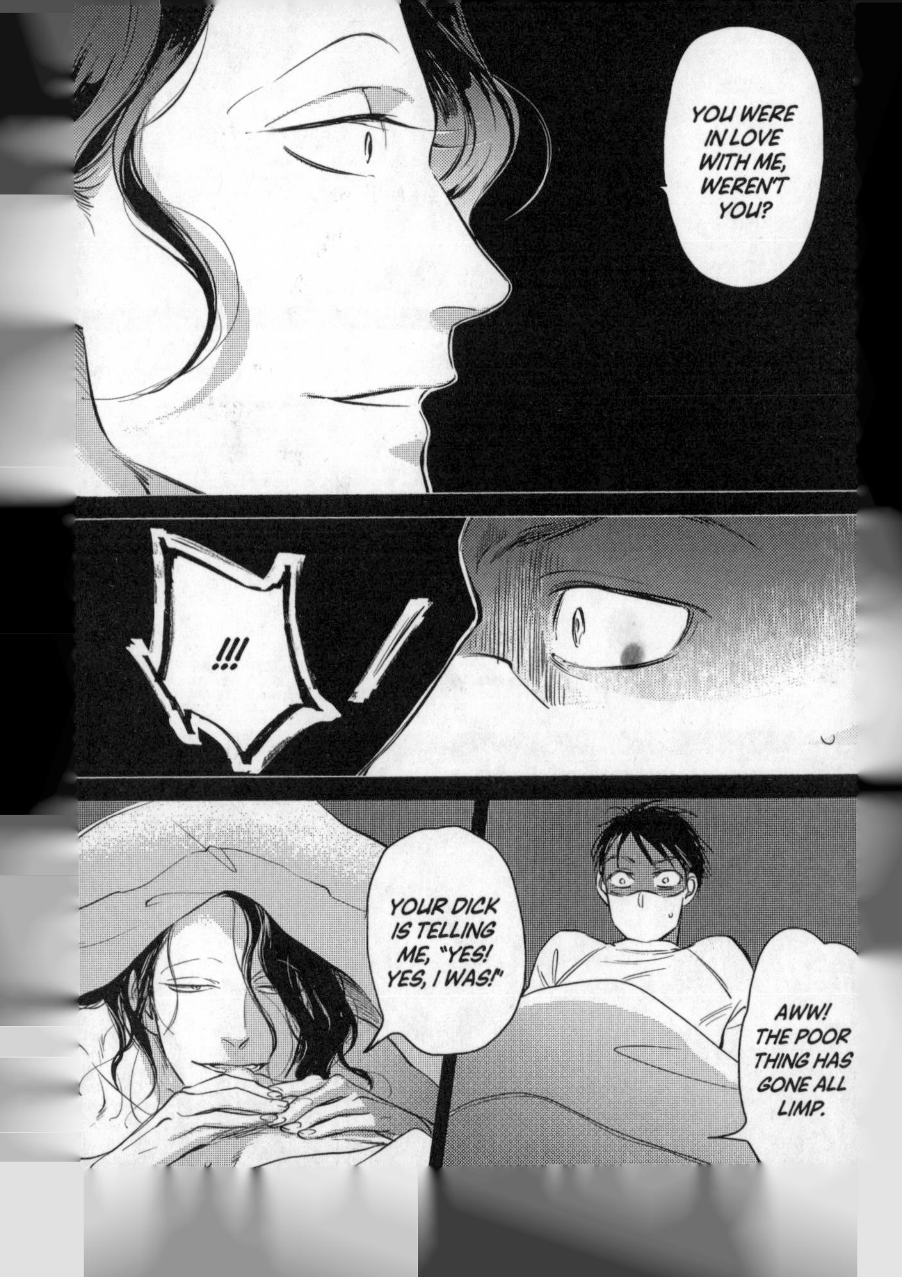
YOU WERE IN LOVE WITH ME, WEREN'T YOU?
!!!
AWW! THE POOR THING HAS GONE ALL LIMP.
YOUR DICK IS TELLING ME, "YES! YES, I WAS!"

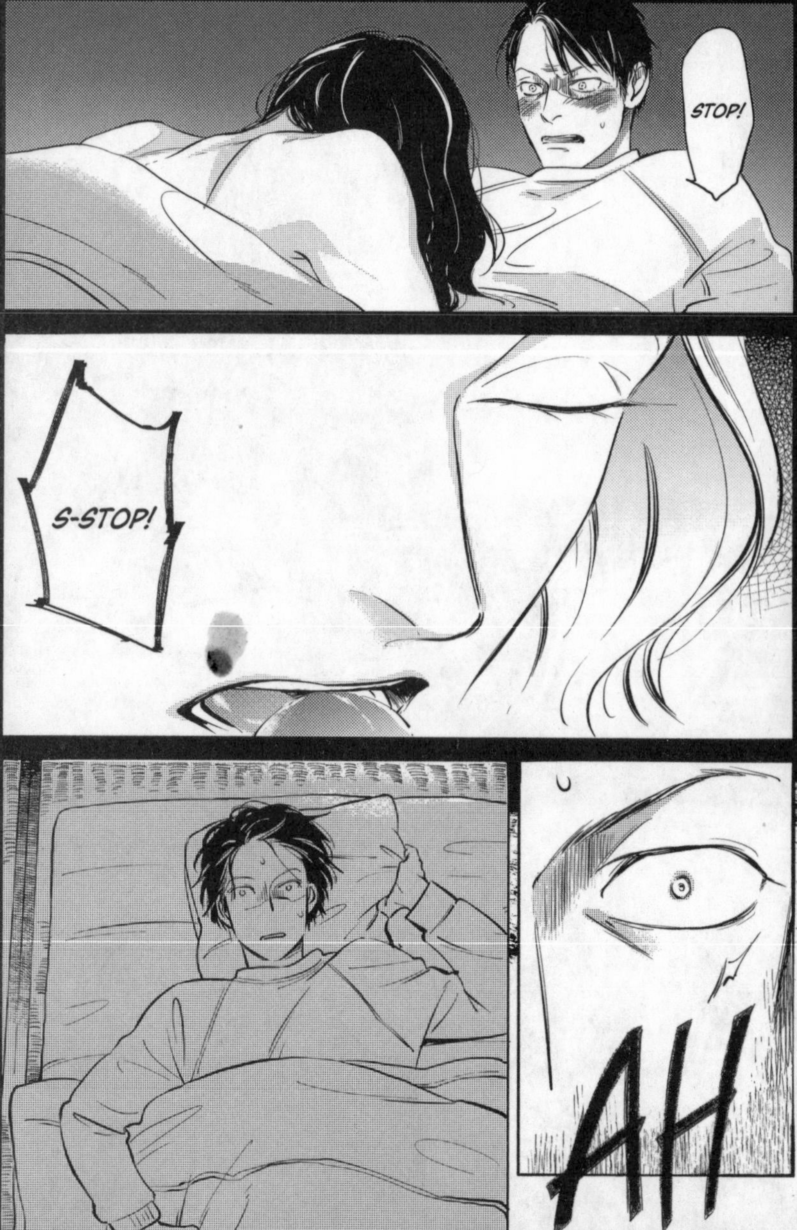
STOP!
S-STOP!
AH

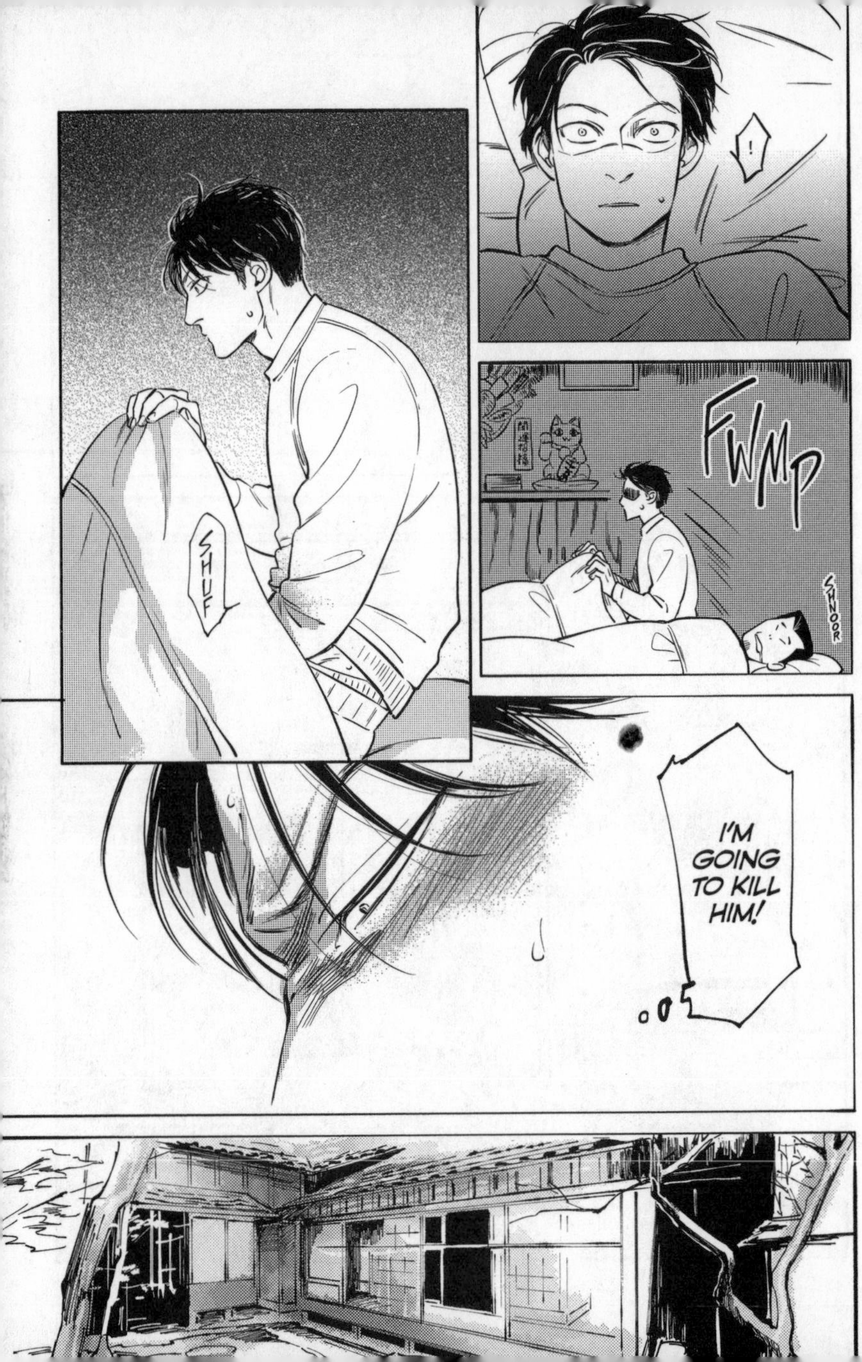
!
FWMP
SHNOOR
SHUF
I'M GOING TO KILL HIM!

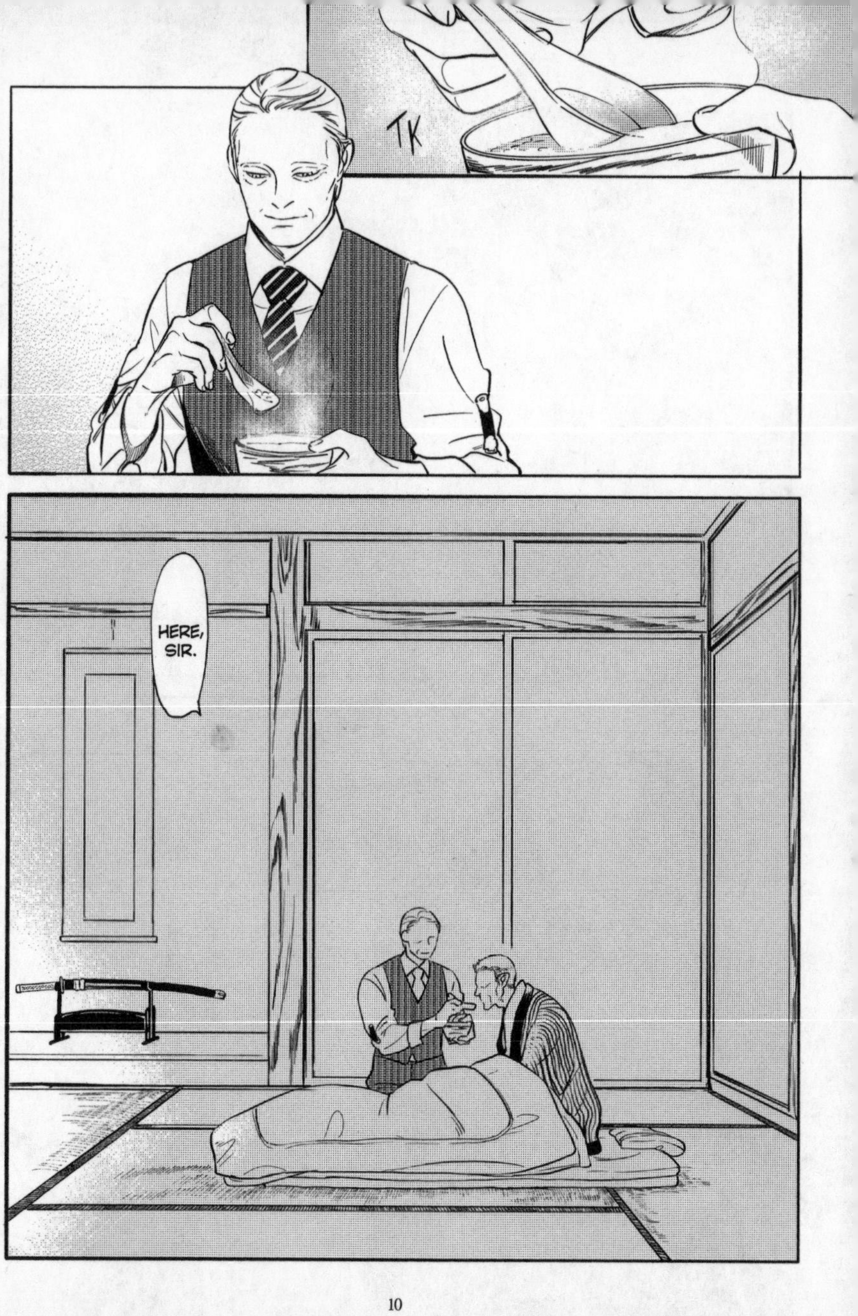
TK
HERE, SIR.

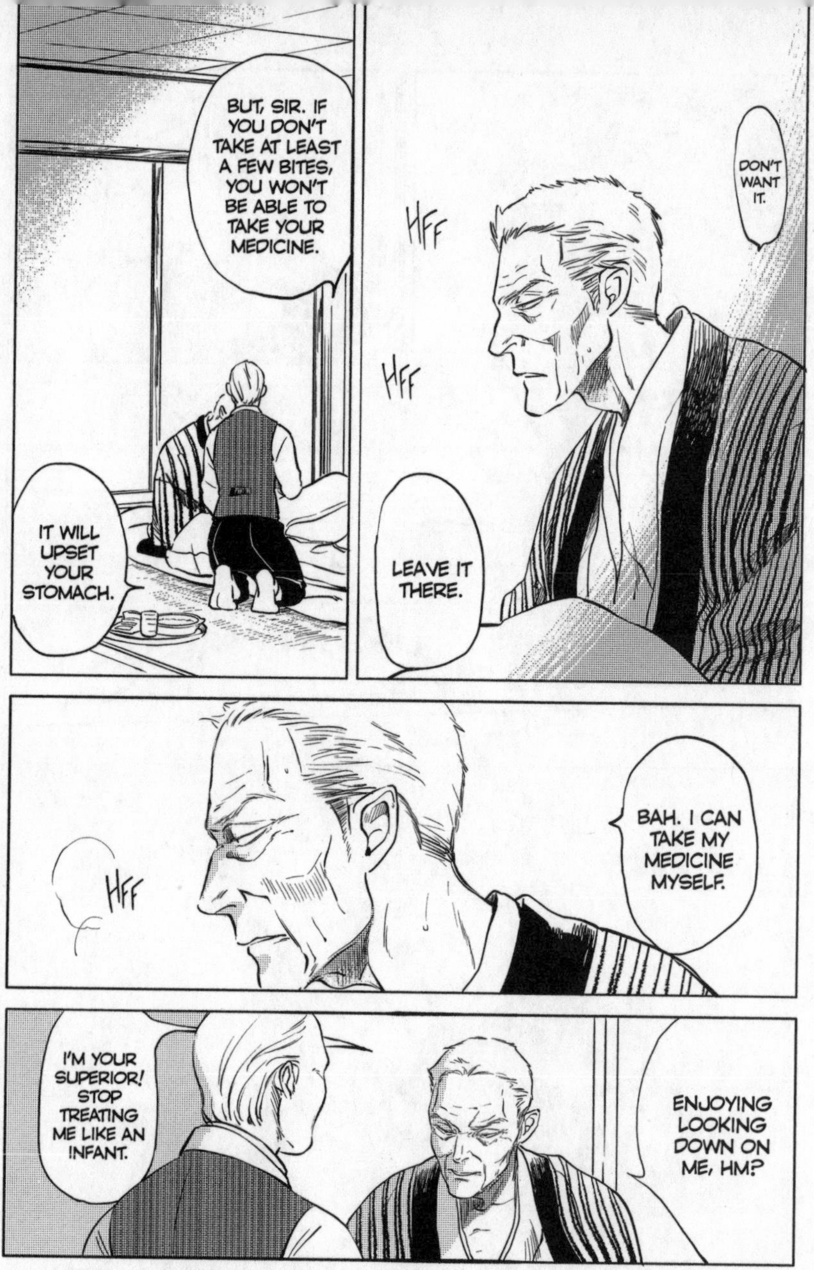
DON'T WANT IT.
HFF
HFF
LEAVE IT THERE.
BUT, SIR. IF YOU DON'T TAKE AT LEAST A FEW BITES, YOU WON'T BE ABLE TO TAKE YOUR MEDICINE.
IT WILL UPSET YOUR STOMACH.
BAH. I CAN TAKE MY MEDICINE MYSELF.
HFF
ENJOYING LOOKING DOWN ON ME, HM?
I'M YOUR SUPERIOR! STOP TREATING ME LIKE AN INFANT.

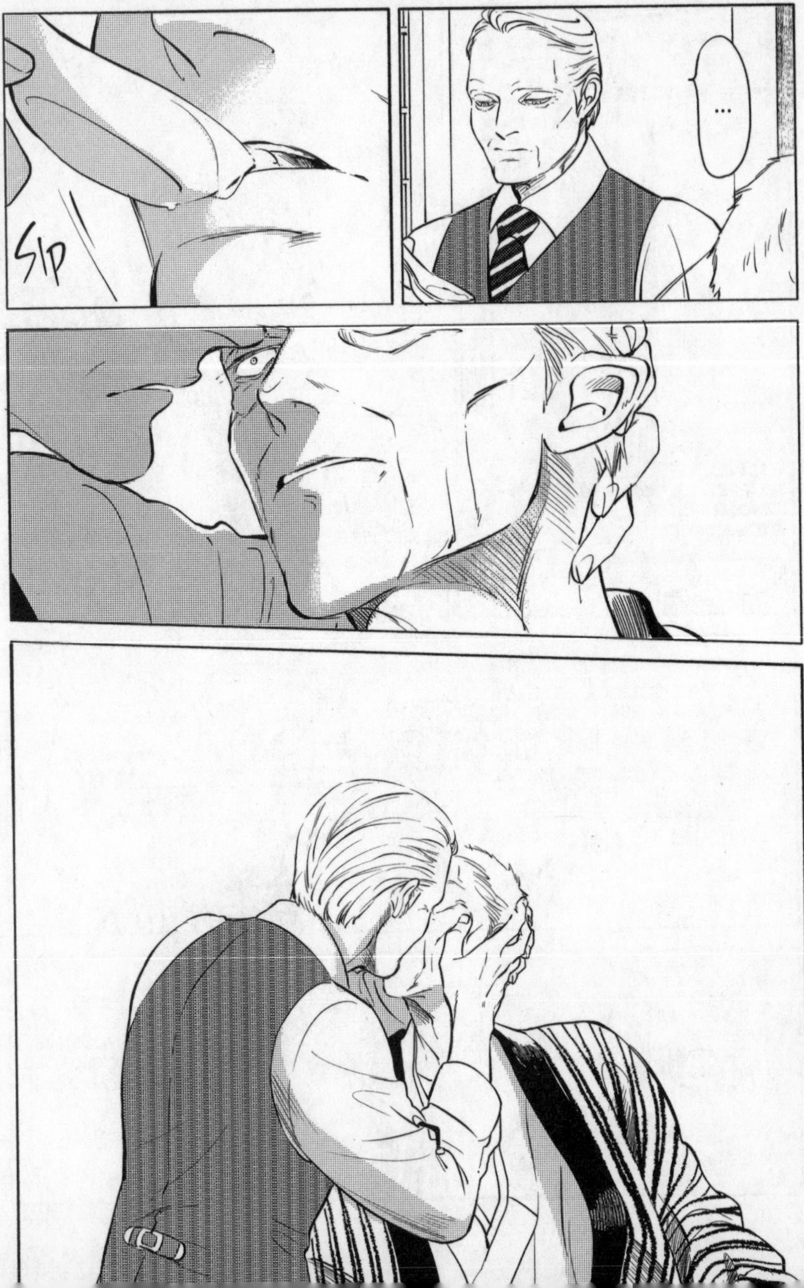
...
Slp

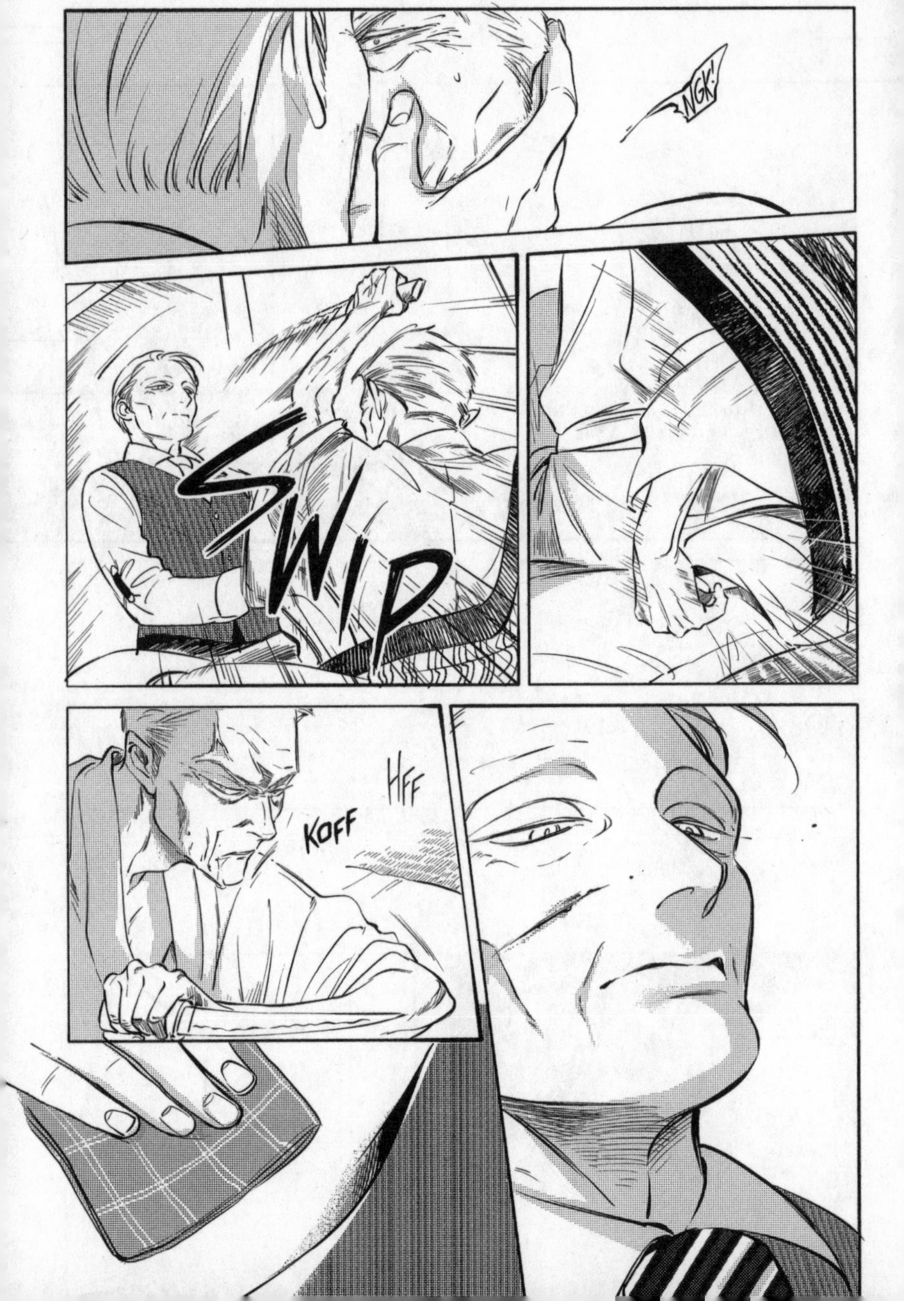
NGK!
SWIP
HFF
KOFF

YOU WILL LIVE, SIR.
NO MATTER WHAT IT TAKES.
DON'T BOTHER LYING! I HEARD EVERYTHING FROM MR. KOGA DIRECTLY!

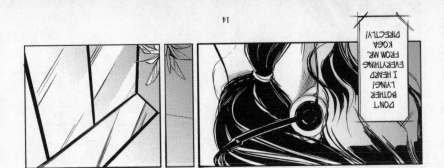

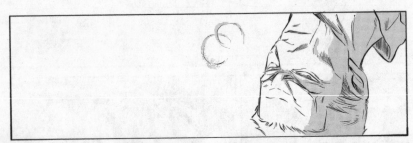

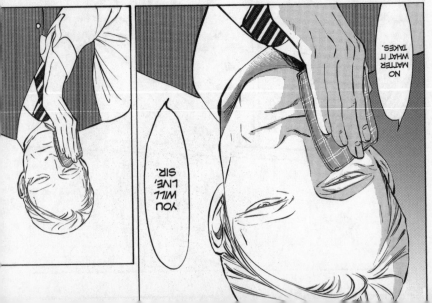

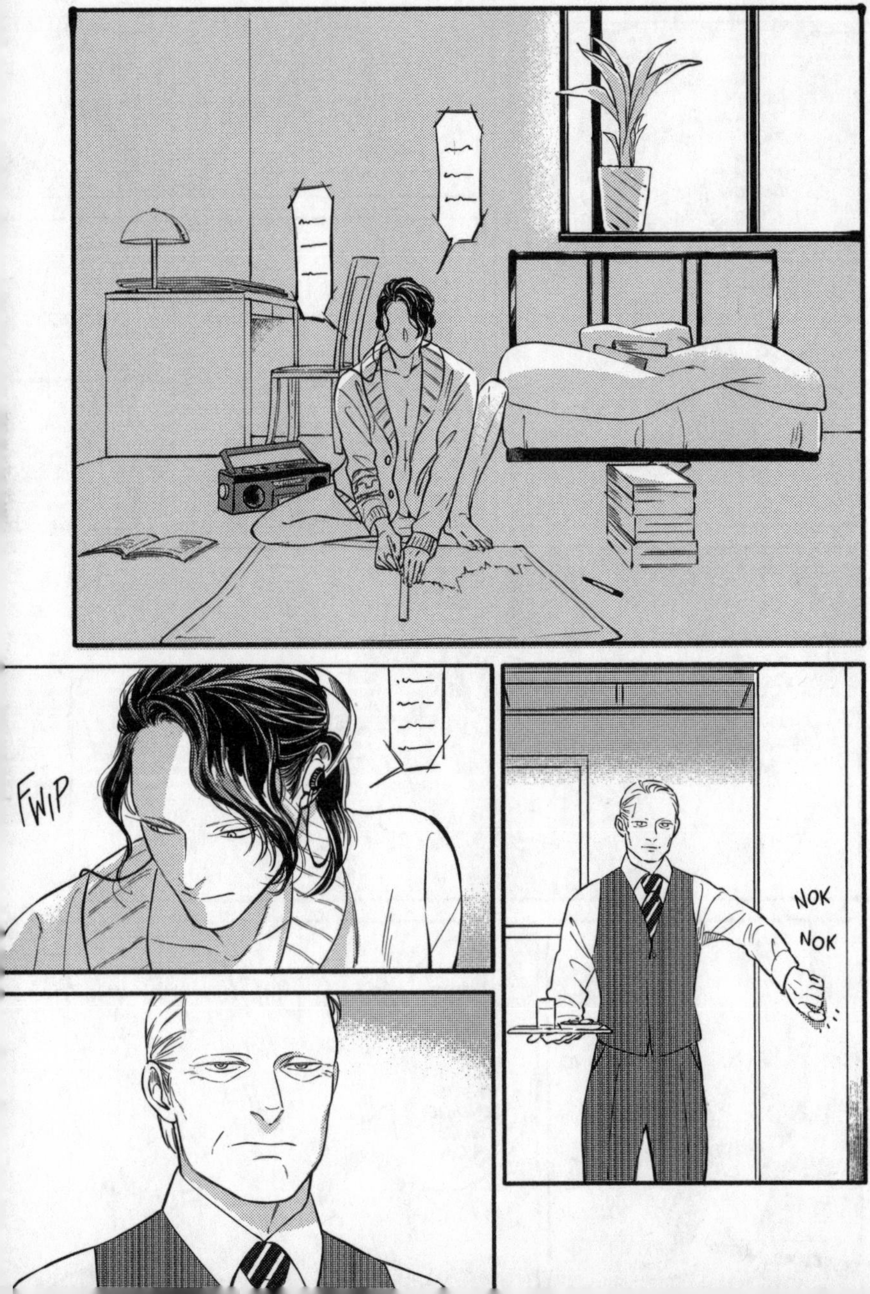
NOK
NOK
FWIP

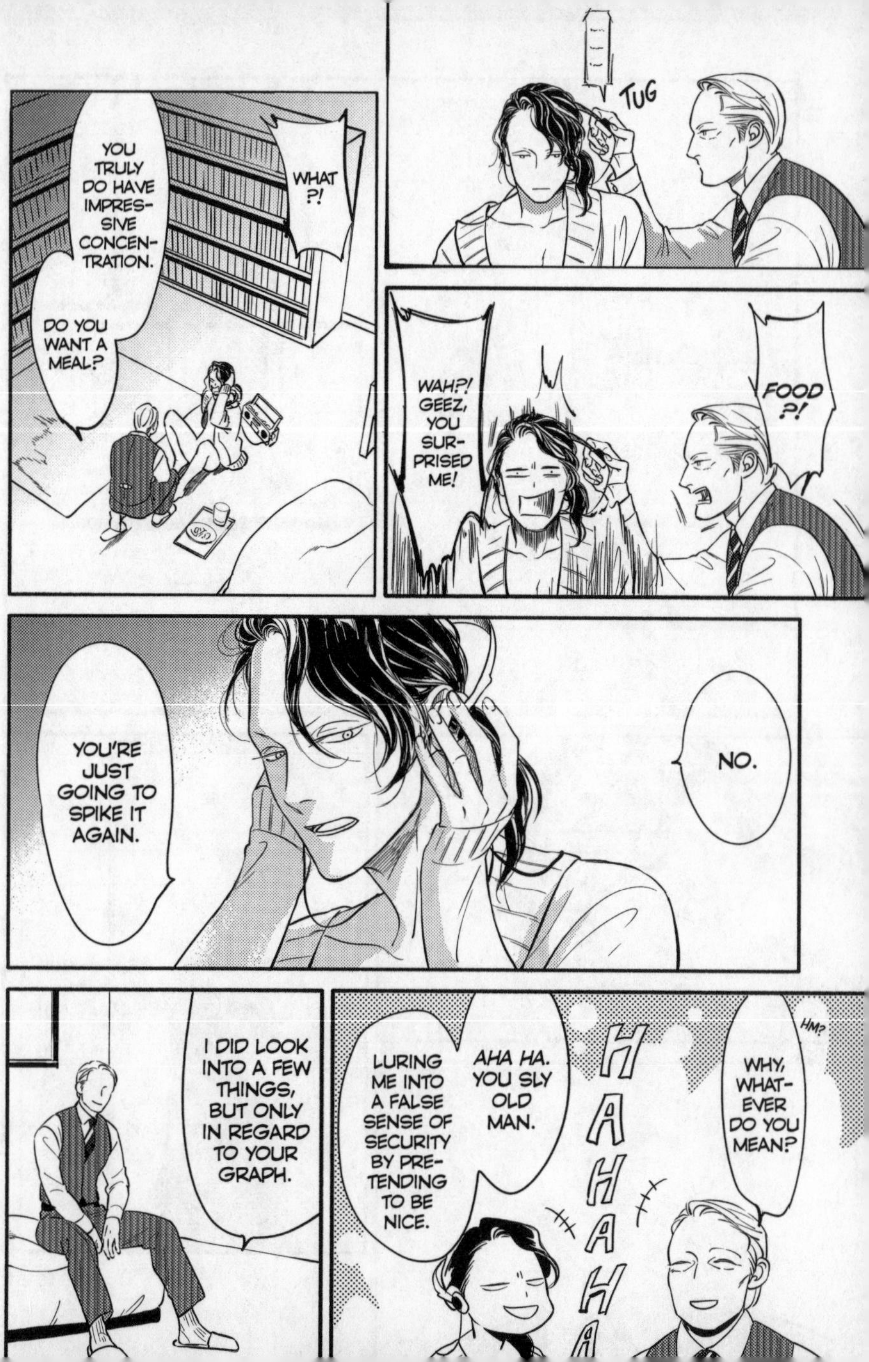
...
TUG
FOOD ?!
WAH?! GEEZ, YOU SURPRISED ME!
WHAT ?!
YOU TRULY DO HAVE IMPRESSIVE CONCENTRATION.
DO YOU WANT A MEAL?
NO.
YOU'RE JUST GOING TO SPIKE IT AGAIN.
HM?
WHY, WHATEVER DO YOU MEAN?
HAHAHA
AHA HA. YOU SLY OLD MAN.
LURING ME INTO A FALSE SENSE OF SECURITY BY PRETENDING TO BE NICE.
I DID LOOK INTO A FEW THINGS, BUT ONLY IN REGARD TO YOUR GRAPH.

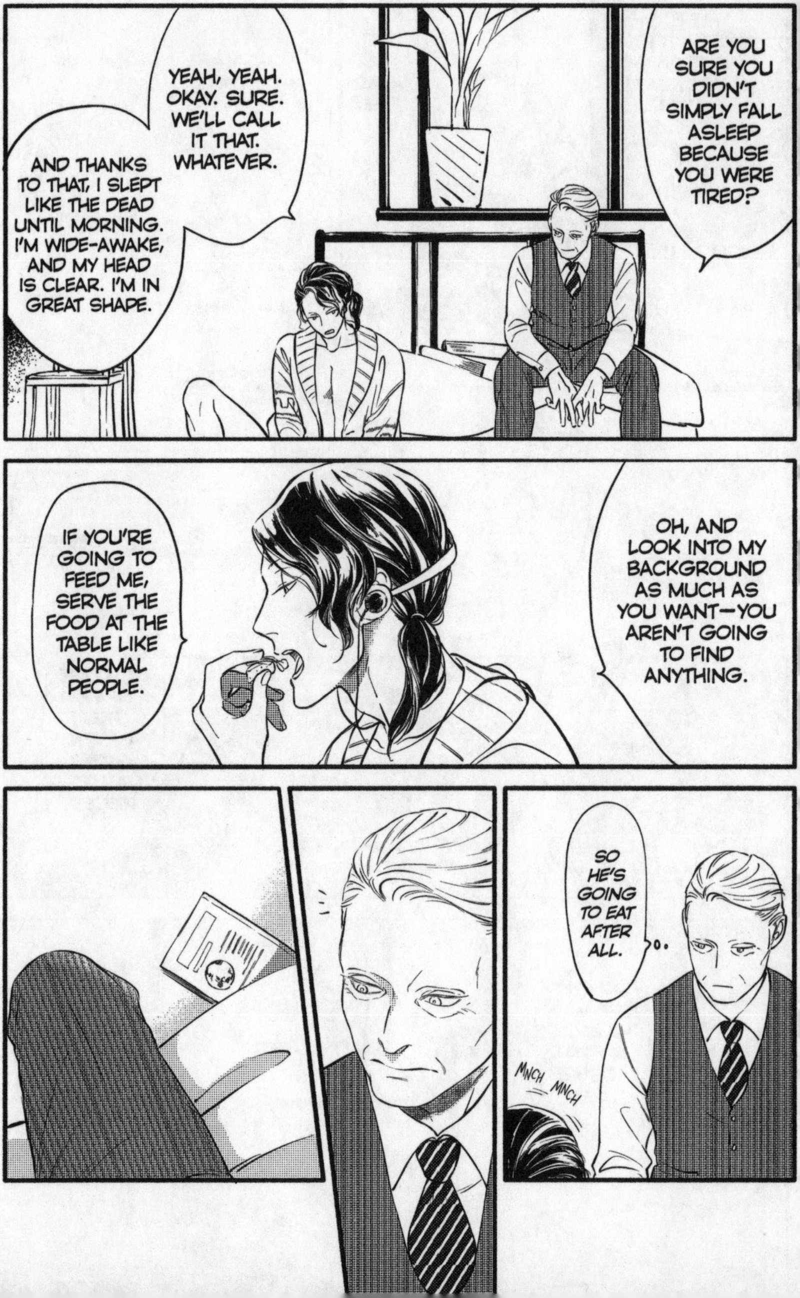
ARE YOU SURE YOU DIDN'T SIMPLY FALL ASLEEP BECAUSE YOU WERE TIRED?
YEAH, YEAH. OKAY. SURE. WE'LL CALL IT THAT. WHATEVER.
AND THANKS TO THAT, I SLEPT LIKE THE DEAD UNTIL MORNING. I'M WIDE-AWAKE, AND MY HEAD IS CLEAR. I'M IN GREAT SHAPE.
OH, AND LOOK INTO MY BACKGROUND AS MUCH AS YOU WANT—YOU AREN'T GOING TO FIND ANYTHING.
IF YOU'RE GOING TO FEED ME, SERVE THE FOOD AT THE TABLE LIKE NORMAL PEOPLE.
SO HE'S GOING TO EAT AFTER ALL.
MNCH MNCH

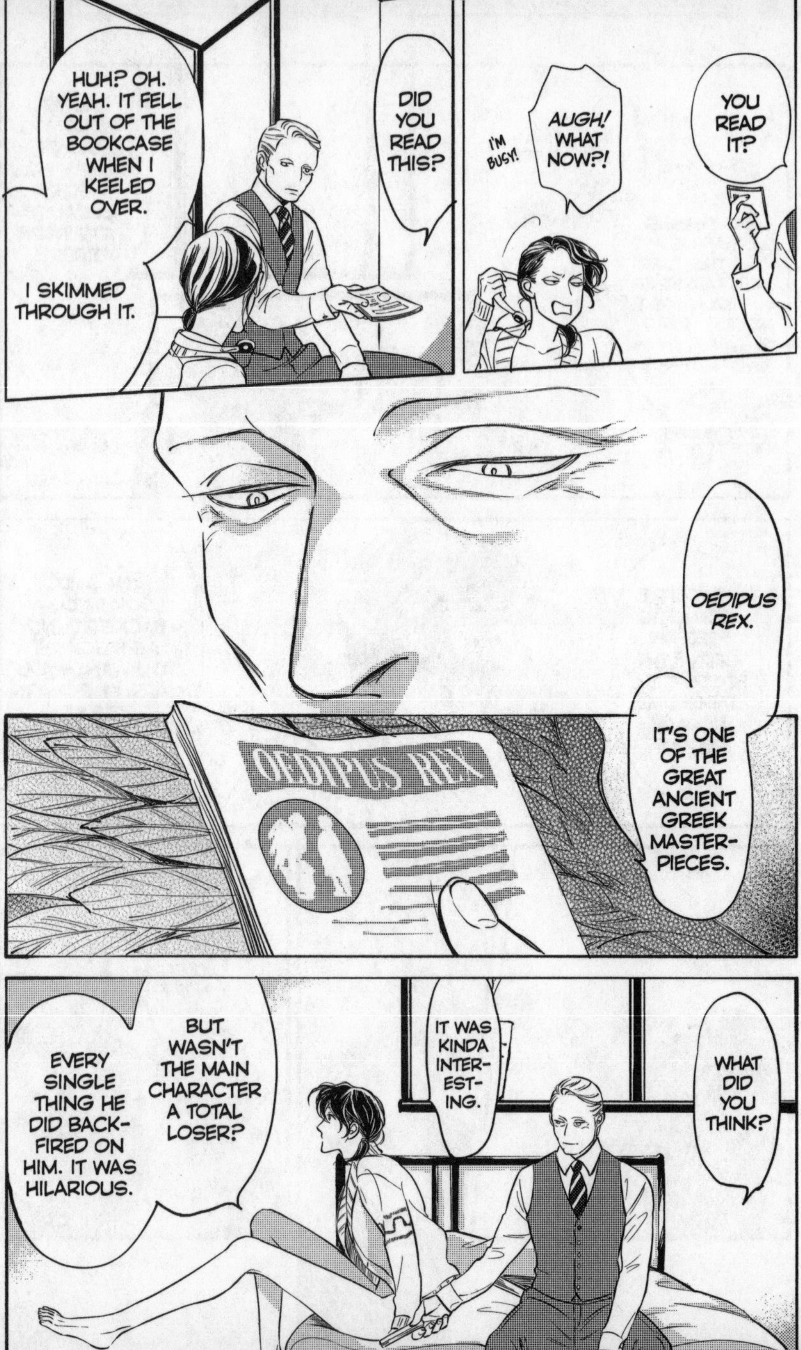
YOU READ IT?
AUGH! WHAT NOW?!
I'M BUSY!
DID YOU READ THIS?
HUH? OH. YEAH. IT FELL OUT OF THE BOOKCASE WHEN I KEELED OVER.
I SKIMMED THROUGH IT.
OEDIPUS REX.
IT'S ONE OF THE GREAT ANCIENT GREEK MASTER-PIECES.
OEDIPUS REX
WHAT DID YOU THINK?
IT WAS KINDA INTER-EST-ING.
BUT WASN'T THE MAIN CHARACTER A TOTAL LOSER?
EVERY SINGLE THING HE DID BACK-FIRED ON HIM. IT WAS HILARIOUS.

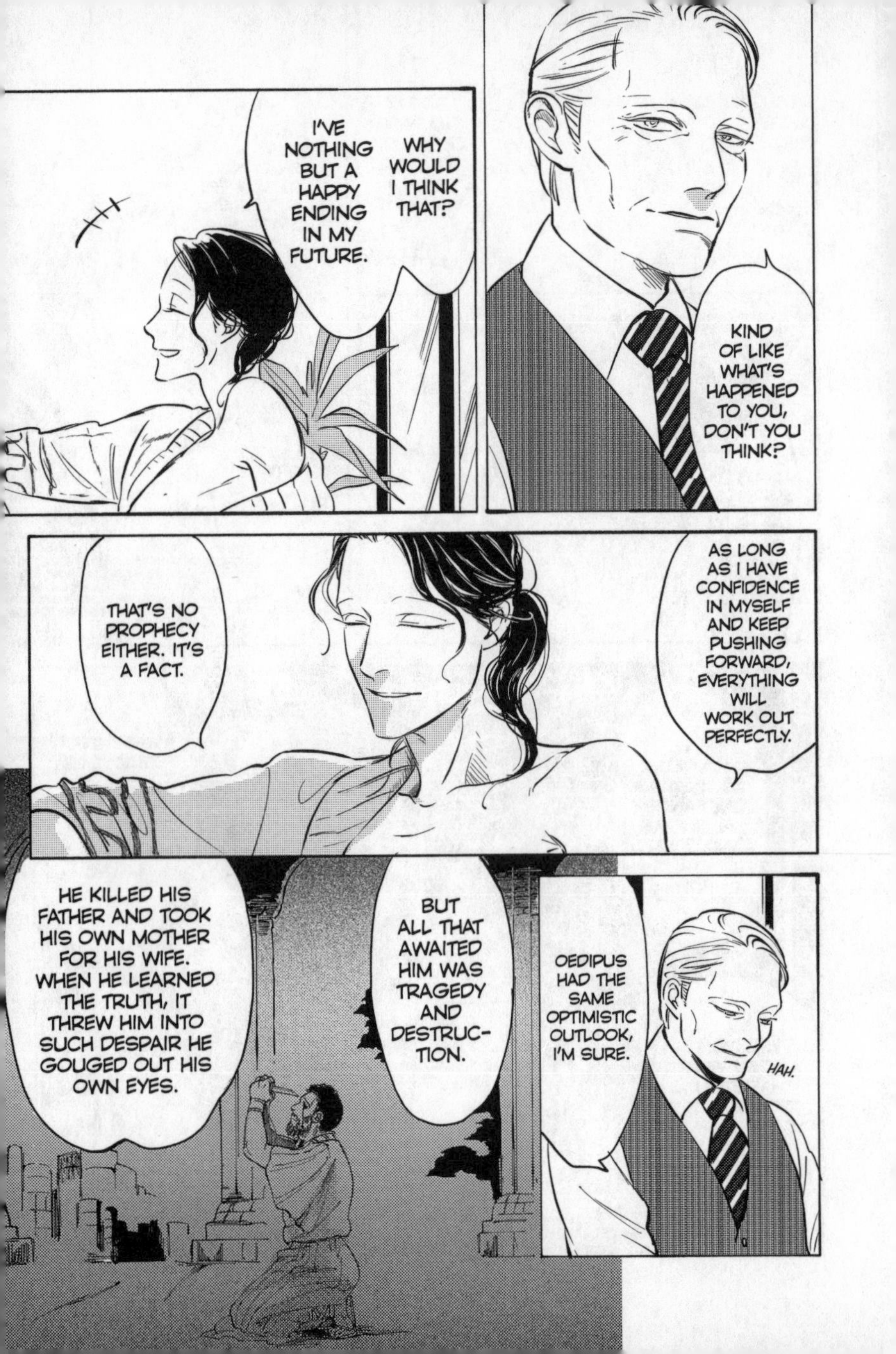
KIND OF LIKE WHAT'S HAPPENED TO YOU, DON'T YOU THINK?
WHY WOULD I THINK THAT?
I'VE NOTHING BUT A HAPPY ENDING IN MY FUTURE.
AS LONG AS I HAVE CONFIDENCE IN MYSELF AND KEEP PUSHING FORWARD, EVERYTHING WILL WORK OUT PERFECTLY.
THAT'S NO PROPHECY EITHER. IT'S A FACT.
OEDIPUS HAD THE SAME OPTIMISTIC OUTLOOK, I'M SURE.
HAH.
BUT ALL THAT AWAITED HIM WAS TRAGEDY AND DESTRUC-TION.
HE KILLED HIS FATHER AND TOOK HIS OWN MOTHER FOR HIS WIFE. WHEN HE LEARNED THE TRUTH, IT THREW HIM INTO SUCH DESPAIR HE GOUGED OUT HIS OWN EYES.

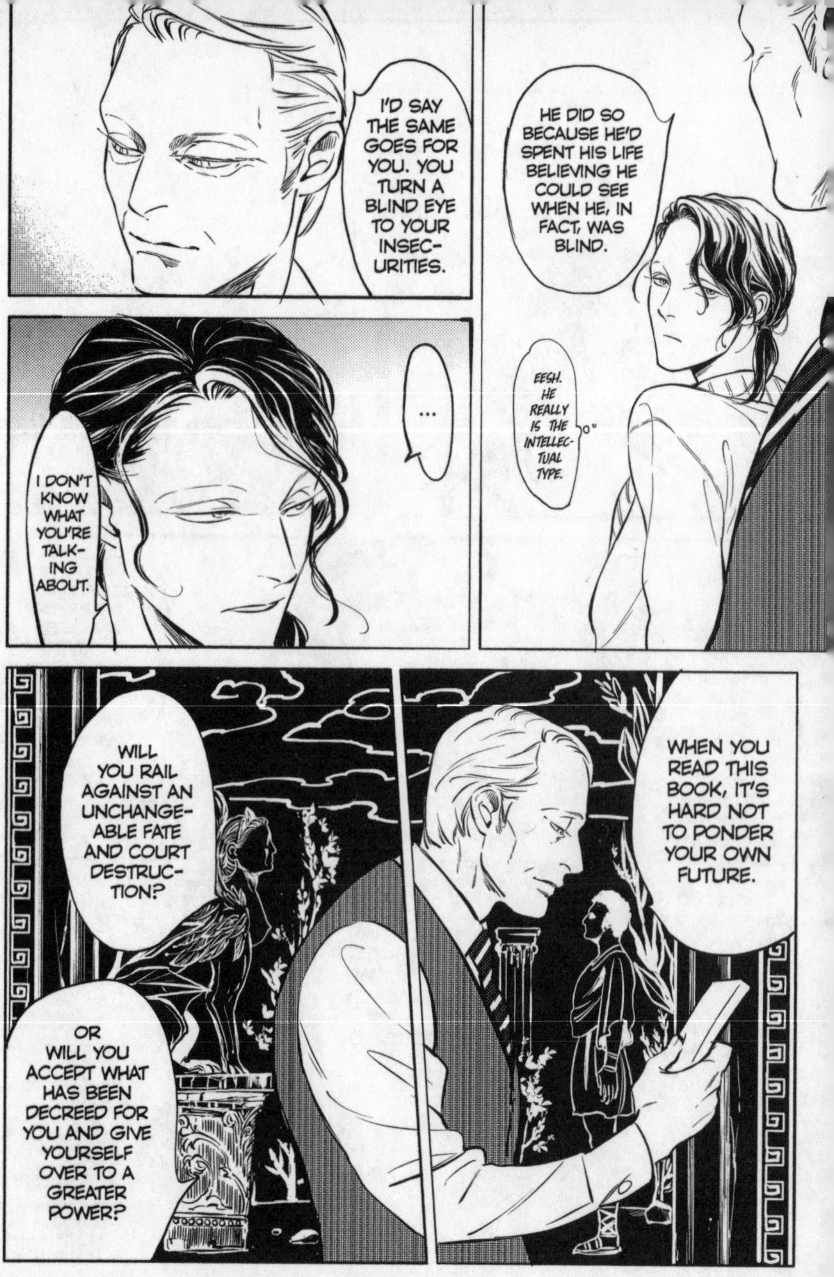
HE DID SO BECAUSE HE'D SPENT HIS LIFE BELIEVING HE COULD SEE WHEN HE, IN FACT, WAS BLIND.
EESH. HE REALLY IS THE INTELLECTUAL TYPE.
I'D SAY THE SAME GOES FOR YOU. YOU TURN A BLIND EYE TO YOUR INSECURITIES.
...
I DON'T KNOW WHAT YOU'RE TALKING ABOUT.
WHEN YOU READ THIS BOOK, IT'S HARD NOT TO PONDER YOUR OWN FUTURE.
WILL YOU RAIL AGAINST AN UNCHANGEABLE FATE AND COURT DESTRUCTION?
OR WILL YOU ACCEPT WHAT HAS BEEN DECREED FOR YOU AND GIVE YOURSELF OVER TO A GREATER POWER?

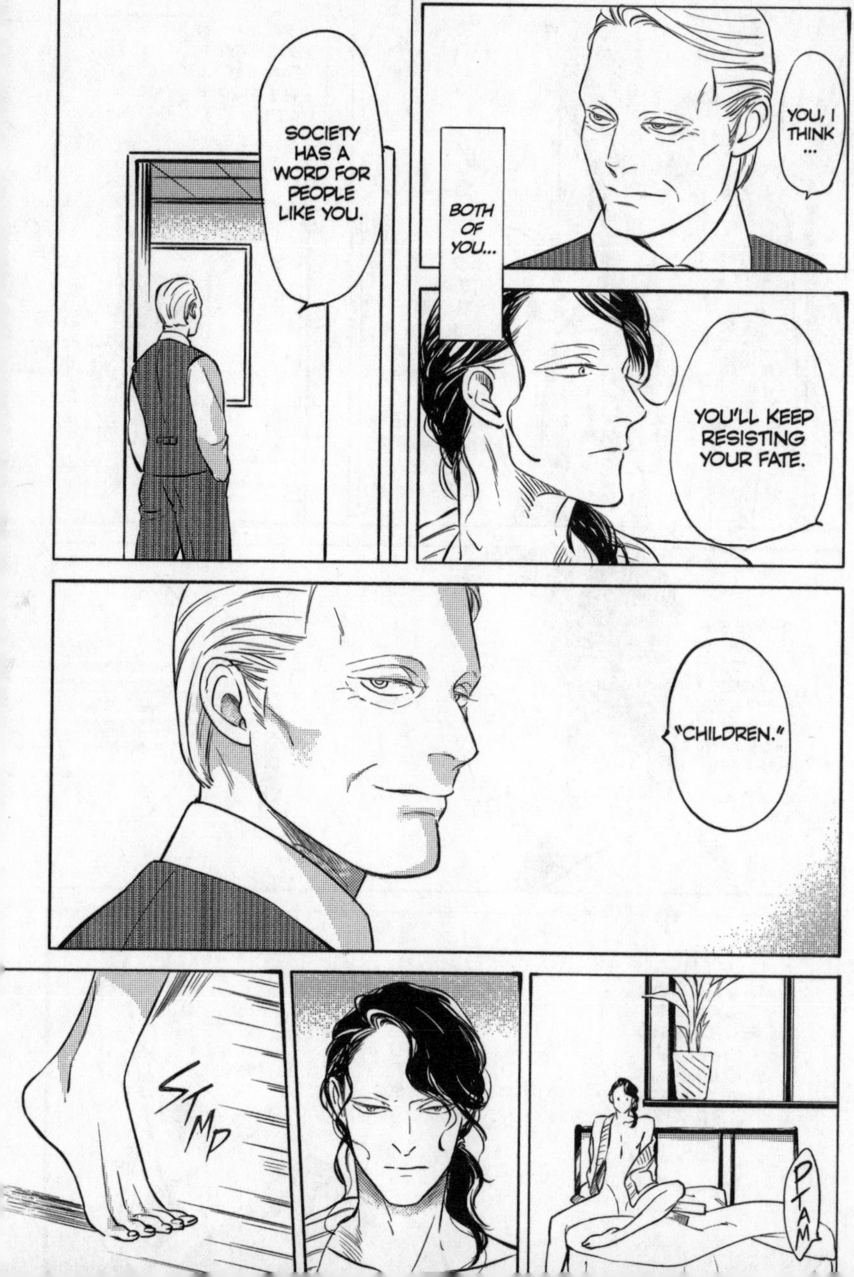
YOU, I THINK ...
BOTH OF YOU...
YOU'LL KEEP RESISTING YOUR FATE.
SOCIETY HAS A WORD FOR PEOPLE LIKE YOU.
"CHILDREN."
PTAM
STMP

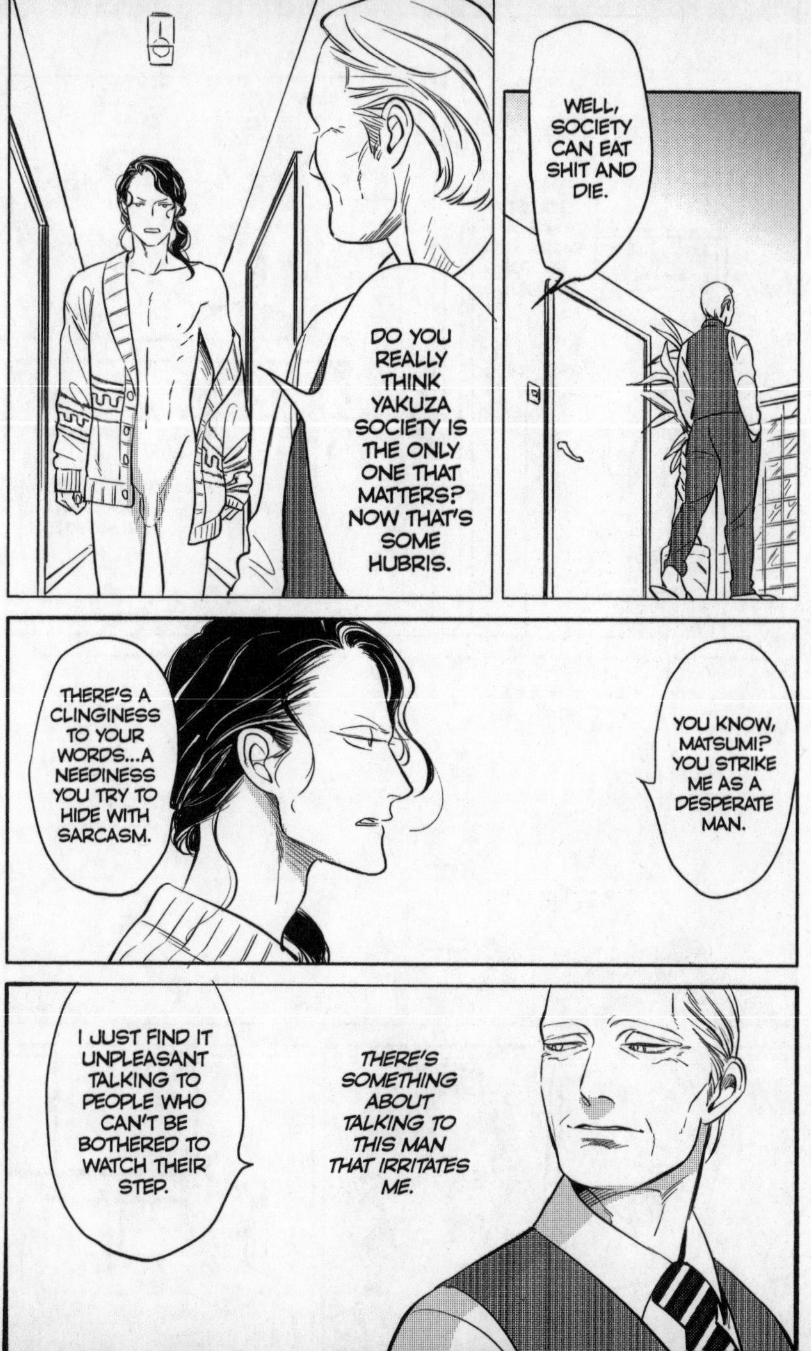
WELL, SOCIETY CAN EAT SHIT AND DIE.
DO YOU REALLY THINK YAKUZA SOCIETY IS THE ONLY ONE THAT MATTERS? NOW THAT'S SOME HUBRIS.
YOU KNOW, MATSUMI? YOU STRIKE ME AS A DESPERATE MAN.
THERE'S A CLINGINESS TO YOUR WORDS...A NEEDINESS YOU TRY TO HIDE WITH SARCASM.
THERE'S SOMETHING ABOUT TALKING TO THIS MAN THAT IRRITATES ME.
I JUST FIND IT UNPLEASANT TALKING TO PEOPLE WHO CAN'T BE BOTHERED TO WATCH THEIR STEP.

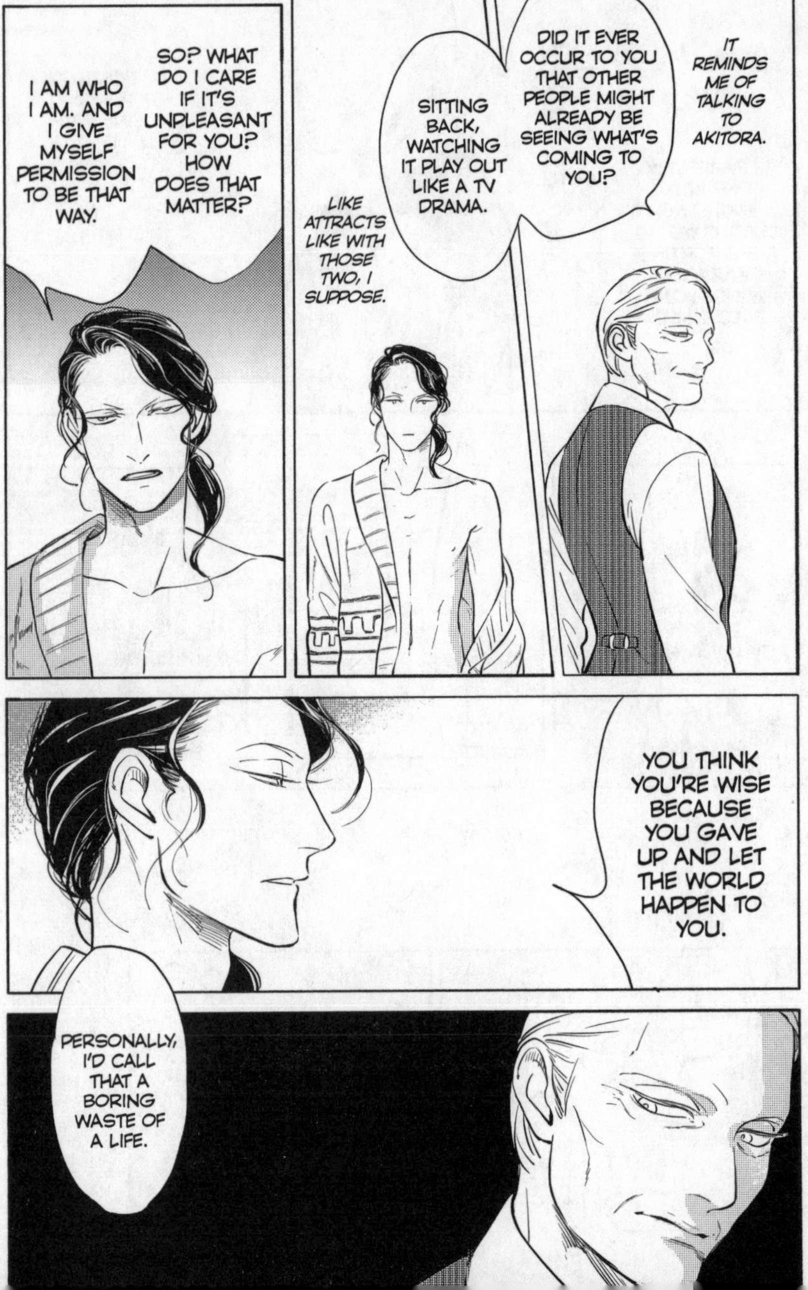
IT REMINDS ME OF TALKING TO AKITORA.
DID IT EVER OCCUR TO YOU THAT OTHER PEOPLE MIGHT ALREADY BE SEEING WHAT'S COMING TO YOU?
SITTING BACK, WATCHING IT PLAY OUT LIKE A TV DRAMA.
LIKE ATTRACTS LIKE WITH THOSE TWO, I SUPPOSE.
SO? WHAT DO I CARE IF IT'S UNPLEASANT FOR YOU? HOW DOES THAT MATTER?
I AM WHO I AM. AND I GIVE MYSELF PERMISSION TO BE THAT WAY.
YOU THINK YOU'RE WISE BECAUSE YOU GAVE UP AND LET THE WORLD HAPPEN TO YOU.
PERSONALLY, I'D CALL THAT A BORING WASTE OF A LIFE.

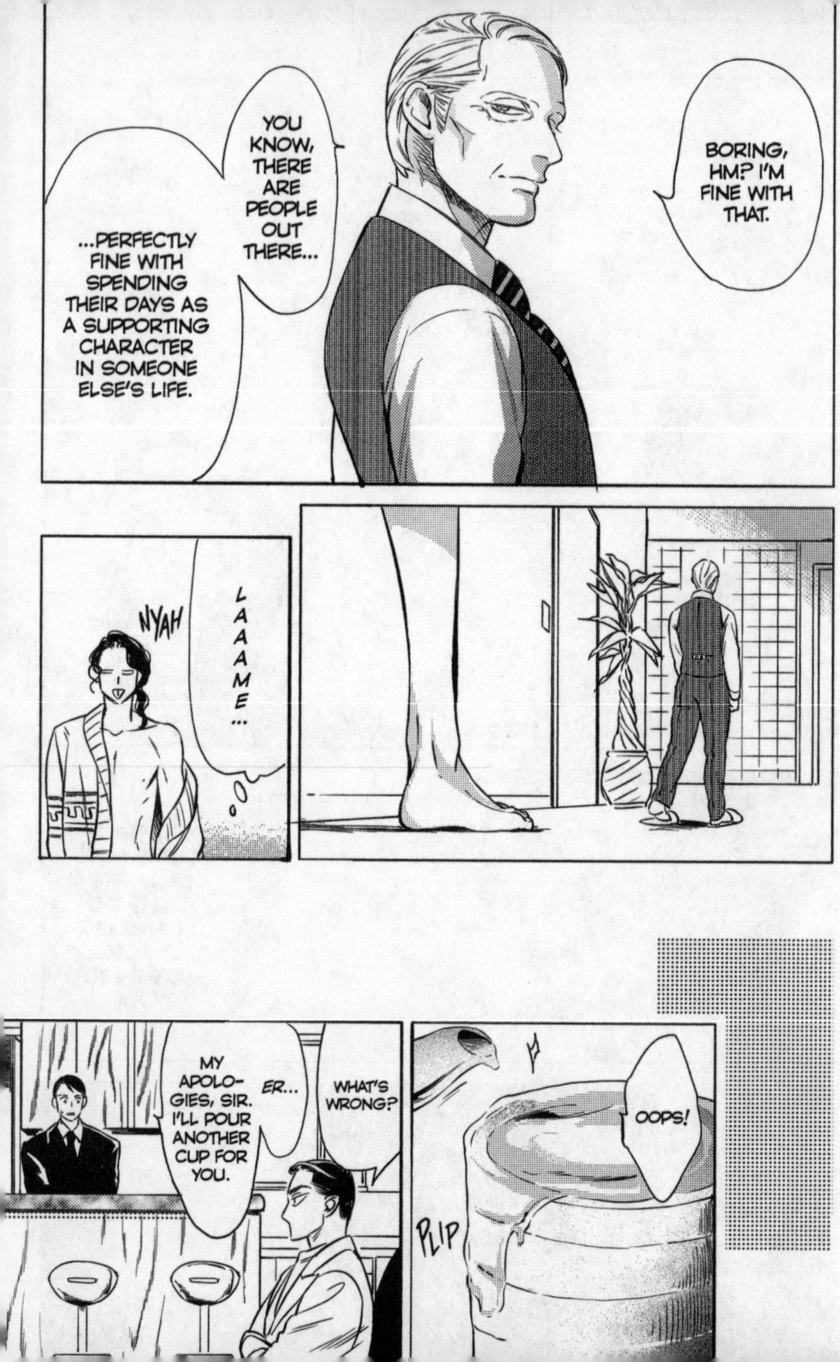
BORING, HM? I'M FINE WITH THAT.
YOU KNOW, THERE ARE PEOPLE OUT THERE...
...PERFECTLY FINE WITH SPENDING THEIR DAYS AS A SUPPORTING CHARACTER IN SOMEONE ELSE'S LIFE.
LAAAME...
NYAH
OOPS!
PLIP
WHAT'S WRONG?
ER...
MY APOLOGIES, SIR. I'LL POUR ANOTHER CUP FOR YOU.

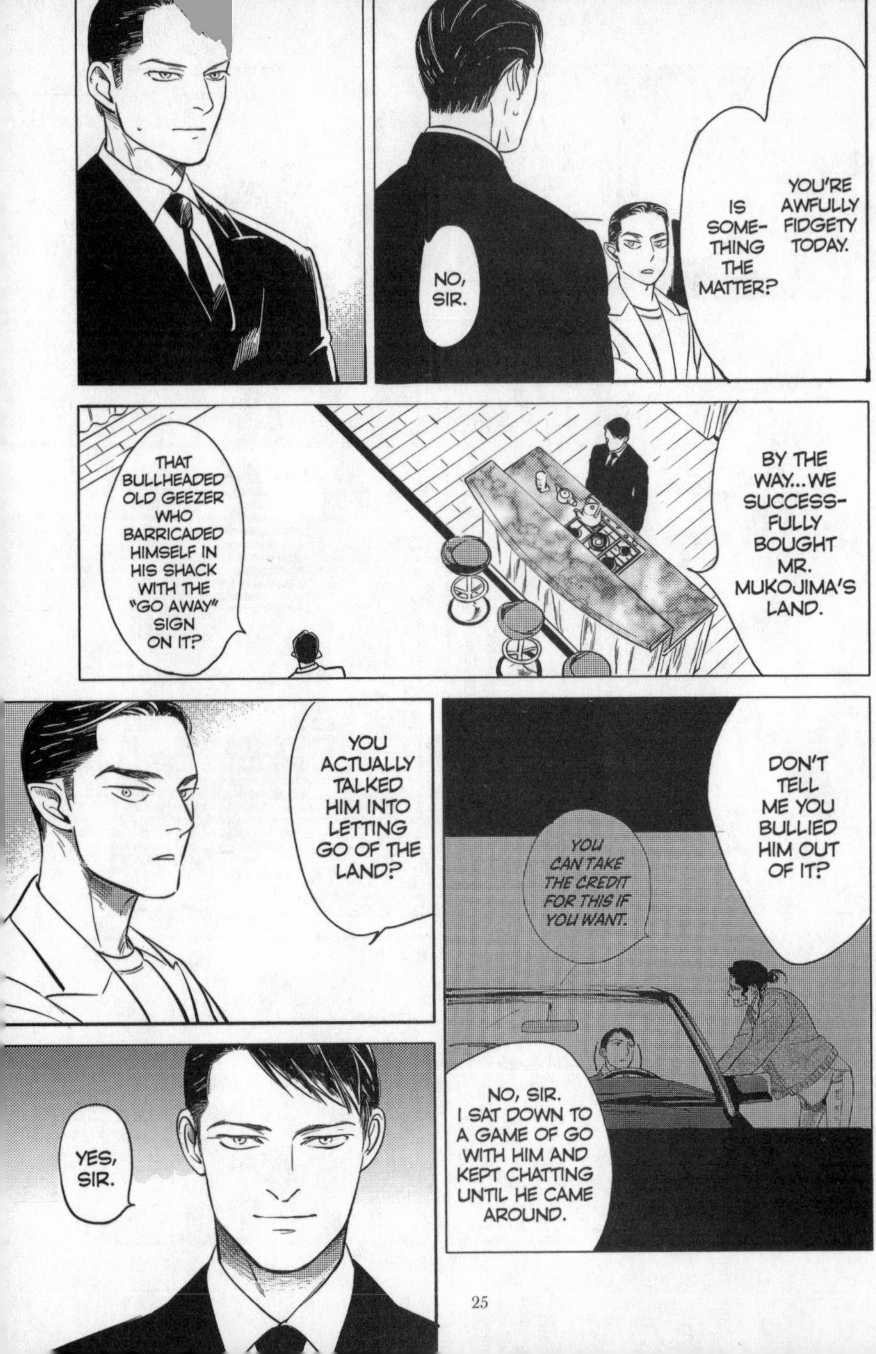
YOU'RE AWFULLY FIDGETY TODAY.
IS SOMETHING THE MATTER?
NO, SIR.
BY THE WAY...WE SUCCESSFULLY BOUGHT MR. MUKOJIMA'S LAND.
THAT BULLHEADED OLD GEEZER WHO BARRICADED HIMSELF IN HIS SHACK WITH THE "GO AWAY" SIGN ON IT?
DON'T TELL ME YOU BULLIED HIM OUT OF IT?
YOU CAN TAKE THE CREDIT FOR THIS IF YOU WANT.
NO, SIR. I SAT DOWN TO A GAME OF GO WITH HIM AND KEPT CHATTING UNTIL HE CAME AROUND.
YOU ACTUALLY TALKED HIM INTO LETTING GO OF THE LAND?
YES, SIR.

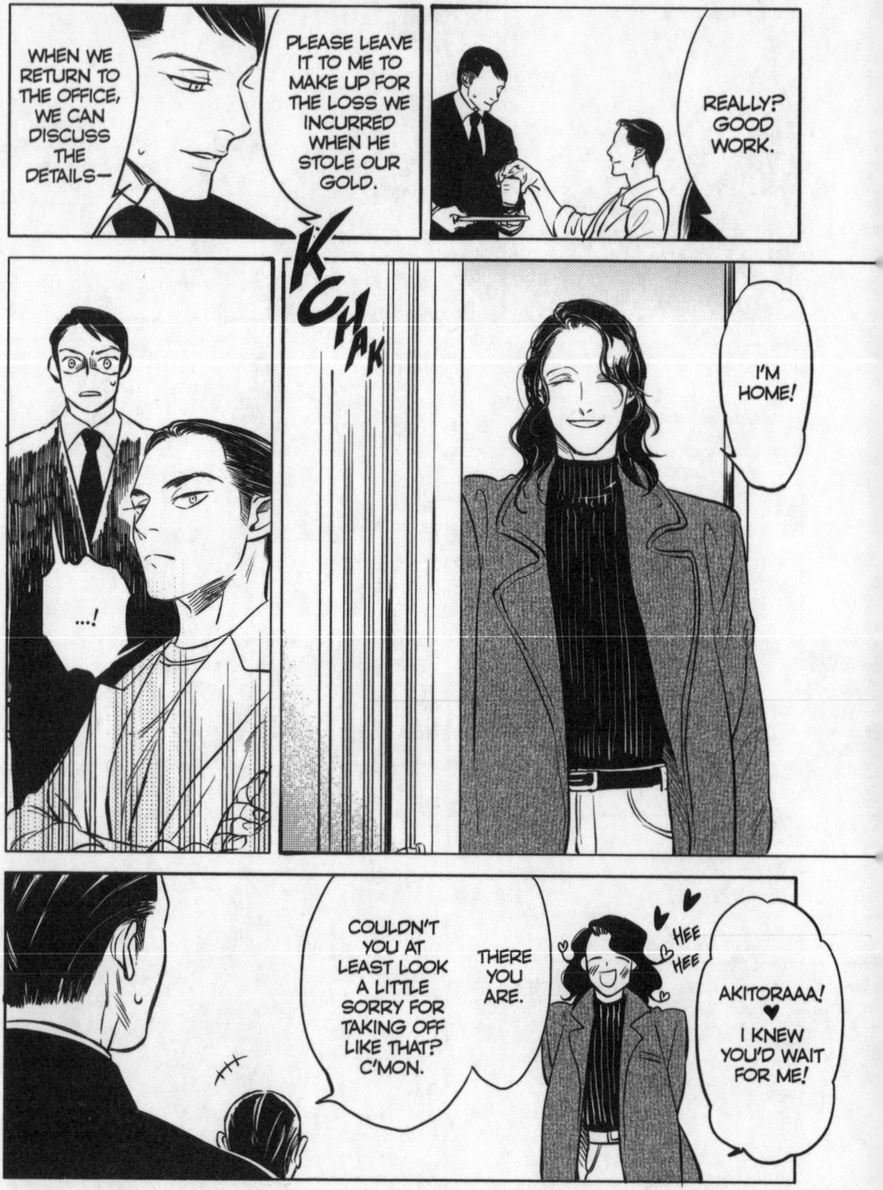
REALLY? GOOD WORK.
PLEASE LEAVE IT TO ME TO MAKE UP FOR THE LOSS WE INCURRED WHEN HE STOLE OUR GOLD.
WHEN WE RETURN TO THE OFFICE, WE CAN DISCUSS THE DETAILS—
I'M HOME!
KCHAK
...!
AKITORAAA! ♥ I KNEW YOU'D WAIT FOR ME!
HEE HEE
THERE YOU ARE.
COULDN'T YOU AT LEAST LOOK A LITTLE SORRY FOR TAKING OFF LIKE THAT? C'MON.

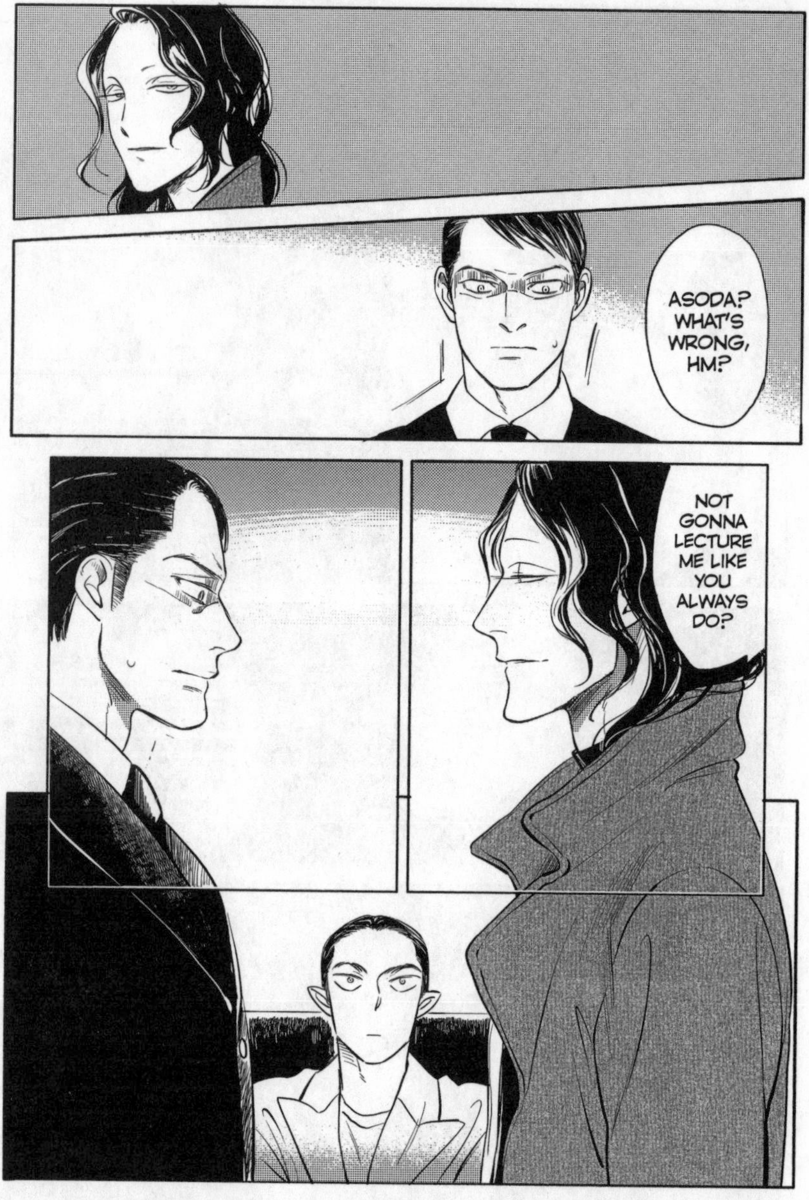
ASODA? WHAT'S WRONG, HM?
NOT GONNA LECTURE ME LIKE YOU ALWAYS DO?

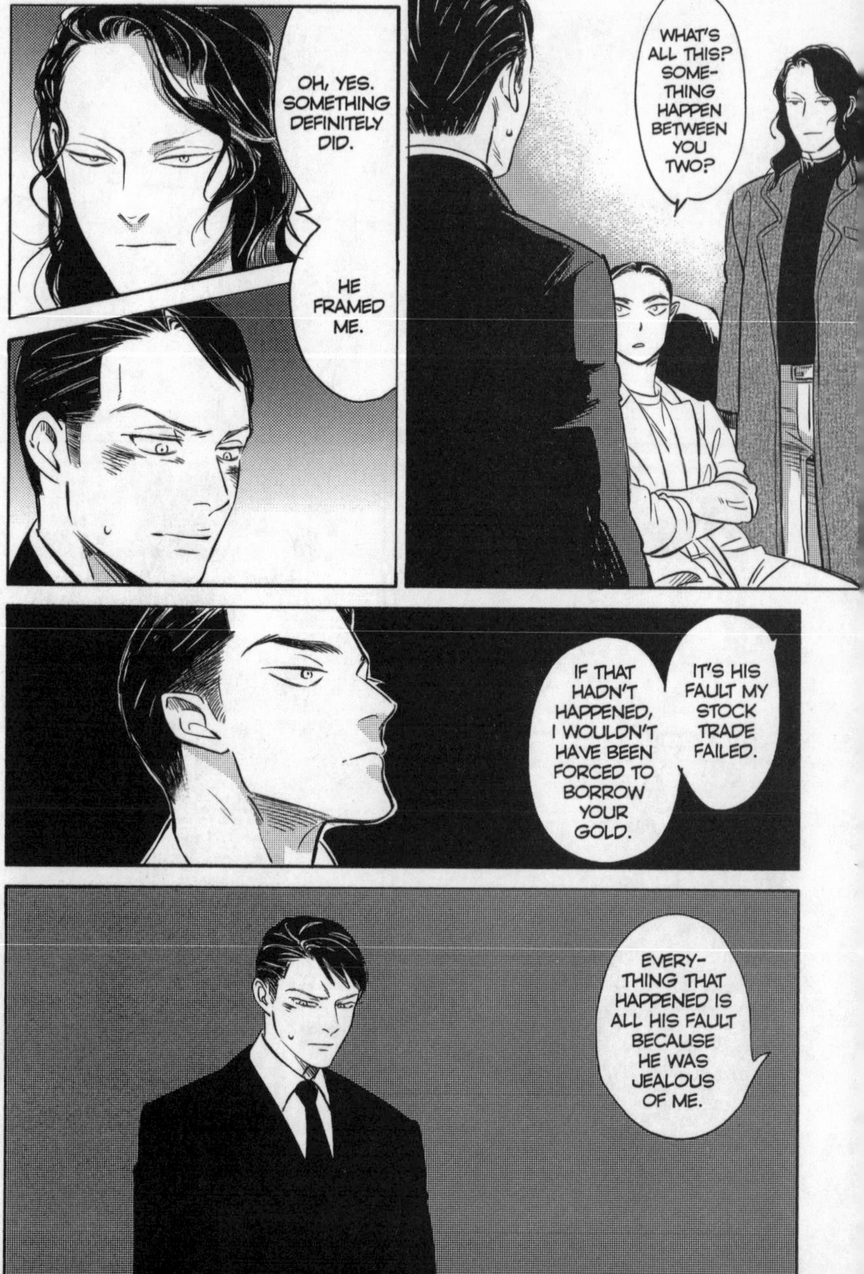
WHAT'S ALL THIS? SOME-THING HAPPEN BETWEEN YOU TWO?
OH, YES. SOMETHING DEFINITELY DID.
HE FRAMED ME.
IT'S HIS FAULT MY STOCK TRADE FAILED.
IF THAT HADN'T HAPPENED, I WOULDN'T HAVE BEEN FORCED TO BORROW YOUR GOLD.
EVERY-THING THAT HAPPENED IS ALL HIS FAULT BECAUSE HE WAS JEALOUS OF ME.

SIGH
WHAT ARE YOU TALKING ABOUT?
LIKE ALWAYS, ALL YOU DO IS BLUFF AND POSTURE.
I SEE. SO YOU HAVE THE GUTS TO AT LEAST PLAY INNOCENT, HM?
LAST NIGHT YOU TURNED TAIL PRACTICALLY IN TEARS.
BUT, Y'KNOW?
HOW LONG WILL YOU BE ABLE TO HANG ON TO THAT BRAVE FACE WHEN YOU HEAR THIS?
WHA ...?!
!
WAIT A MINUTE. ISN'T THAT MY CASSETTE PLAYER?
OOPS!
UM, CAN WE IGNORE THAT PART FOR NOW?

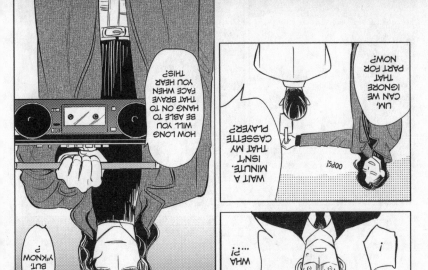

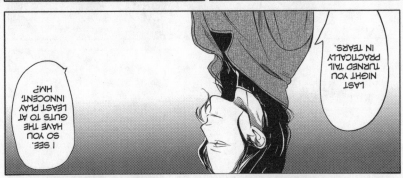

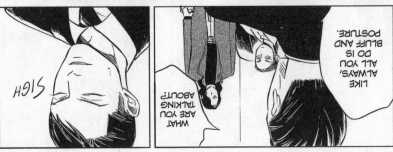

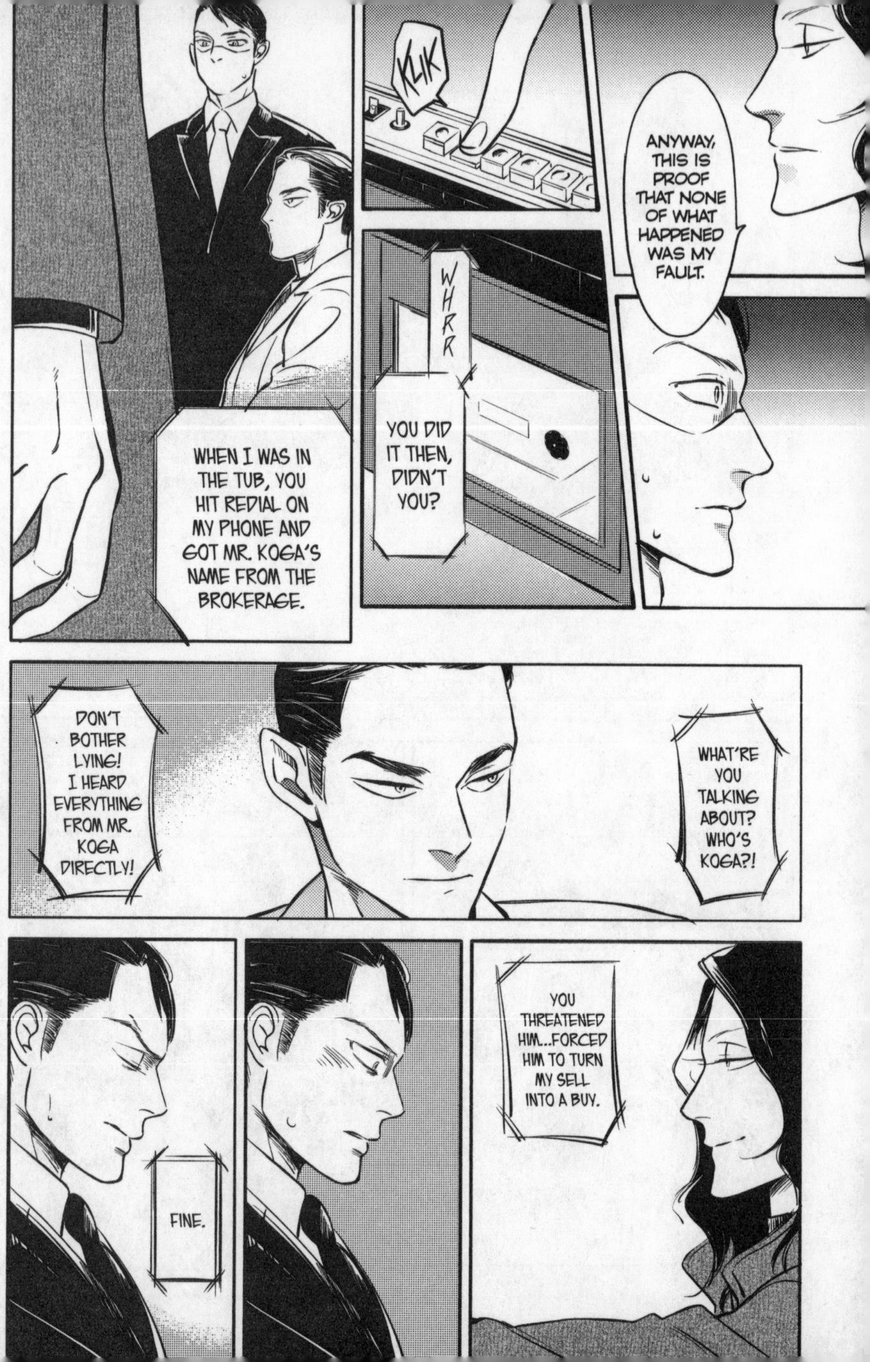
ANYWAY, THIS IS PROOF THAT NONE OF WHAT HAPPENED WAS MY FAULT.
KLIK
WHRR
YOU DID IT THEN, DIDN'T YOU?
WHEN I WAS IN THE TUB, YOU HIT REDIAL ON MY PHONE AND GOT MR. KOGA'S NAME FROM THE BROKERAGE.
WHAT'RE YOU TALKING ABOUT? WHO'S KOGA?!
DON'T BOTHER LYING! I HEARD EVERYTHING FROM MR. KOGA DIRECTLY!
YOU THREATENED HIM...FORCED HIM TO TURN MY SELL INTO A BUY.
FINE.

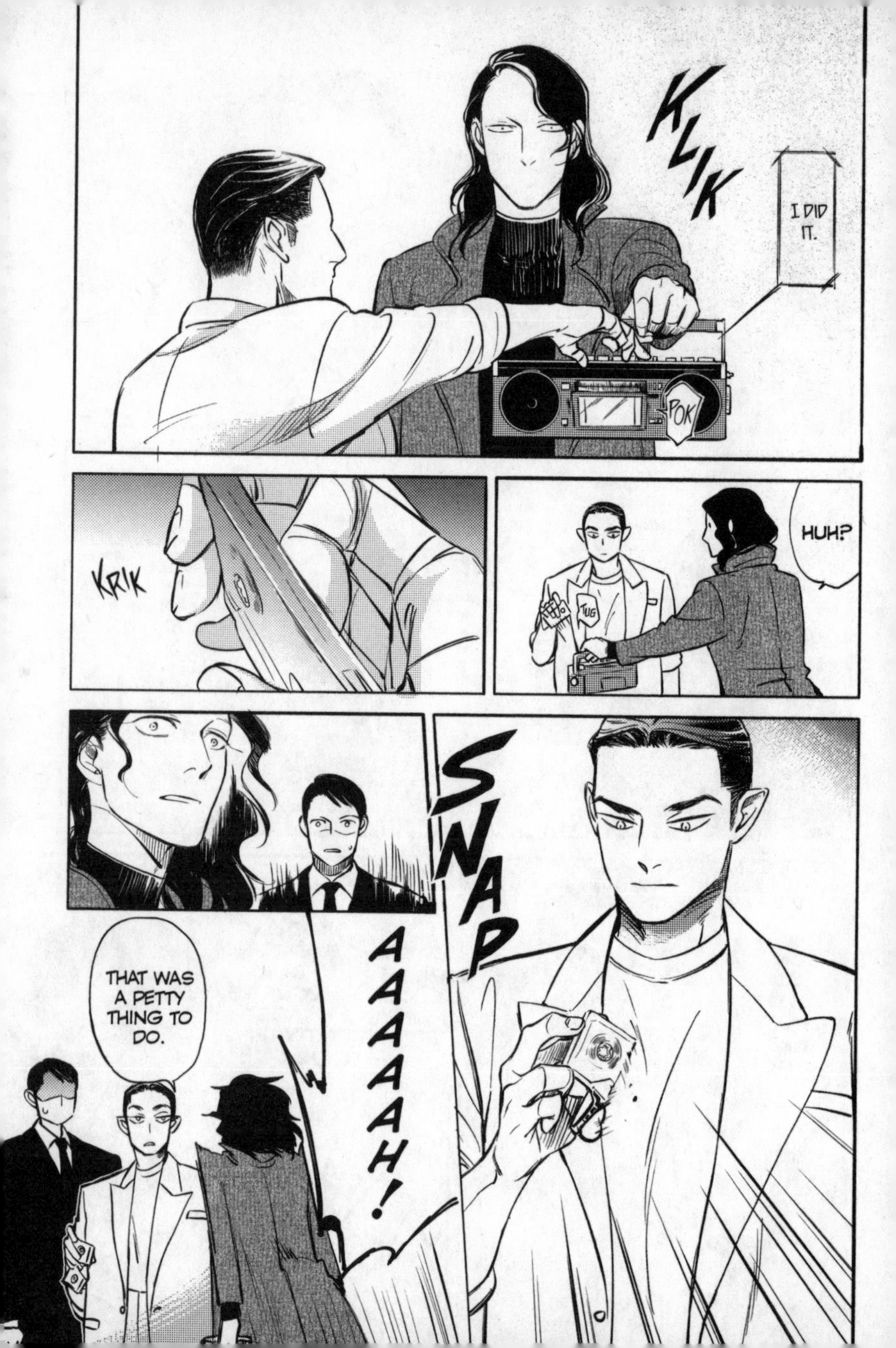
I DID IT.
KLIK
POK
HUH?
TUG
KRIK
SNAP
AAAAAAH!
THAT WAS A PETTY THING TO DO.

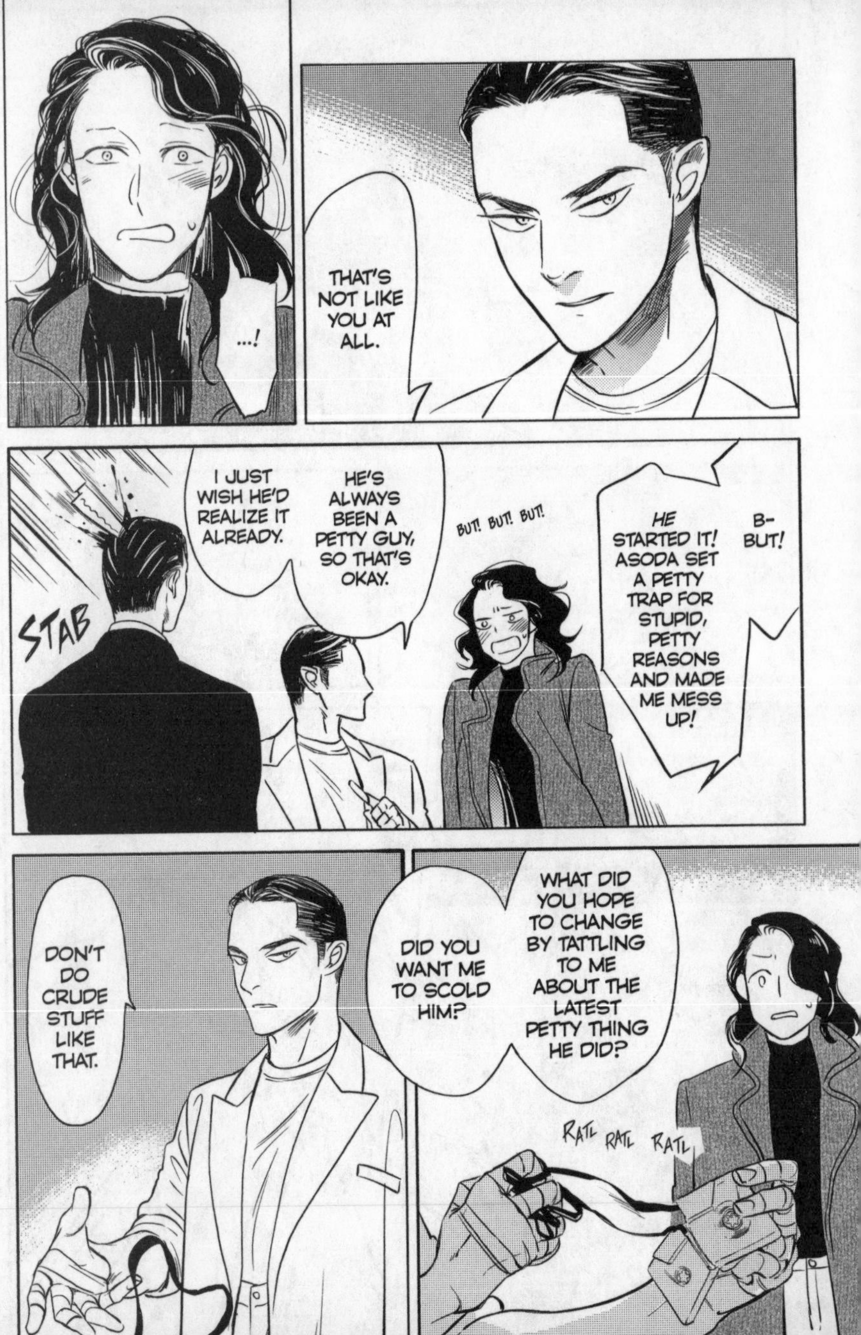
THAT'S NOT LIKE YOU AT ALL.
...!
B- BUT!
HE STARTED IT! ASODA SET A PETTY TRAP FOR STUPID, PETTY REASONS AND MADE ME MESS UP!
BUT! BUT! BUT!
HE'S ALWAYS BEEN A PETTY GUY, SO THAT'S OKAY.
I JUST WISH HE'D REALIZE IT ALREADY.
STAB
WHAT DID YOU HOPE TO CHANGE BY TATTLING TO ME ABOUT THE LATEST PETTY THING HE DID?
DID YOU WANT ME TO SCOLD HIM?
RATL RATL RATL
DON'T DO CRUDE STUFF LIKE THAT.

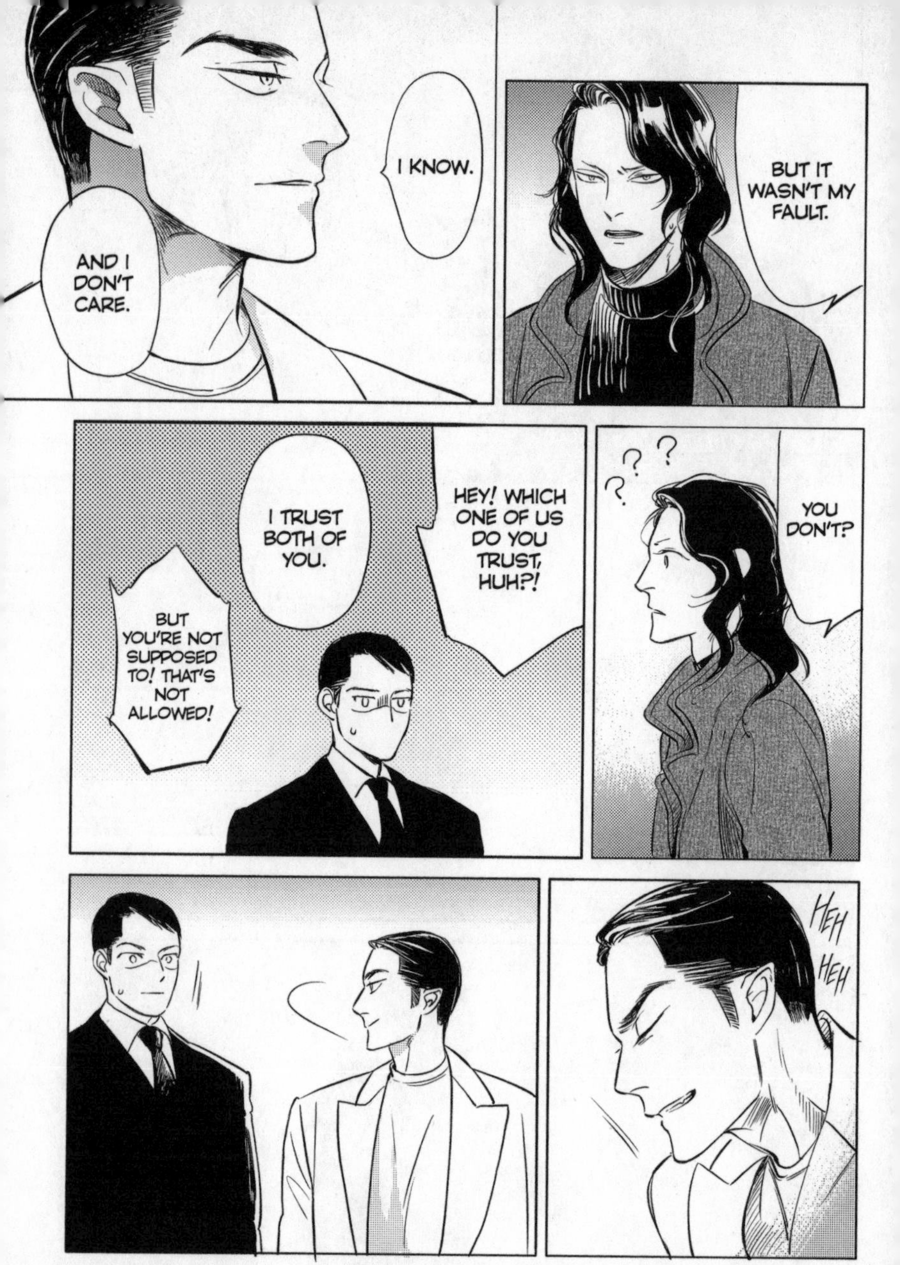
BUT IT WASN'T MY FAULT.
I KNOW.
AND I DON'T CARE.
YOU DON'T?
HEY! WHICH ONE OF US DO YOU TRUST, HUH?!
I TRUST BOTH OF YOU.
BUT YOU'RE NOT SUPPOSED TO! THAT'S NOT ALLOWED!
HEH HEH

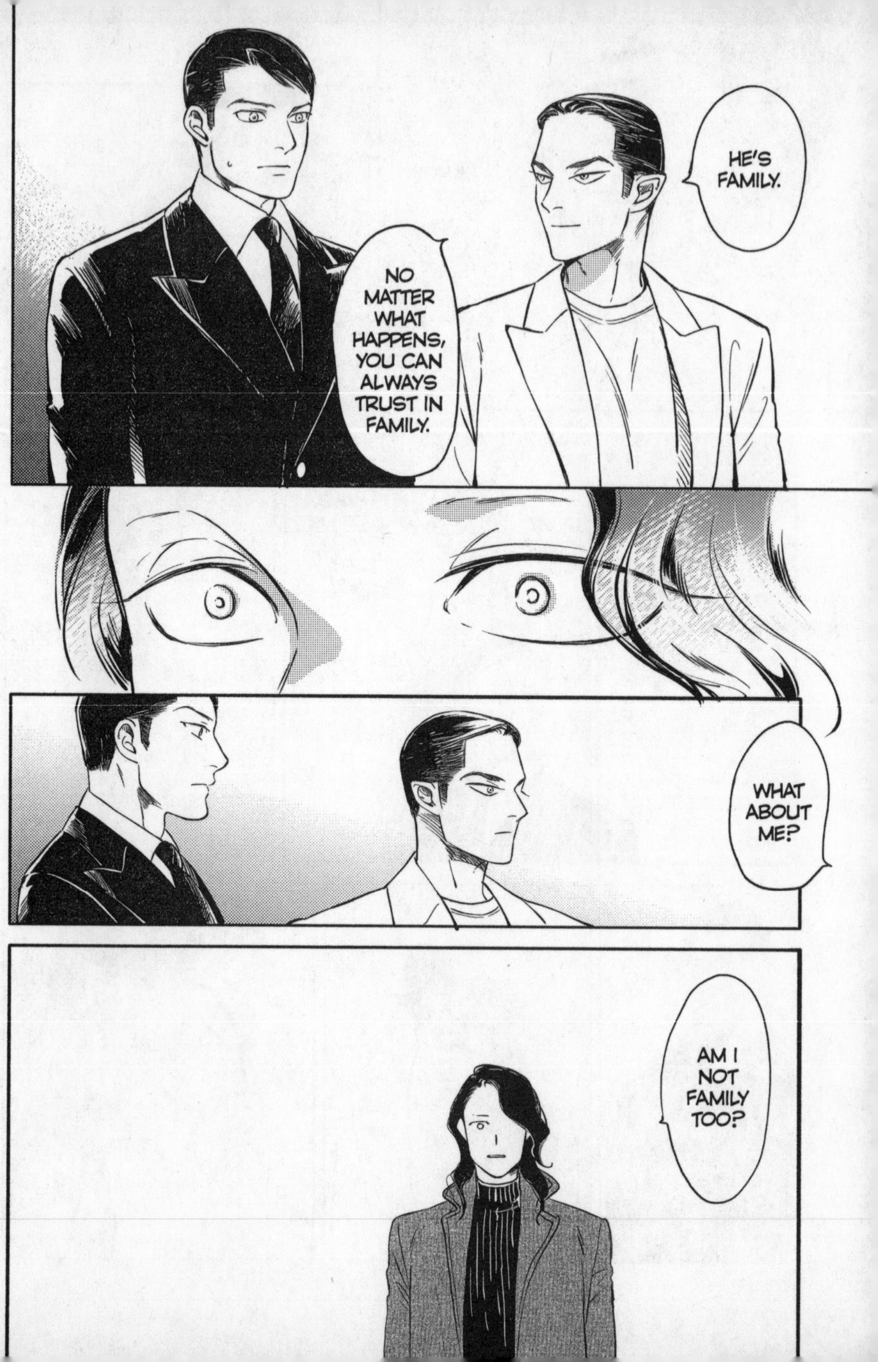
HE'S FAMILY.
NO MATTER WHAT HAPPENS, YOU CAN ALWAYS TRUST IN FAMILY.
WHAT ABOUT ME?
AM I NOT FAMILY TOO?

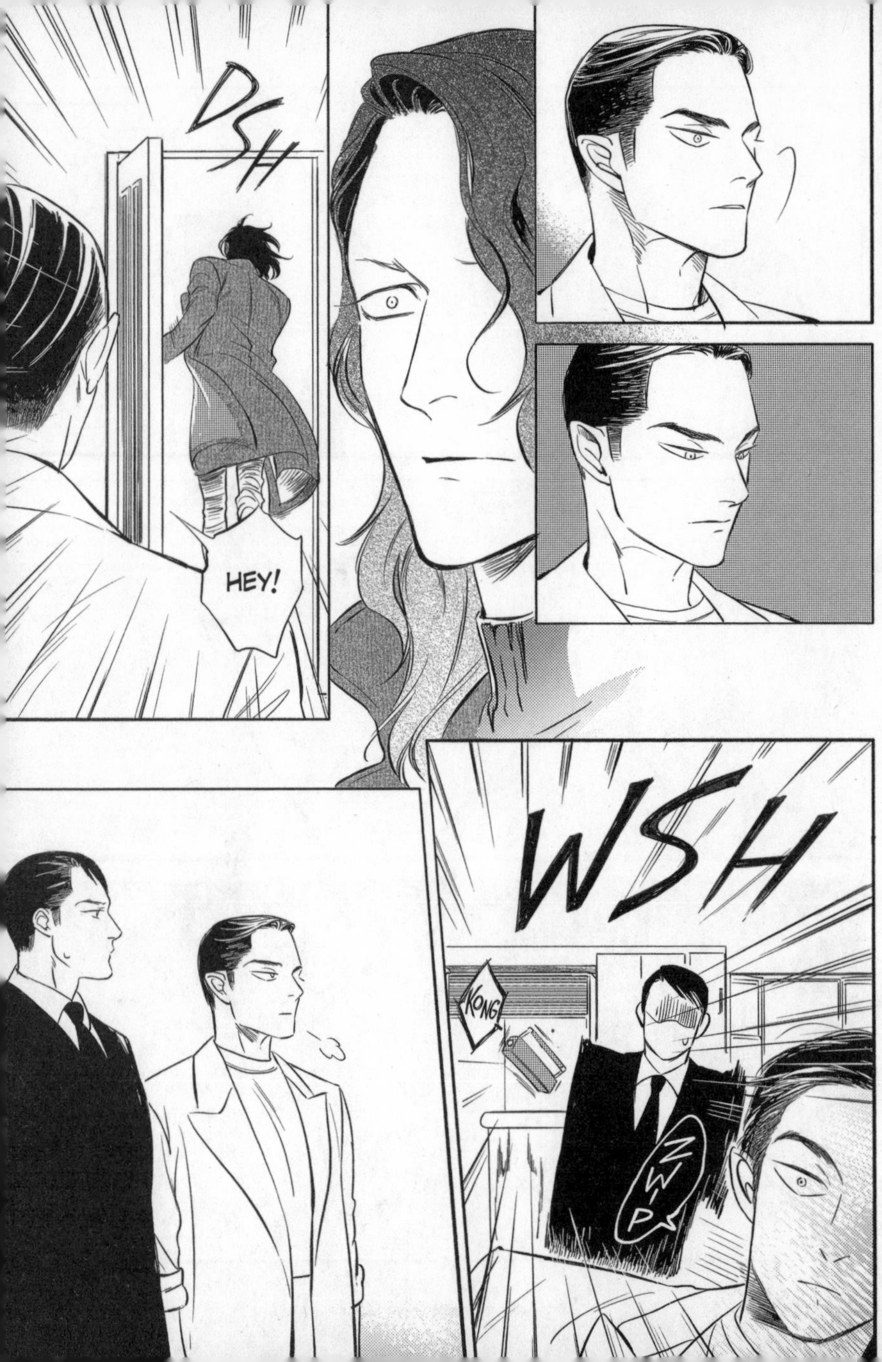
DSH
HEY!
WSH
KONG
ZWIP

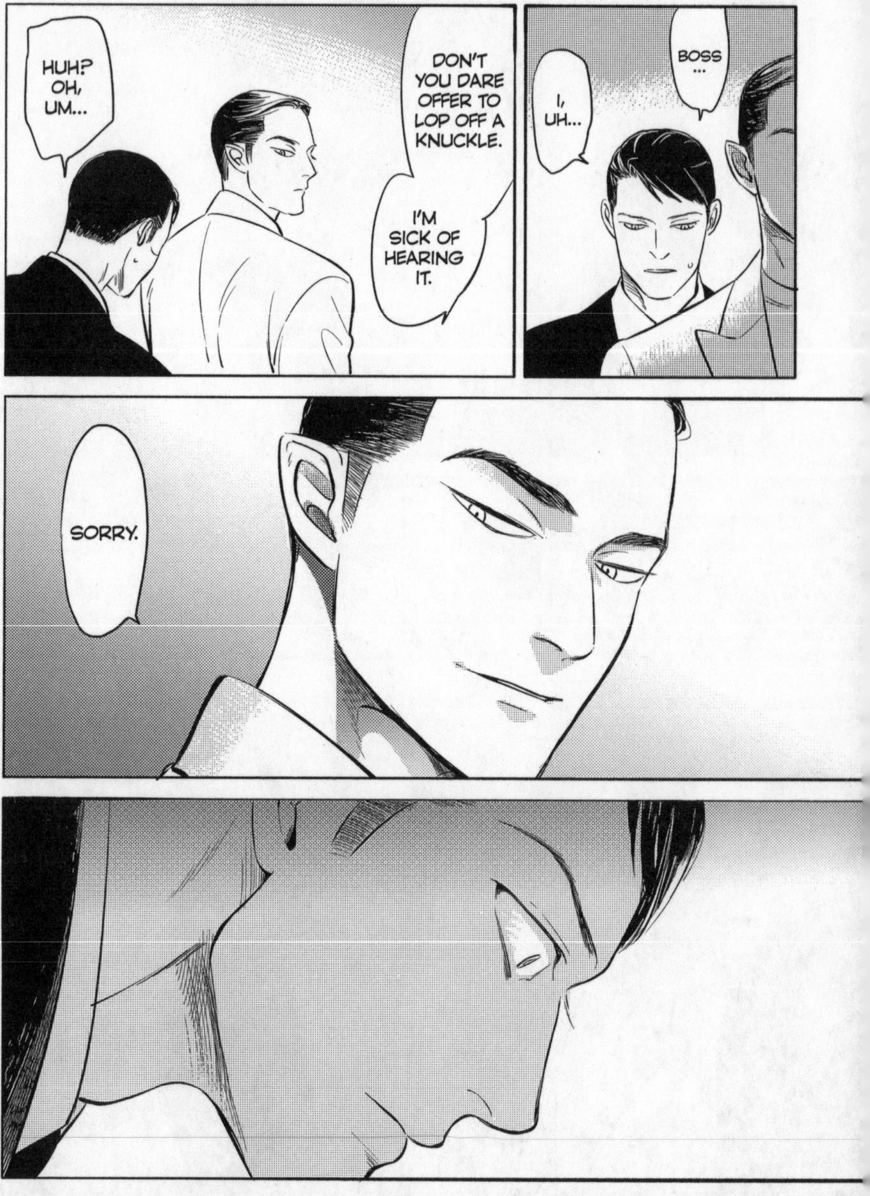
BOSS ...
I, UH...
DON'T YOU DARE OFFER TO LOP OFF A KNUCKLE.
HUH? OH, UM...
I'M SICK OF HEARING IT.
SORRY.

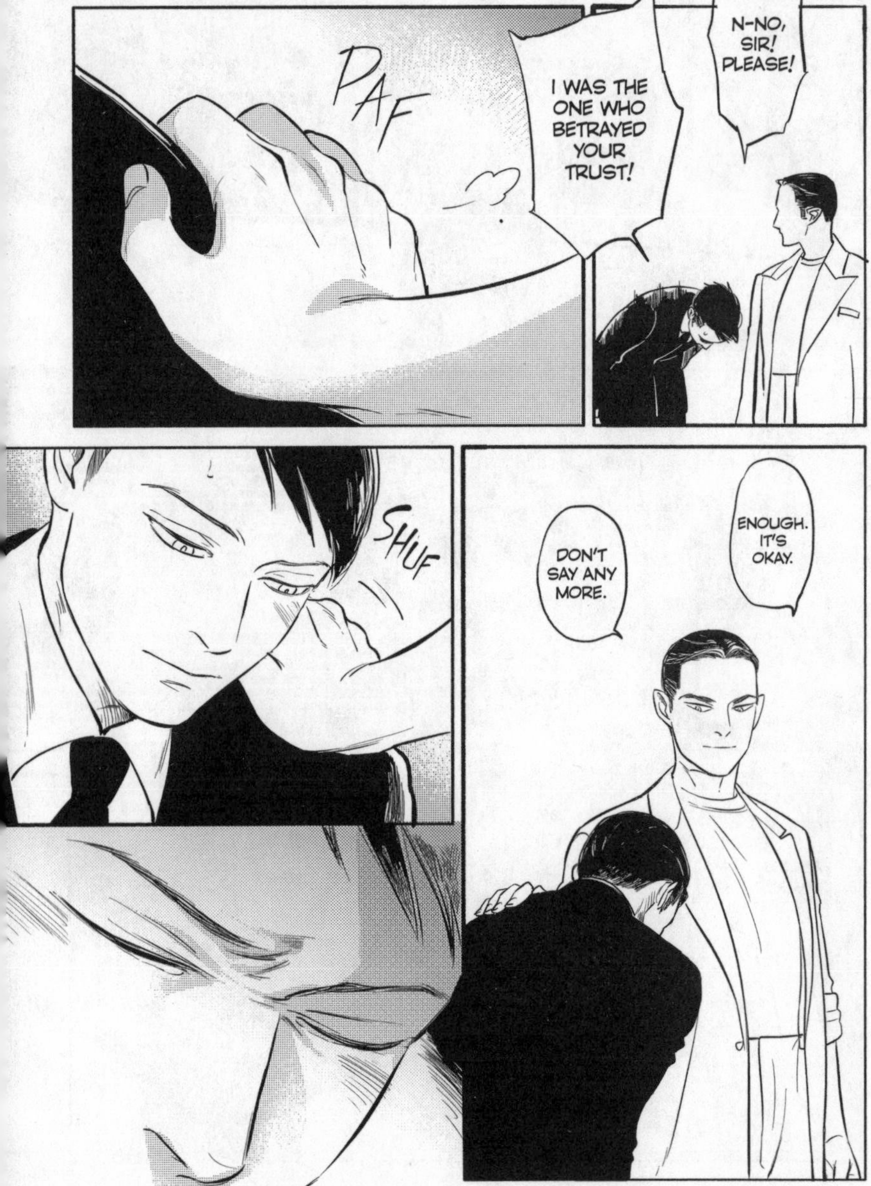
N-NO, SIR! PLEASE!
I WAS THE ONE WHO BETRAYED YOUR TRUST!
PAF
ENOUGH. IT'S OKAY.
DON'T SAY ANY MORE.
SHUF

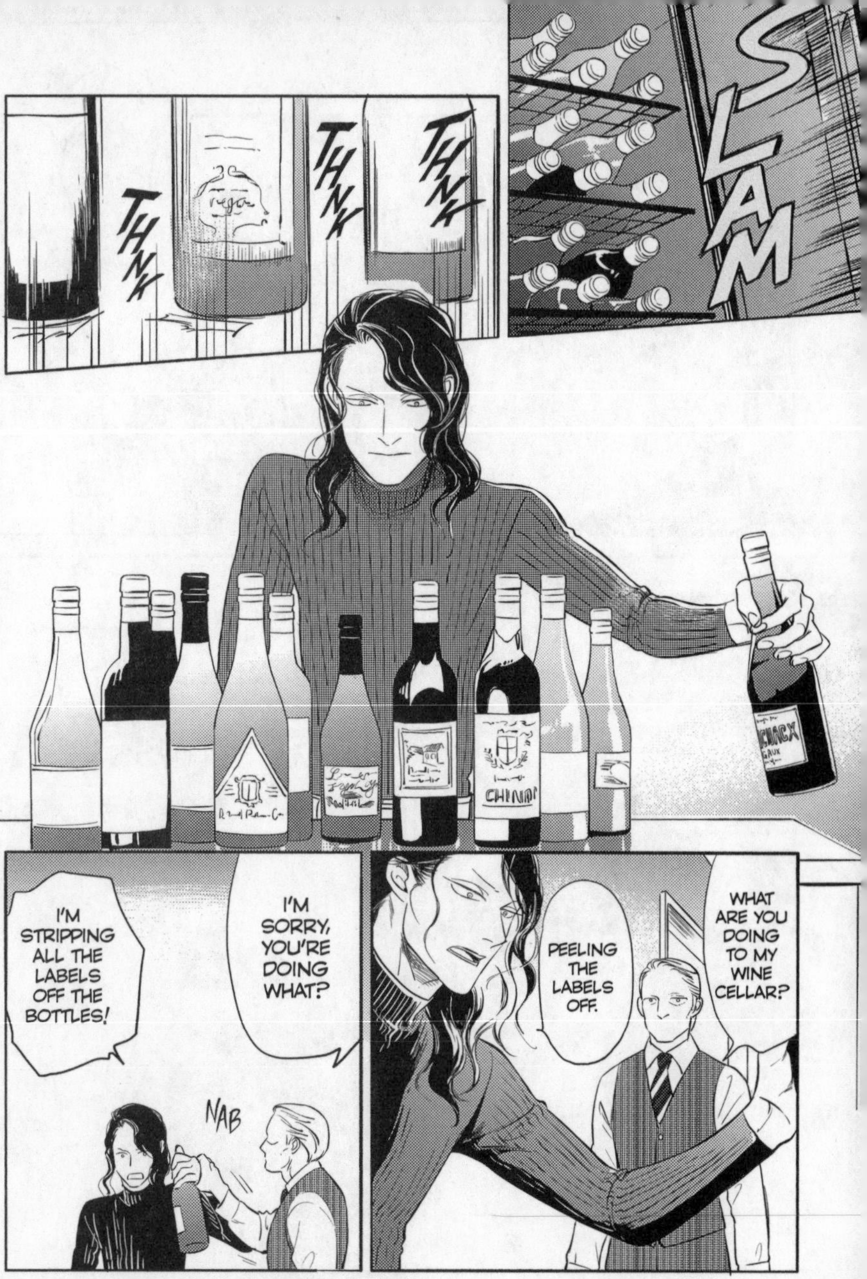
SLAM
THNK
THNK
THNK
WHAT ARE YOU DOING TO MY WINE CELLAR?
PEELING THE LABELS OFF.
I'M SORRY, YOU'RE DOING WHAT?
I'M STRIPPING ALL THE LABELS OFF THE BOTTLES!
NAB

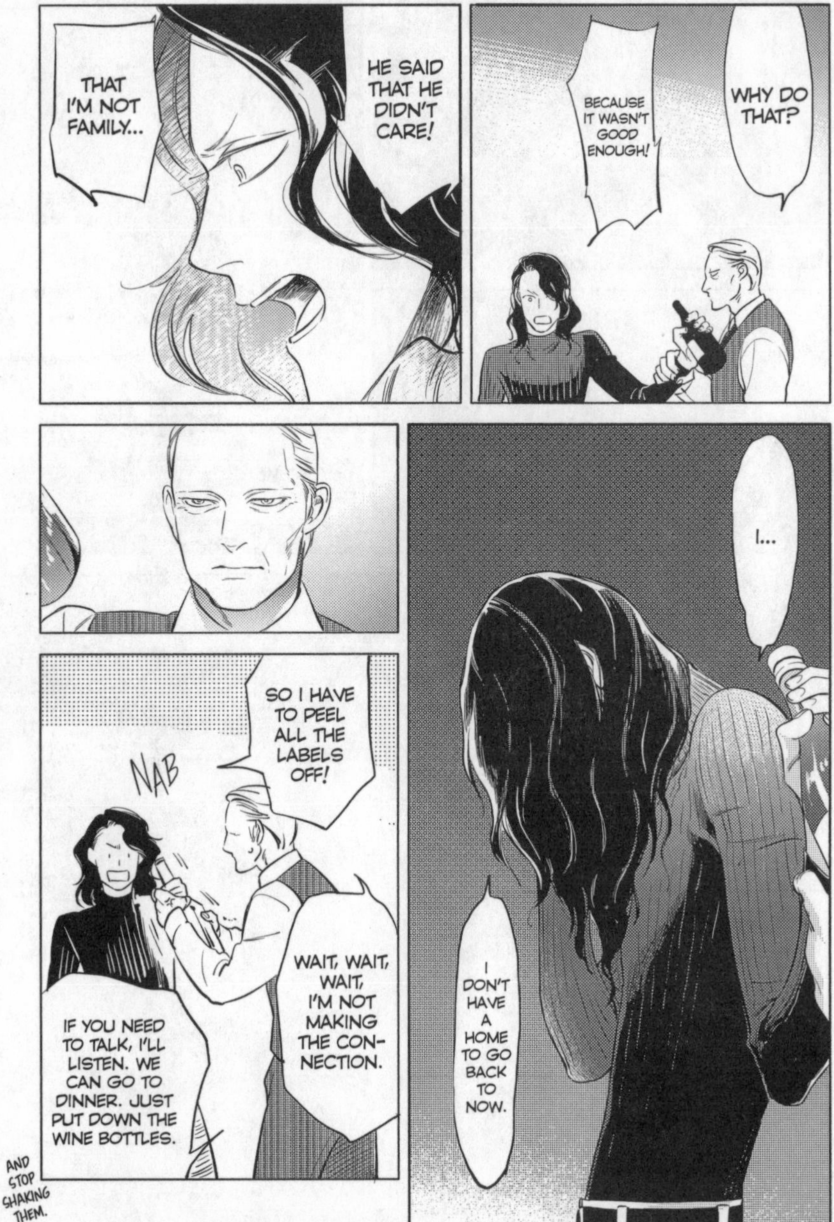
WHY DO THAT?
BECAUSE IT WASN'T GOOD ENOUGH!
HE SAID THAT HE DIDN'T CARE!
THAT I'M NOT FAMILY...
I...
I DON'T HAVE A HOME TO GO BACK TO NOW.
SO I HAVE TO PEEL ALL THE LABELS OFF!
NAB
WAIT, WAIT, WAIT, I'M NOT MAKING THE CONNECTION.
IF YOU NEED TO TALK, I'LL LISTEN. WE CAN GO TO DINNER. JUST PUT DOWN THE WINE BOTTLES.
AND STOP SHAKING THEM.

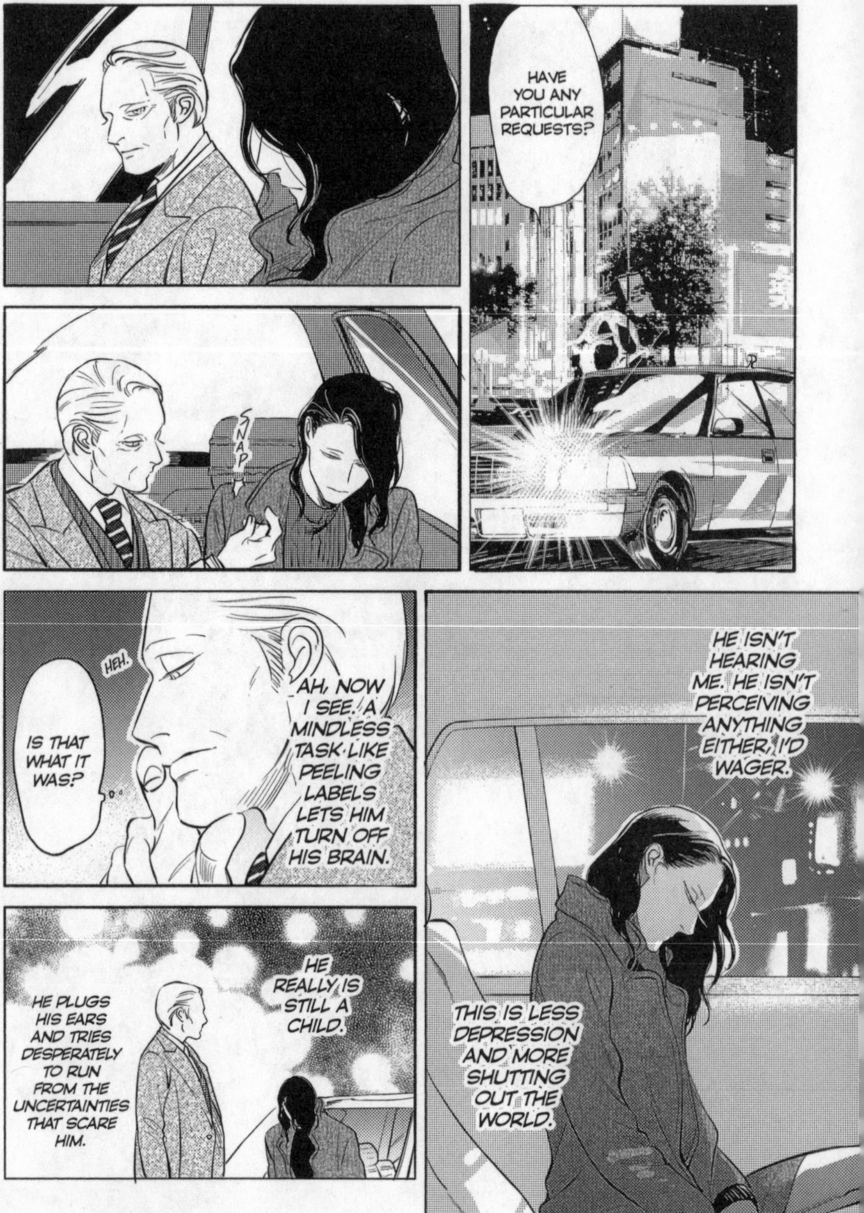
HAVE YOU ANY PARTICULAR REQUESTS?
SNAP
HE ISN'T HEARING ME. HE ISN'T PERCEIVING ANYTHING EITHER, I'D WAGER.
THIS IS LESS DEPRESSION AND MORE SHUTTING OUT THE WORLD.
HEH.
AH, NOW I SEE. A MINDLESS TASK LIKE PEELING LABELS LETS HIM TURN OFF HIS BRAIN.
IS THAT WHAT IT WAS?
HE REALLY IS STILL A CHILD.
HE PLUGS HIS EARS AND TRIES DESPERATELY TO RUN FROM THE UNCERTAINTIES THAT SCARE HIM.

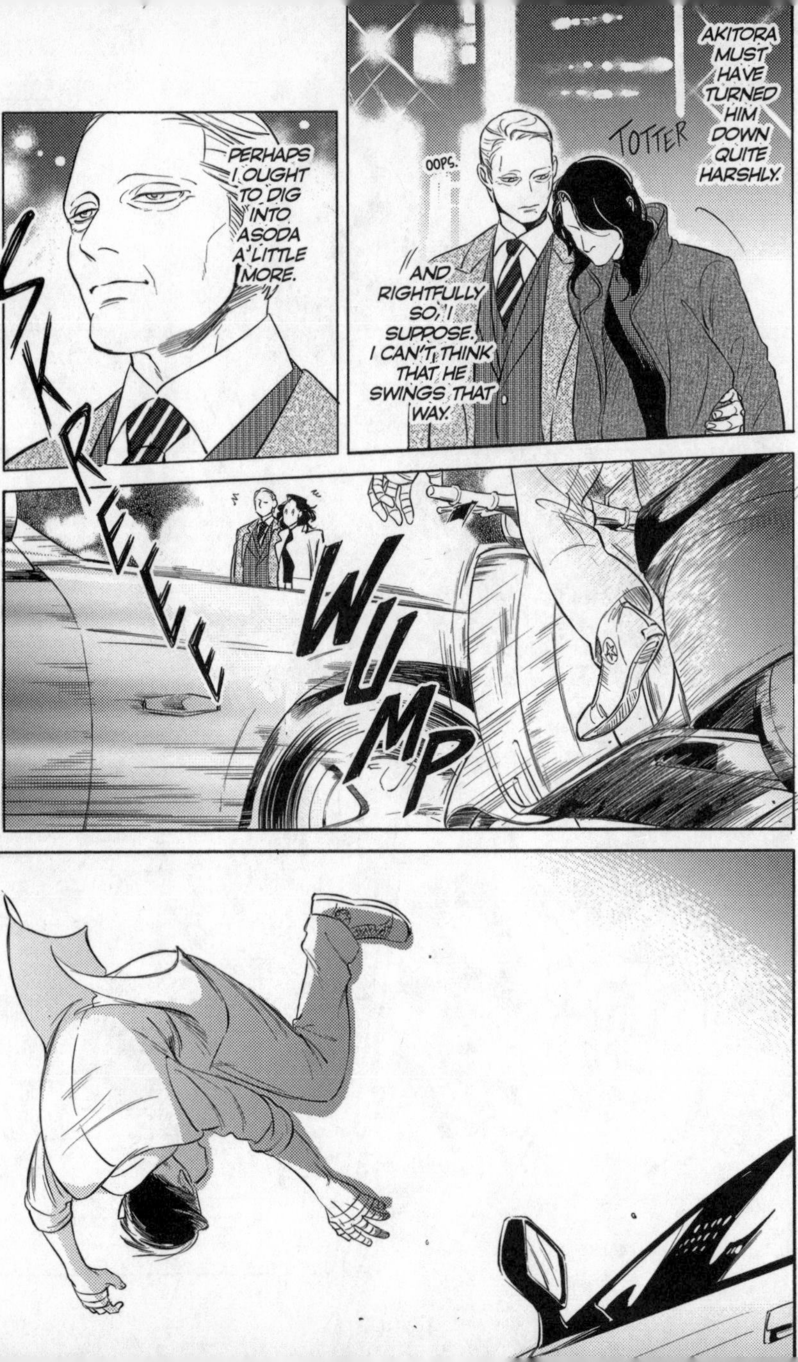
AKITORA MUST HAVE TURNED HIM DOWN QUITE HARSHLY.
TOTTER
OOPS.
AND RIGHTFULLY SO, I SUPPOSE. I CAN'T THINK THAT HE SWINGS THAT WAY.
PERHAPS I OUGHT TO DIG INTO ASODA A LITTLE MORE.
SKREEEEE
WUMP

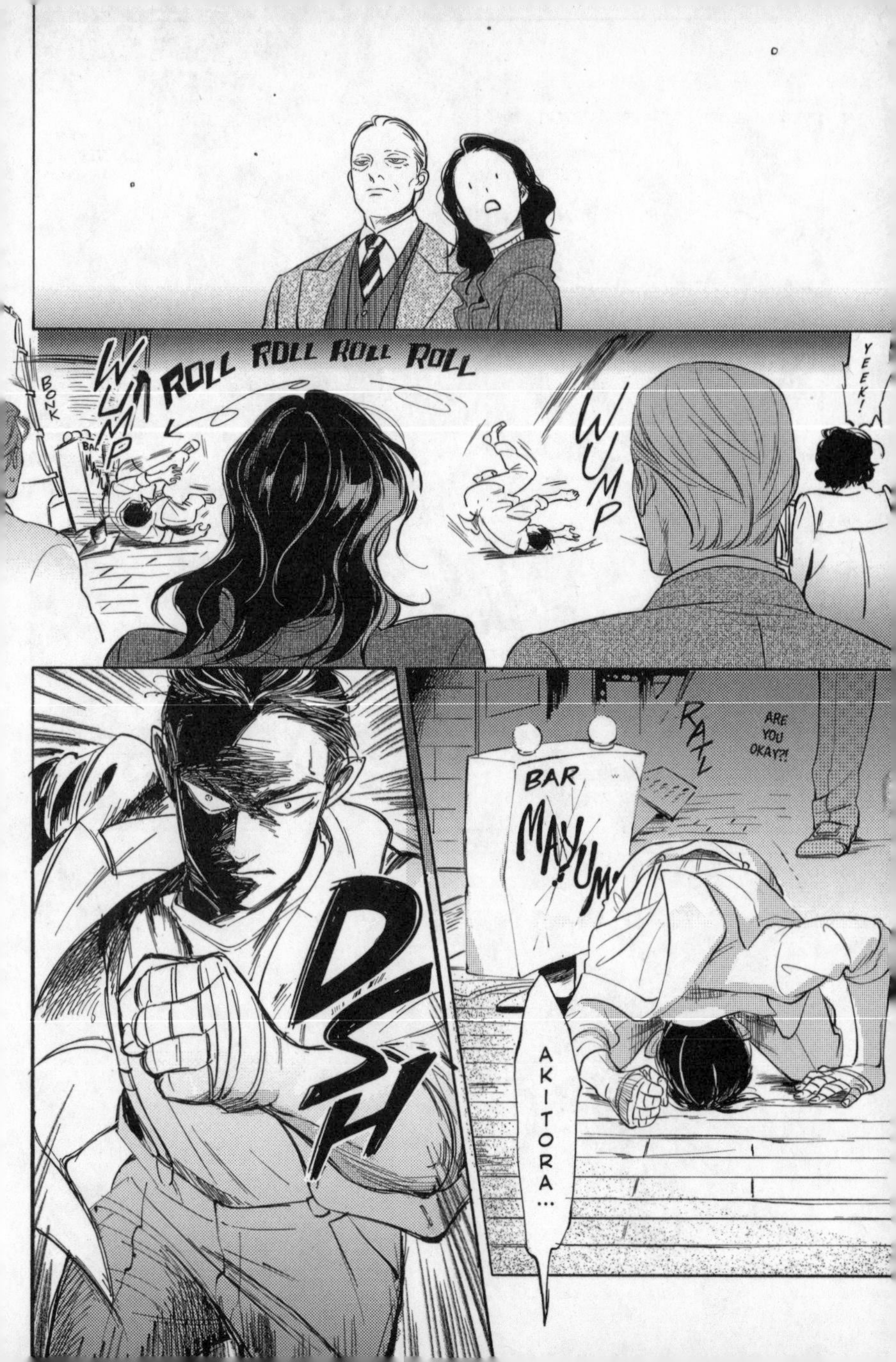
YEEK!
WUMP
ROLL ROLL ROLL ROLL
WUMP
BONK
ARE YOU OKAY?!
RATTLE
BAR MAYUMI
AKITORA...
DSH

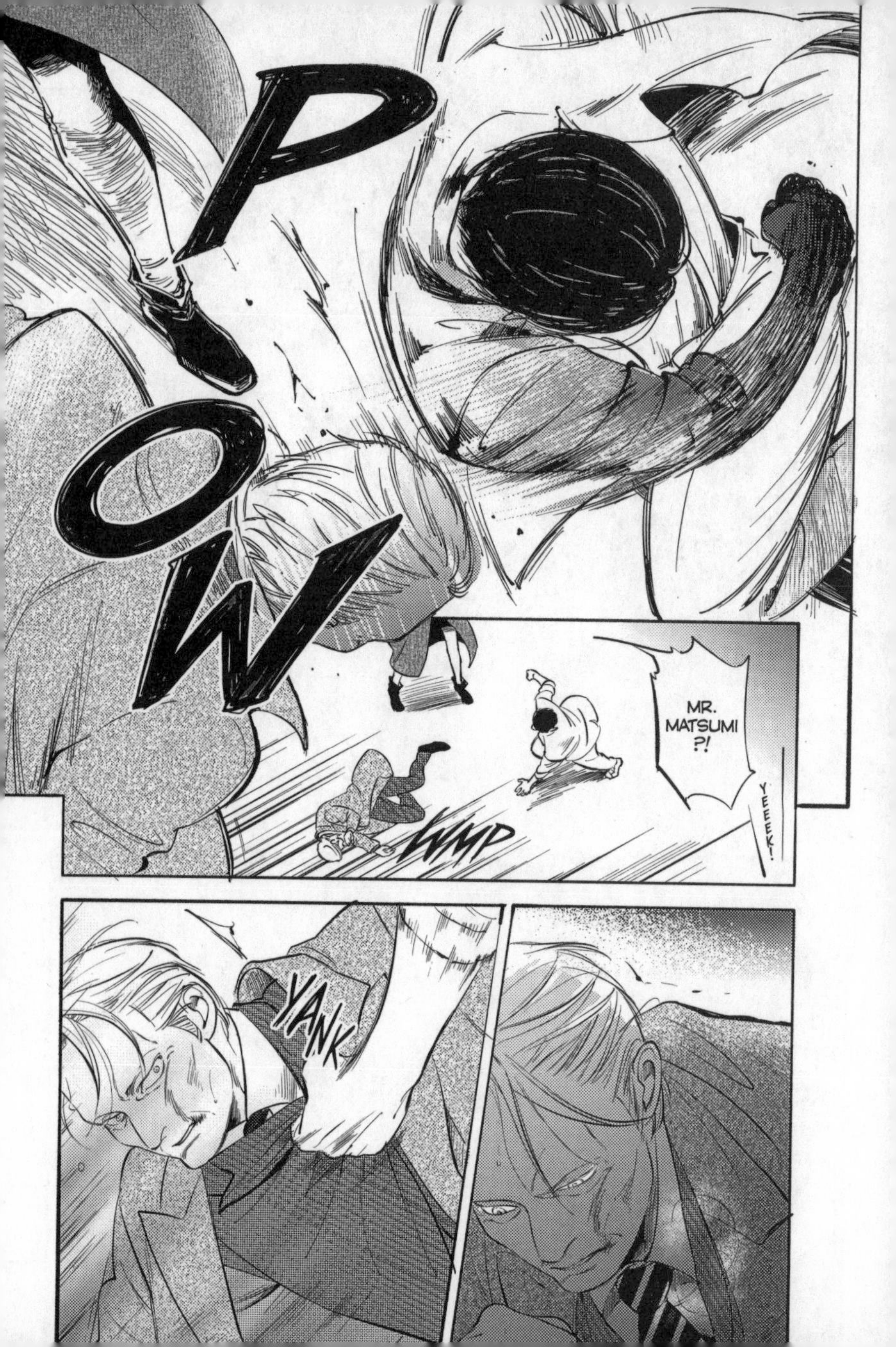
POW
YEEEK!
MR. MATSUMI ?!
WMP
…
YANK

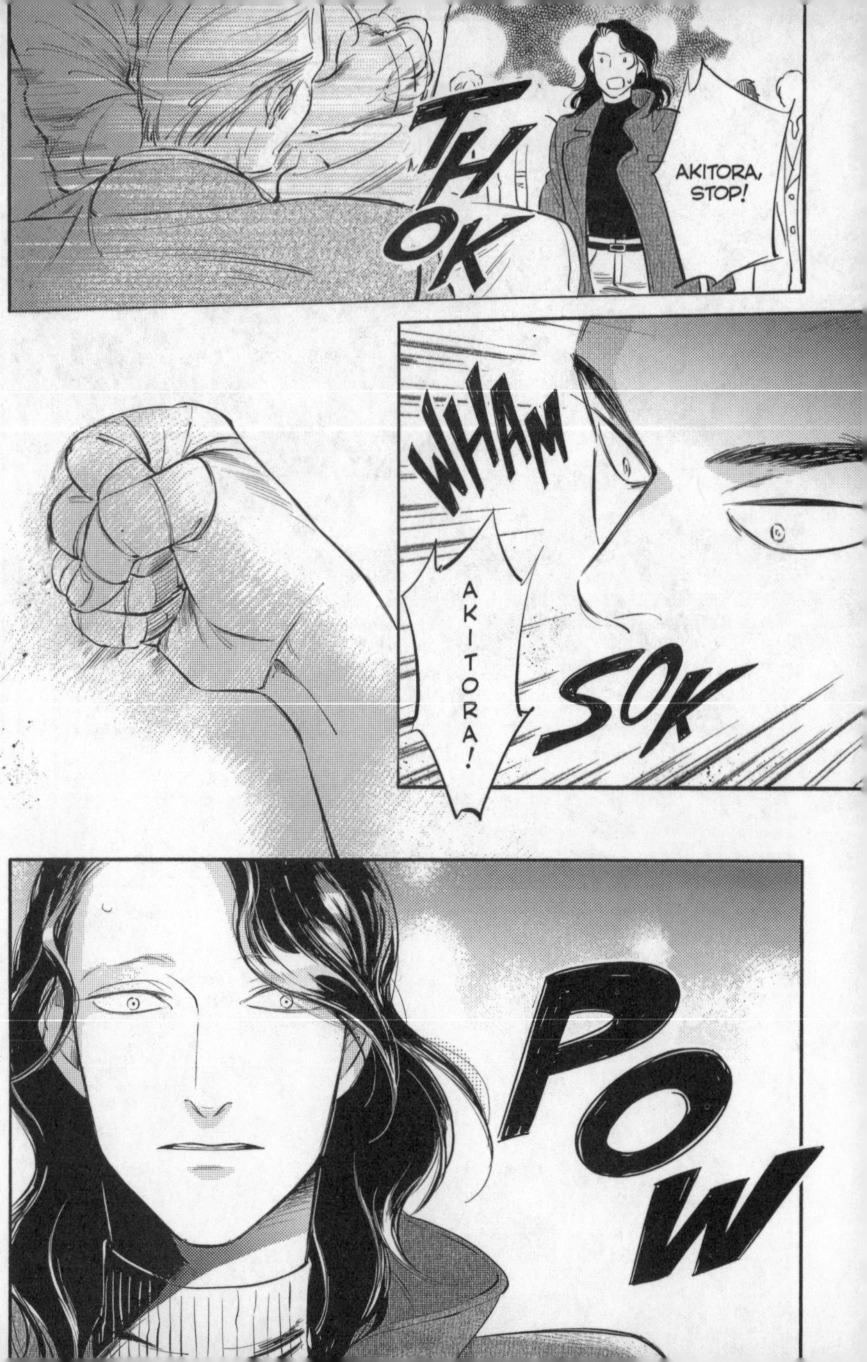
AKITORA, STOP!
THOK
WHAM
SOK
AKITORA!
POW

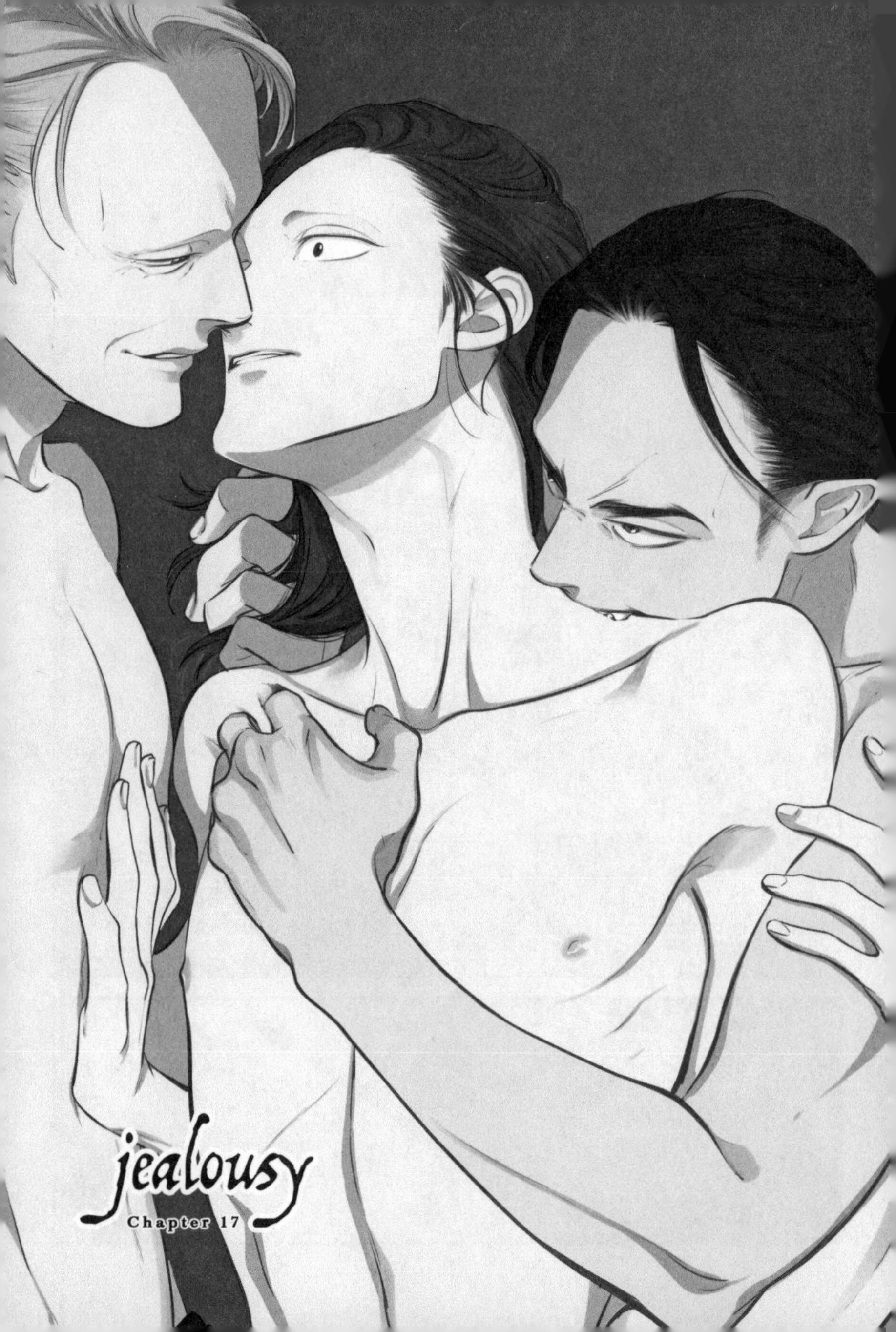
jealousy
Chapter 17

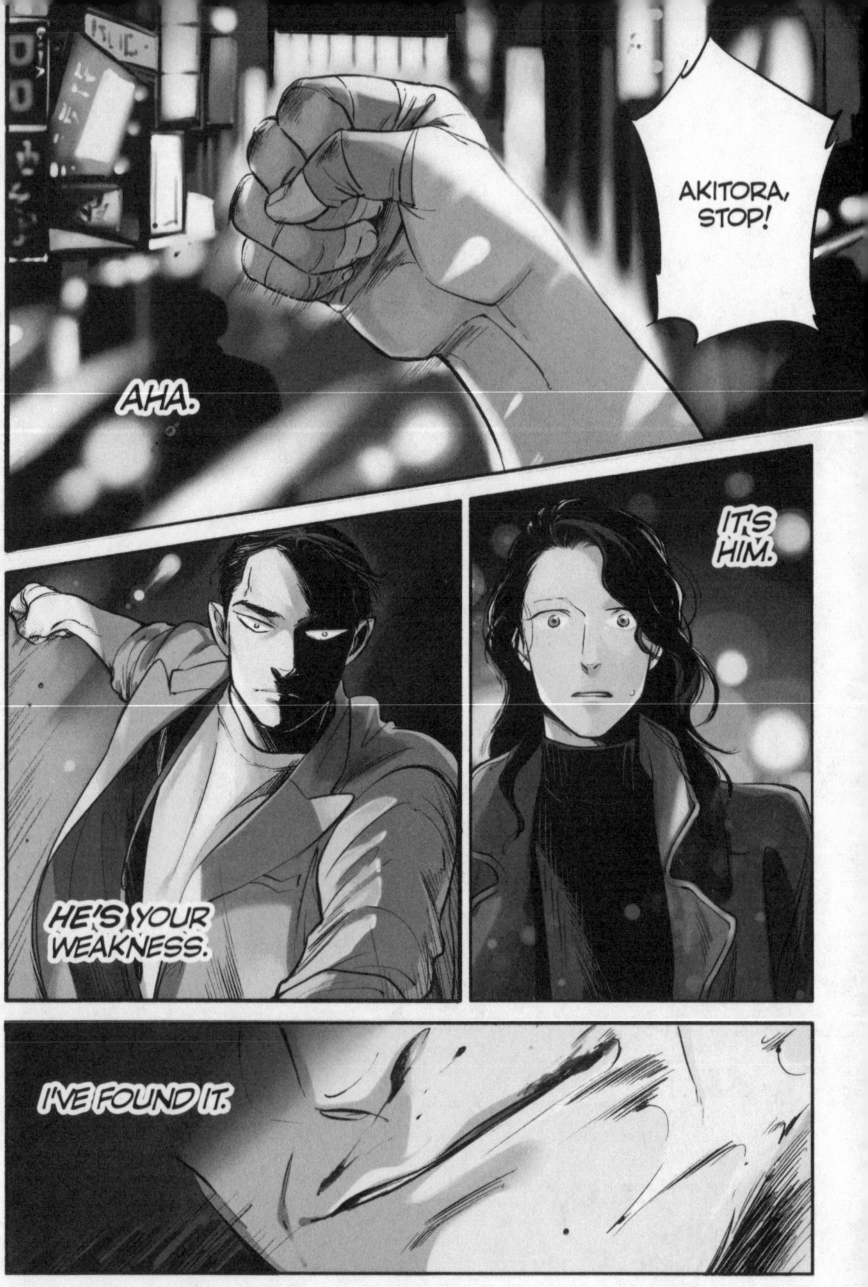
AKITORA, STOP!
AHA.
IT'S HIM.
HE'S YOUR WEAKNESS.
I'VE FOUND IT.

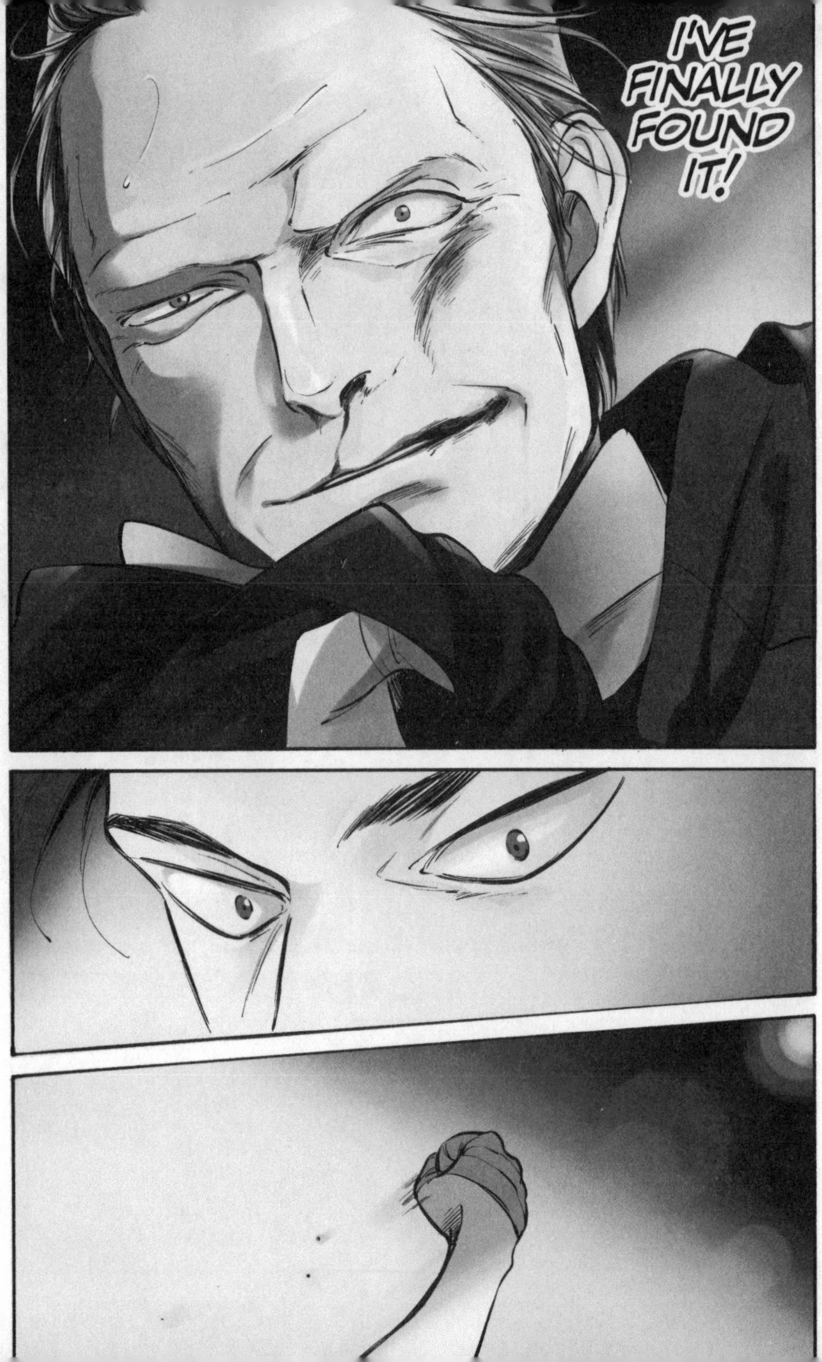
I'VE FINALLY FOUND IT!

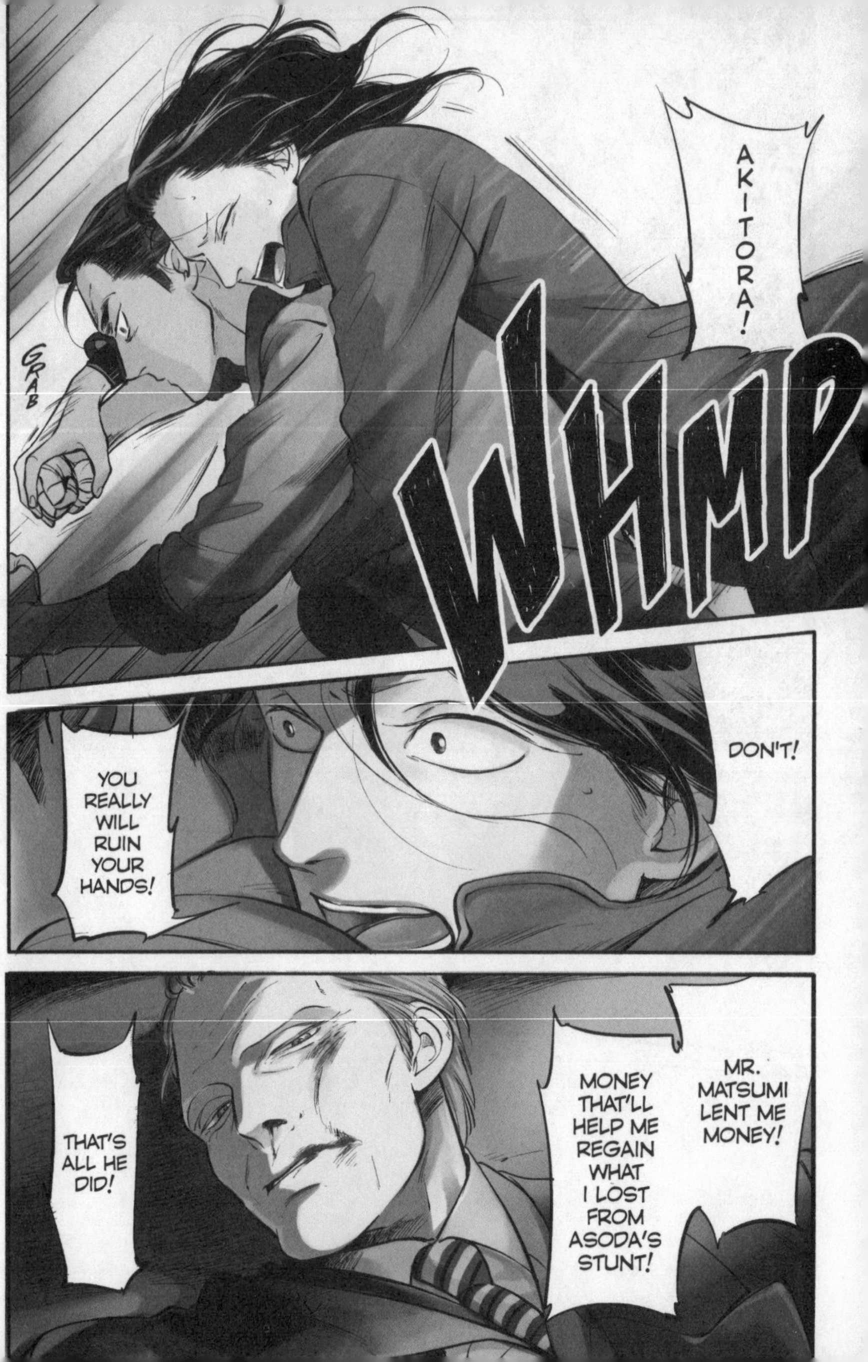
AKITORA!
WHMP
GRAB
DON'T!
YOU REALLY WILL RUIN YOUR HANDS!
MR. MATSUMI LENT ME MONEY!
MONEY THAT'LL HELP ME REGAIN WHAT I LOST FROM ASODA'S STUNT!
THAT'S ALL HE DID!

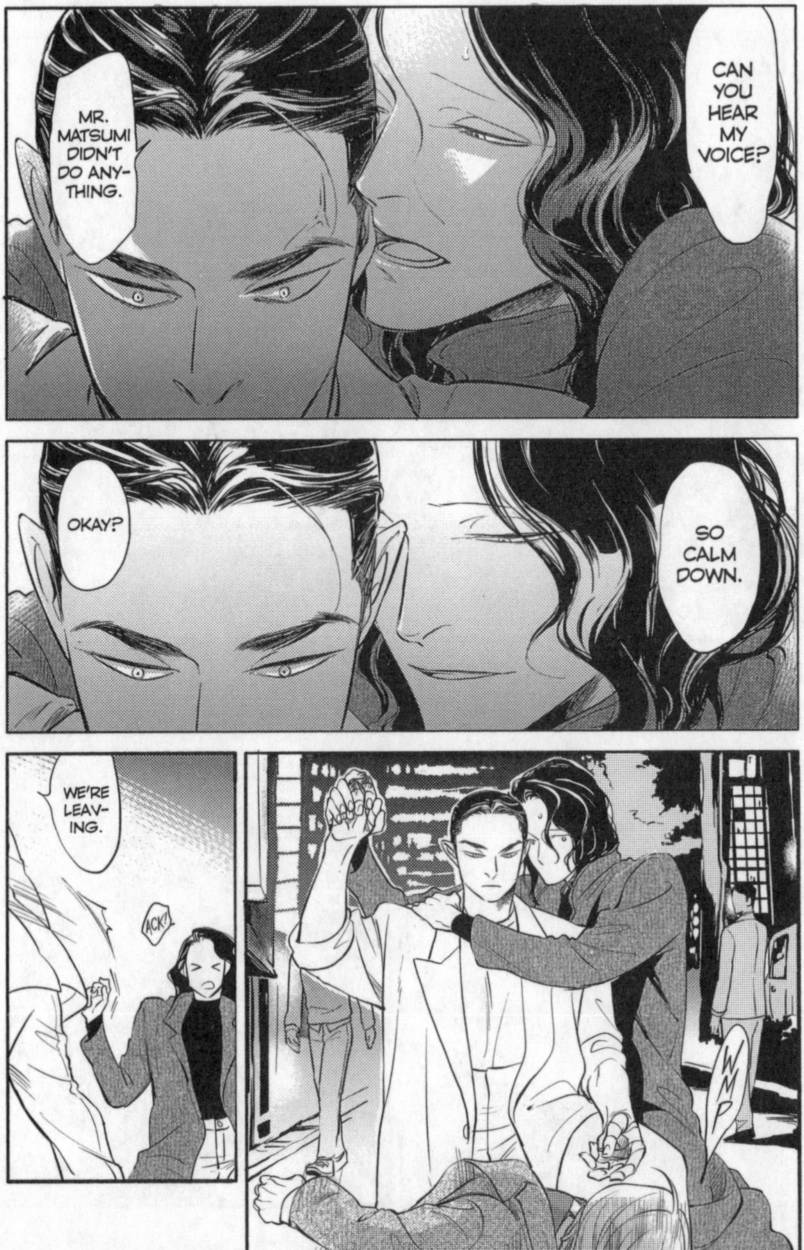
CAN YOU HEAR MY VOICE?
MR. MATSUMI DIDN'T DO ANY-THING.
SO CALM DOWN.
OKAY?
WMP
ACK!
WE'RE LEAV-ING.

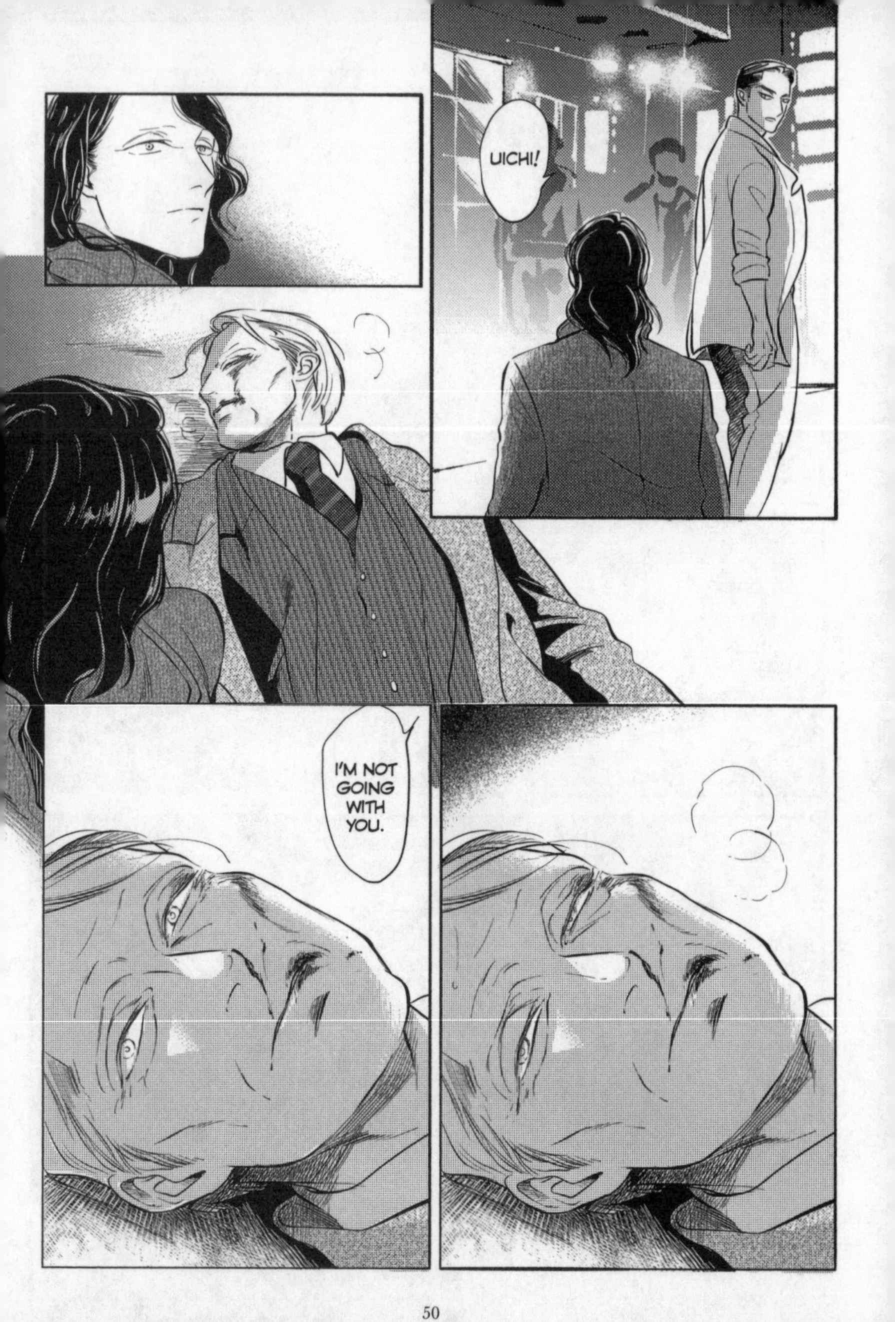
UICHI!
I'M NOT GOING WITH YOU.

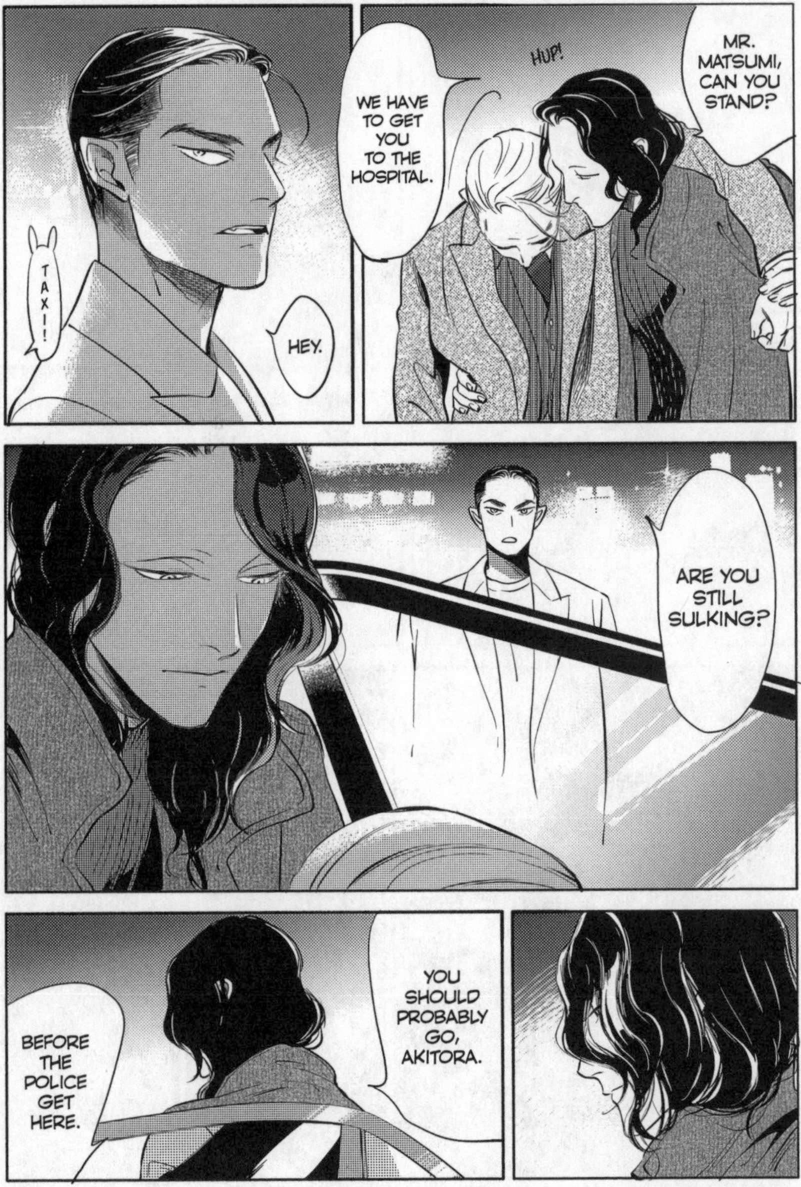
MR. MATSUMI, CAN YOU STAND?
HUP!
WE HAVE TO GET YOU TO THE HOSPITAL.
HEY.
TAXI!
ARE YOU STILL SULKING?
YOU SHOULD PROBABLY GO, AKITORA.
BEFORE THE POLICE GET HERE.

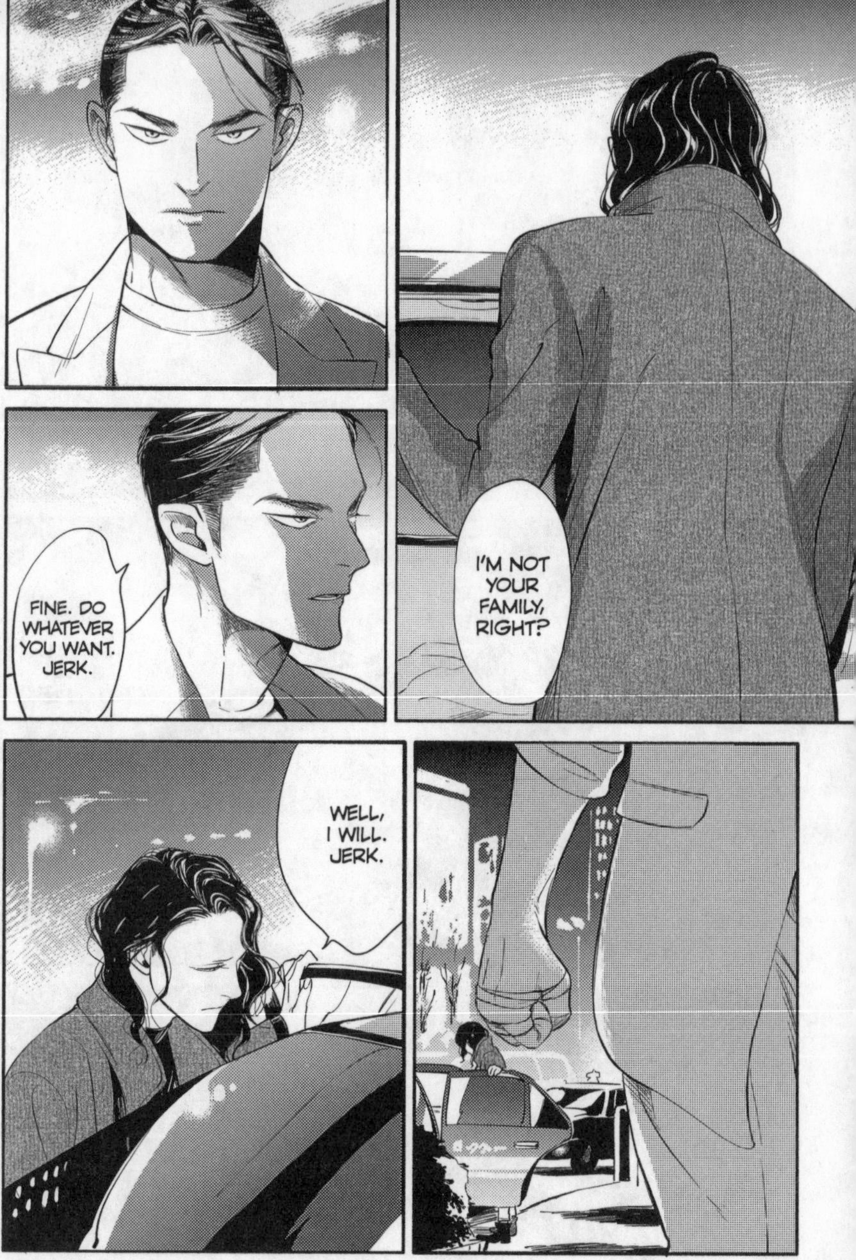
I'M NOT YOUR FAMILY, RIGHT?
FINE. DO WHATEVER YOU WANT. JERK.
WELL, I WILL. JERK.

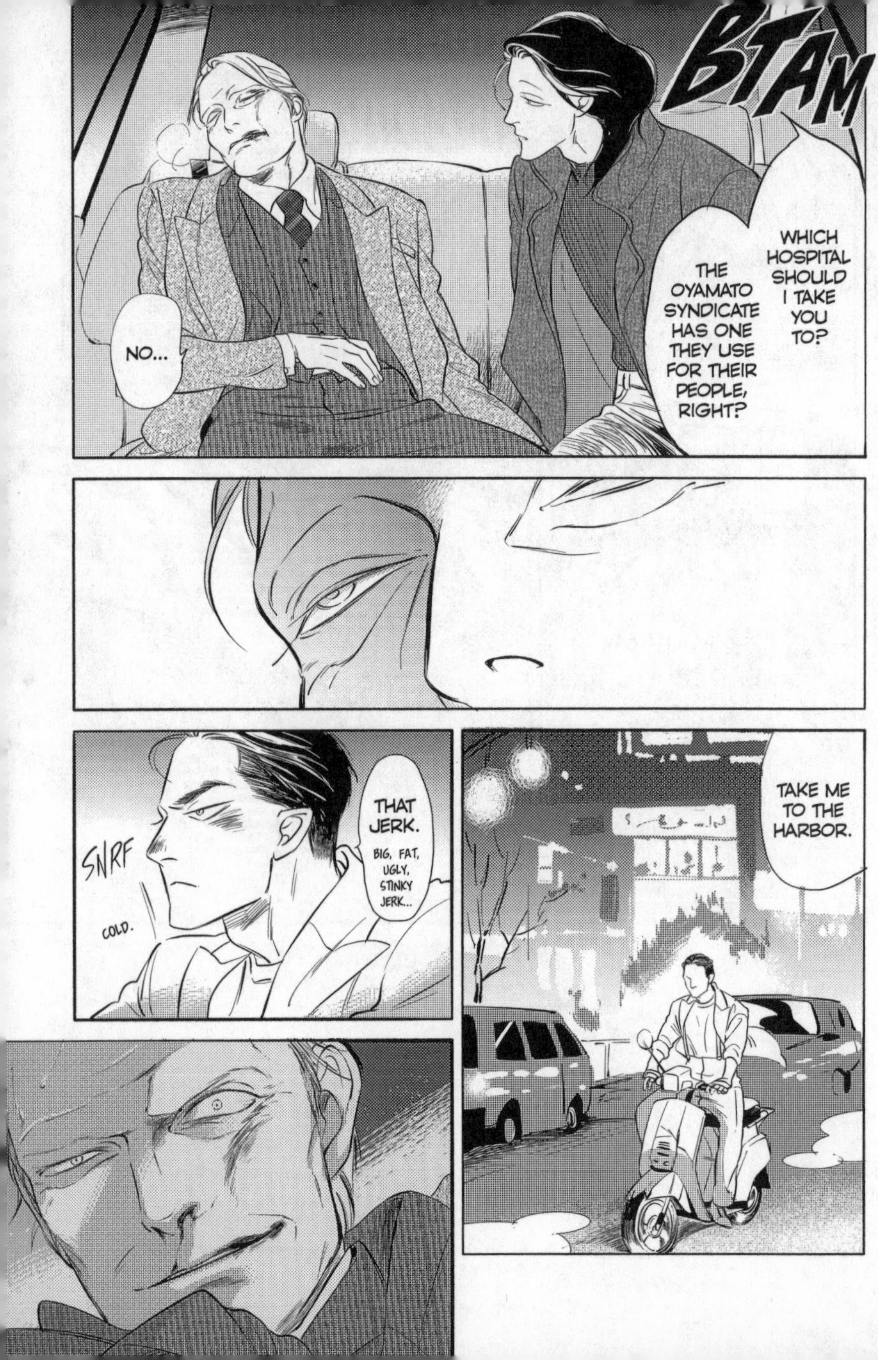
BTAM
WHICH HOSPITAL SHOULD I TAKE YOU TO?
THE OYAMATO SYNDICATE HAS ONE THEY USE FOR THEIR PEOPLE, RIGHT?
NO...
TAKE ME TO THE HARBOR.
THAT JERK.
BIG, FAT, UGLY, STINKY JERK...
SNRF
COLD.

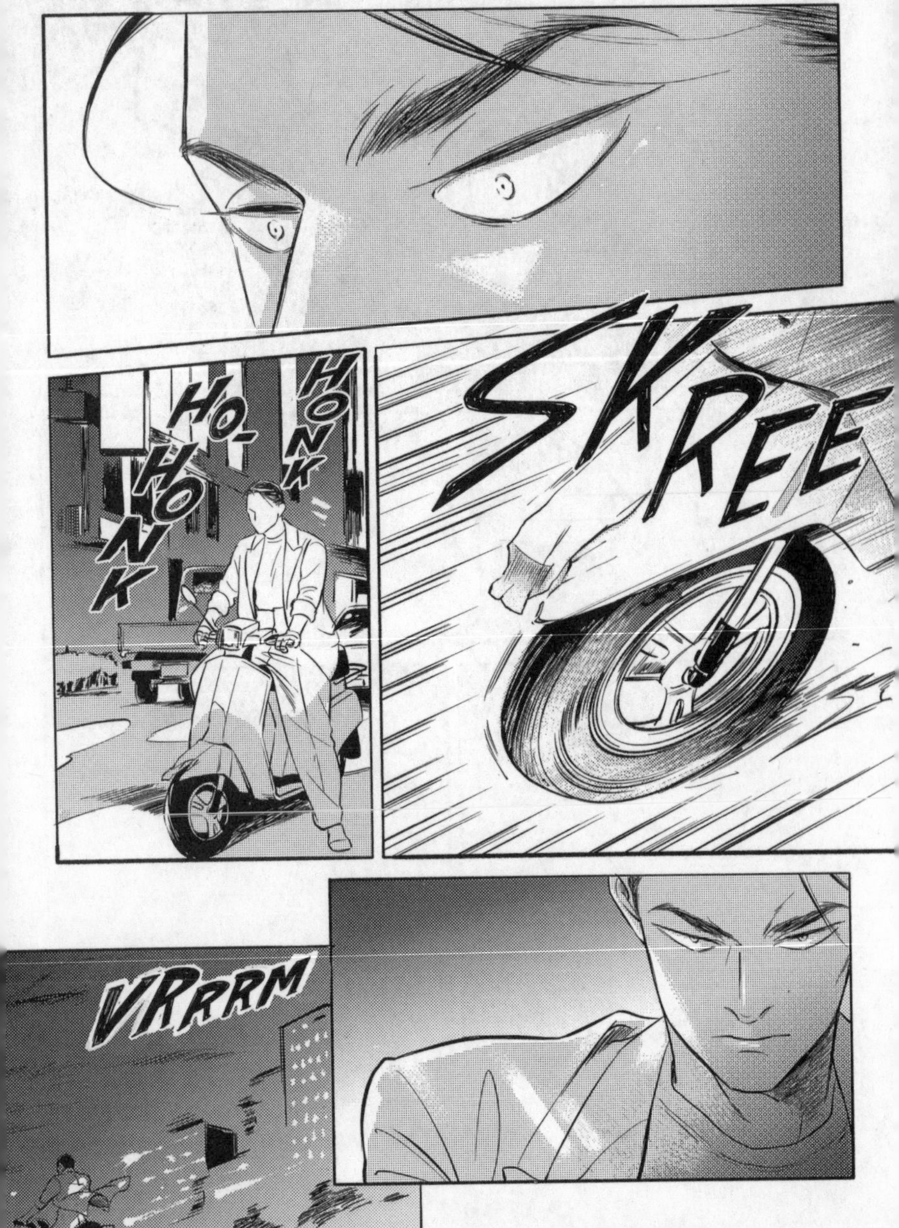
SKREE
HONK
HO-HONK
VRRRM

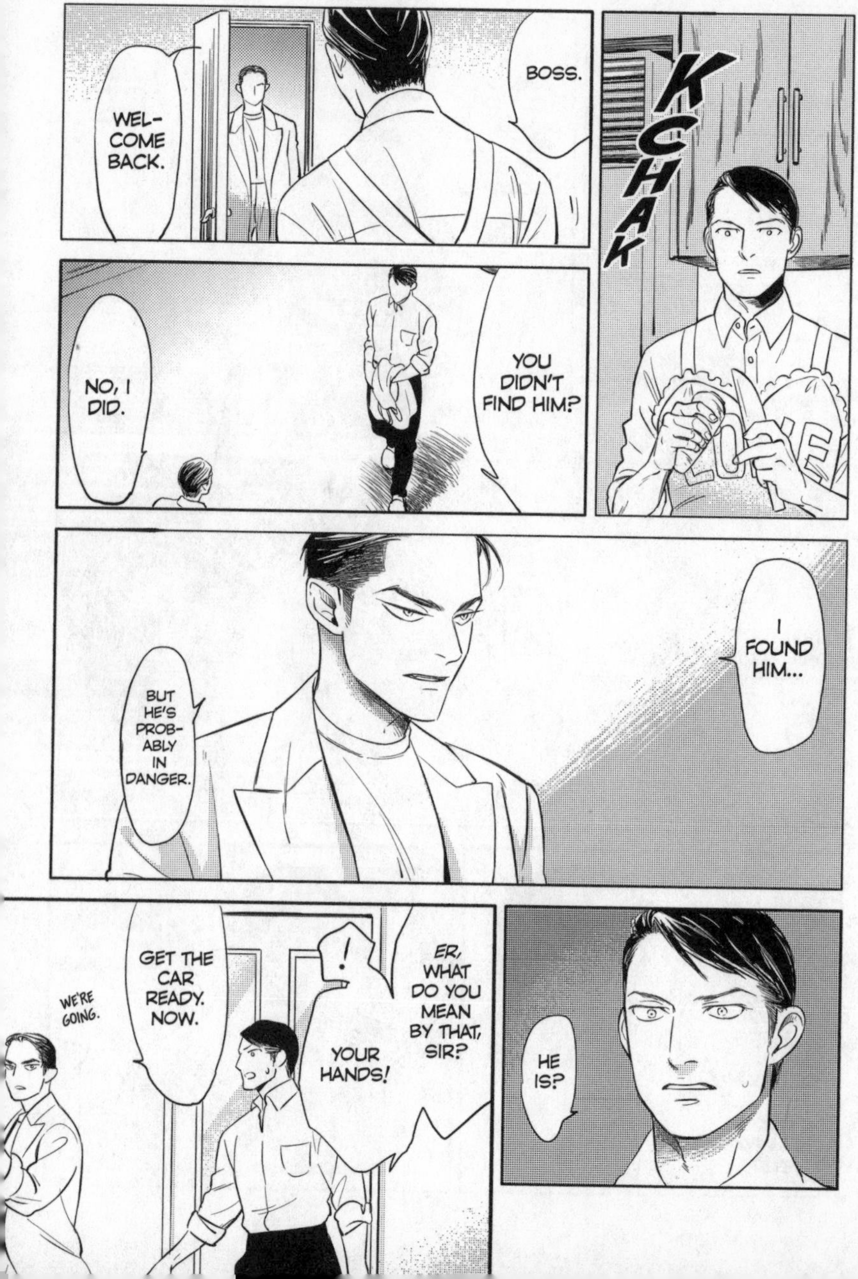
KCHAK
BOSS.
WEL-COME BACK.
YOU DIDN'T FIND HIM?
NO, I DID.
I FOUND HIM...
BUT HE'S PROB-ABLY IN DANGER.
HE IS?
ER, WHAT DO YOU MEAN BY THAT, SIR?
YOUR HANDS!
!
GET THE CAR READY. NOW.
WE'RE GOING.

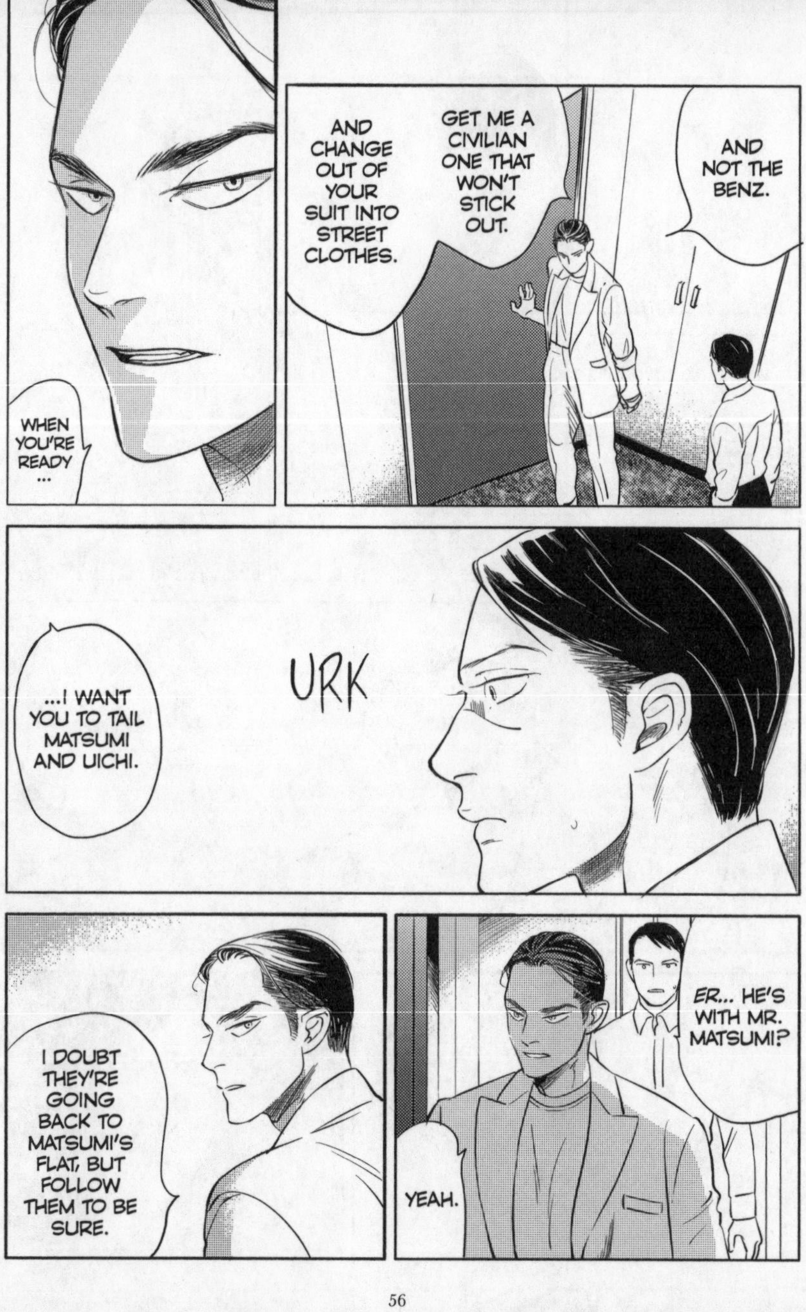
AND NOT THE BENZ.
GET ME A CIVILIAN ONE THAT WON'T STICK OUT.
AND CHANGE OUT OF YOUR SUIT INTO STREET CLOTHES.
WHEN YOU'RE READY ...
...I WANT YOU TO TAIL MATSUMI AND UICHI.
URK
ER... HE'S WITH MR. MATSUMI?
YEAH.
I DOUBT THEY'RE GOING BACK TO MATSUMI'S FLAT, BUT FOLLOW THEM TO BE SURE.

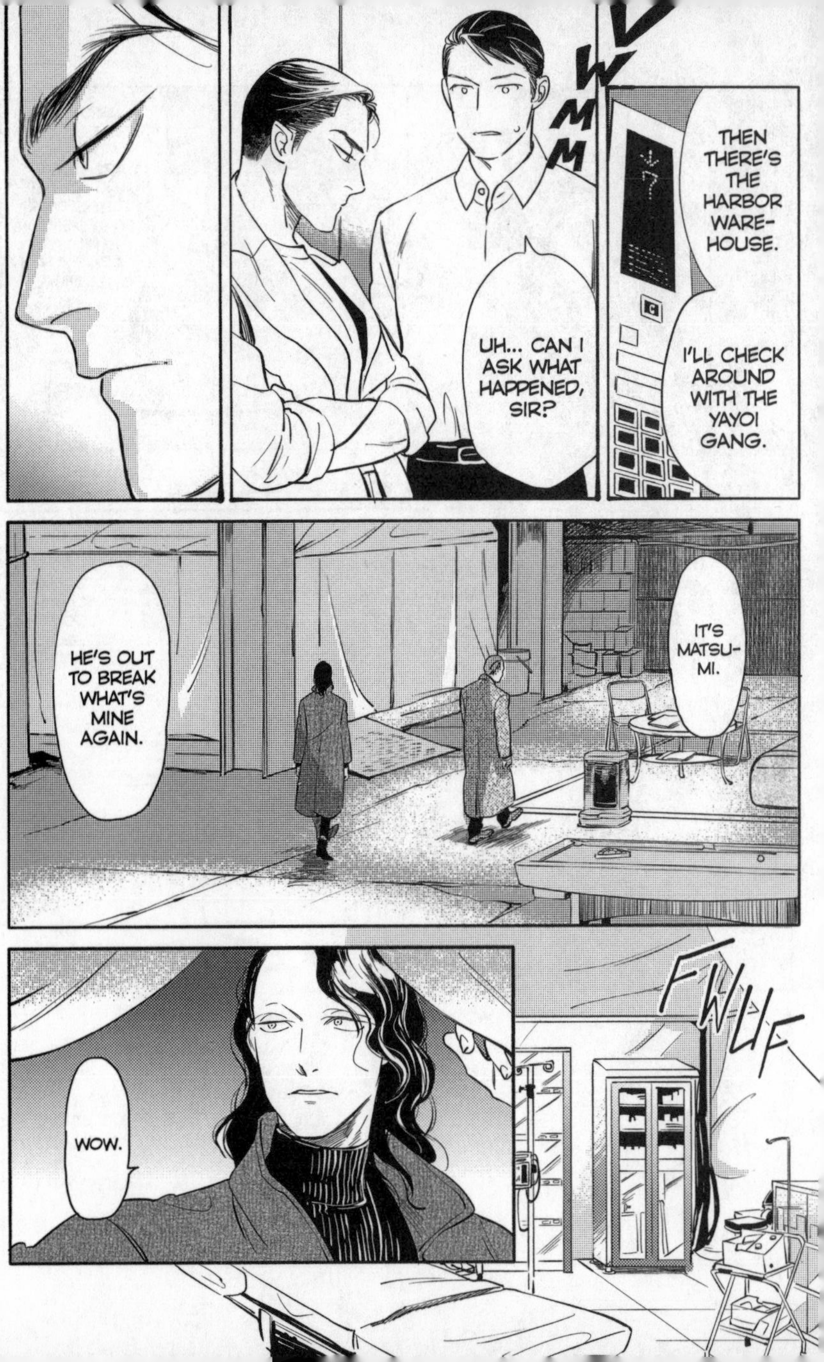
THEN THERE'S THE HARBOR WARE-HOUSE.
I'LL CHECK AROUND WITH THE YAYOI GANG.
VWMM
UH... CAN I ASK WHAT HAPPENED, SIR?
IT'S MATSU-MI.
HE'S OUT TO BREAK WHAT'S MINE AGAIN.
FWUF
WOW.

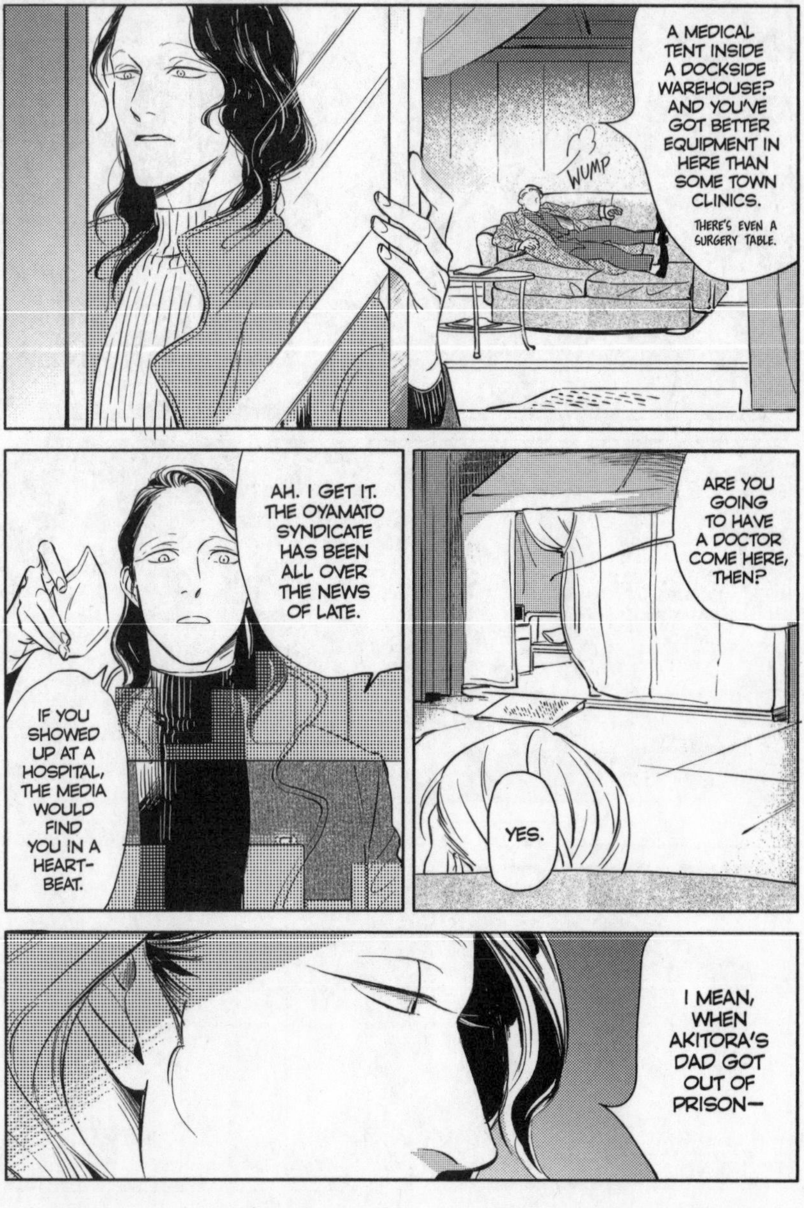
A MEDICAL TENT INSIDE A DOCKSIDE WAREHOUSE? AND YOU'VE GOT BETTER EQUIPMENT IN HERE THAN SOME TOWN CLINICS.
THERE'S EVEN A SURGERY TABLE.
WUMP
ARE YOU GOING TO HAVE A DOCTOR COME HERE, THEN?
YES.
AH. I GET IT. THE OYAMATO SYNDICATE HAS BEEN ALL OVER THE NEWS OF LATE.
IF YOU SHOWED UP AT A HOSPITAL, THE MEDIA WOULD FIND YOU IN A HEART-BEAT.
I MEAN, WHEN AKITORA'S DAD GOT OUT OF PRISON—

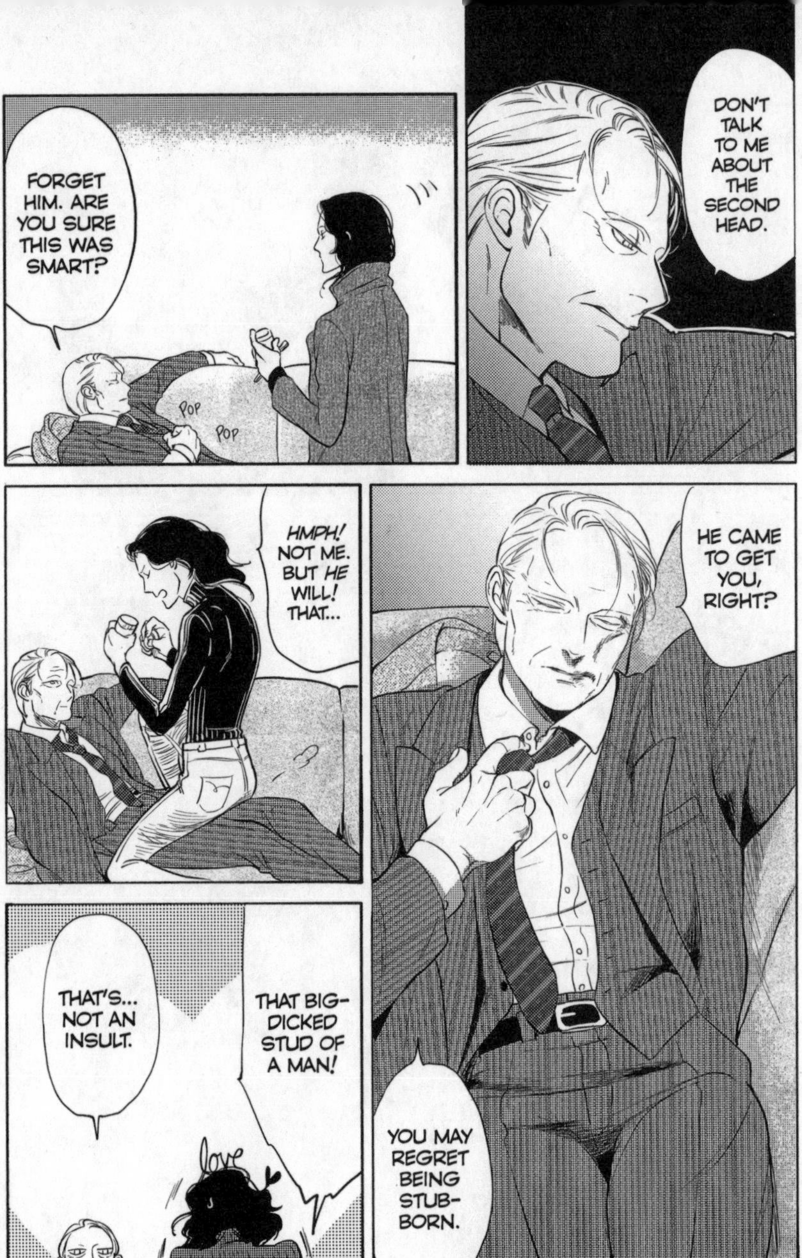
DON'T TALK TO ME ABOUT THE SECOND HEAD.
FORGET HIM. ARE YOU SURE THIS WAS SMART?
POP
POP
HE CAME TO GET YOU, RIGHT?
YOU MAY REGRET BEING STUB-BORN.
HMPH! NOT ME. BUT *HE* WILL! THAT...
THAT BIG-DICKED STUD OF A MAN!
THAT'S... NOT AN INSULT.
love

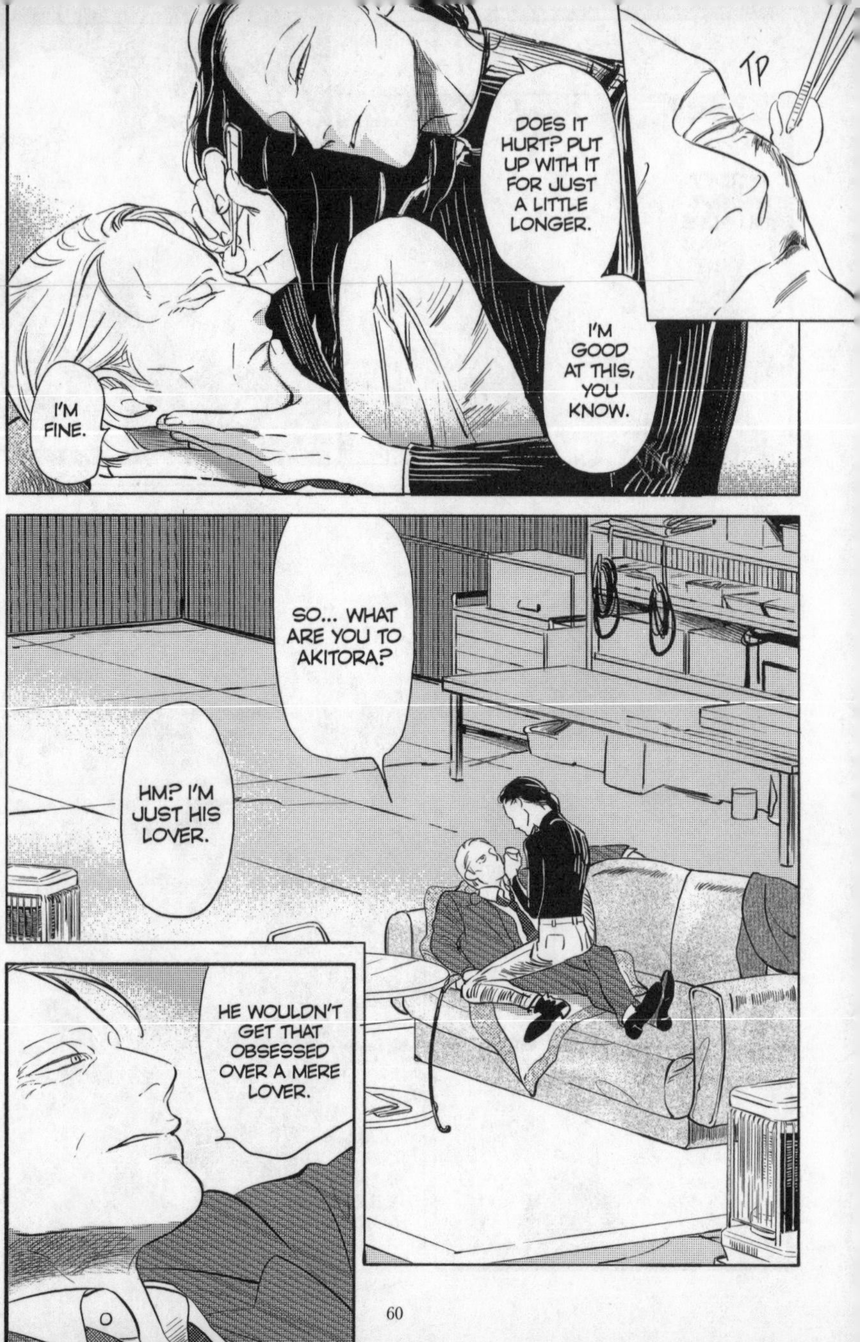
TP
DOES IT HURT? PUT UP WITH IT FOR JUST A LITTLE LONGER.
I'M GOOD AT THIS, YOU KNOW.
I'M FINE.
SO... WHAT ARE YOU TO AKITORA?
HM? I'M JUST HIS LOVER.
HE WOULDN'T GET THAT OBSESSED OVER A MERE LOVER.

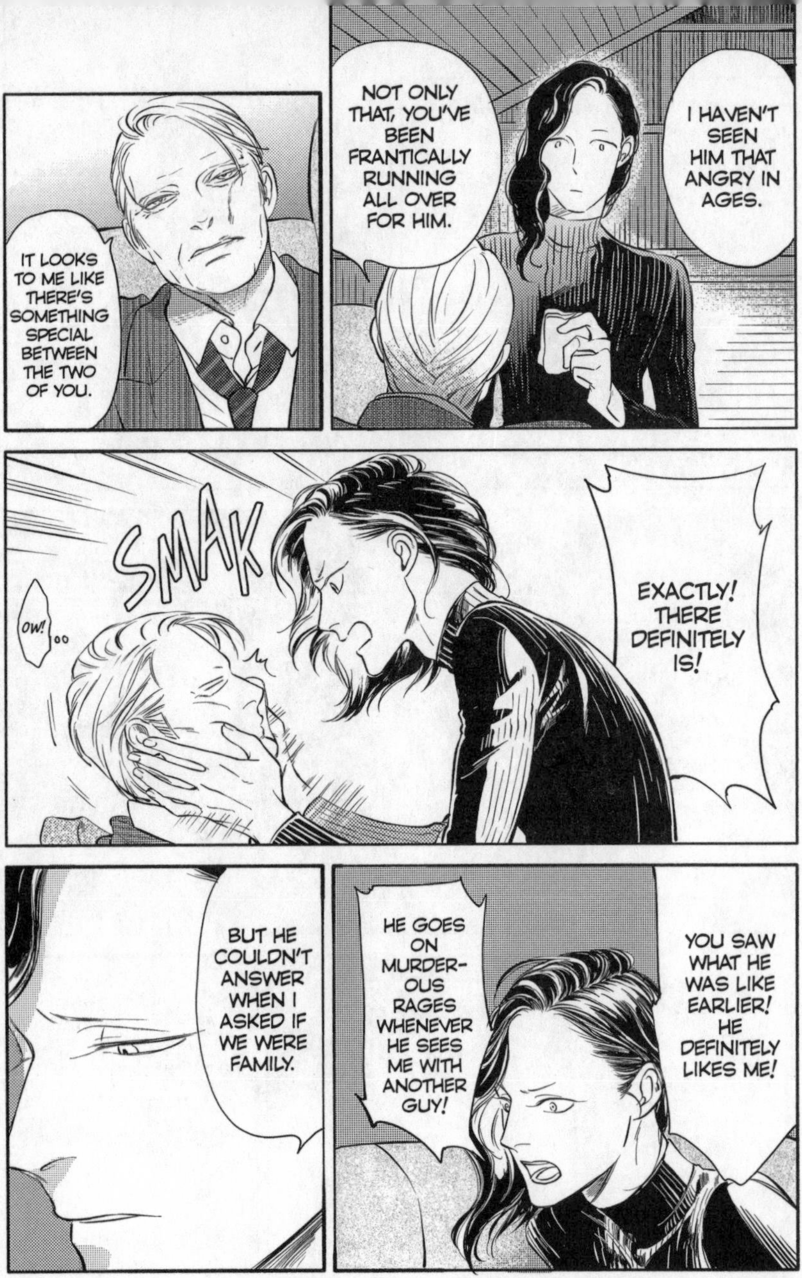
I HAVEN'T SEEN HIM THAT ANGRY IN AGES.
NOT ONLY THAT, YOU'VE BEEN FRANTICALLY RUNNING ALL OVER FOR HIM.
IT LOOKS TO ME LIKE THERE'S SOMETHING SPECIAL BETWEEN THE TWO OF YOU.
EXACTLY! THERE DEFINITELY IS!
SMAK
OW!
YOU SAW WHAT HE WAS LIKE EARLIER! HE DEFINITELY LIKES ME!
HE GOES ON MURDER-OUS RAGES WHENEVER HE SEES ME WITH ANOTHER GUY!
BUT HE COULDN'T ANSWER WHEN I ASKED IF WE WERE FAMILY.

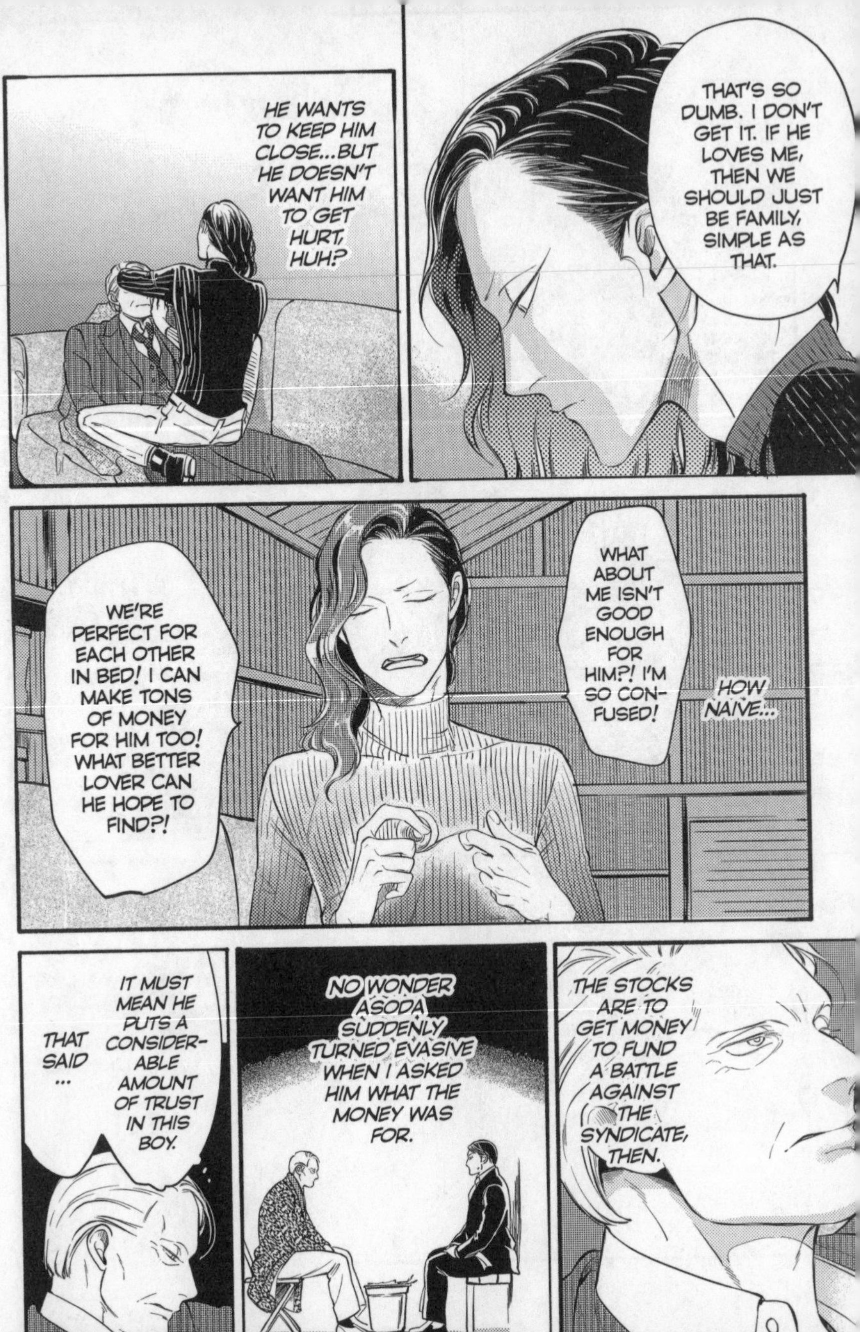
THAT'S SO DUMB. I DON'T GET IT. IF HE LOVES ME, THEN WE SHOULD JUST BE FAMILY, SIMPLE AS THAT.
HE WANTS TO KEEP HIM CLOSE...BUT HE DOESN'T WANT HIM TO GET HURT, HUH?
HOW NAIVE...
WHAT ABOUT ME ISN'T GOOD ENOUGH FOR HIM?! I'M SO CON-FUSED!
WE'RE PERFECT FOR EACH OTHER IN BED! I CAN MAKE TONS OF MONEY FOR HIM TOO! WHAT BETTER LOVER CAN HE HOPE TO FIND?!
THE STOCKS ARE TO GET MONEY TO FUND A BATTLE AGAINST THE SYNDICATE, THEN.
NO WONDER ASODA SUDDENLY TURNED EVASIVE WHEN I ASKED HIM WHAT THE MONEY WAS FOR.
IT MUST MEAN HE PUTS A CONSIDER-ABLE AMOUNT OF TRUST IN THIS BOY.
THAT SAID...

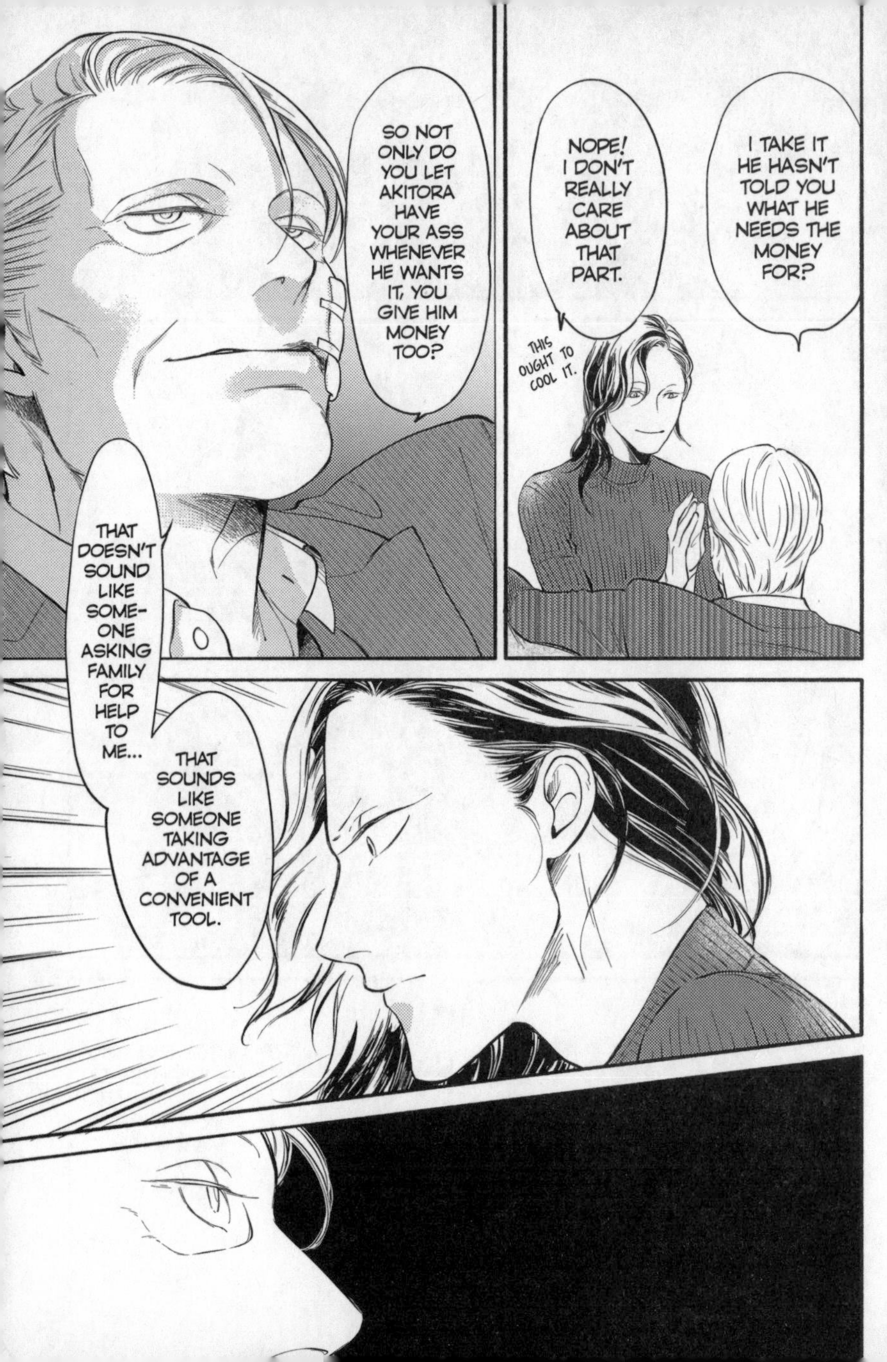
I TAKE IT HE HASN'T TOLD YOU WHAT HE NEEDS THE MONEY FOR?
NOPE! I DON'T REALLY CARE ABOUT THAT PART.
THIS OUGHT TO COOL IT.
SO NOT ONLY DO YOU LET AKITORA HAVE YOUR ASS WHENEVER HE WANTS IT, YOU GIVE HIM MONEY TOO?
THAT DOESN'T SOUND LIKE SOME-ONE ASKING FAMILY FOR HELP TO ME...
THAT SOUNDS LIKE SOMEONE TAKING ADVANTAGE OF A CONVENIENT TOOL.

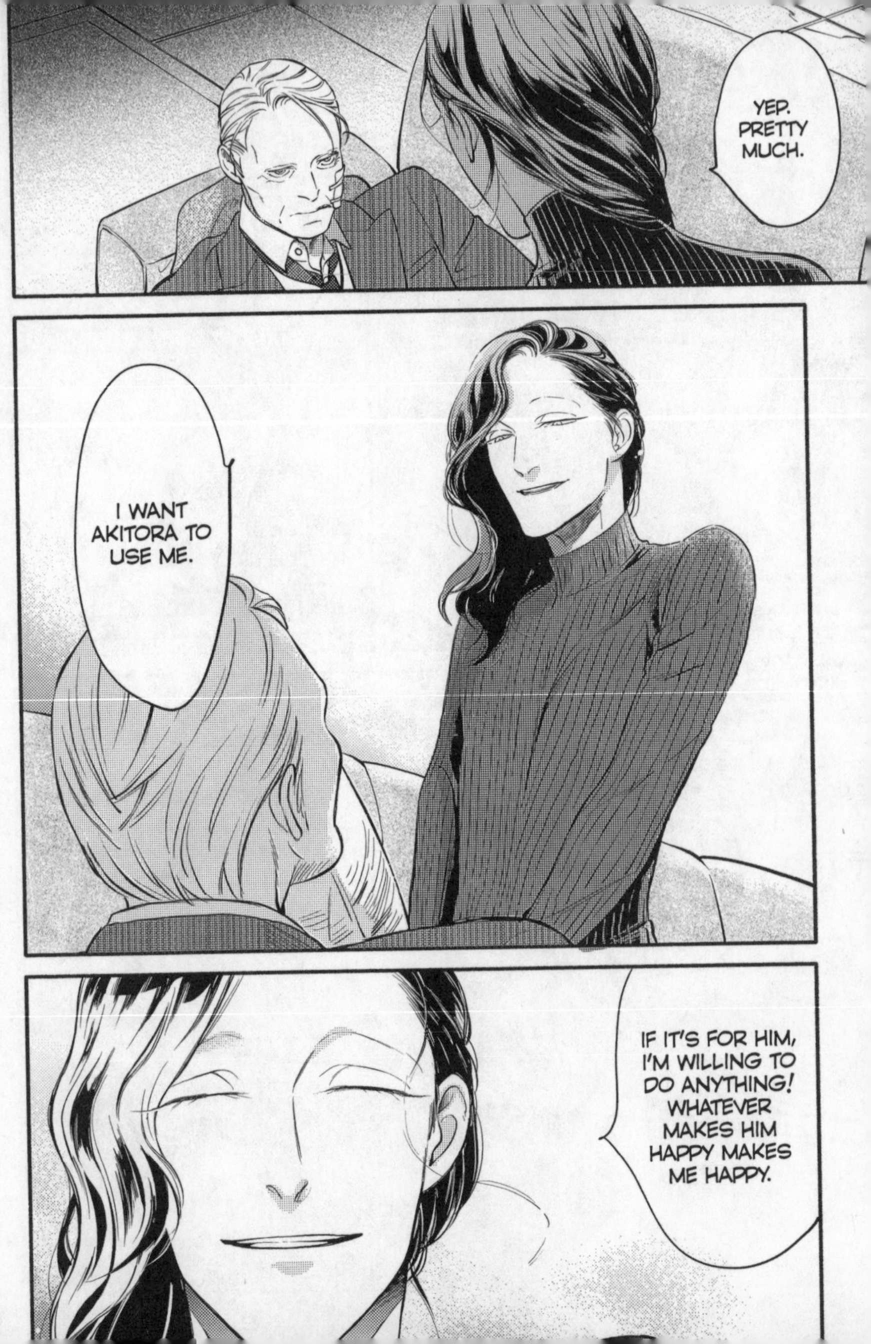
YEP. PRETTY MUCH.
I WANT AKITORA TO USE ME.
IF IT'S FOR HIM, I'M WILLING TO DO ANYTHING! WHATEVER MAKES HIM HAPPY MAKES ME HAPPY.

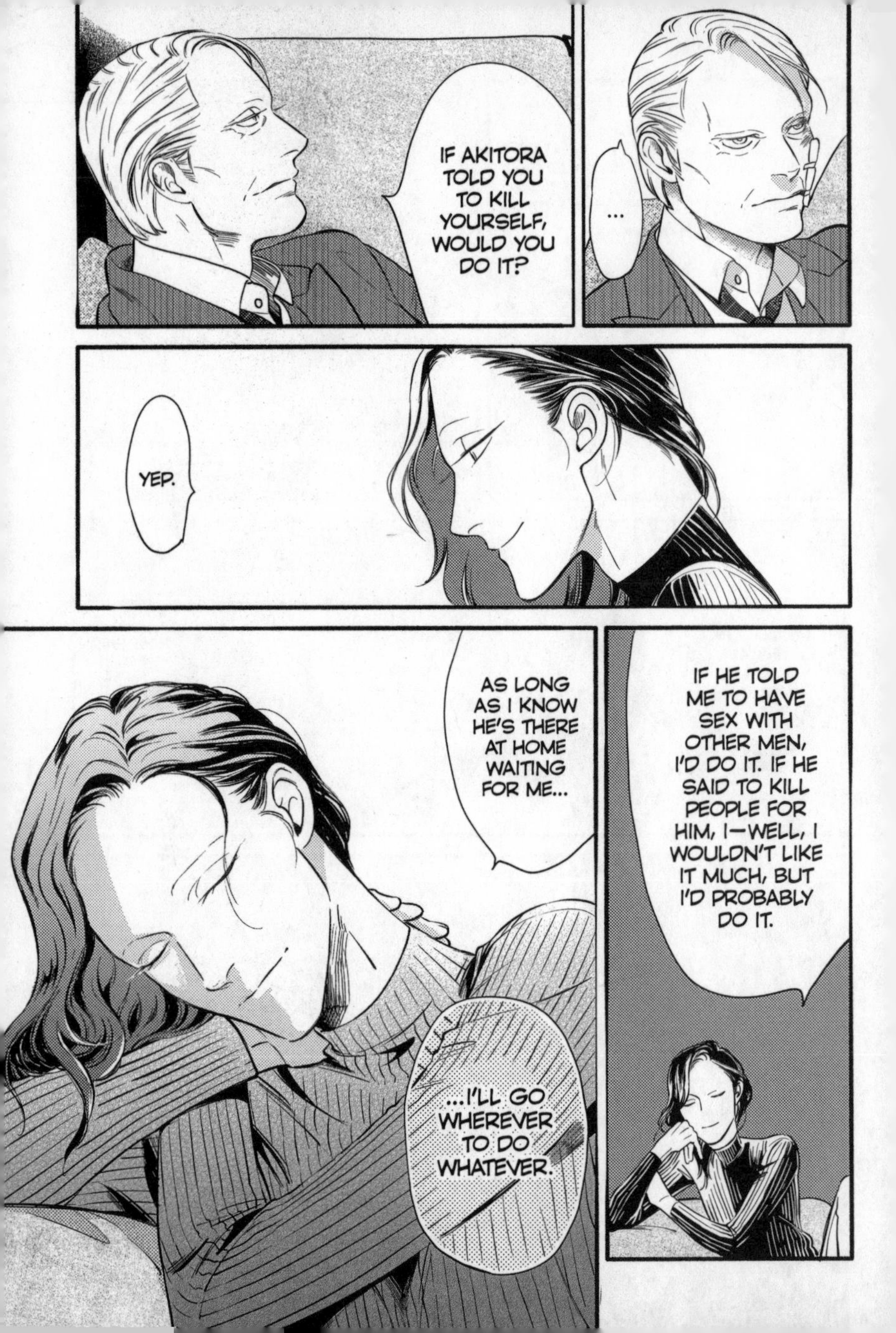
...
IF AKITORA TOLD YOU TO KILL YOURSELF, WOULD YOU DO IT?
YEP.
IF HE TOLD ME TO HAVE SEX WITH OTHER MEN, I'D DO IT. IF HE SAID TO KILL PEOPLE FOR HIM, I—WELL, I WOULDN'T LIKE IT MUCH, BUT I'D PROBABLY DO IT.
AS LONG AS I KNOW HE'S THERE AT HOME WAITING FOR ME...
...I'LL GO WHEREVER TO DO WHATEVER.

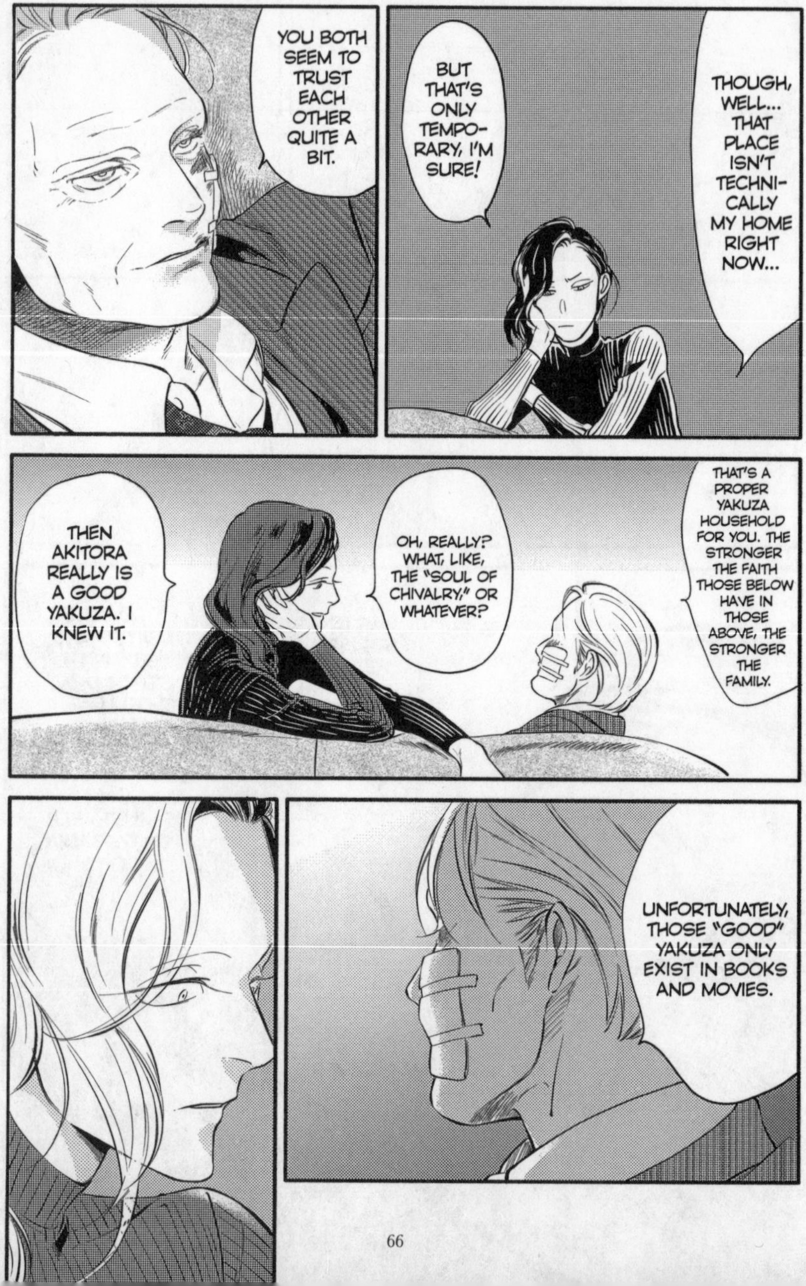
THOUGH, WELL... THAT PLACE ISN'T TECHNICALLY MY HOME RIGHT NOW...
BUT THAT'S ONLY TEMPORARY, I'M SURE!
YOU BOTH SEEM TO TRUST EACH OTHER QUITE A BIT.
THAT'S A PROPER YAKUZA HOUSEHOLD FOR YOU. THE STRONGER THE FAITH THOSE BELOW HAVE IN THOSE ABOVE, THE STRONGER THE FAMILY.
OH, REALLY? WHAT, LIKE, THE "SOUL OF CHIVALRY," OR WHATEVER?
THEN AKITORA REALLY IS A GOOD YAKUZA. I KNEW IT.
UNFORTUNATELY, THOSE "GOOD" YAKUZA ONLY EXIST IN BOOKS AND MOVIES.

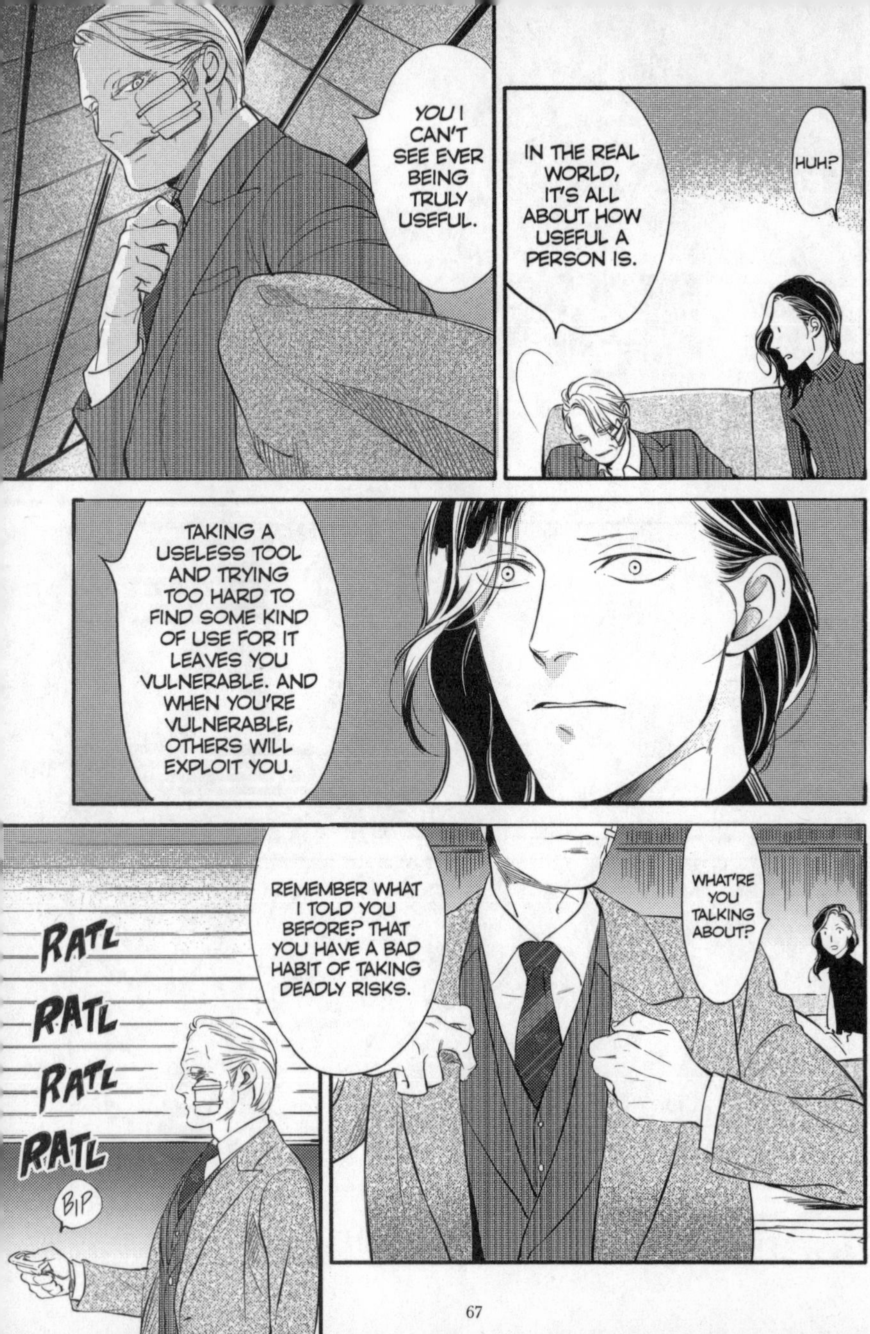
HUH?
IN THE REAL WORLD, IT'S ALL ABOUT HOW USEFUL A PERSON IS.
YOU I CAN'T SEE EVER BEING TRULY USEFUL.
TAKING A USELESS TOOL AND TRYING TOO HARD TO FIND SOME KIND OF USE FOR IT LEAVES YOU VULNERABLE. AND WHEN YOU'RE VULNERABLE, OTHERS WILL EXPLOIT YOU.
WHAT'RE YOU TALKING ABOUT?
REMEMBER WHAT I TOLD YOU BEFORE? THAT YOU HAVE A BAD HABIT OF TAKING DEADLY RISKS.
RATL
RATL
RATL
RATL
BIP

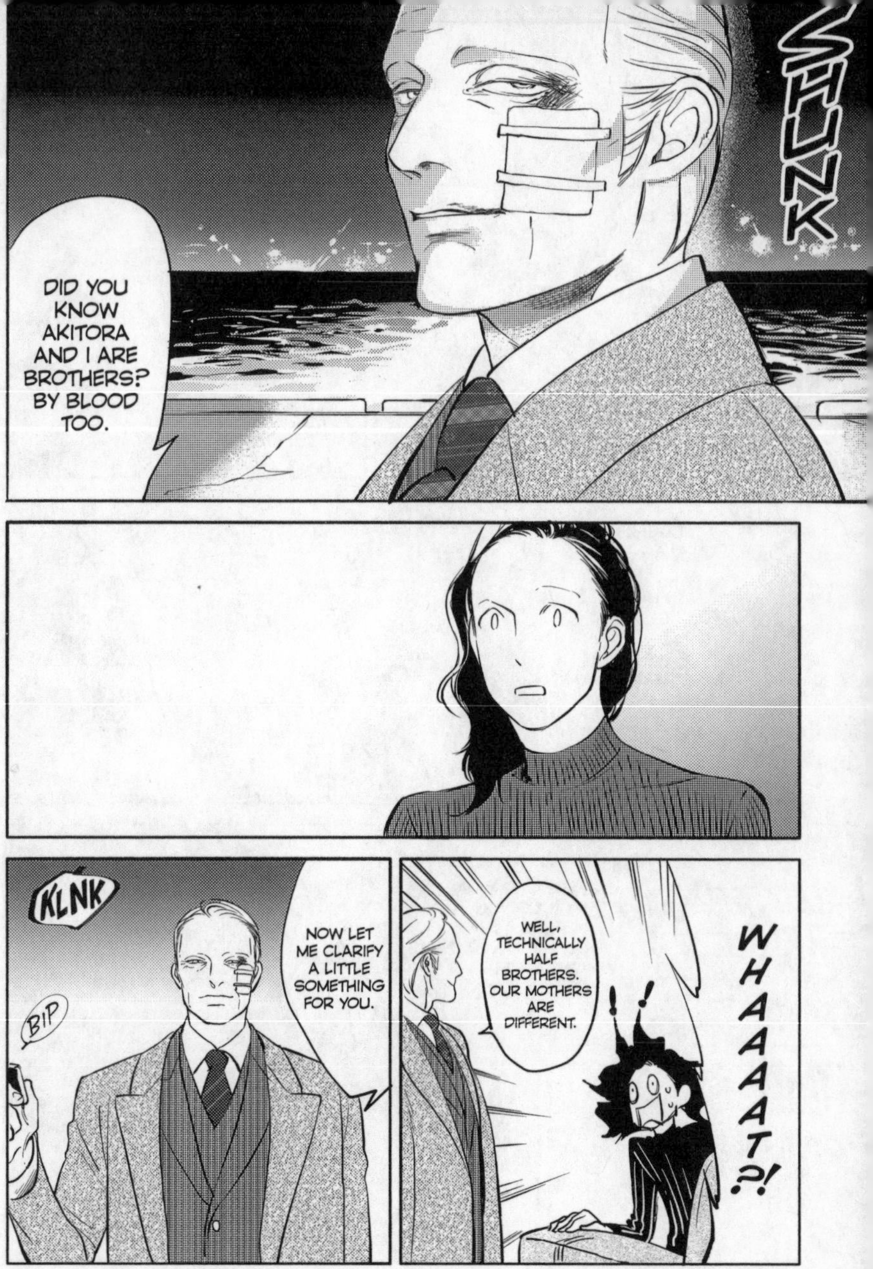
SHUNK
DID YOU KNOW AKITORA AND I ARE BROTHERS? BY BLOOD TOO.
WELL, TECHNICALLY HALF BROTHERS. OUR MOTHERS ARE DIFFERENT.
WHAAAAAT?!
KLNK
NOW LET ME CLARIFY A LITTLE SOMETHING FOR YOU.
BIP

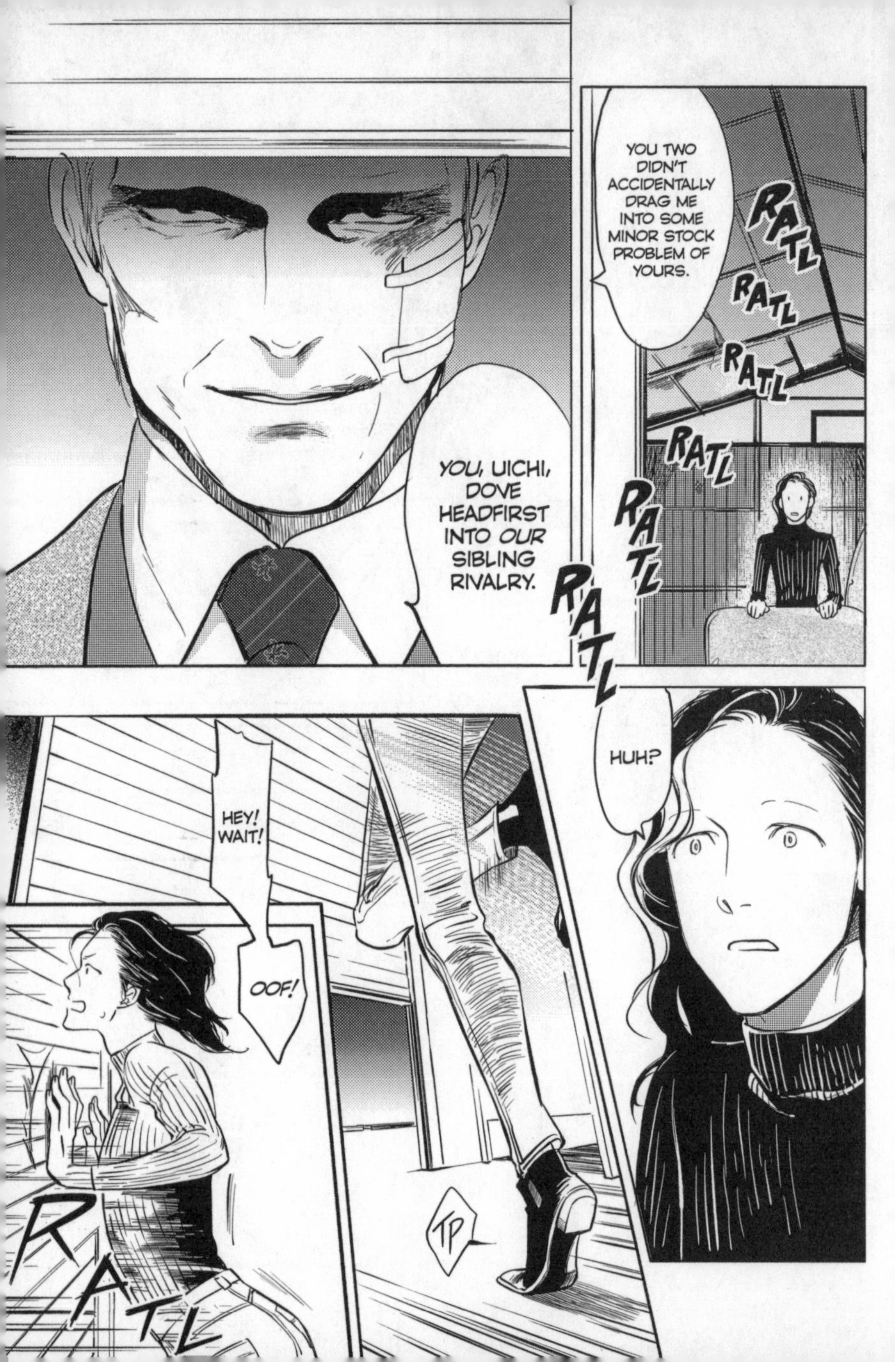
YOU TWO DIDN'T ACCIDENTALLY DRAG ME INTO SOME MINOR STOCK PROBLEM OF YOURS.
RATL RATL RATL RATL RATL RATL
YOU, UICHI, DOVE HEADFIRST INTO OUR SIBLING RIVALRY.
HUH?
TP
HEY! WAIT!
OOF!
RATL

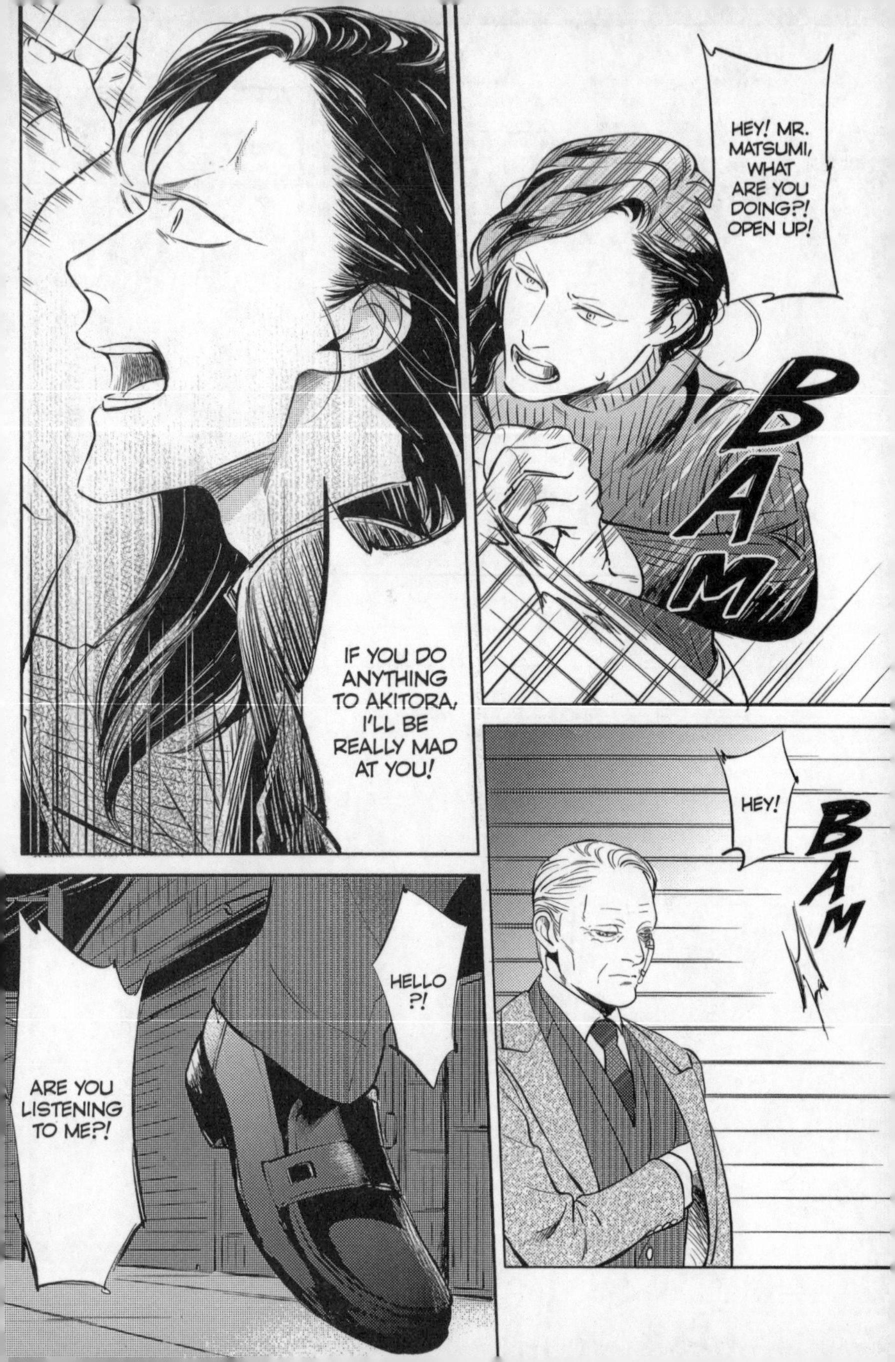
HEY! MR. MATSUMI, WHAT ARE YOU DOING?! OPEN UP!
BAM
IF YOU DO ANYTHING TO AKITORA, I'LL BE REALLY MAD AT YOU!
HEY!
BAM
HELLO ?!
ARE YOU LISTENING TO ME?!

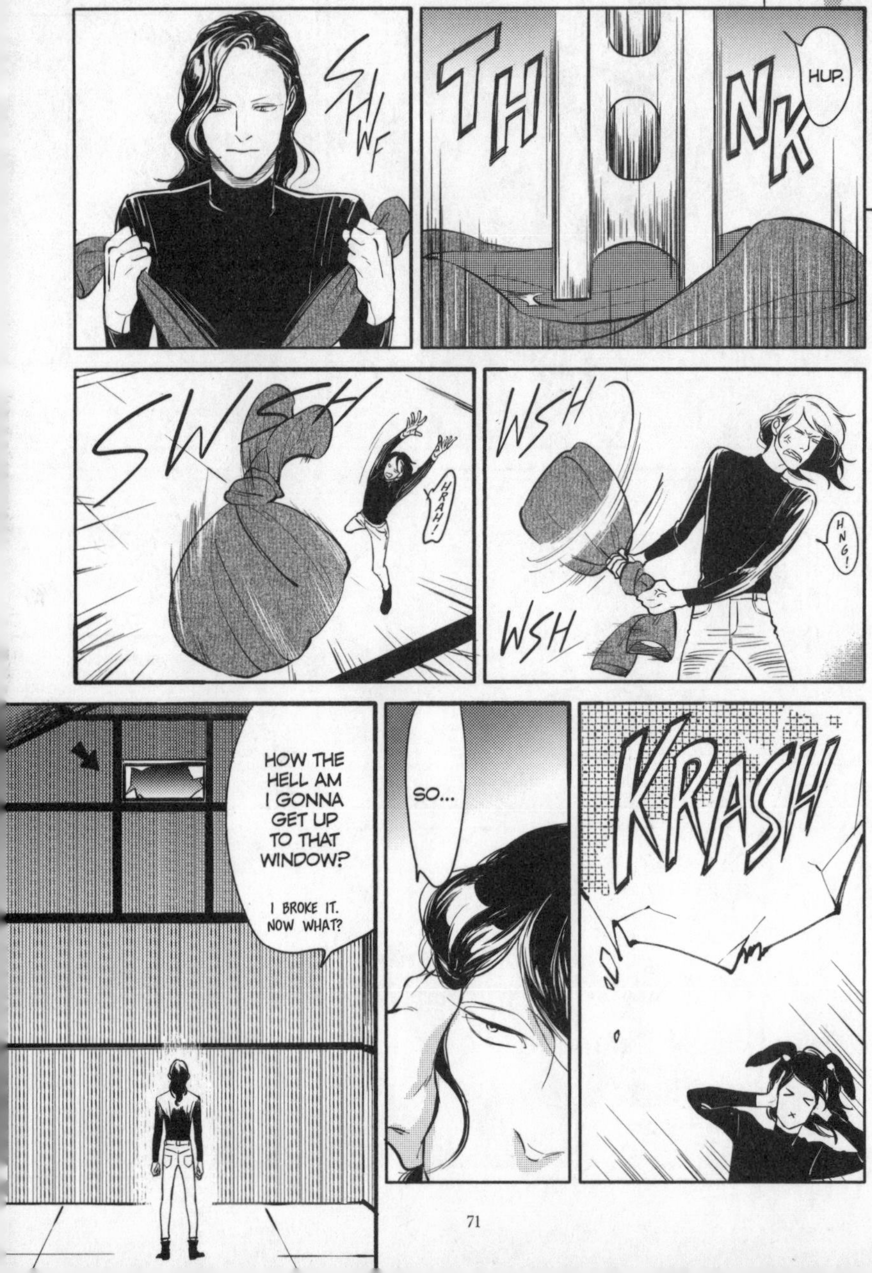
THUNK
HUP.
SHWF
WSH
HNG!
WSH
SWSH
HRAH!
KRASH
SO...
HOW THE HELL AM I GONNA GET UP TO THAT WINDOW?
I BROKE IT. NOW WHAT?

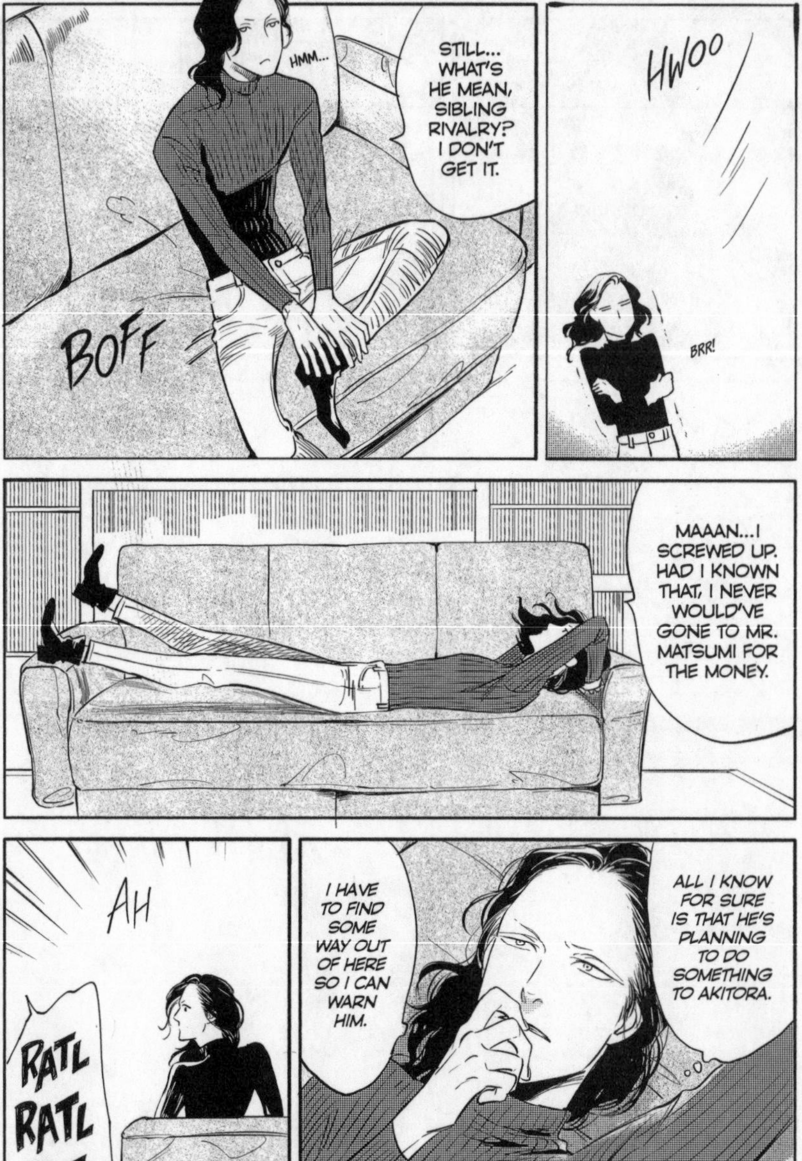
HWOO
BRR!
HMM...
STILL... WHAT'S HE MEAN, SIBLING RIVALRY? I DON'T GET IT.
BOFF
MAAAN...I SCREWED UP. HAD I KNOWN THAT, I NEVER WOULD'VE GONE TO MR. MATSUMI FOR THE MONEY.
ALL I KNOW FOR SURE IS THAT HE'S PLANNING TO DO SOMETHING TO AKITORA.
I HAVE TO FIND SOME WAY OUT OF HERE SO I CAN WARN HIM.
AH
RATL RATL RATL

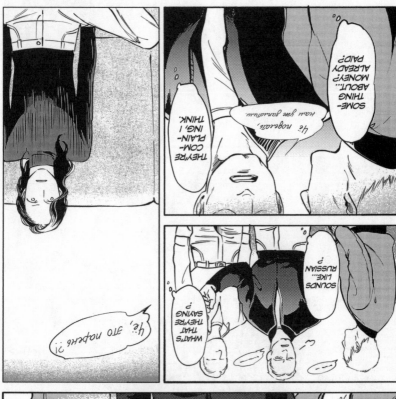

Здаров.
Чё, это парень ?!
WHAT'S THAT THEY'RE SAYING ?
SOUNDS LIKE... RUSSIAN ?
Чё поделать, нам уже заплатили.
THEY'RE COM-PLAIN-ING, I THINK.
SOME-THING ABOUT... MONEY? ALREADY PAID?

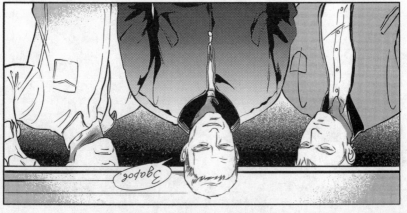

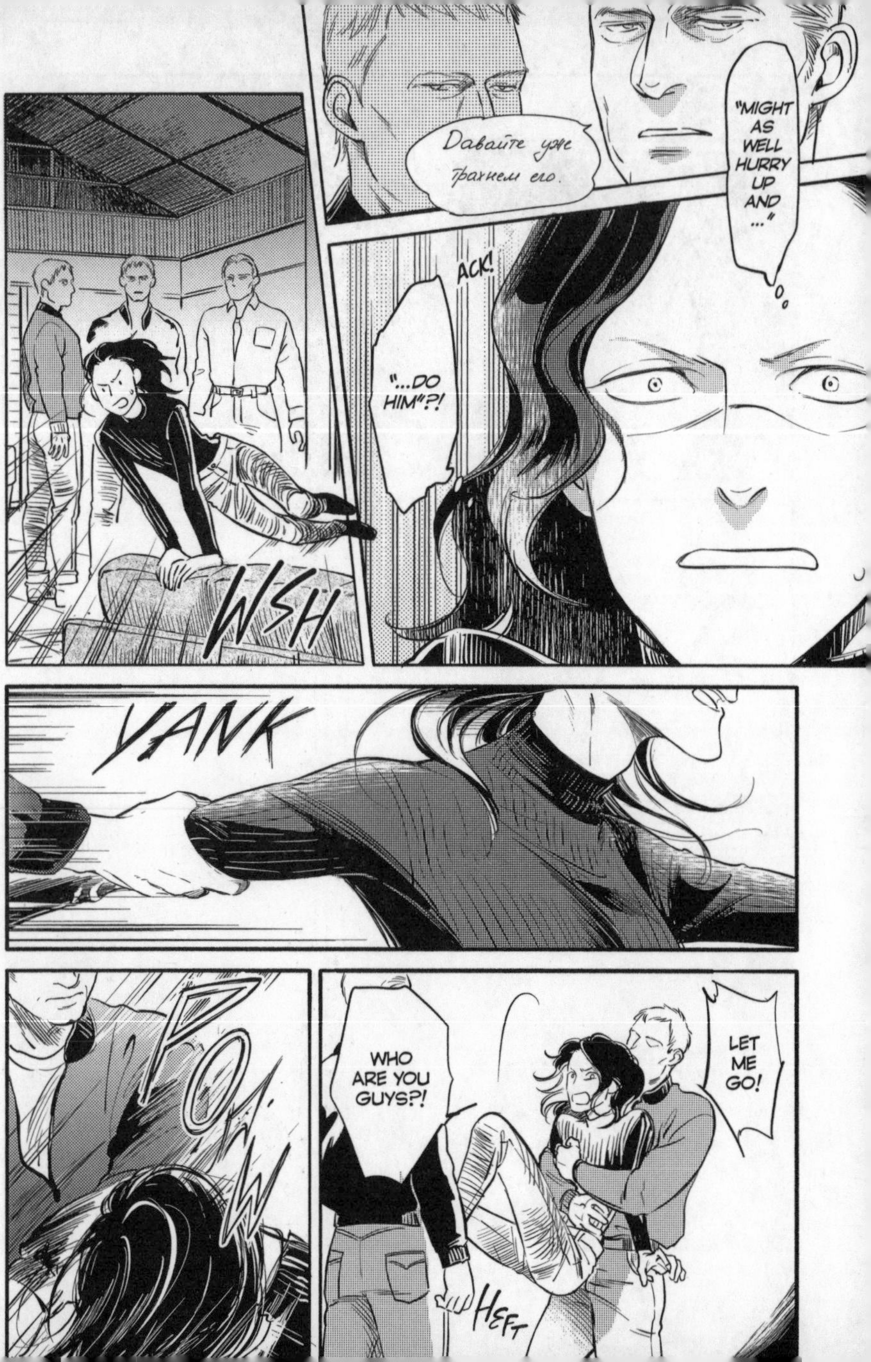
"MIGHT AS WELL HURRY UP AND..."
Давайте уже трахнем его.
ACK!
"...DO HIM"?!
WSH
VANK
LET ME GO!
WHO ARE YOU GUYS?!
HEFT
POW

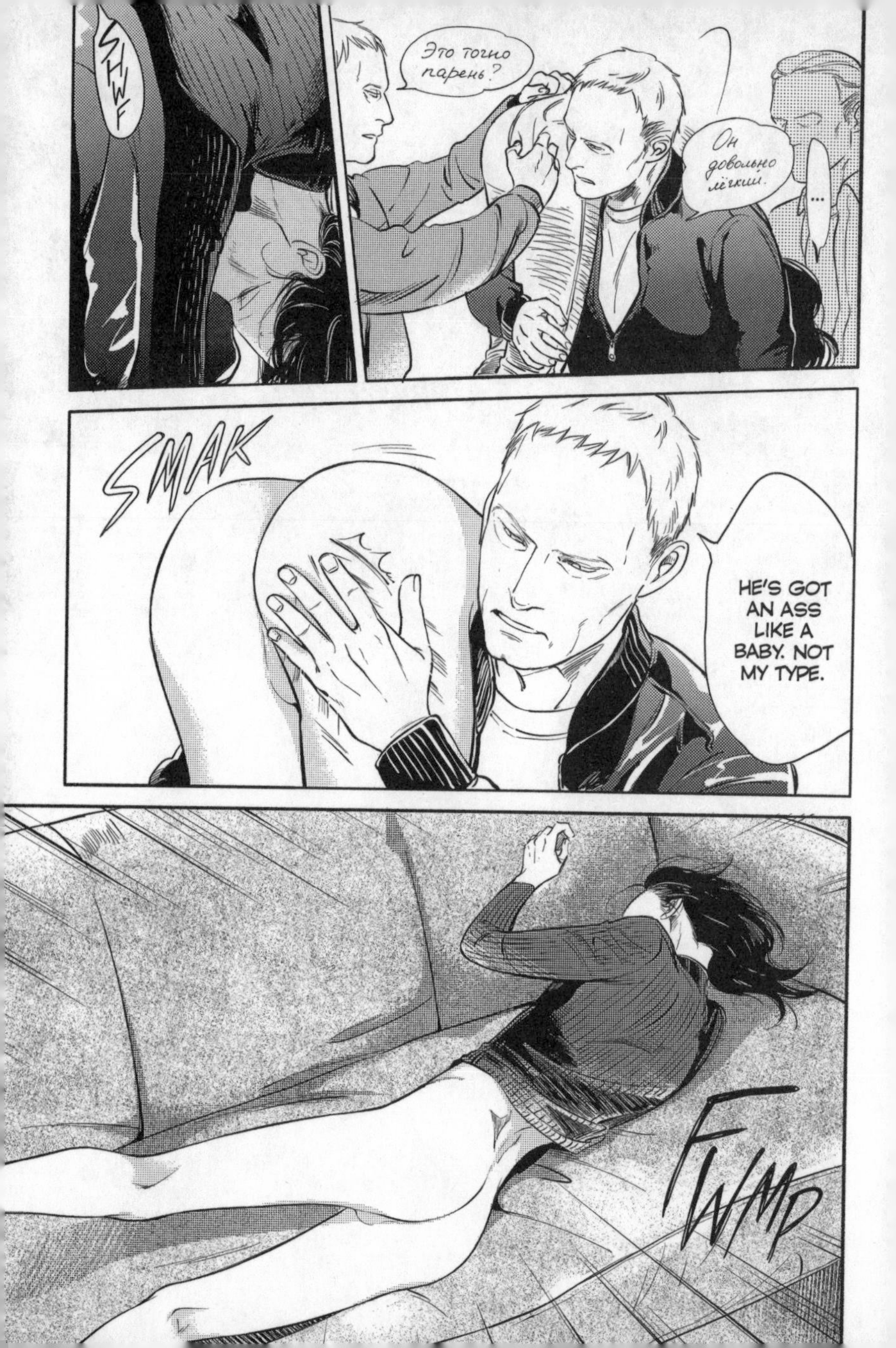
Это точно парень?
Он довольно лёгкий.
...
SHWF
SMAK
HE'S GOT AN ASS LIKE A BABY. NOT MY TYPE.
FWMP

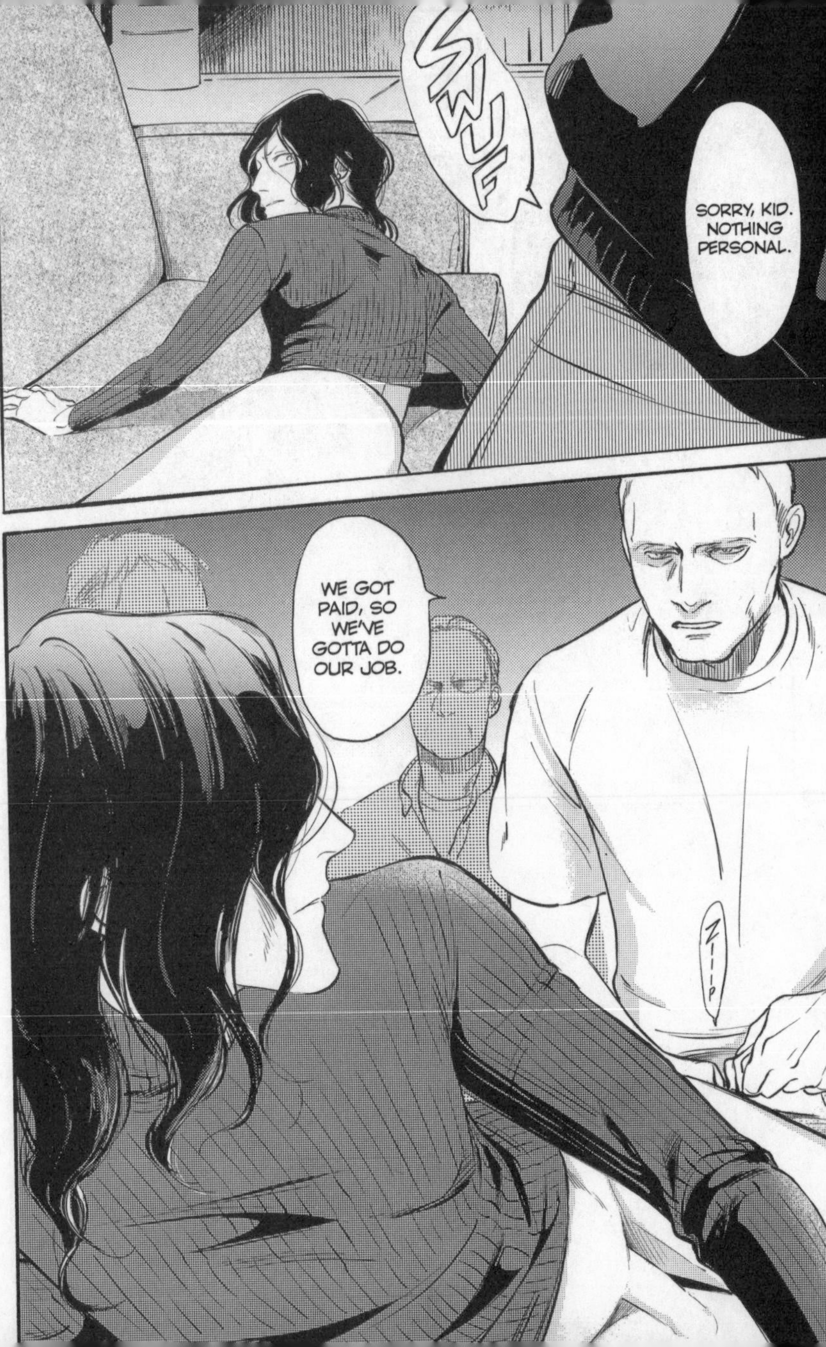
SORRY, KID. NOTHING PERSONAL.
SWUF
ZIIP
WE GOT PAID, SO WE'VE GOTTA DO OUR JOB.

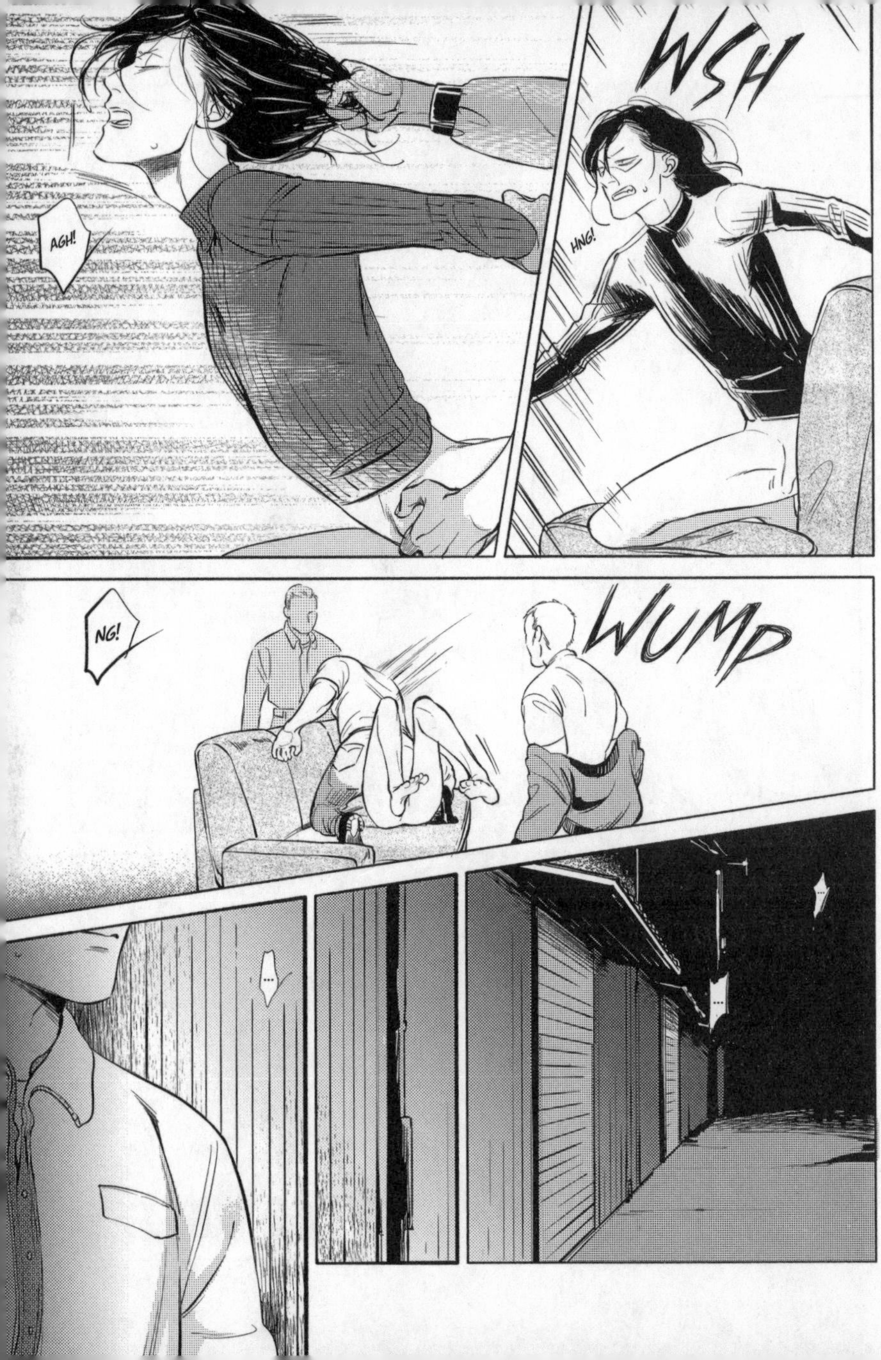
WSH
HNG!
AGH!
WUMP
NG!
...
...
...

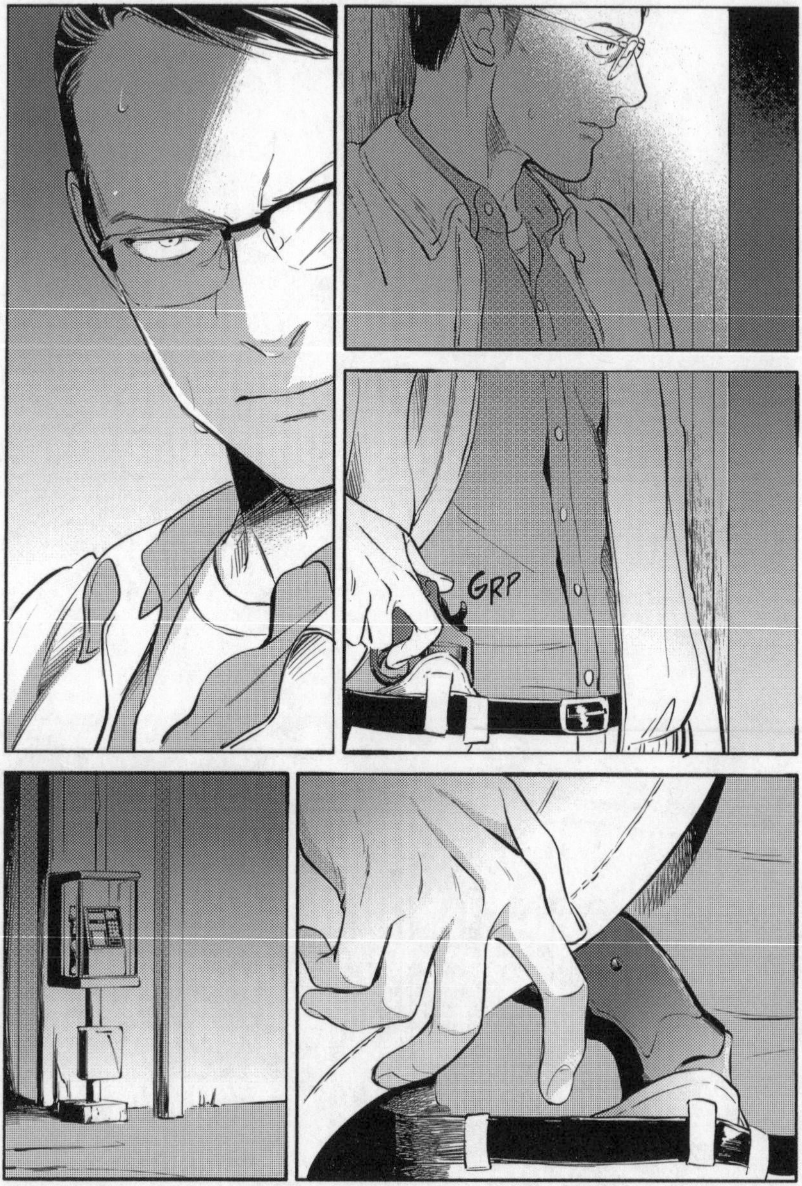
GRP

HE'S NOT AT THE HARBOR WARE- HOUSE.

NO, SIR.

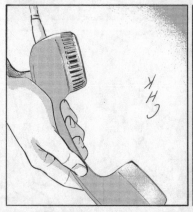

CHK

IT'S ASODA.

BOSS.

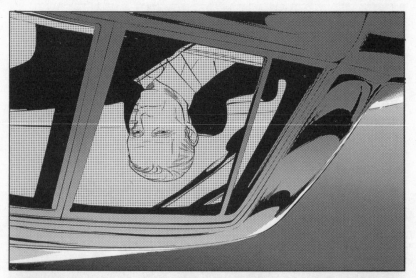

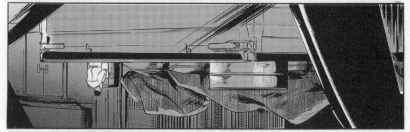

I'LL CONTINUE SEARCHING THE AREA, SIR.

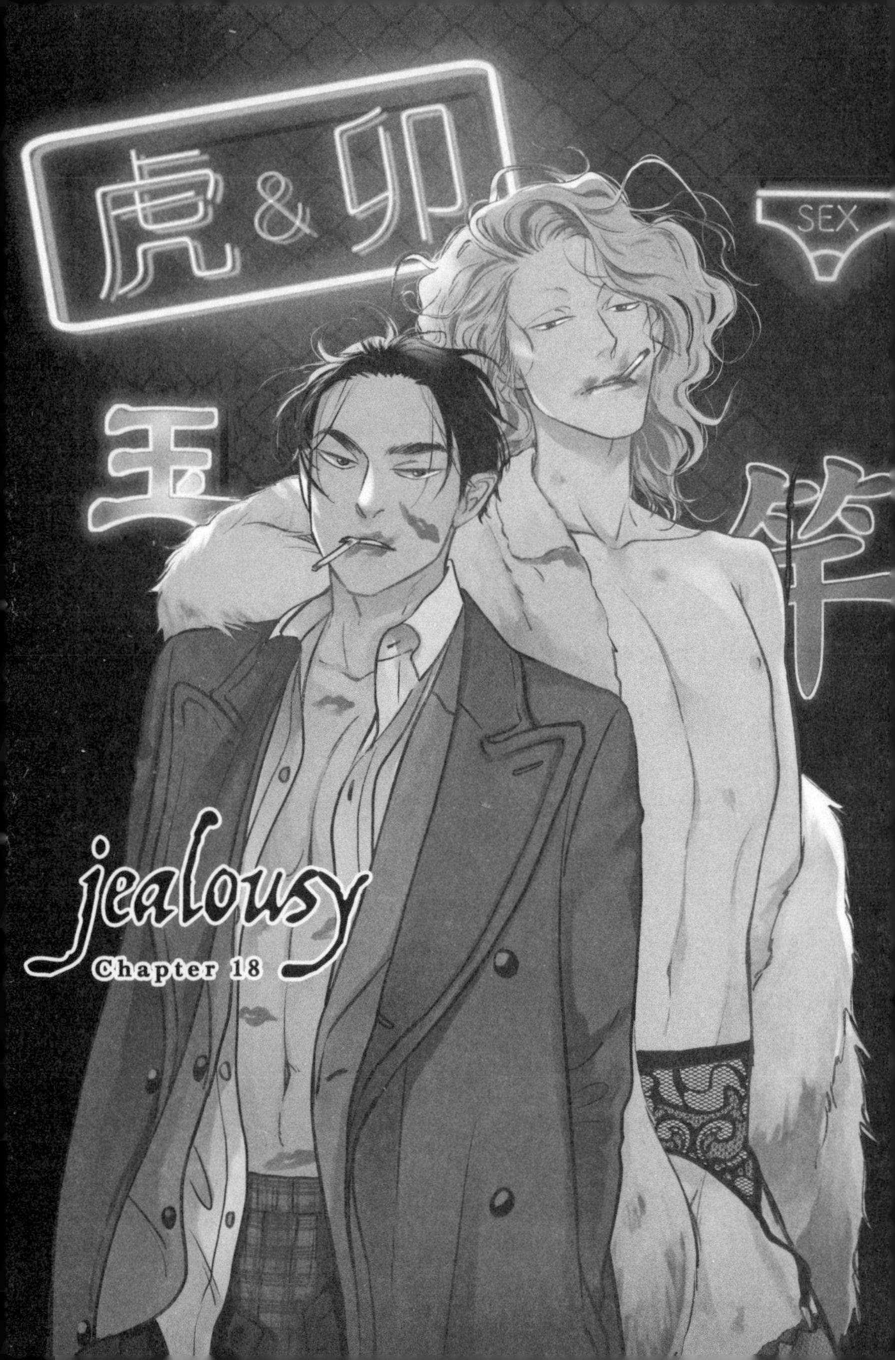
虎&卯
SEX
王
jealousy
Chapter 18

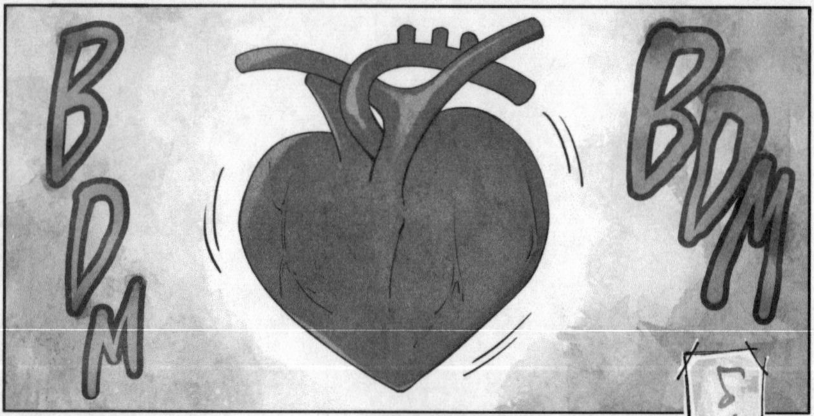
BDM
BDM
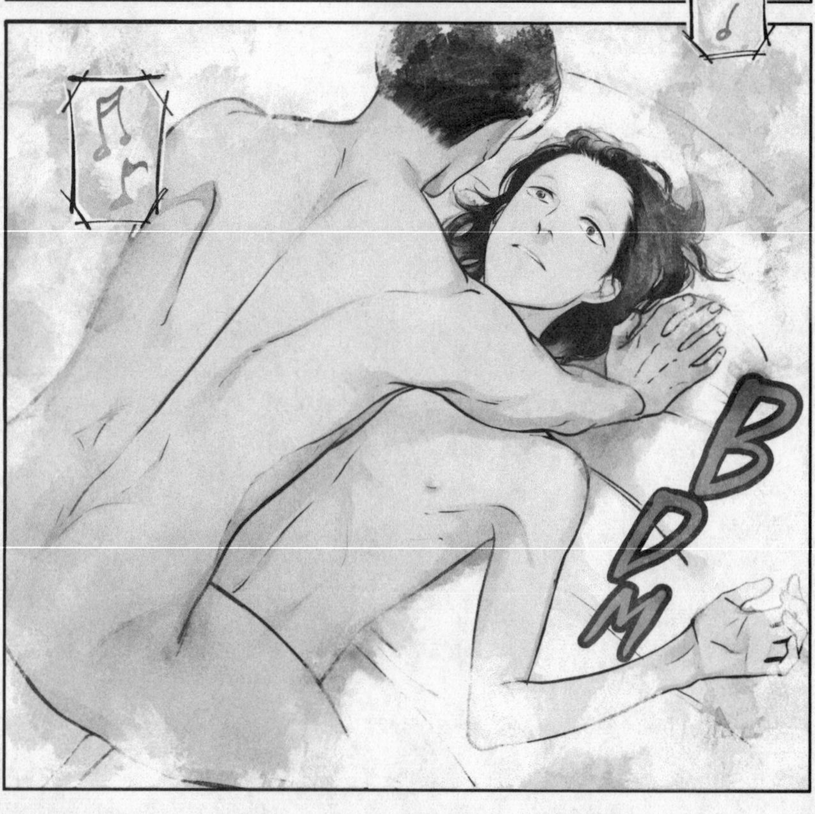
BDM

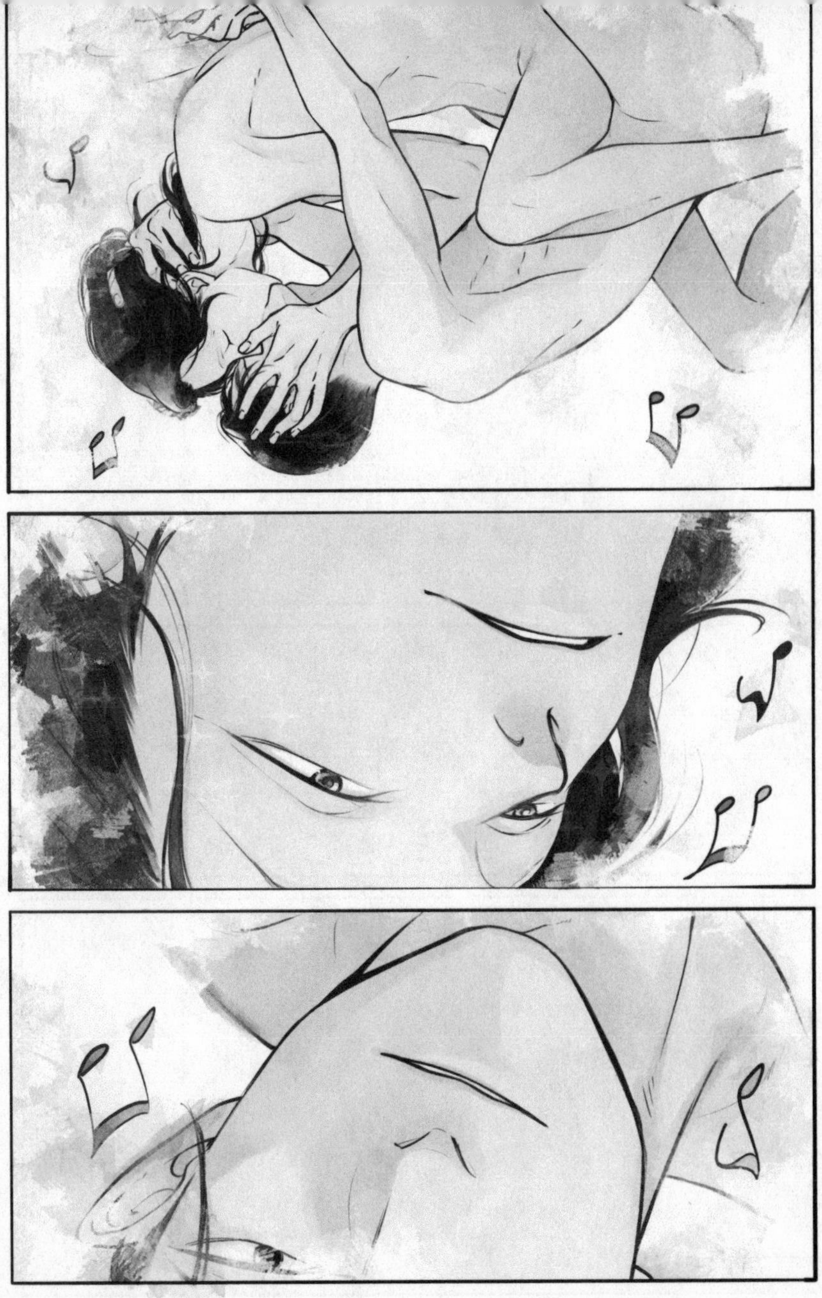

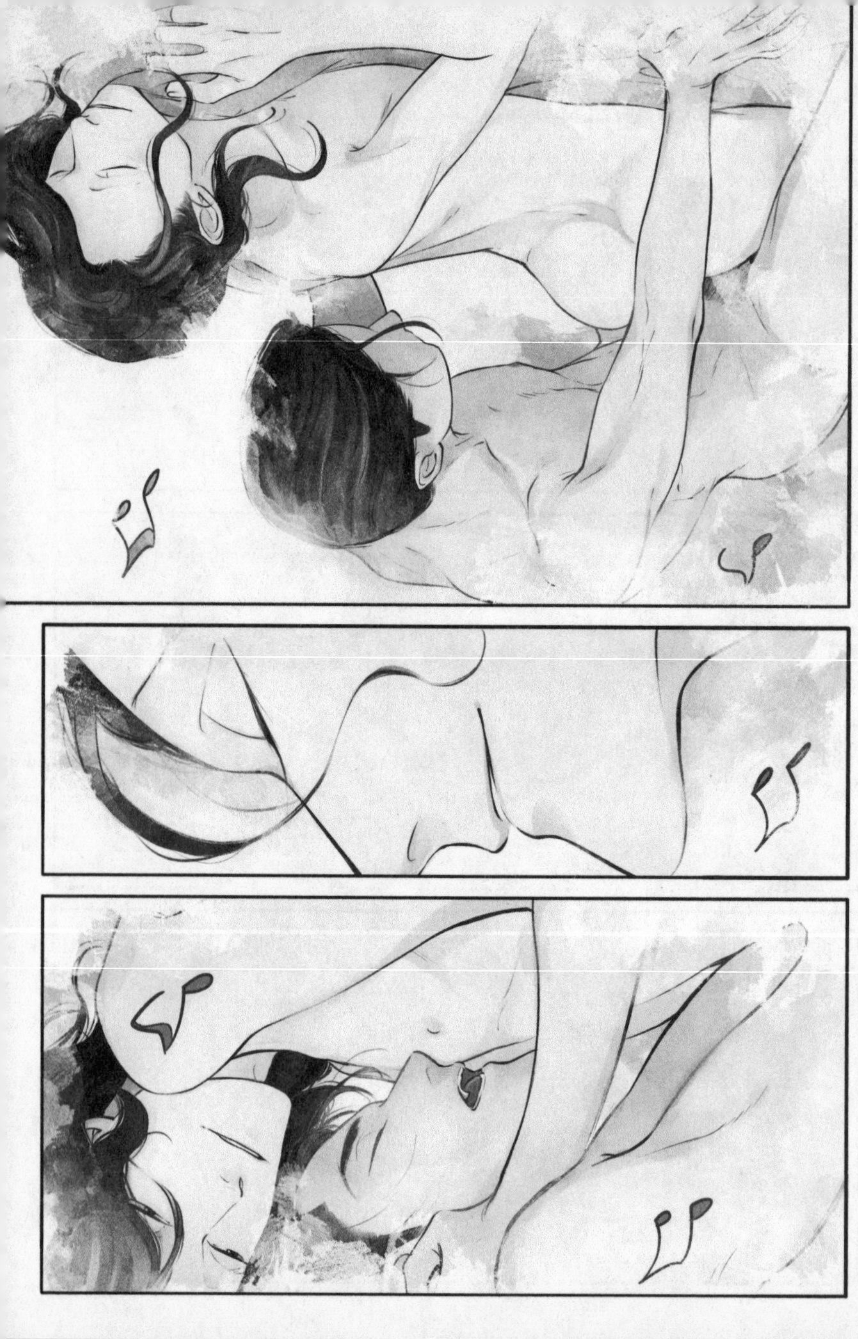

HAA
THP
HAA
THP
HAA
AGH
THP
TAK
N!
THP
SWF

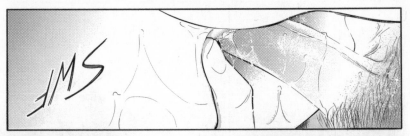

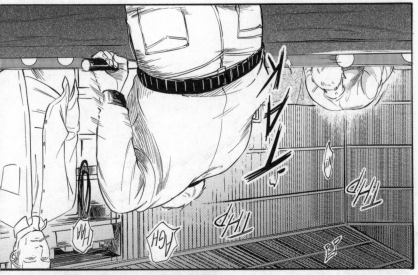

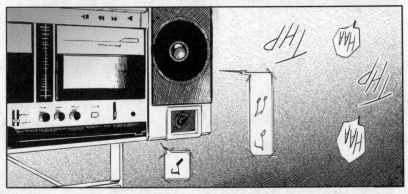

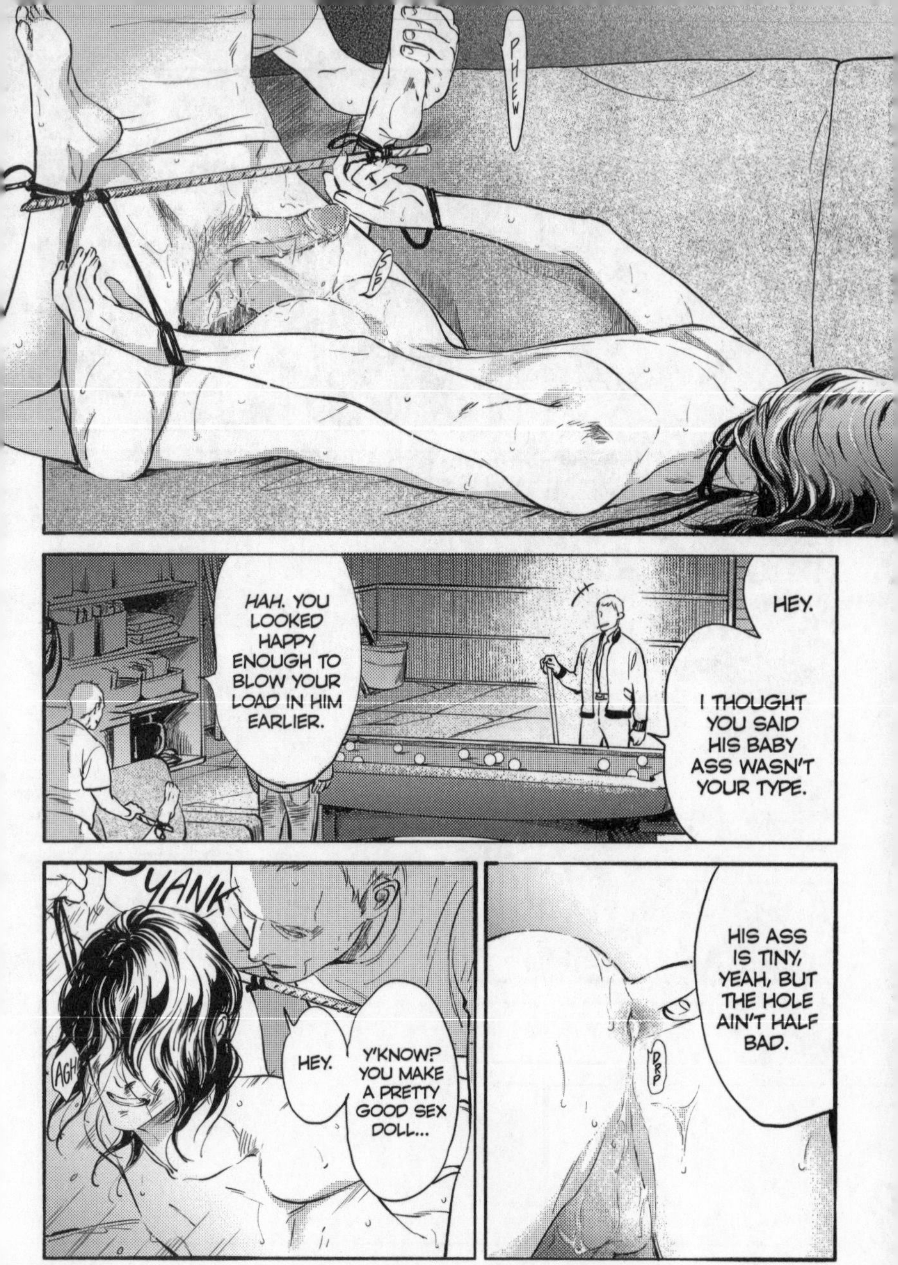
PHEW
HEY.
I THOUGHT YOU SAID HIS BABY ASS WASN'T YOUR TYPE.
HAH. YOU LOOKED HAPPY ENOUGH TO BLOW YOUR LOAD IN HIM EARLIER.
HIS ASS IS TINY, YEAH, BUT THE HOLE AIN'T HALF BAD.
DRP
YANK
HEY.
Y'KNOW? YOU MAKE A PRETTY GOOD SEX DOLL...
AGH

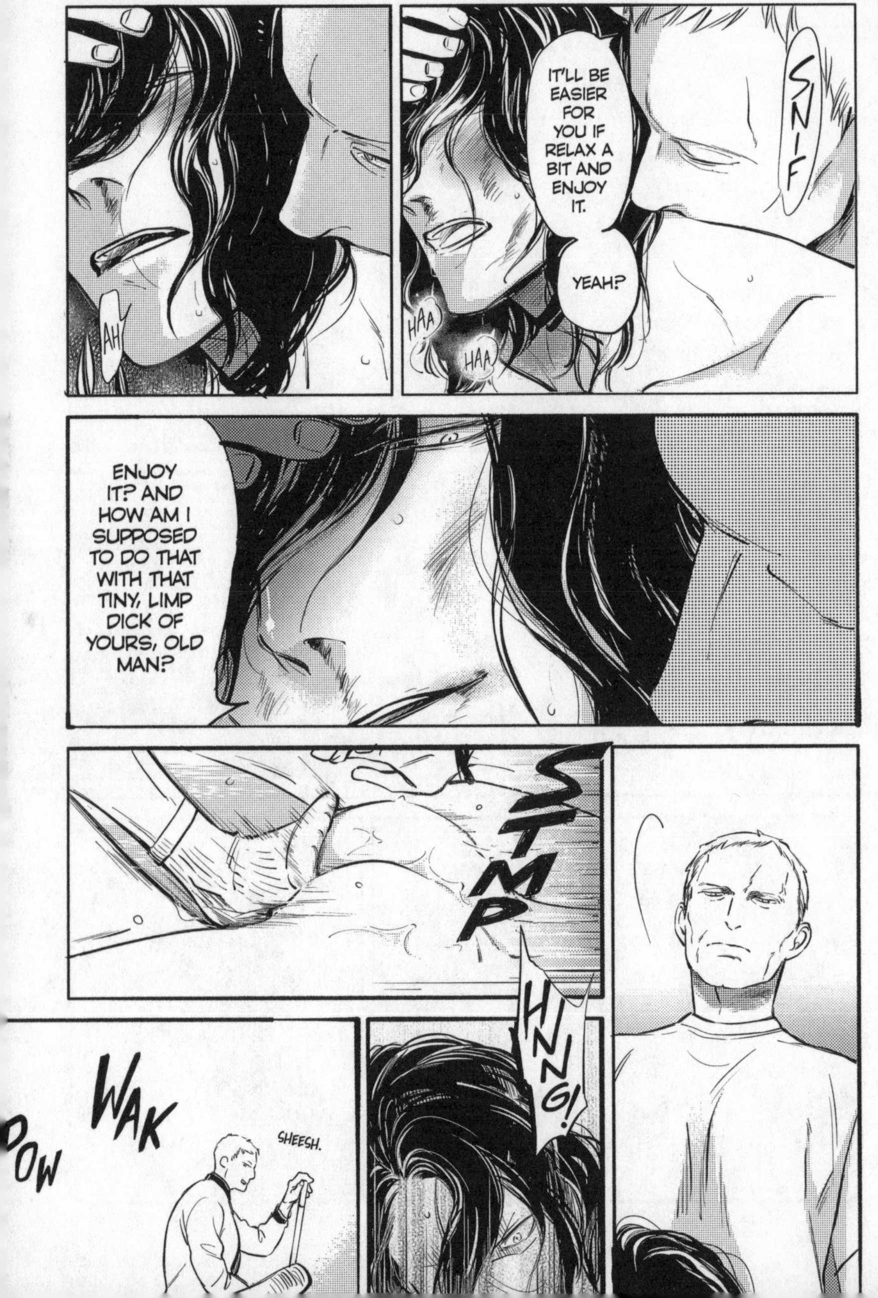
SNIF
IT'LL BE EASIER FOR YOU IF RELAX A BIT AND ENJOY IT.
YEAH?
HAA
HAA
AH
ENJOY IT? AND HOW AM I SUPPOSED TO DO THAT WITH THAT TINY, LIMP DICK OF YOURS, OLD MAN?
STMP
HNNG!
SHEESH.
WAK
DOW

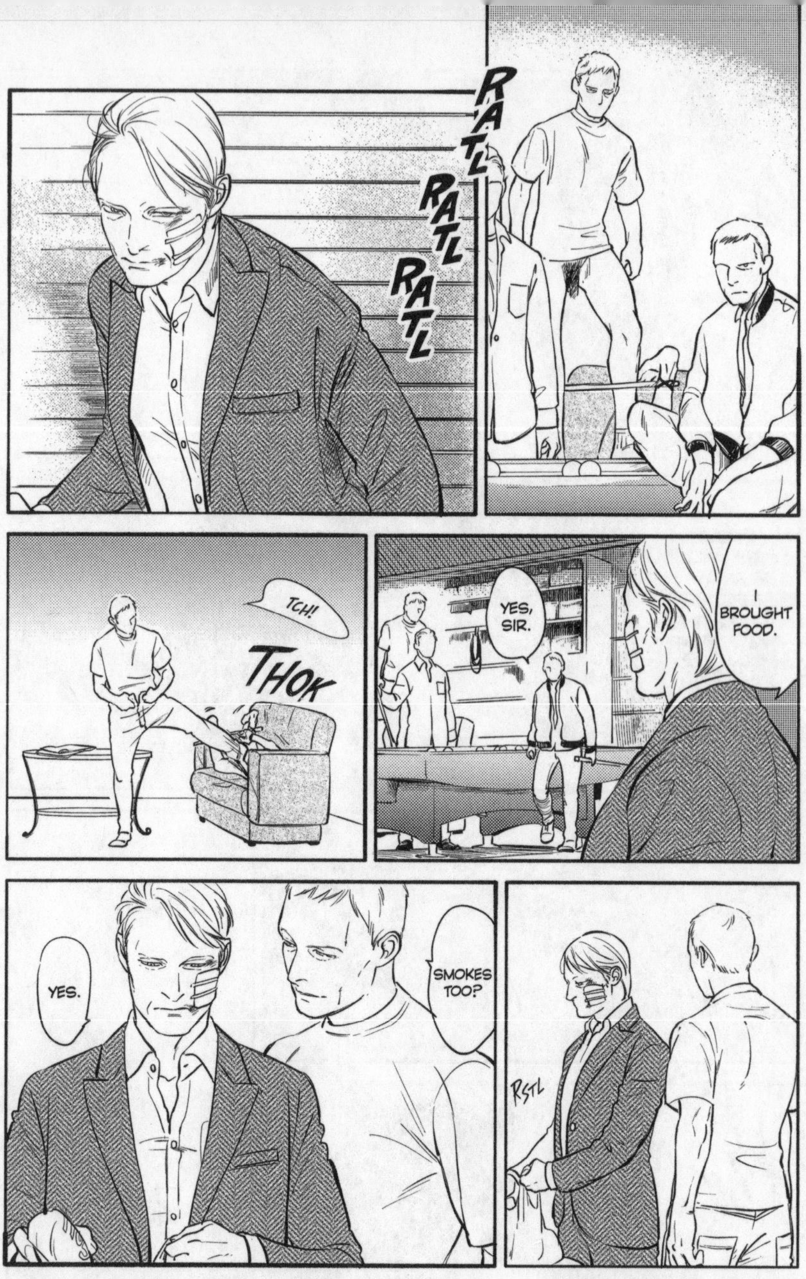
RATL
RATL
RATL
I BROUGHT FOOD.
YES, SIR.
TCH!
THOK
RSTL
SMOKES TOO?
YES.

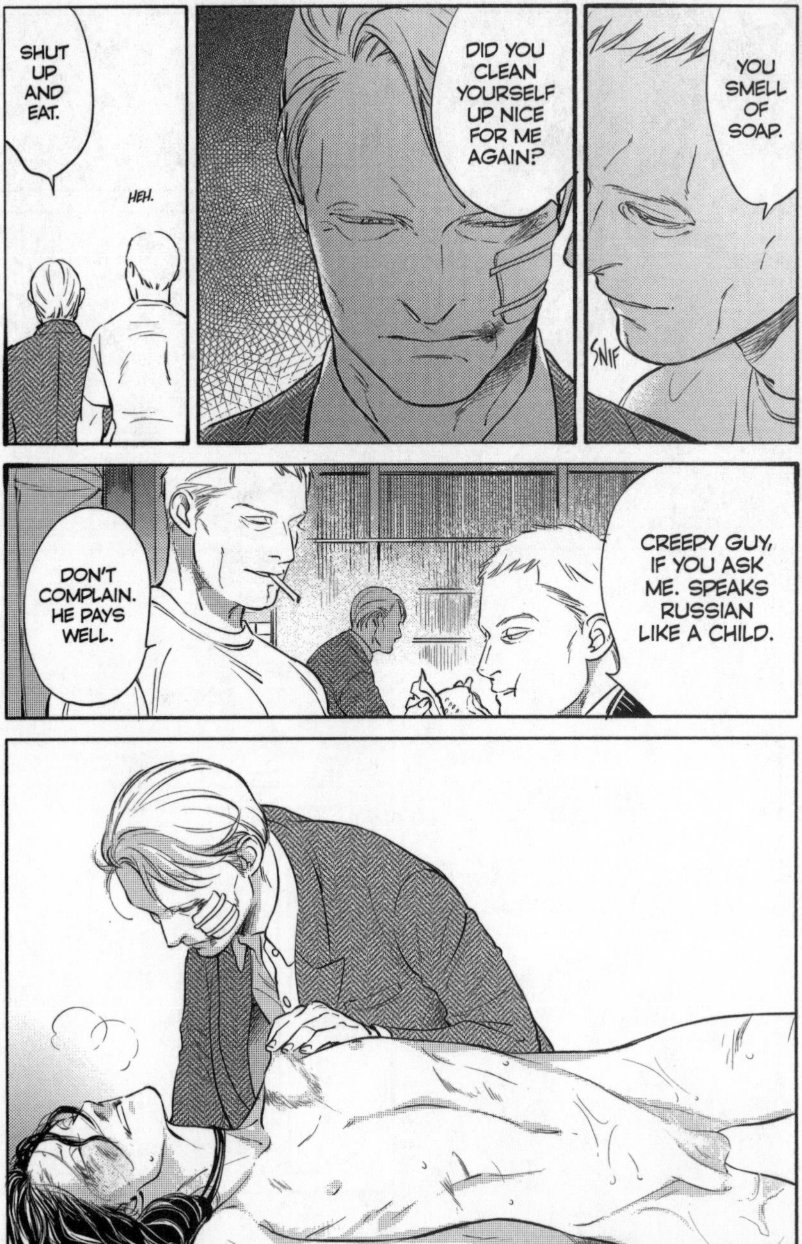
YOU SMELL OF SOAP.
SNIF
DID YOU CLEAN YOURSELF UP NICE FOR ME AGAIN?
SHUT UP AND EAT.
HEH.
CREEPY GUY, IF YOU ASK ME. SPEAKS RUSSIAN LIKE A CHILD.
DON'T COMPLAIN. HE PAYS WELL.

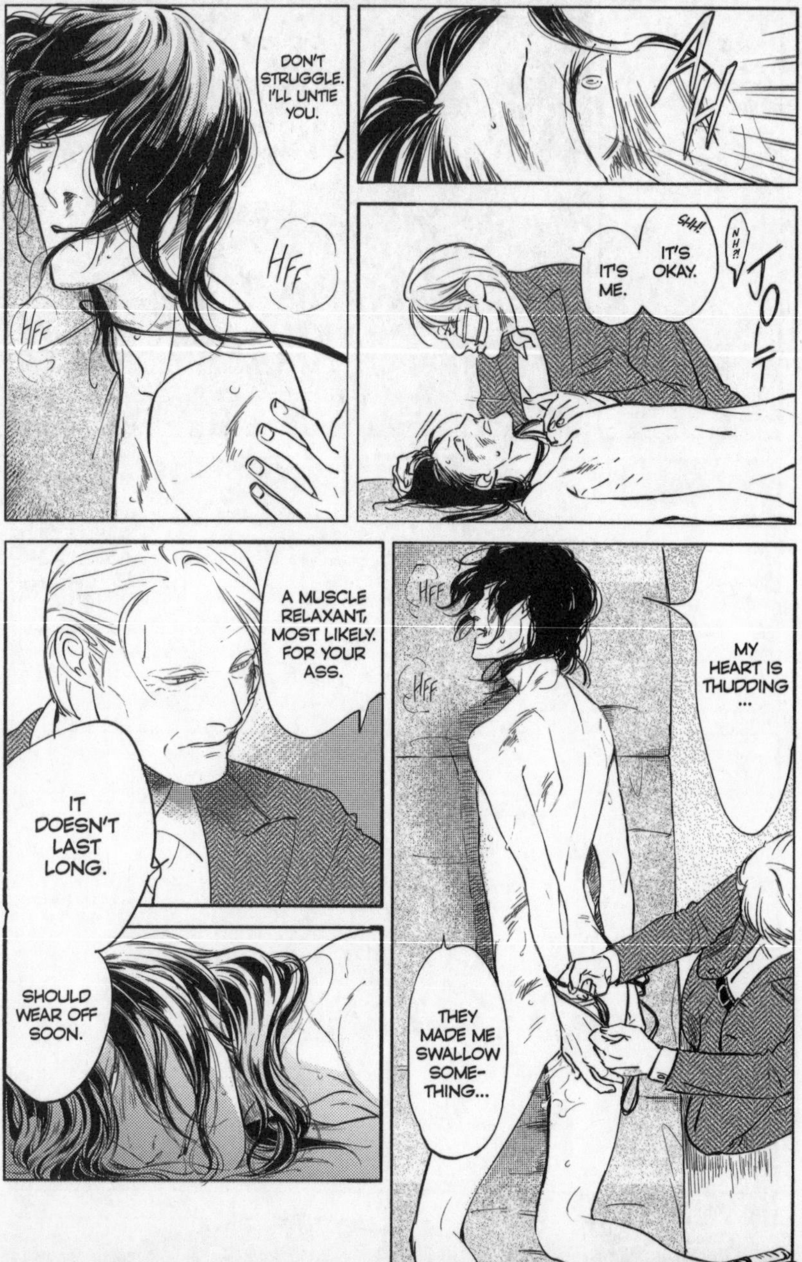
AH
JOLT
NH?!
SHH!
IT'S OKAY.
IT'S ME.
DON'T STRUGGLE. I'LL UNTIE YOU.
HFF
HFF
HFF
HFF
MY HEART IS THUDDING ...
THEY MADE ME SWALLOW SOME-THING...
A MUSCLE RELAXANT, MOST LIKELY. FOR YOUR ASS.
IT DOESN'T LAST LONG.
SHOULD WEAR OFF SOON.

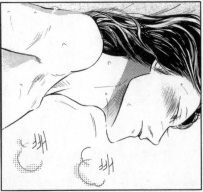

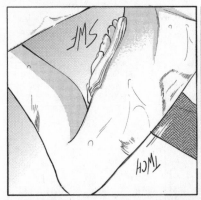

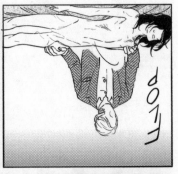

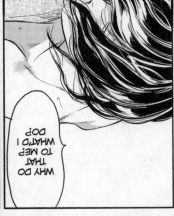

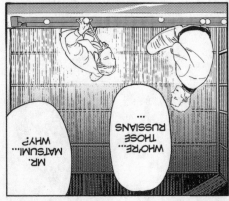

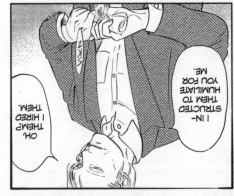

MR. MATSUMI... WHY?
WHO'RE... THOSE RUSSIANS ...
WHY DO THAT TO ME? WHAT'D I DO?
OH, THEM? I HIRED THEM.
I IN-STRUCTED THEM TO HUMILIATE YOU FOR ME.
SKZ
FLOP
TWCH
SWF
HFF
HFF

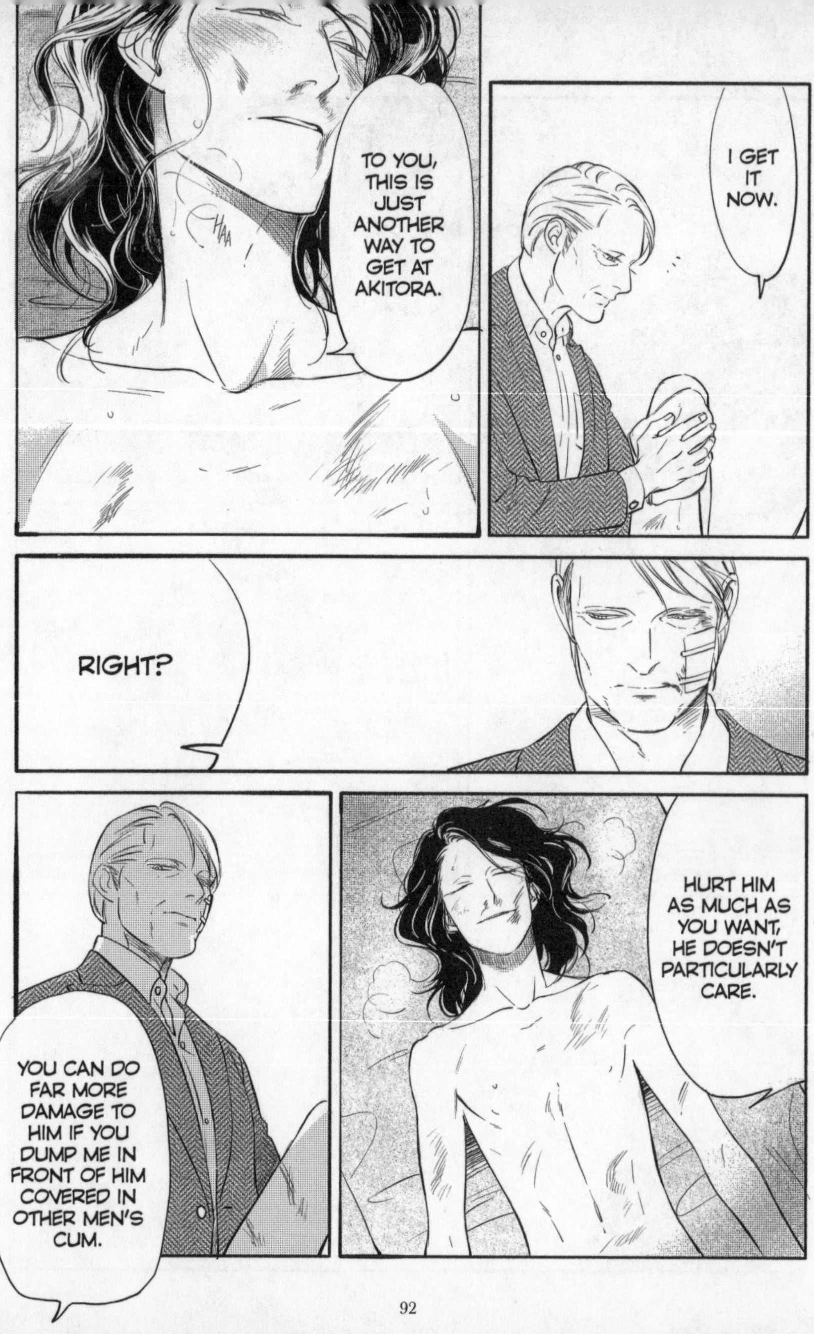
I GET IT NOW.
TO YOU, THIS IS JUST ANOTHER WAY TO GET AT AKITORA.
HAA
RIGHT?
HURT HIM AS MUCH AS YOU WANT, HE DOESN'T PARTICULARLY CARE.
YOU CAN DO FAR MORE DAMAGE TO HIM IF YOU DUMP ME IN FRONT OF HIM COVERED IN OTHER MEN'S CUM.

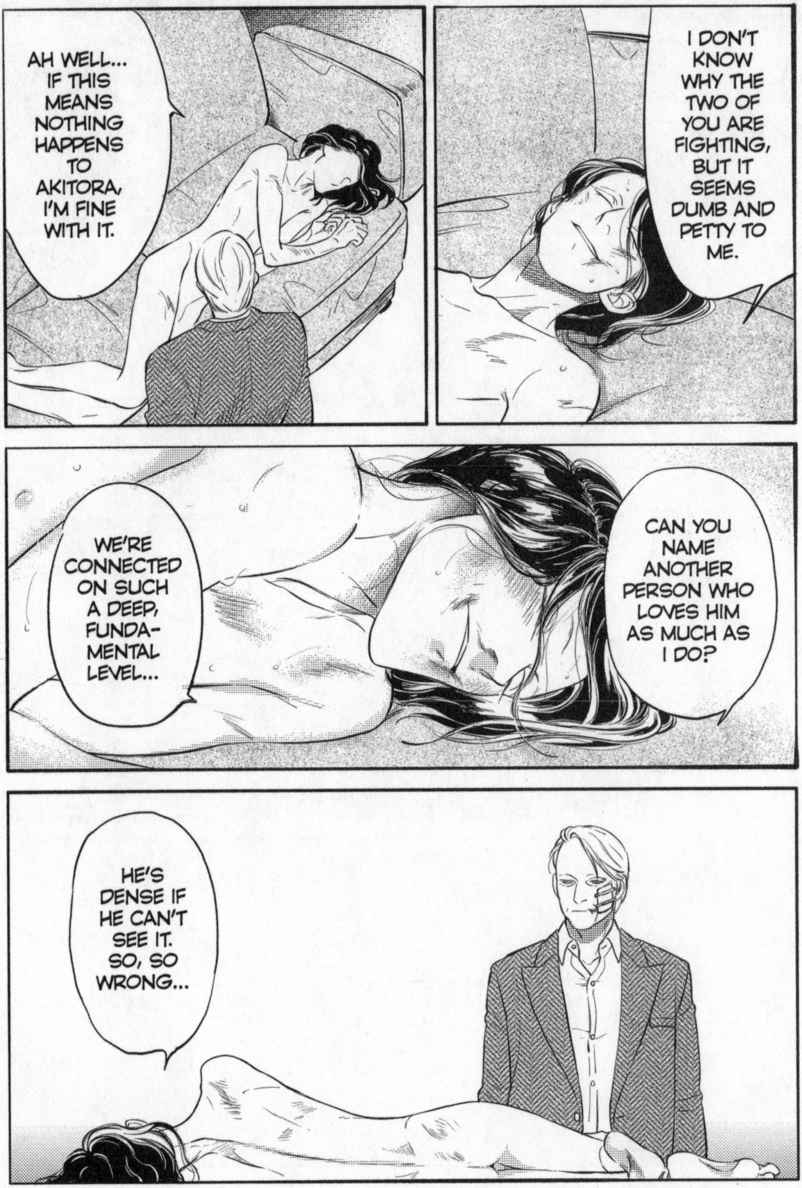
I DON'T KNOW WHY THE TWO OF YOU ARE FIGHTING, BUT IT SEEMS DUMB AND PETTY TO ME.
AH WELL... IF THIS MEANS NOTHING HAPPENS TO AKITORA, I'M FINE WITH IT.
CAN YOU NAME ANOTHER PERSON WHO LOVES HIM AS MUCH AS I DO?
WE'RE CONNECTED ON SUCH A DEEP, FUNDAMENTAL LEVEL...
HE'S DENSE IF HE CAN'T SEE IT. SO, SO WRONG...

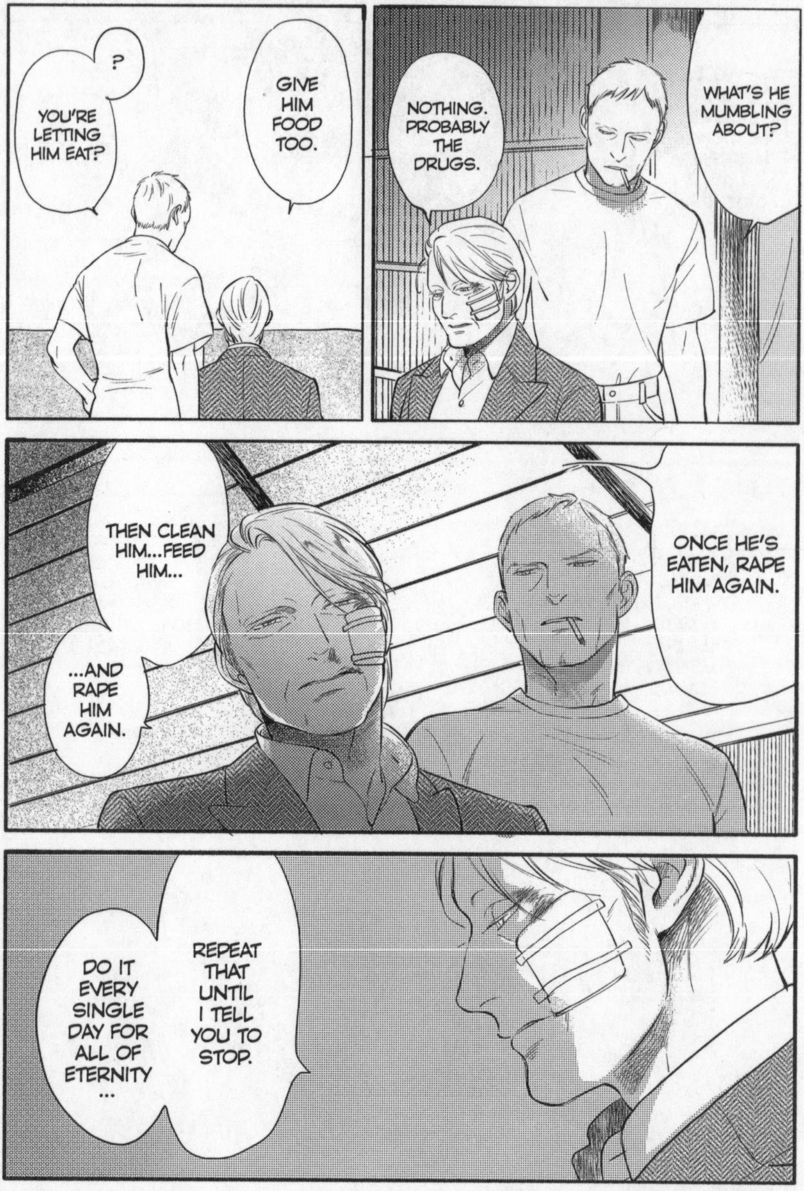
WHAT'S HE MUMBLING ABOUT?
NOTHING. PROBABLY THE DRUGS.
GIVE HIM FOOD TOO.
?
YOU'RE LETTING HIM EAT?
ONCE HE'S EATEN, RAPE HIM AGAIN.
THEN CLEAN HIM...FEED HIM...
...AND RAPE HIM AGAIN.
REPEAT THAT UNTIL I TELL YOU TO STOP.
DO IT EVERY SINGLE DAY FOR ALL OF ETERNITY ...

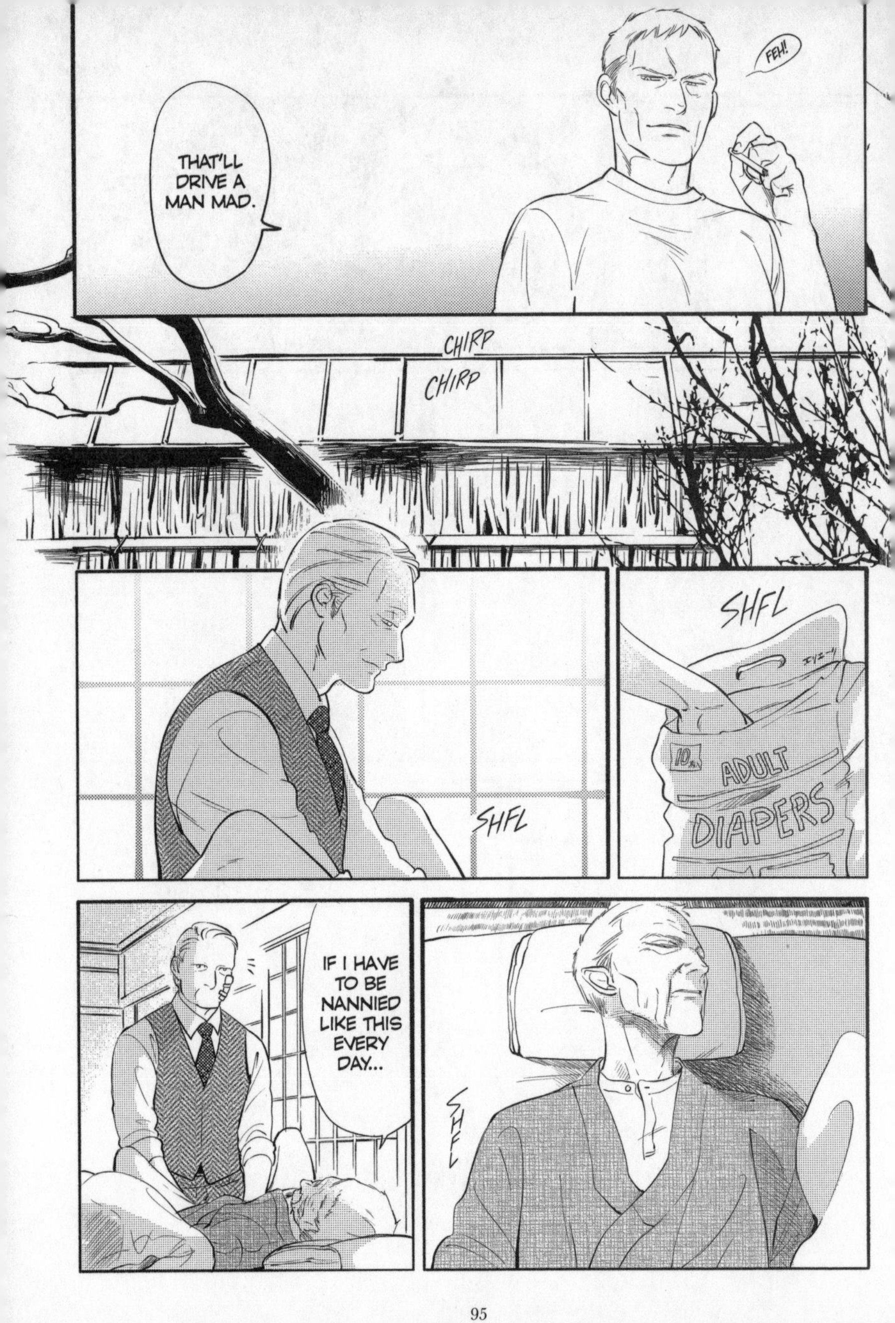
FEH!
THAT'LL DRIVE A MAN MAD.
CHIRP
CHIRP
SHFL
10
ADULT DIAPERS
SHFL
SHFL
IF I HAVE TO BE NANNIED LIKE THIS EVERY DAY...

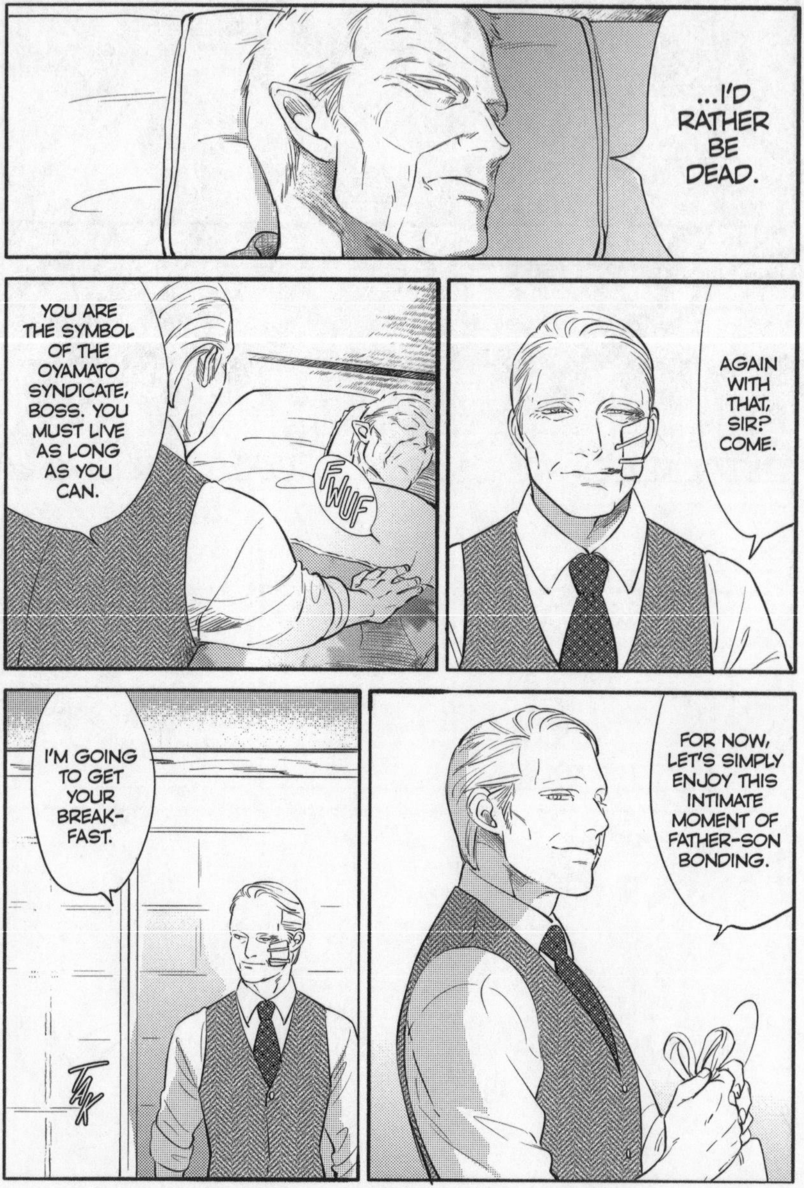
...I'D RATHER BE DEAD.
AGAIN WITH THAT, SIR? COME.
YOU ARE THE SYMBOL OF THE OYAMATO SYNDICATE, BOSS. YOU MUST LIVE AS LONG AS YOU CAN.
FWUF
FOR NOW, LET'S SIMPLY ENJOY THIS INTIMATE MOMENT OF FATHER-SON BONDING.
I'M GOING TO GET YOUR BREAK-FAST.
TAK

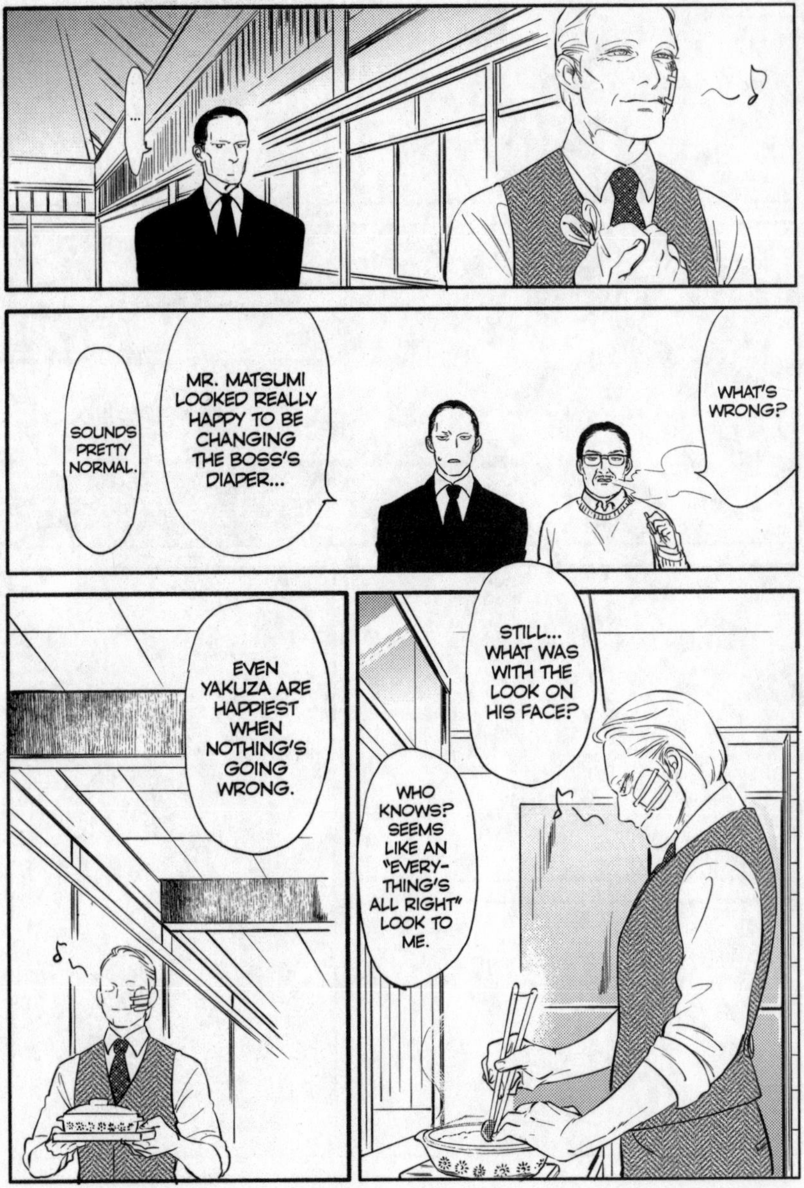
...
WHAT'S WRONG?
MR. MATSUMI LOOKED REALLY HAPPY TO BE CHANGING THE BOSS'S DIAPER...
SOUNDS PRETTY NORMAL.
STILL... WHAT WAS WITH THE LOOK ON HIS FACE?
WHO KNOWS? SEEMS LIKE AN "EVERY-THING'S ALL RIGHT" LOOK TO ME.
EVEN YAKUZA ARE HAPPIEST WHEN NOTHING'S GOING WRONG.

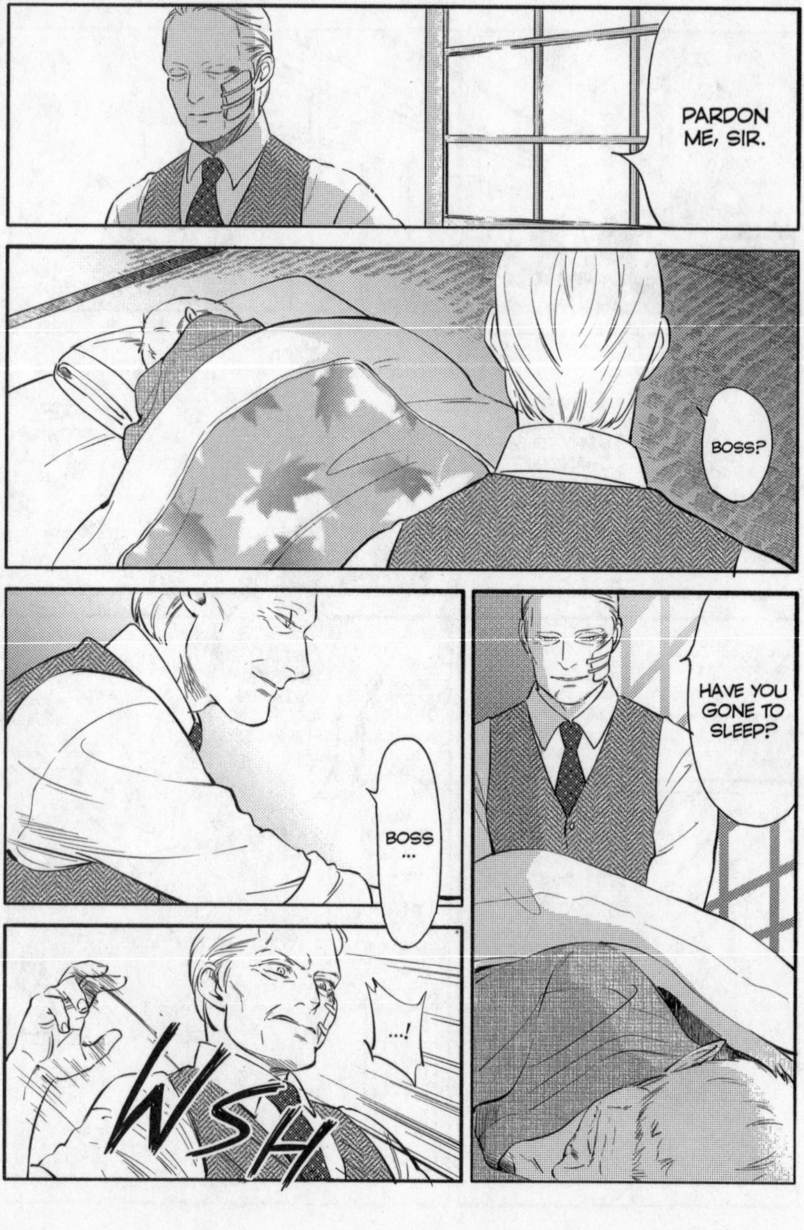
PARDON ME, SIR.
BOSS?
HAVE YOU GONE TO SLEEP?
BOSS ...
...!
WSH

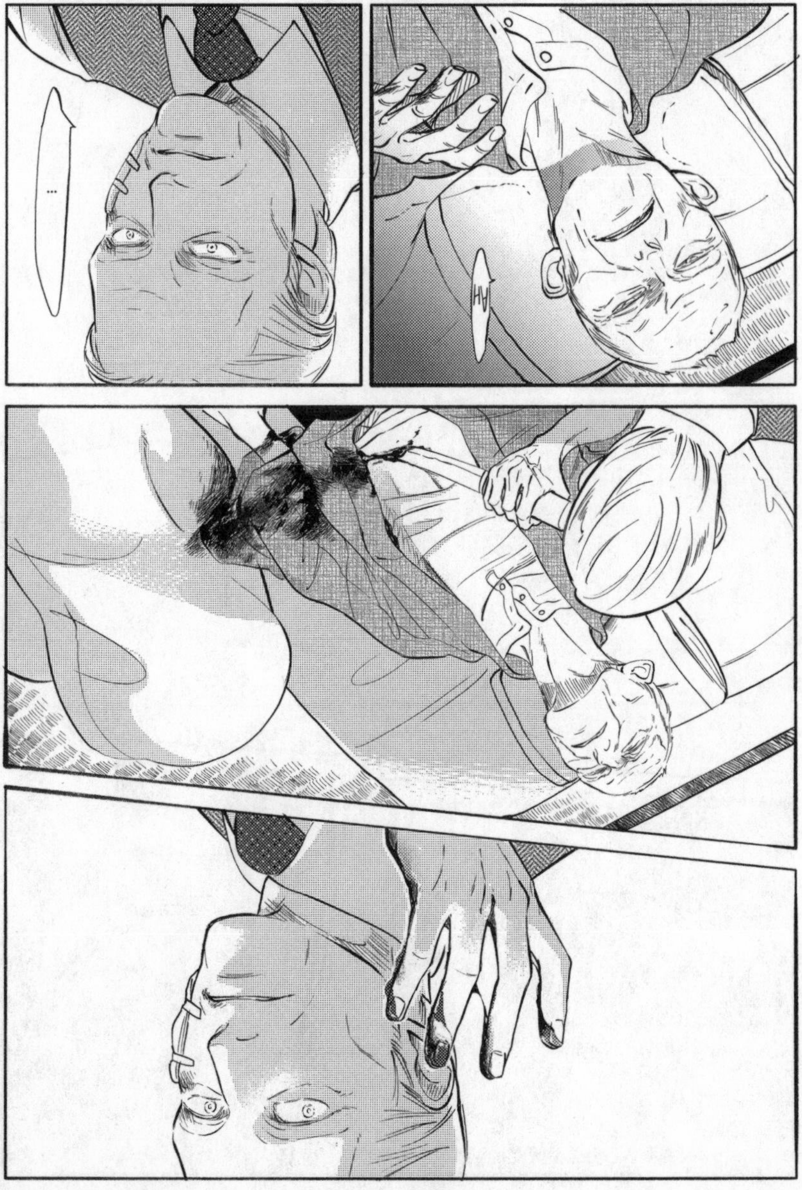
AH
...

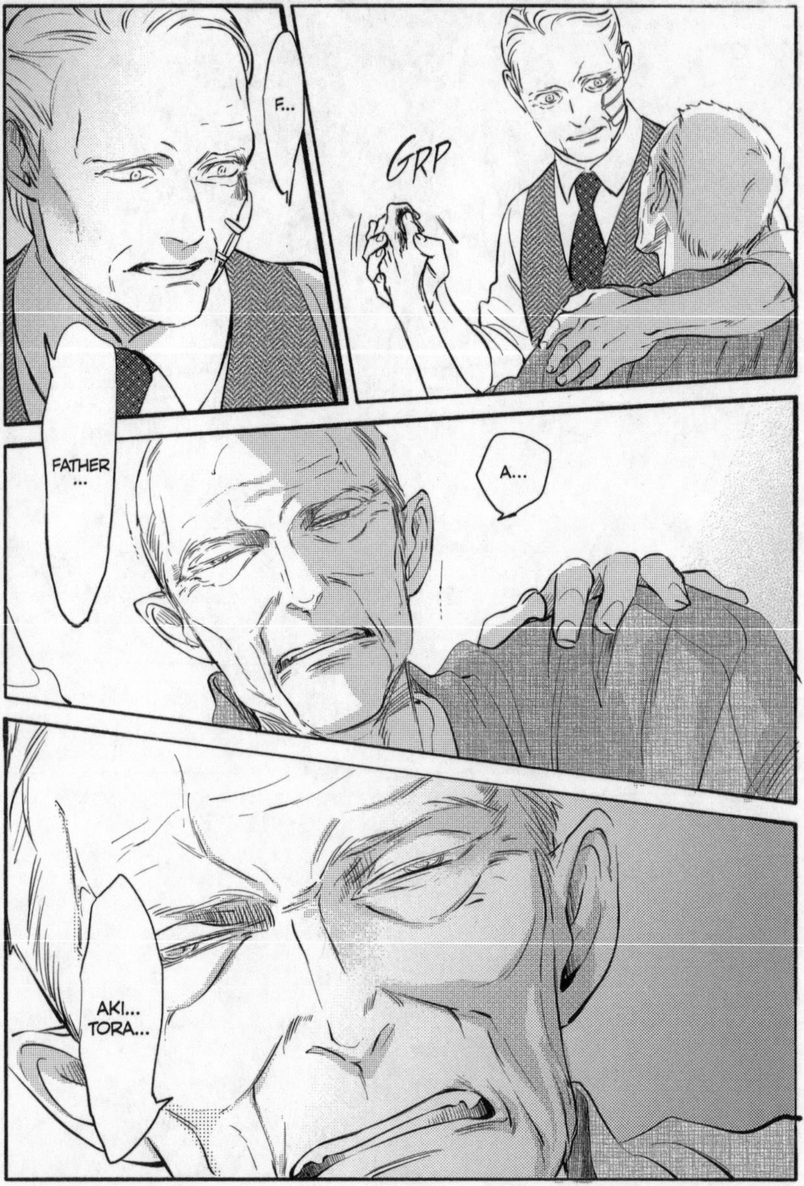
GRP
F...
FATHER...
A...
AKI... TORA...

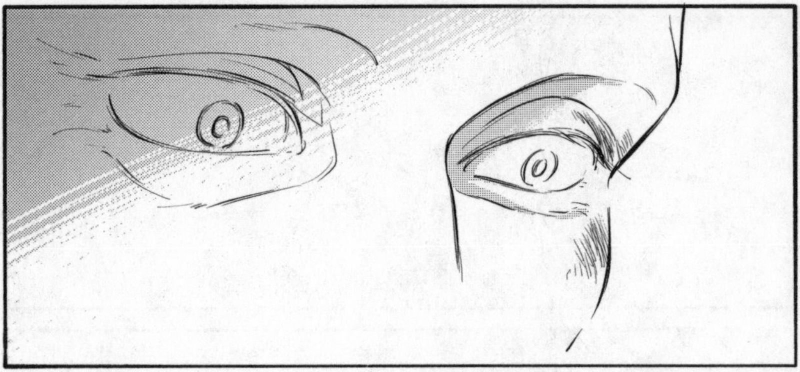

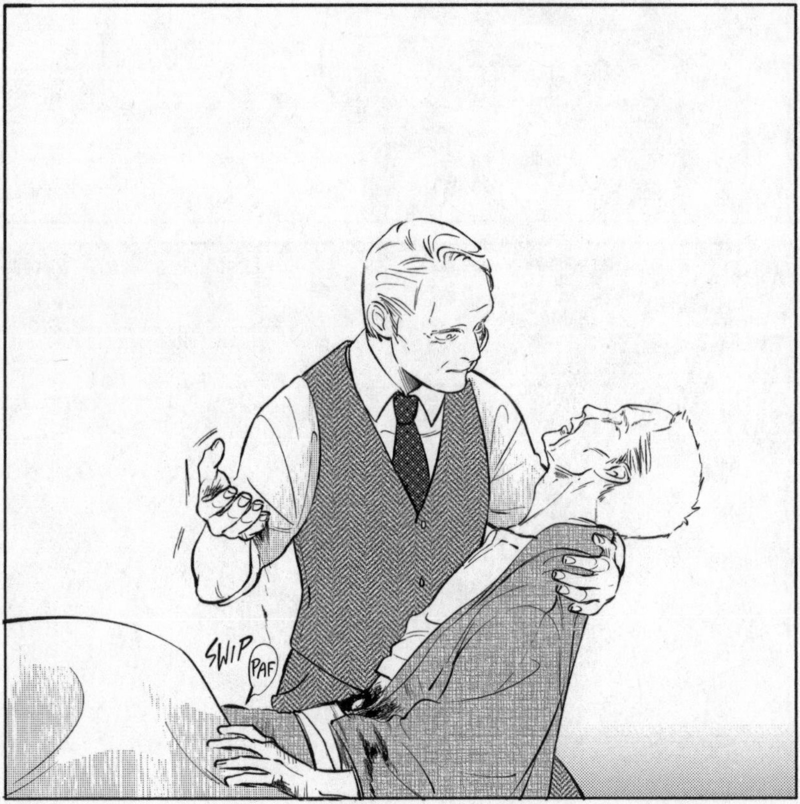
SWIP
PAF

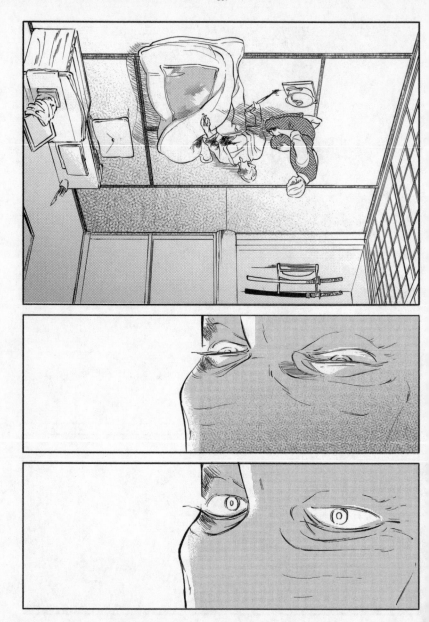

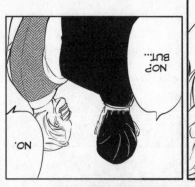

NO.

NO? BUT...

SIR....

SHOULDN'T WE CONTACT YOUNG MASTER AKITORA?

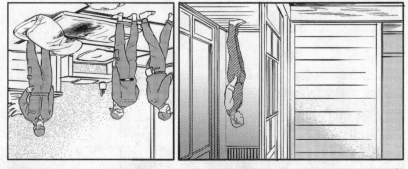

POLICE

...
R-RIGHT...
WE'LL SAY THAT I WAS THE ONE TO DISCOVER THE SECOND HEAD, THEN.
I'LL GO WITH THE POLICE TO EXPLAIN.
GOOD. PLEASE DO.
I HAVE OTHER THINGS TO SEE TO.

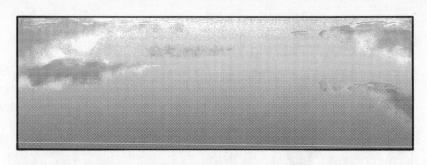

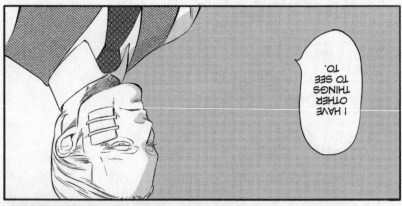

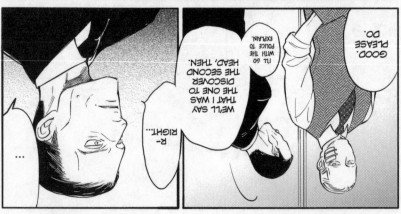

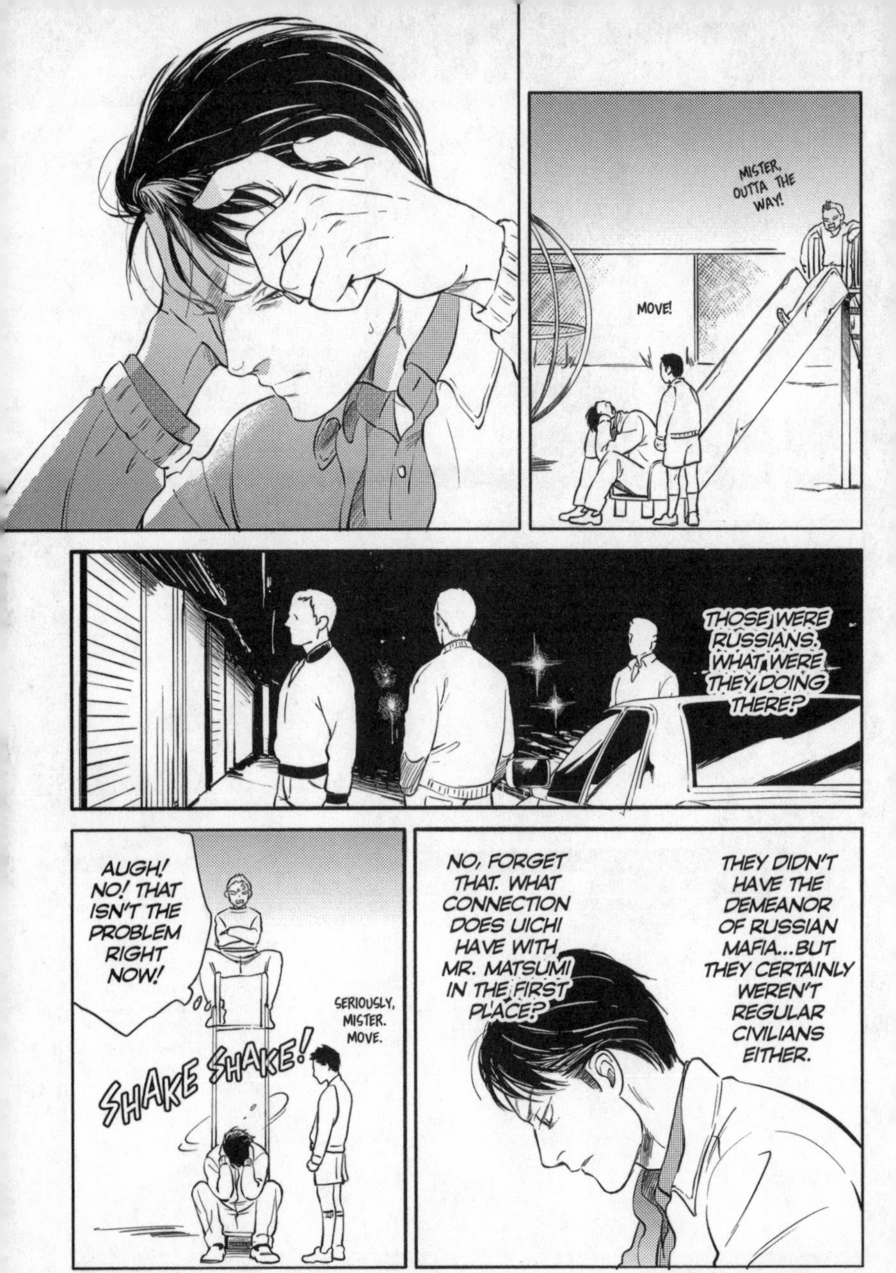
MISTER, OUTTA THE WAY!
MOVE!
THOSE WERE RUSSIANS. WHAT WERE THEY DOING THERE?
NO, FORGET THAT. WHAT CONNECTION DOES UICHI HAVE WITH MR. MATSUMI IN THE FIRST PLACE?
THEY DIDN'T HAVE THE DEMEANOR OF RUSSIAN MAFIA...BUT THEY CERTAINLY WEREN'T REGULAR CIVILIANS EITHER.
AUGH! NO! THAT ISN'T THE PROBLEM RIGHT NOW!
SERIOUSLY, MISTER. MOVE.
SHAKE SHAKE!

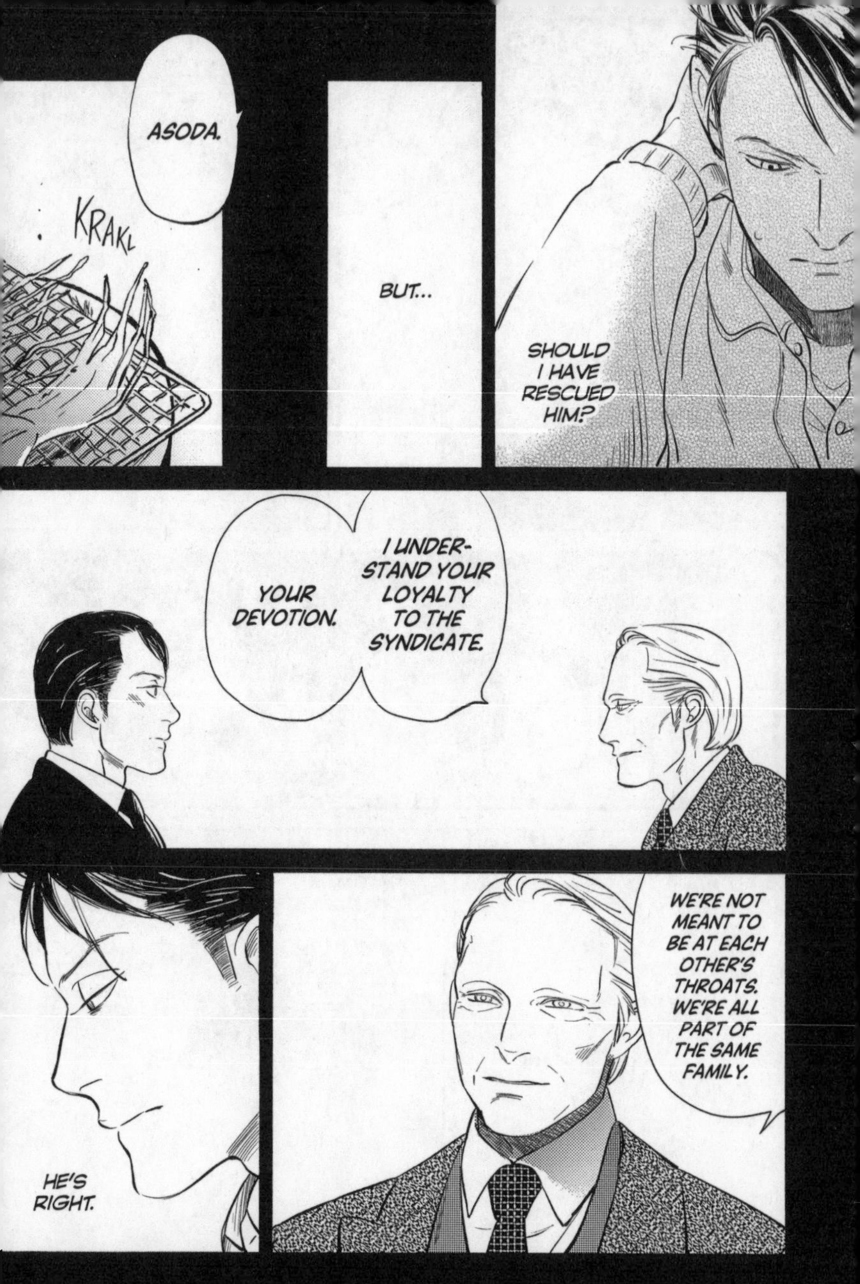
SHOULD I HAVE RESCUED HIM?
BUT...
ASODA.
KRAK!
I UNDER-STAND YOUR LOYALTY TO THE SYNDICATE.
YOUR DEVOTION.
WE'RE NOT MEANT TO BE AT EACH OTHER'S THROATS. WE'RE ALL PART OF THE SAME FAMILY.
HE'S RIGHT.

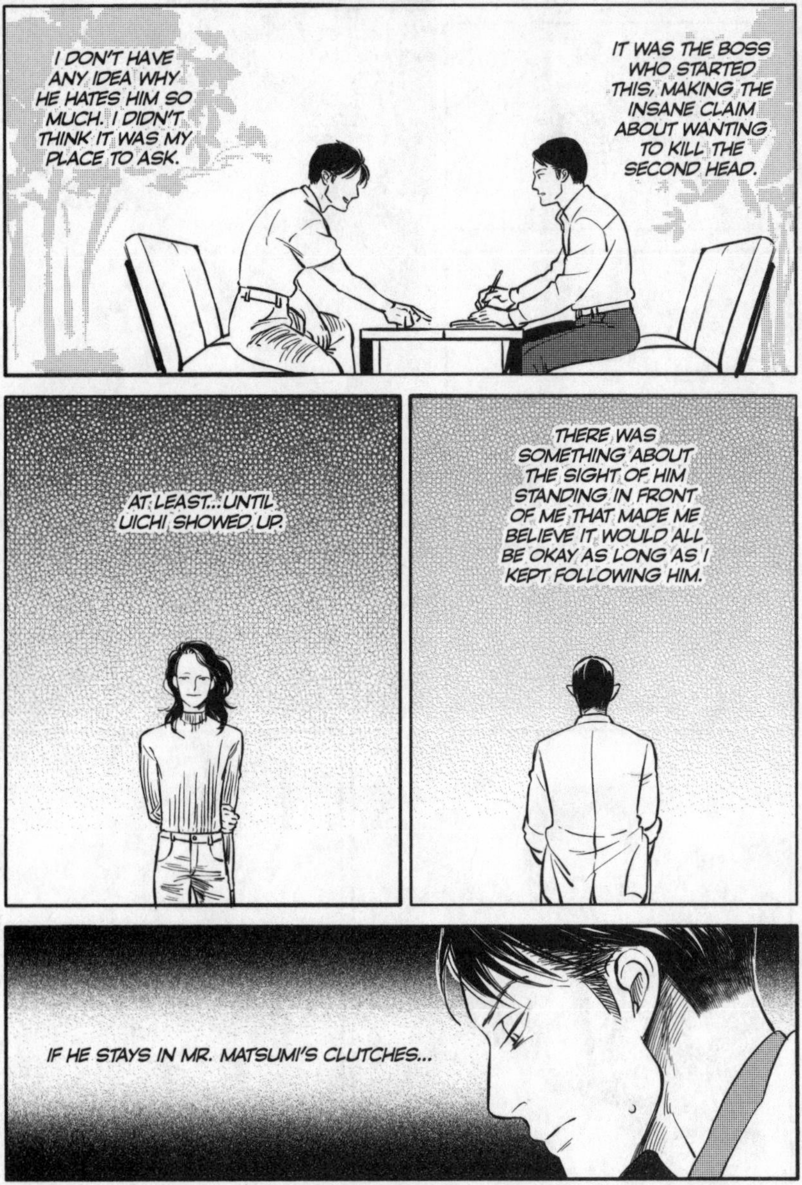
IT WAS THE BOSS WHO STARTED THIS, MAKING THE INSANE CLAIM ABOUT WANTING TO KILL THE SECOND HEAD.
I DON'T HAVE ANY IDEA WHY HE HATES HIM SO MUCH. I DIDN'T THINK IT WAS MY PLACE TO ASK.
THERE WAS SOMETHING ABOUT THE SIGHT OF HIM STANDING IN FRONT OF ME THAT MADE ME BELIEVE IT WOULD ALL BE OKAY AS LONG AS I KEPT FOLLOWING HIM.
AT LEAST...UNTIL UICHI SHOWED UP.
IF HE STAYS IN MR. MATSUMI'S CLUTCHES...

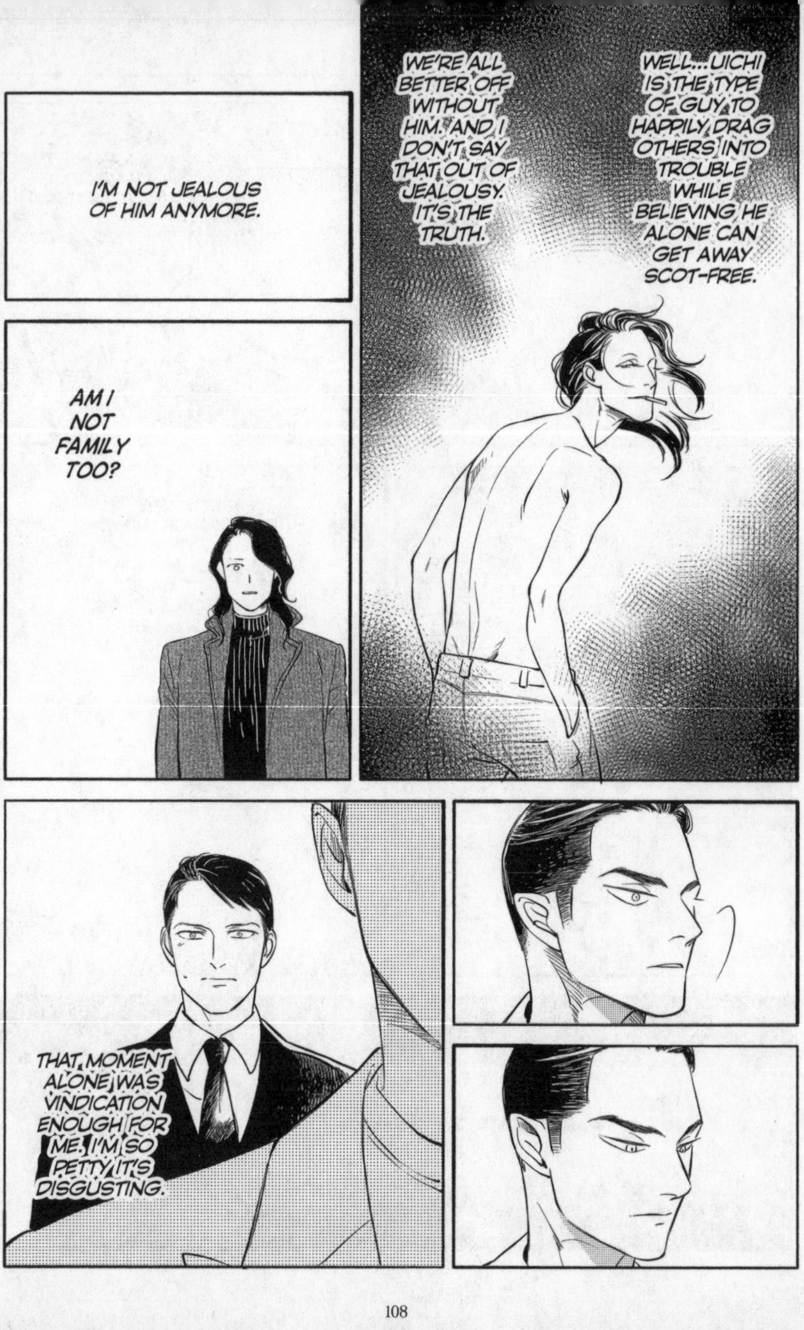
WELL...UICHI IS THE TYPE OF GUY TO HAPPILY DRAG OTHERS INTO TROUBLE WHILE BELIEVING HE ALONE CAN GET AWAY SCOT-FREE.
WE'RE ALL BETTER OFF WITHOUT HIM. AND I DON'T SAY THAT OUT OF JEALOUSY. IT'S THE TRUTH.
I'M NOT JEALOUS OF HIM ANYMORE.
AM I NOT FAMILY TOO?
THAT MOMENT ALONE WAS VINDICATION ENOUGH FOR ME. I'M SO PETTY IT'S DISGUSTING.

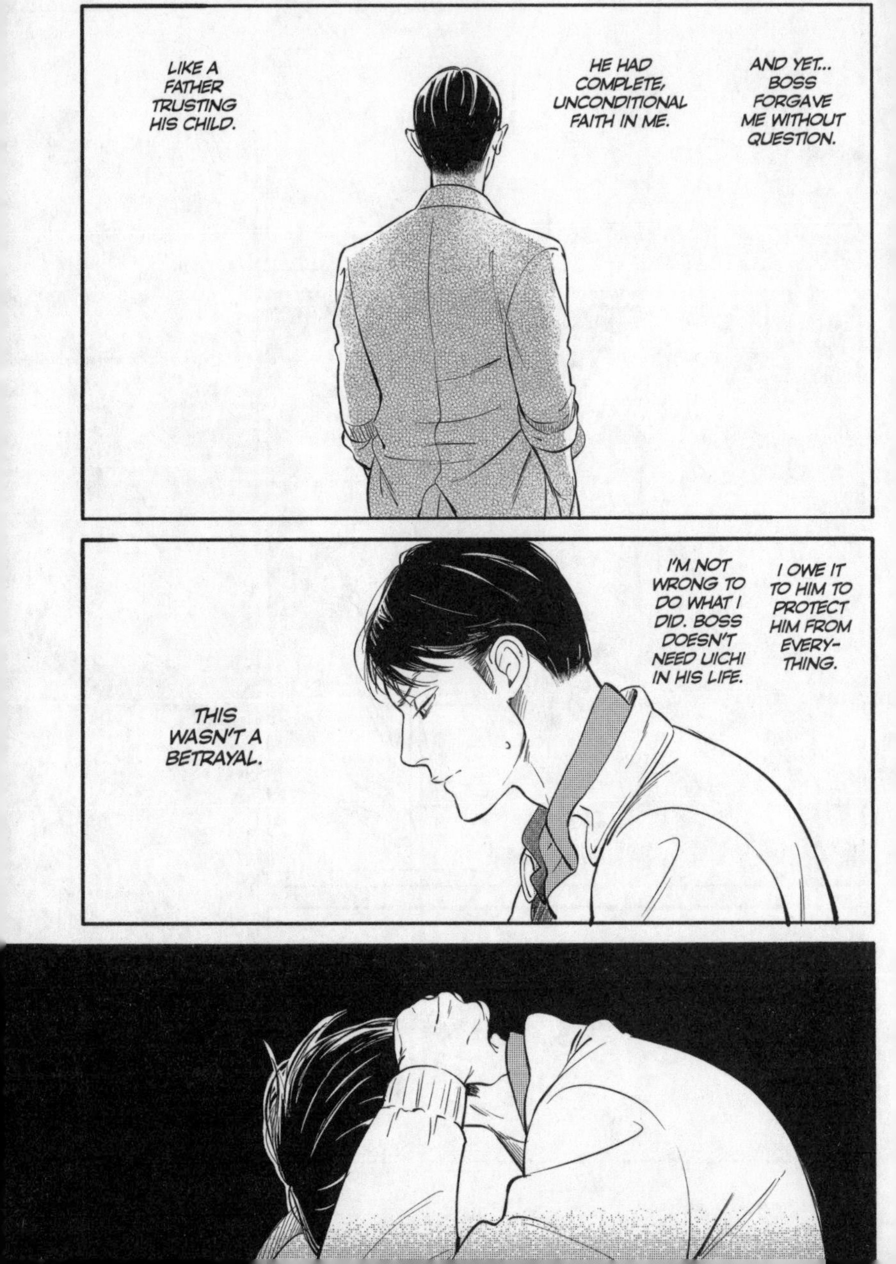
AND YET... BOSS FORGAVE ME WITHOUT QUESTION.
HE HAD COMPLETE, UNCONDITIONAL FAITH IN ME.
LIKE A FATHER TRUSTING HIS CHILD.
I OWE IT TO HIM TO PROTECT HIM FROM EVERY-THING.
I'M NOT WRONG TO DO WHAT I DID. BOSS DOESN'T NEED UICHI IN HIS LIFE.
THIS WASN'T A BETRAYAL.

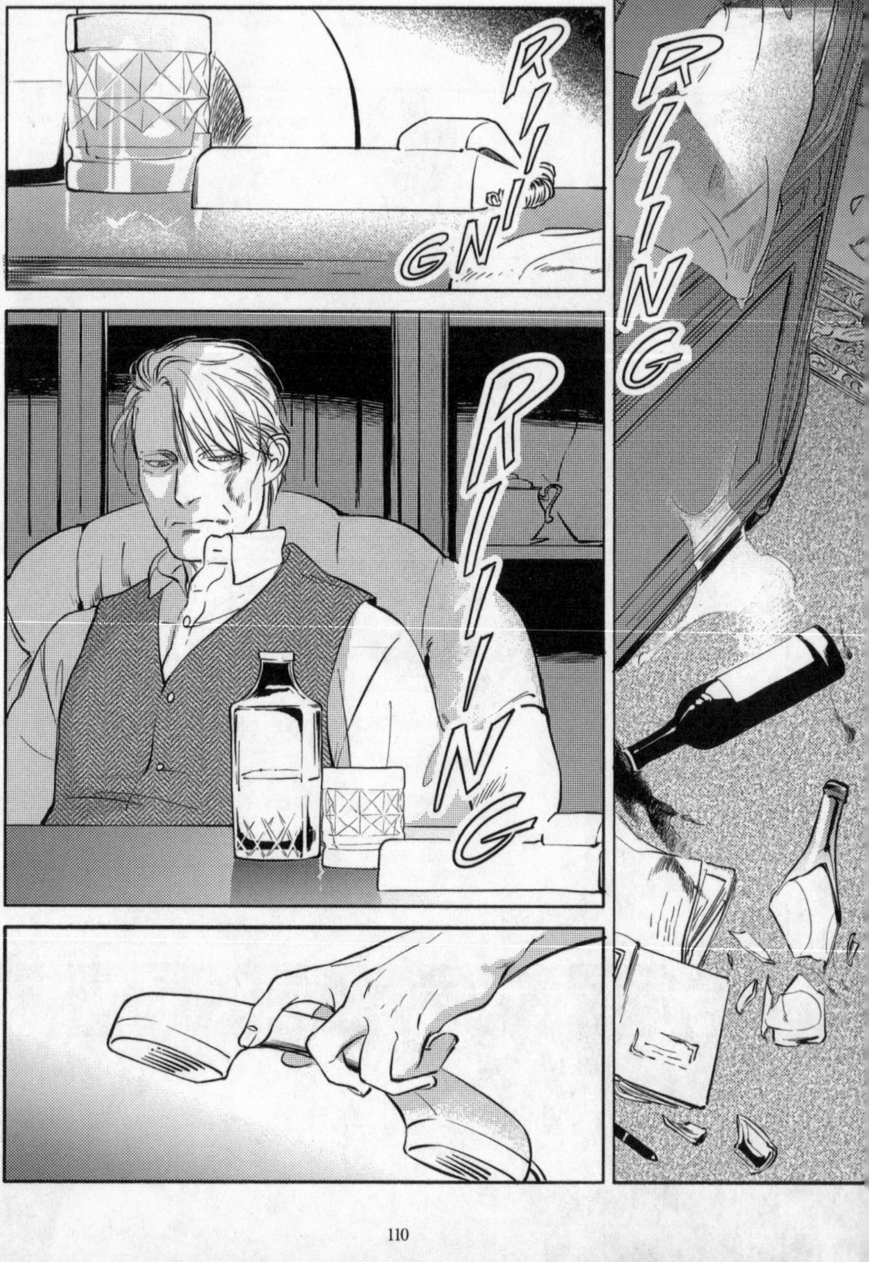
RIIING
RIIING
RIIIING

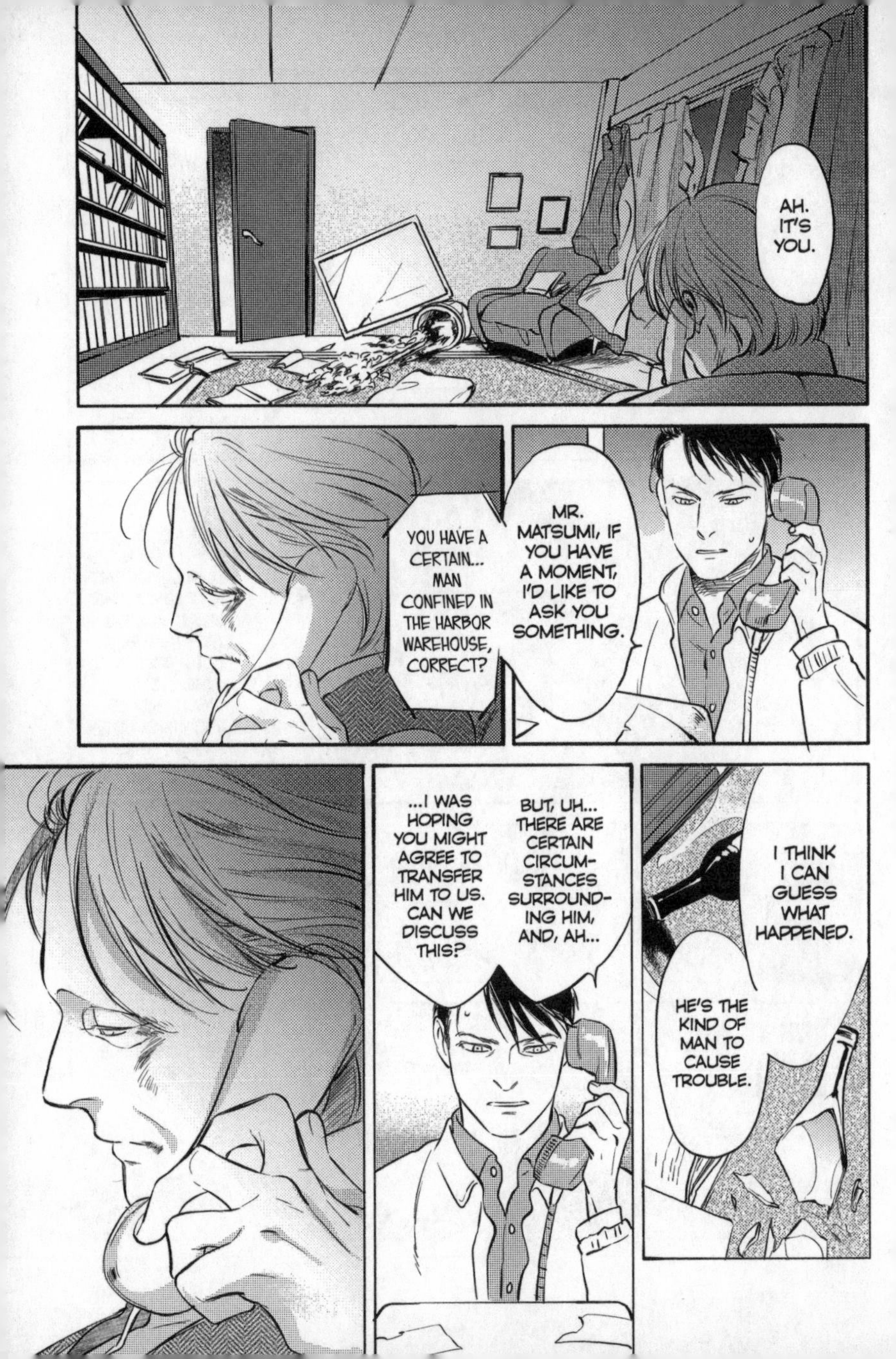
AH. IT'S YOU.
MR. MATSUMI, IF YOU HAVE A MOMENT, I'D LIKE TO ASK YOU SOMETHING.
YOU HAVE A CERTAIN... MAN CONFINED IN THE HARBOR WAREHOUSE, CORRECT?
I THINK I CAN GUESS WHAT HAPPENED.
HE'S THE KIND OF MAN TO CAUSE TROUBLE.
BUT, UH... THERE ARE CERTAIN CIRCUM-STANCES SURROUND-ING HIM, AND, AH...
...I WAS HOPING YOU MIGHT AGREE TO TRANSFER HIM TO US. CAN WE DISCUSS THIS?

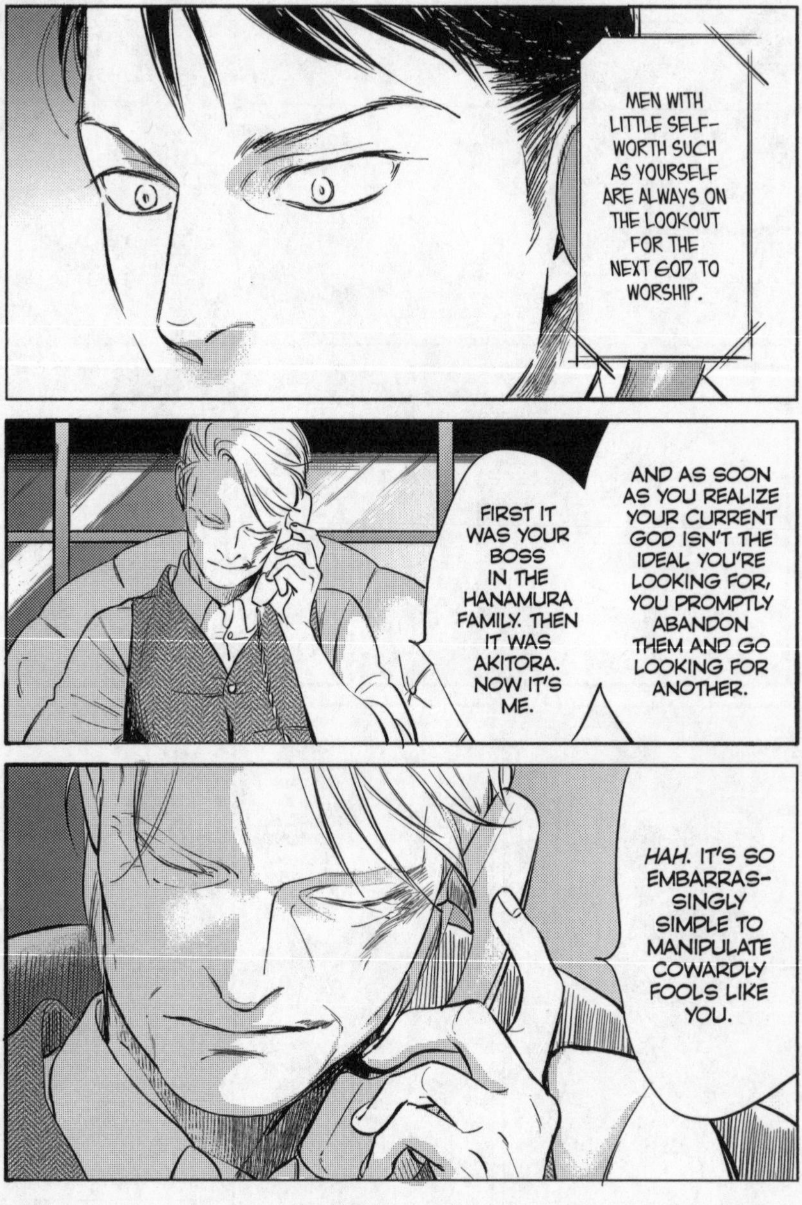
MEN WITH LITTLE SELF-WORTH SUCH AS YOURSELF ARE ALWAYS ON THE LOOKOUT FOR THE NEXT GOD TO WORSHIP.
AND AS SOON AS YOU REALIZE YOUR CURRENT GOD ISN'T THE IDEAL YOU'RE LOOKING FOR, YOU PROMPTLY ABANDON THEM AND GO LOOKING FOR ANOTHER.
FIRST IT WAS YOUR BOSS IN THE HANAMURA FAMILY. THEN IT WAS AKITORA. NOW IT'S ME.
HAH. IT'S SO EMBARRAS-SINGLY SIMPLE TO MANIPULATE COWARDLY FOOLS LIKE YOU.

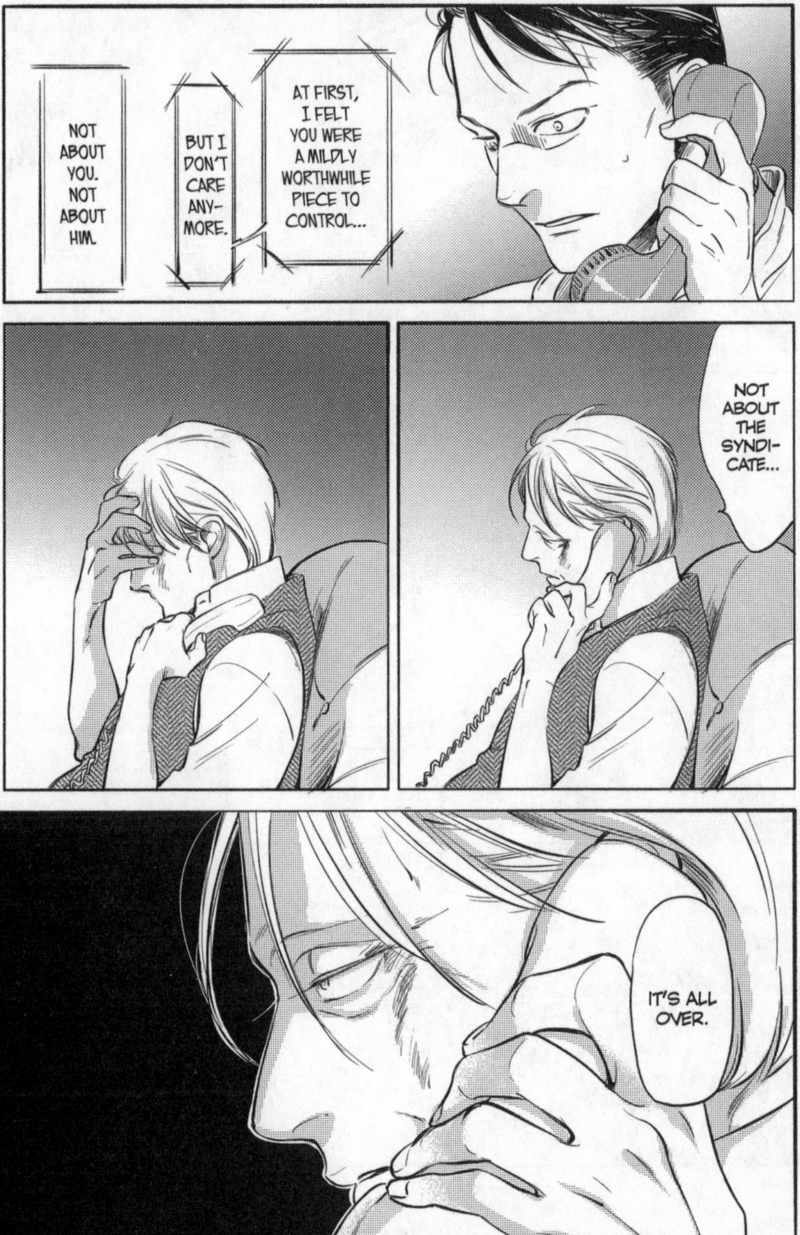
AT FIRST, I FELT YOU WERE A MILDLY WORTHWHILE PIECE TO CONTROL...
BUT I DON'T CARE ANYMORE.
NOT ABOUT YOU. NOT ABOUT HIM.
NOT ABOUT THE SYNDICATE...
IT'S ALL OVER.

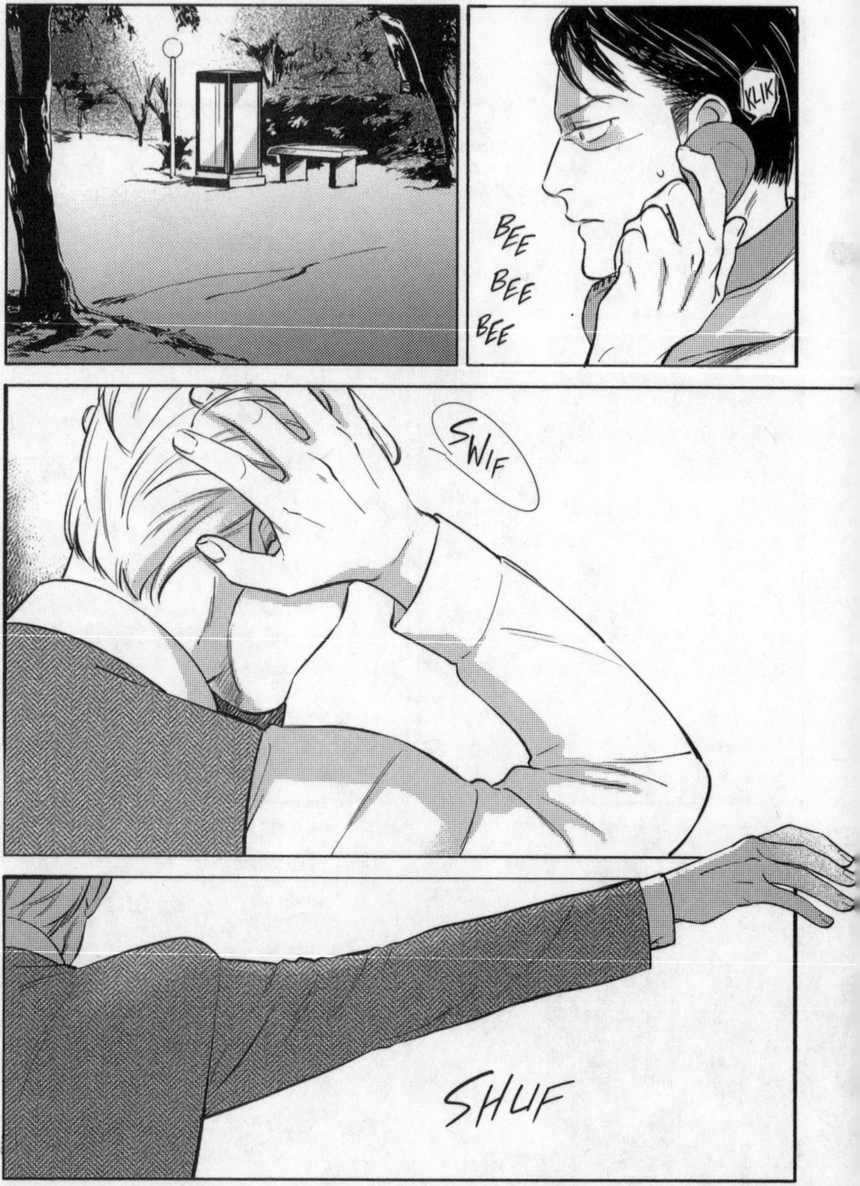
KLIK
BEE
BEE
BEE
SWIF
SHUF

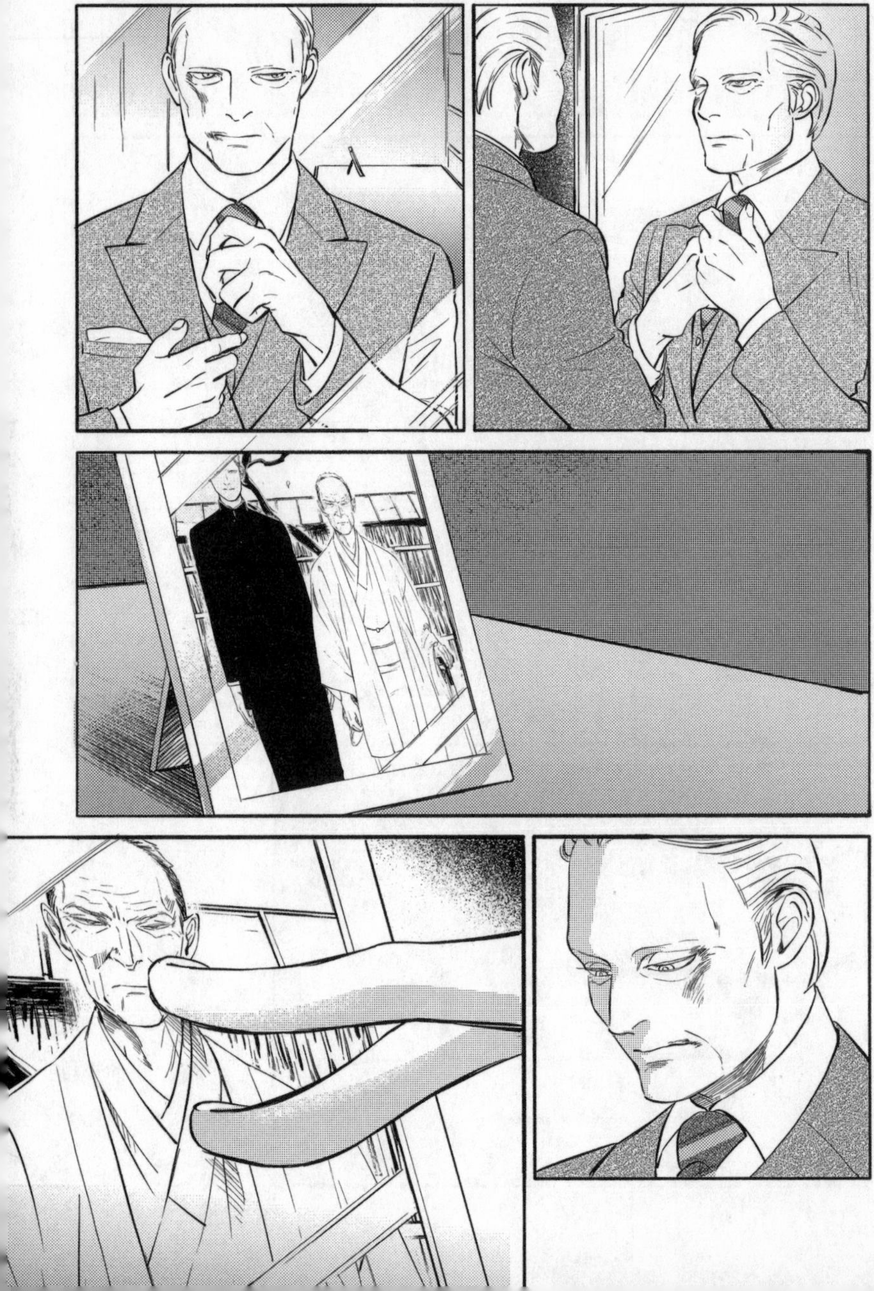

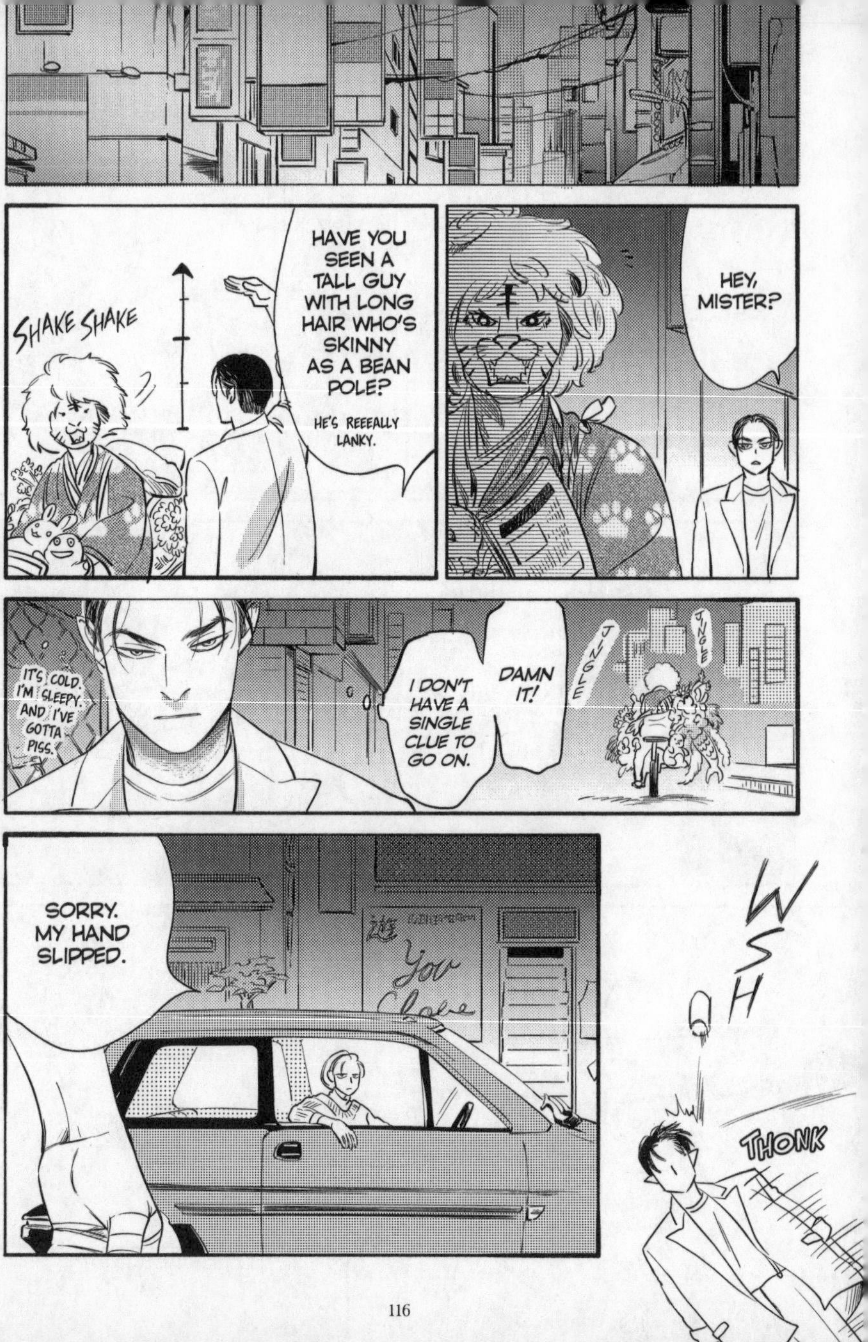
HEY, MISTER?
HAVE YOU SEEN A TALL GUY WITH LONG HAIR WHO'S SKINNY AS A BEAN POLE?
HE'S REEEALLY LANKY.
SHAKE SHAKE
JINGLE
JINGLE
DAMN IT!
I DON'T HAVE A SINGLE CLUE TO GO ON.
IT'S COLD. I'M SLEEPY. AND I'VE GOTTA PISS.
WSH
THONK
SORRY. MY HAND SLIPPED.

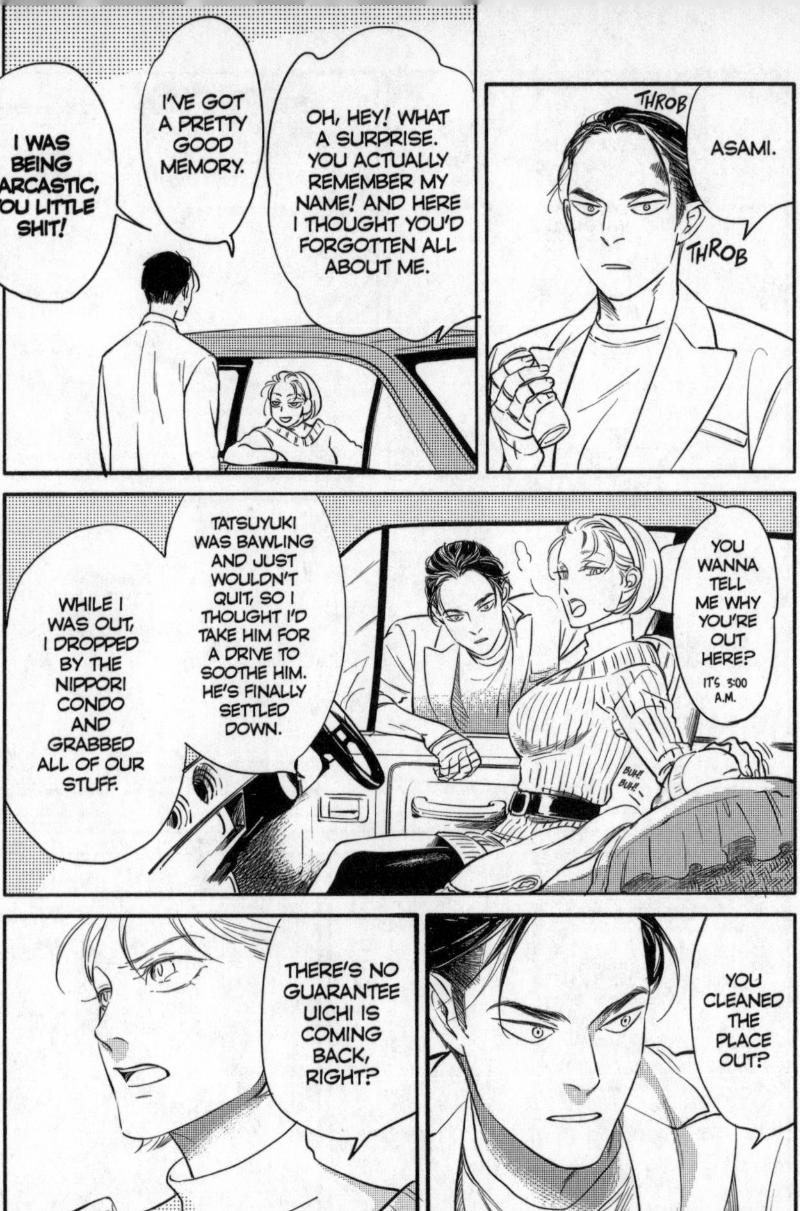

THROB
ASAMI.
THROB
OH, HEY! WHAT A SURPRISE. YOU ACTUALLY REMEMBER MY NAME! AND HERE I THOUGHT YOU'D FORGOTTEN ALL ABOUT ME.
I'VE GOT A PRETTY GOOD MEMORY.
I WAS BEING SARCASTIC, YOU LITTLE SHIT!
YOU WANNA TELL ME WHY YOU'RE OUT HERE?
IT'S 3:00 A.M.
BUH! BUH!
TATSUYUKI WAS BAWLING AND JUST WOULDN'T QUIT, SO I THOUGHT I'D TAKE HIM FOR A DRIVE TO SOOTHE HIM. HE'S FINALLY SETTLED DOWN.
WHILE I WAS OUT, I DROPPED BY THE NIPPORI CONDO AND GRABBED ALL OF OUR STUFF.
YOU CLEANED THE PLACE OUT?
THERE'S NO GUARANTEE UICHI IS COMING BACK, RIGHT?

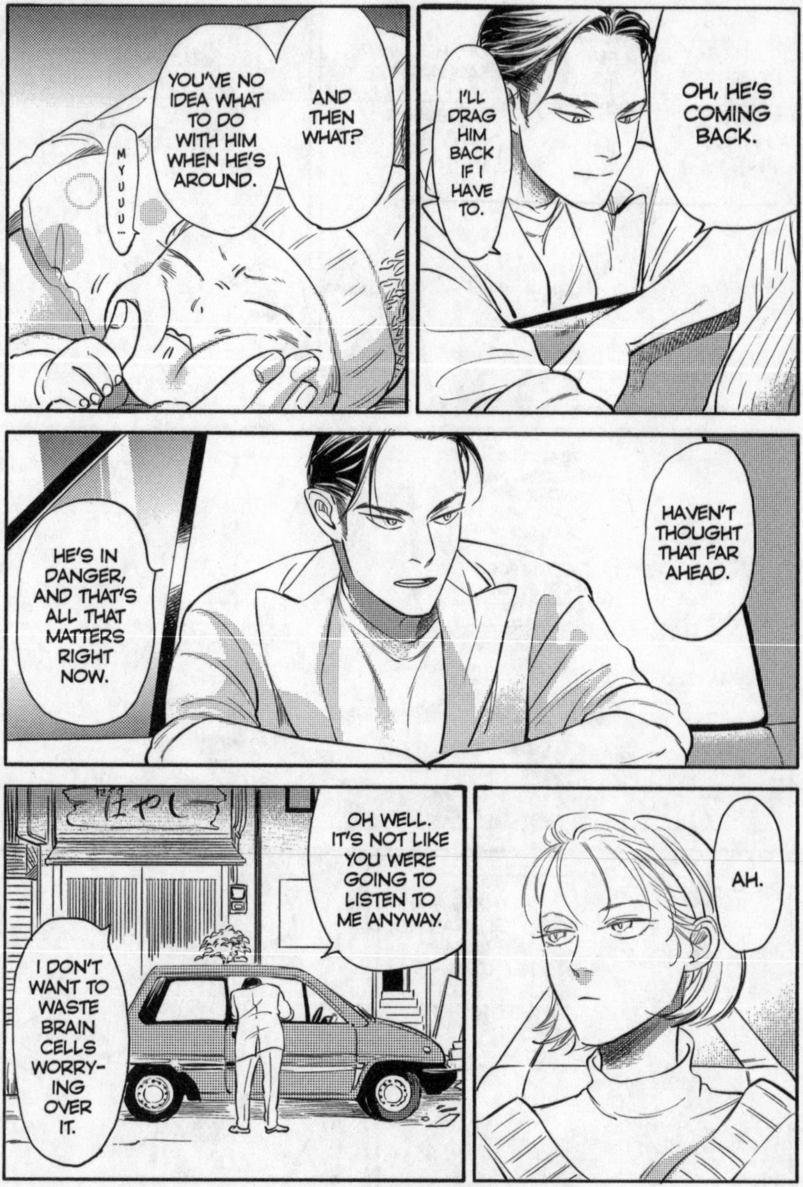
OH, HE'S COMING BACK.
I'LL DRAG HIM BACK IF I HAVE TO.
AND THEN WHAT?
YOU'VE NO IDEA WHAT TO DO WITH HIM WHEN HE'S AROUND.
MYUUU...
HAVEN'T THOUGHT THAT FAR AHEAD.
HE'S IN DANGER, AND THAT'S ALL THAT MATTERS RIGHT NOW.
AH.
OH WELL. IT'S NOT LIKE YOU WERE GOING TO LISTEN TO ME ANYWAY.
I DON'T WANT TO WASTE BRAIN CELLS WORRYING OVER IT.

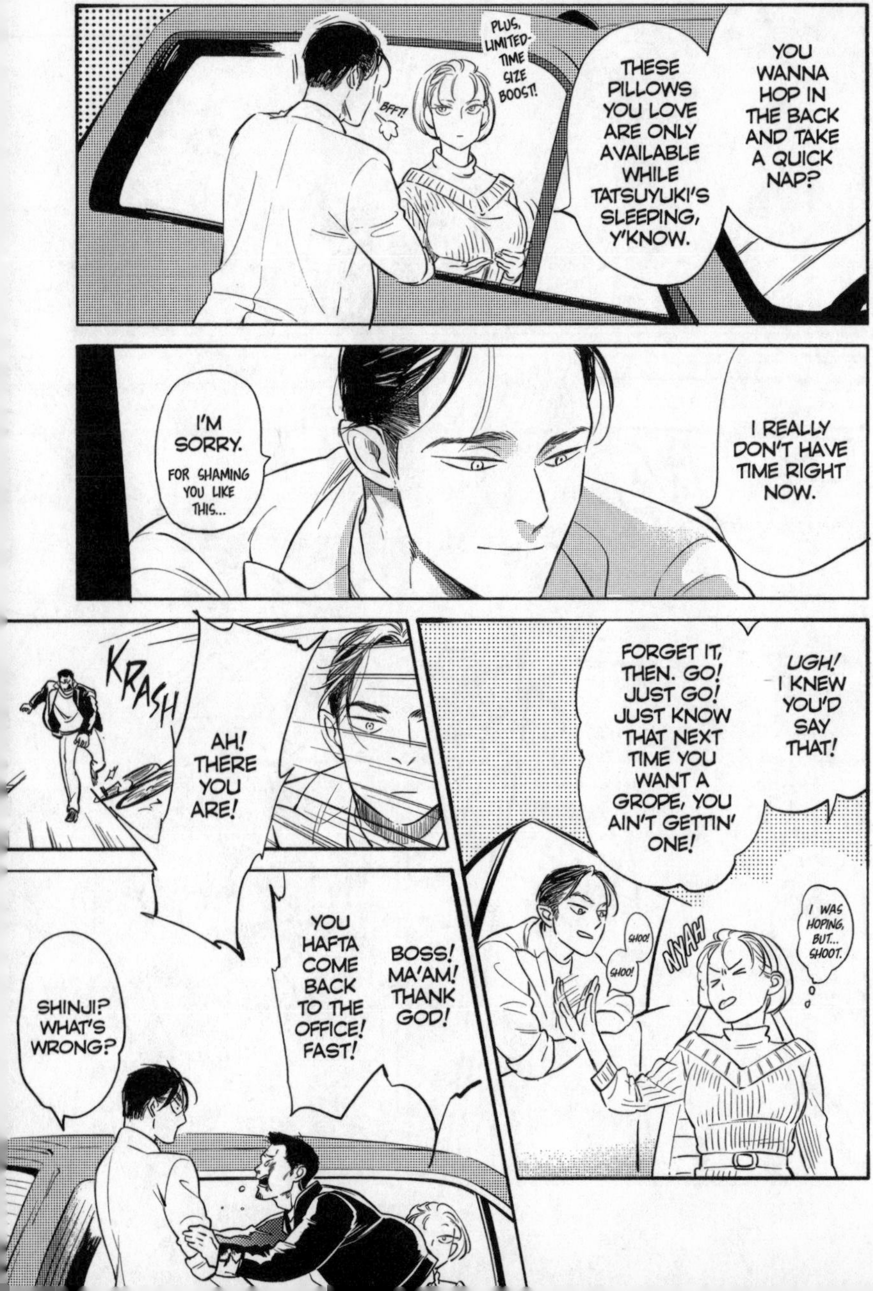
YOU WANNA HOP IN THE BACK AND TAKE A QUICK NAP?
THESE PILLOWS YOU LOVE ARE ONLY AVAILABLE WHILE TATSUYUKI'S SLEEPING, Y'KNOW.
PLUS, LIMITED-TIME SIZE BOOST!
BFFT!
I REALLY DON'T HAVE TIME RIGHT NOW.
I'M SORRY.
FOR SHAMING YOU LIKE THIS...
UGH! I KNEW YOU'D SAY THAT!
FORGET IT, THEN. GO! JUST GO! JUST KNOW THAT NEXT TIME YOU WANT A GROPE, YOU AIN'T GETTIN' ONE!
I WAS HOPING, BUT... SHOOT.
NYAH
SHOO!
SHOO!
AH! THERE YOU ARE!
KRASH
BOSS! MA'AM! THANK GOD!
YOU HAFTA COME BACK TO THE OFFICE! FAST!
SHINJI? WHAT'S WRONG?

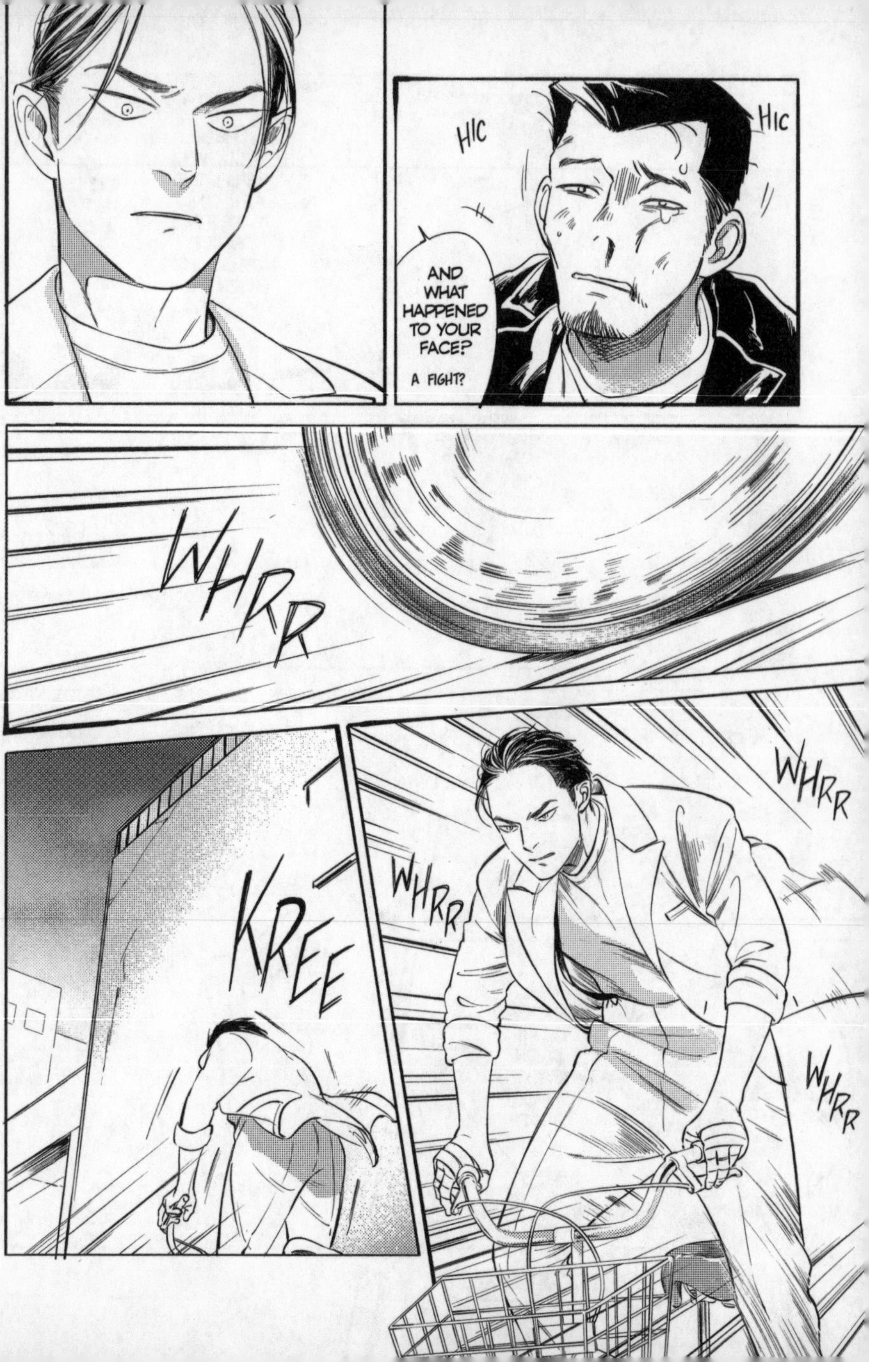
HIC
HIC
AND WHAT HAPPENED TO YOUR FACE?
A FIGHT?
WHRR
WHRR
WHRR
WHRR
KREE

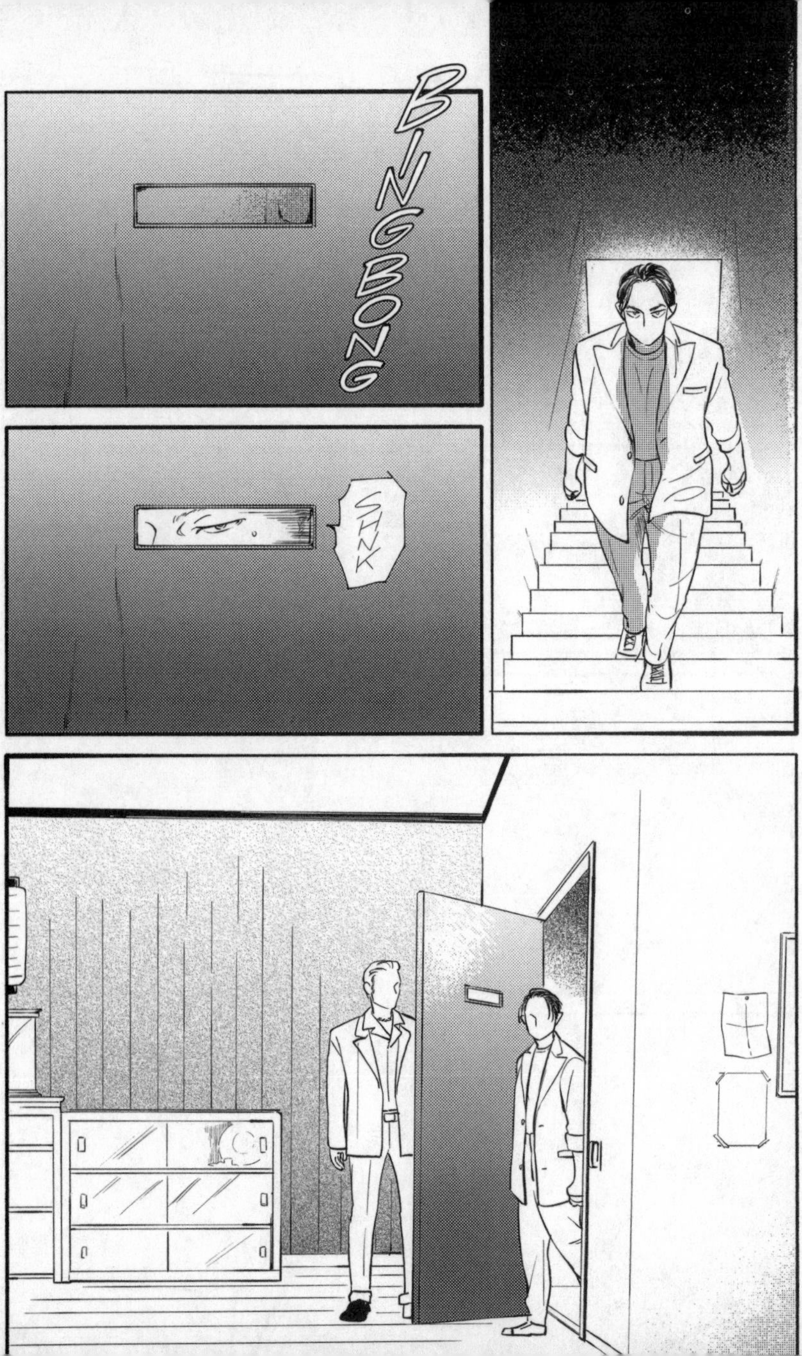
BINGBONG
SHNK

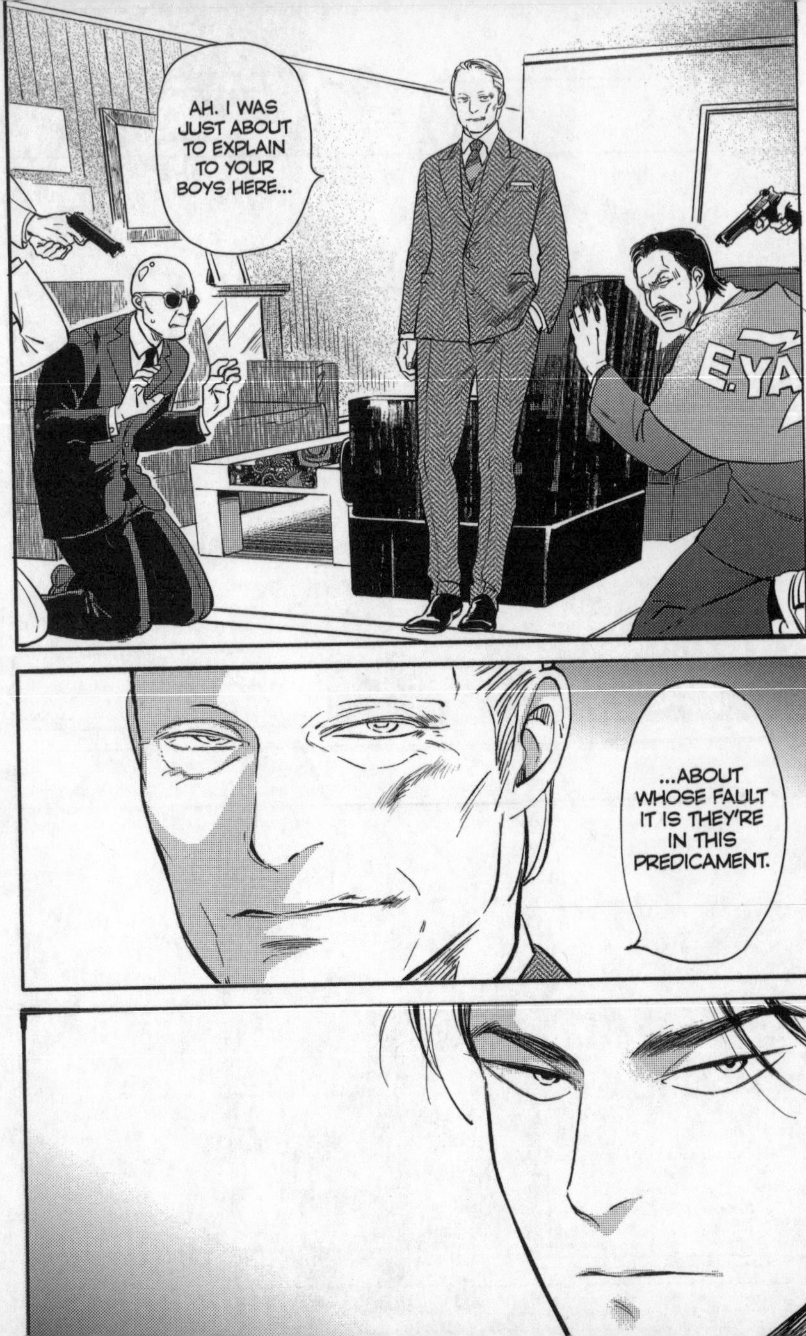
AH. I WAS JUST ABOUT TO EXPLAIN TO YOUR BOYS HERE...
E.YA
...ABOUT WHOSE FAULT IT IS THEY'RE IN THIS PREDICAMENT.

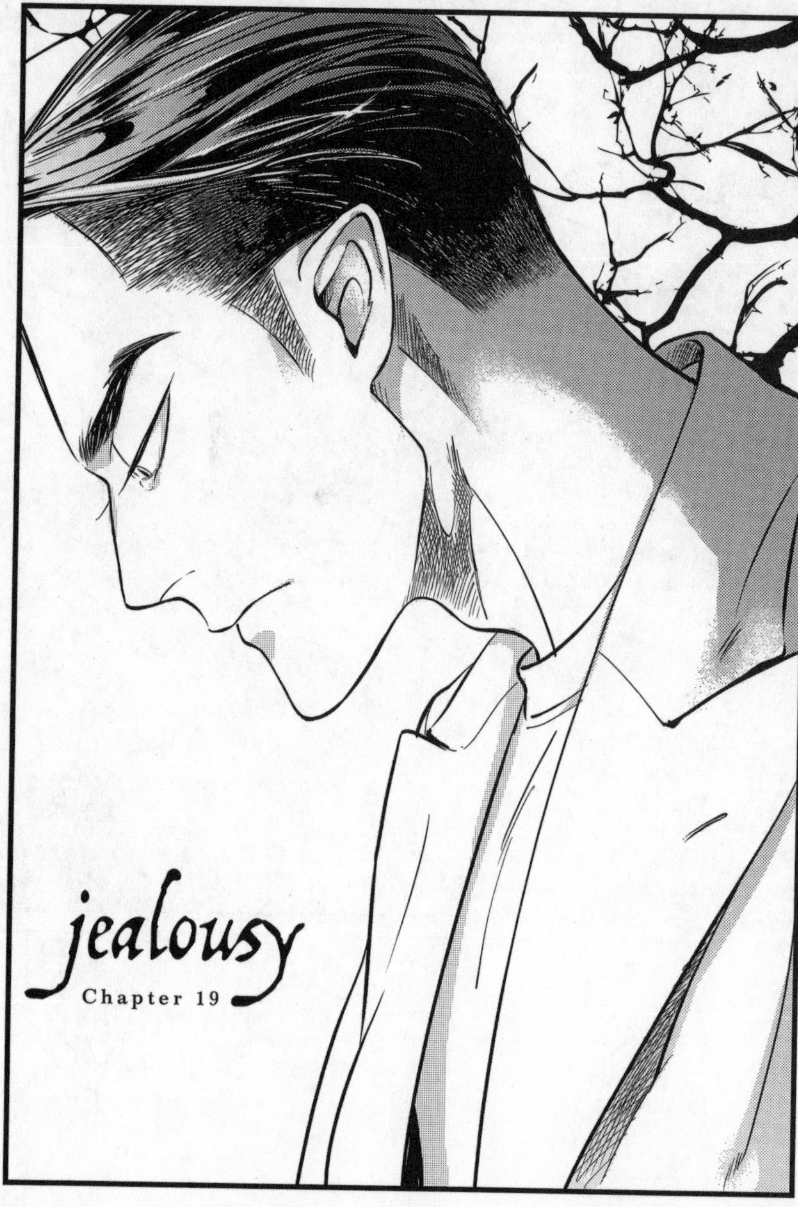
jealousy
Chapter 19

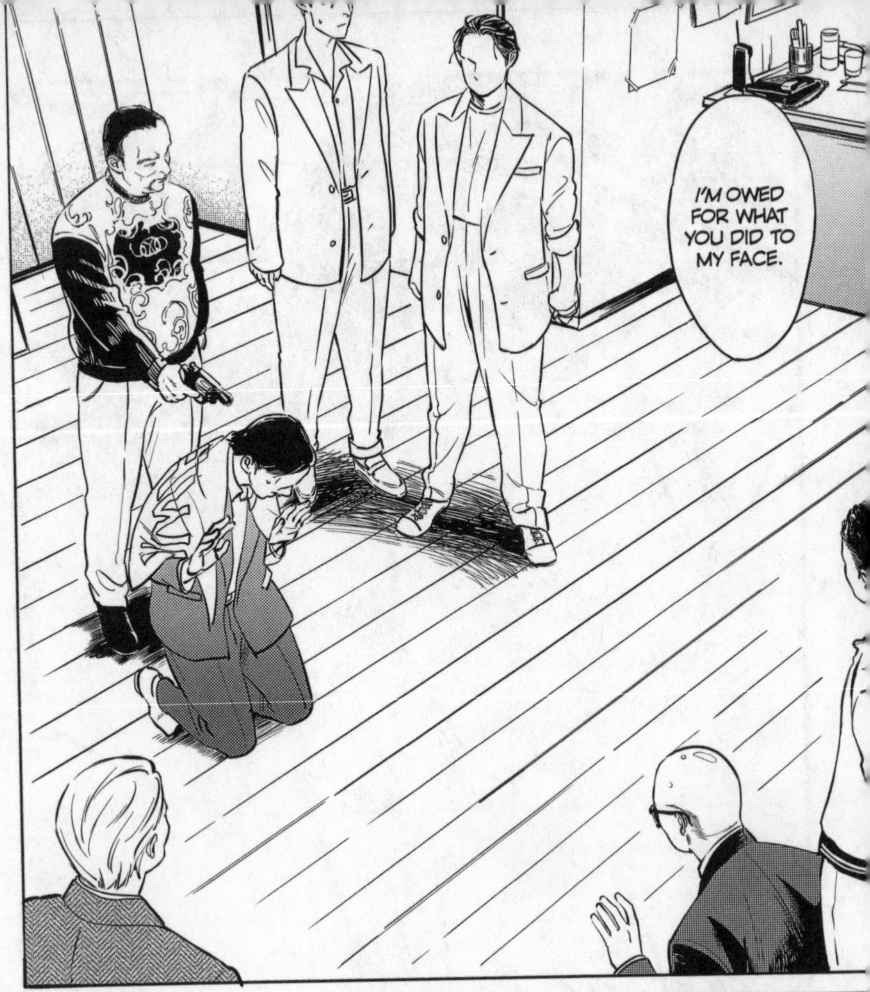
I'M OWED FOR WHAT YOU DID TO MY FACE.
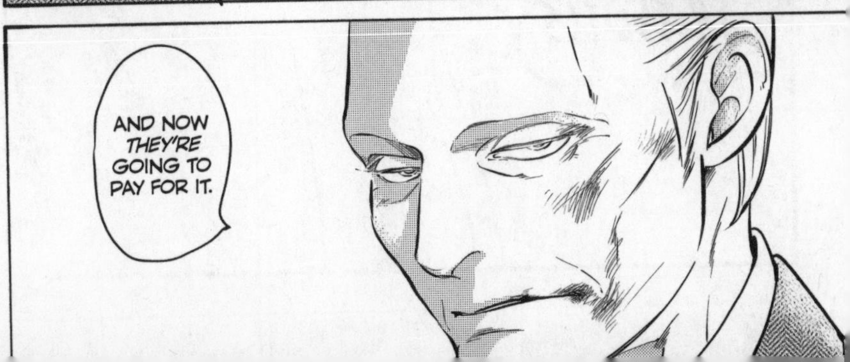
AND NOW THEY'RE GOING TO PAY FOR IT.

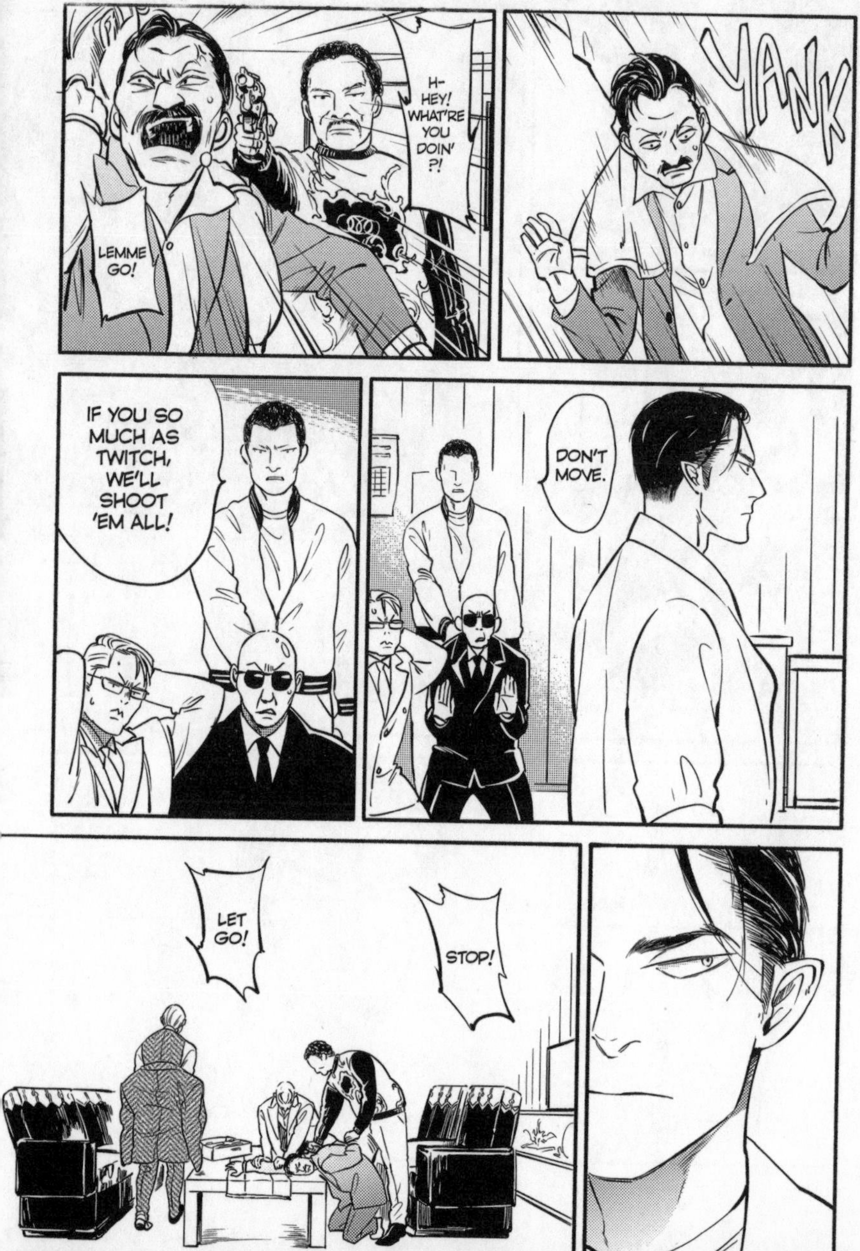
YANK
H- HEY! WHAT'RE YOU DOIN' ?!
LEMME GO!
DON'T MOVE.
IF YOU SO MUCH AS TWITCH, WE'LL SHOOT 'EM ALL!
STOP!
LET GO!

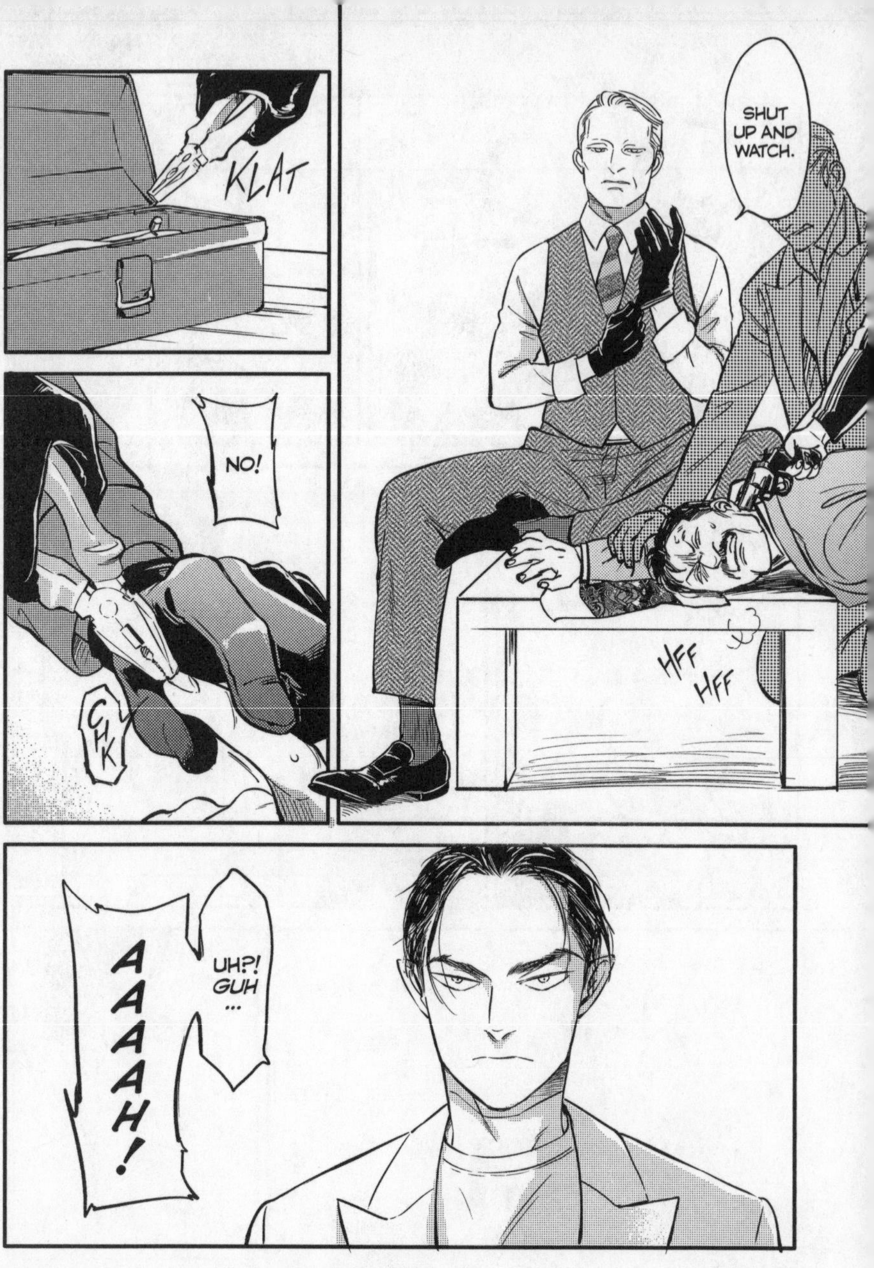
SHUT UP AND WATCH.
HFF HFF
KLAT
NO!
CHK
UH?! GUH ...
AAAAAH!

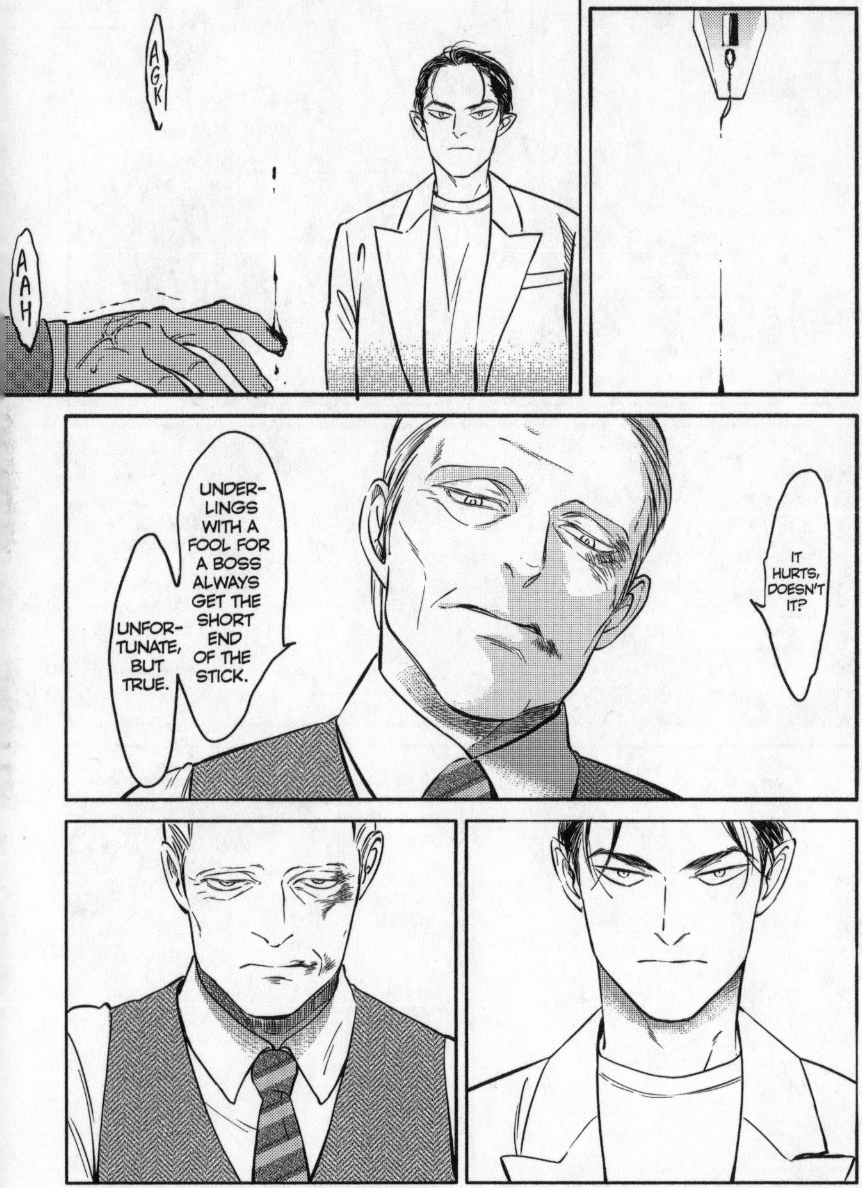
AGK
AAH
IT HURTS, DOESN'T IT?
UNDERLINGS WITH A FOOL FOR A BOSS ALWAYS GET THE SHORT END OF THE STICK.
UNFORTUNATE, BUT TRUE.

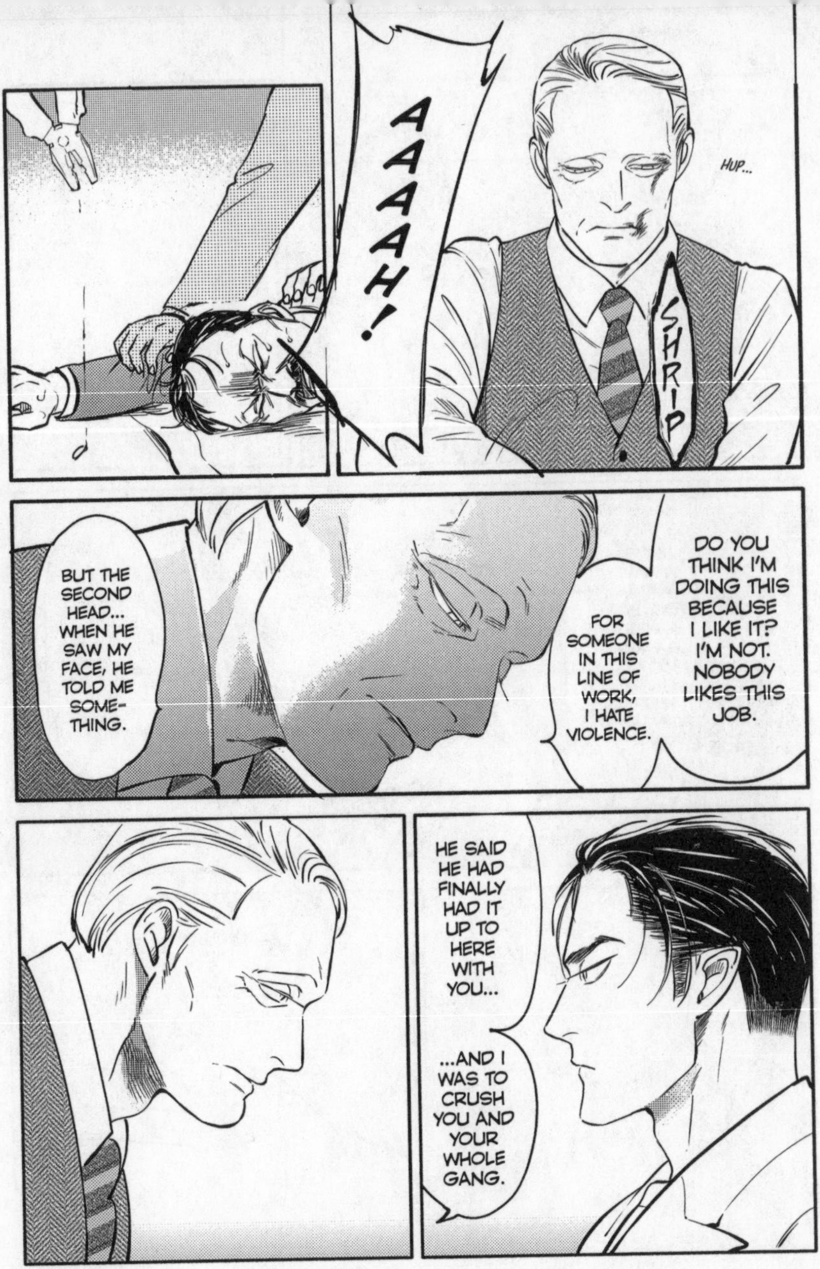
HUP...
SHRIP
AAAAAH!
DO YOU THINK I'M DOING THIS BECAUSE I LIKE IT? I'M NOT. NOBODY LIKES THIS JOB.
FOR SOMEONE IN THIS LINE OF WORK, I HATE VIOLENCE.
BUT THE SECOND HEAD... WHEN HE SAW MY FACE, HE TOLD ME SOME-THING.
HE SAID HE HAD FINALLY HAD IT UP TO HERE WITH YOU...
...AND I WAS TO CRUSH YOU AND YOUR WHOLE GANG.

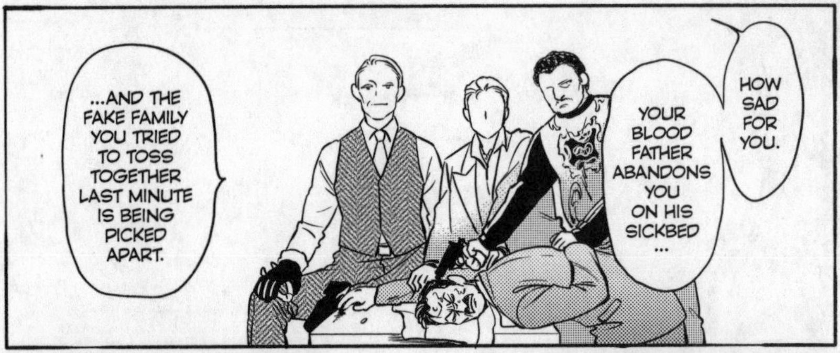
HOW SAD FOR YOU.
YOUR BLOOD FATHER ABANDONS YOU ON HIS SICKBED ...
...AND THE FAKE FAMILY YOU TRIED TO TOSS TOGETHER LAST MINUTE IS BEING PICKED APART.
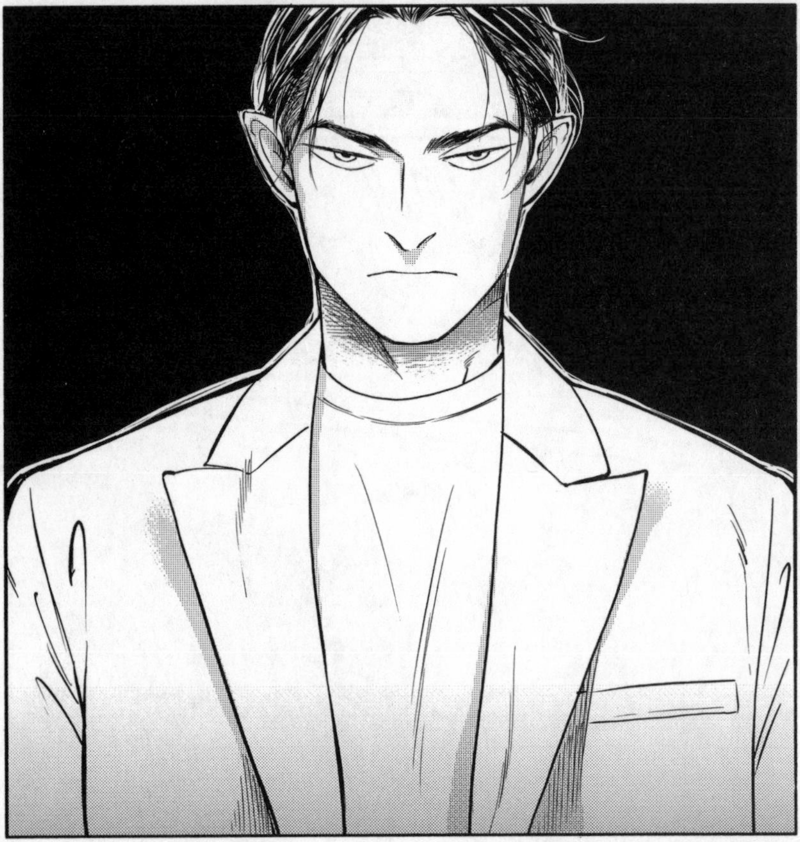

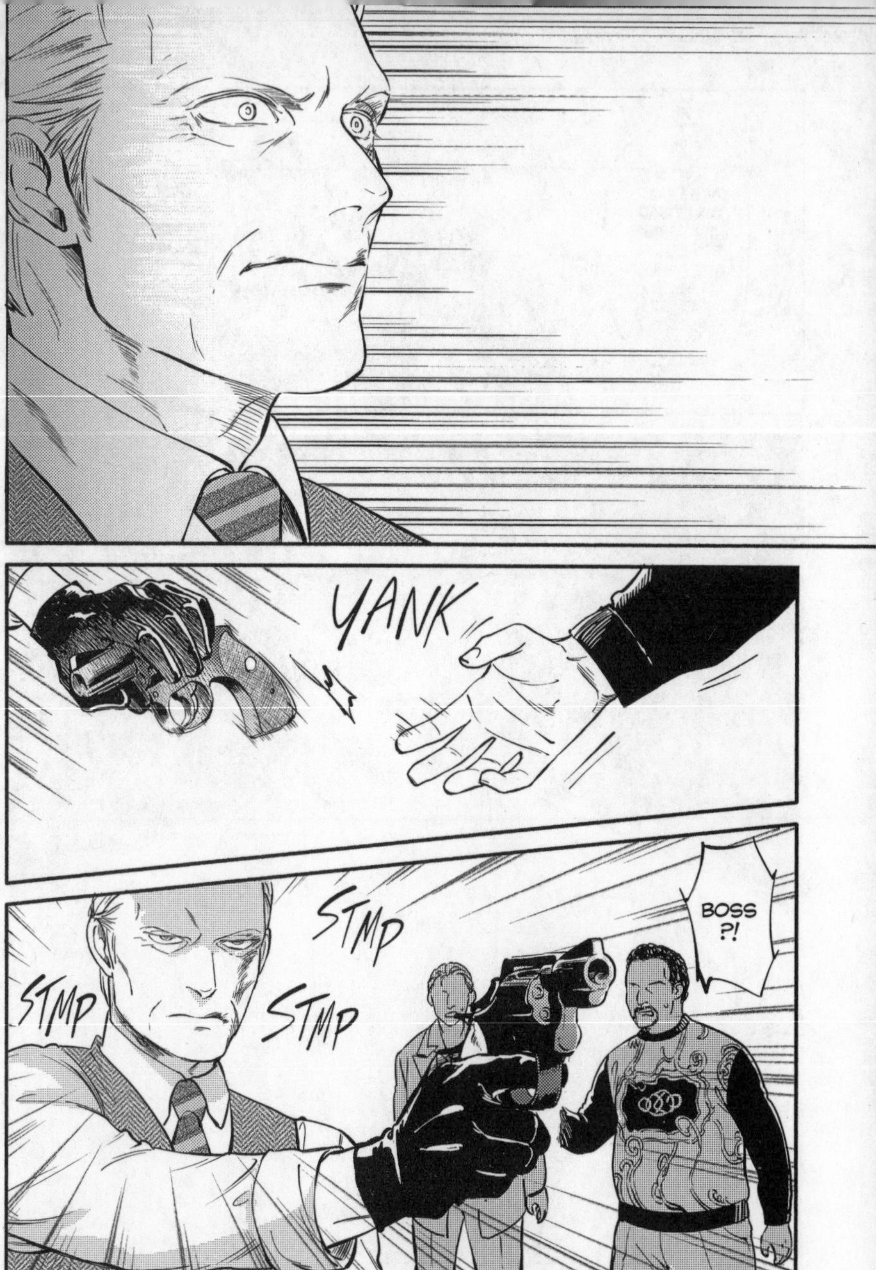
YANK
BOSS ?!
STMP
STMP
STMP

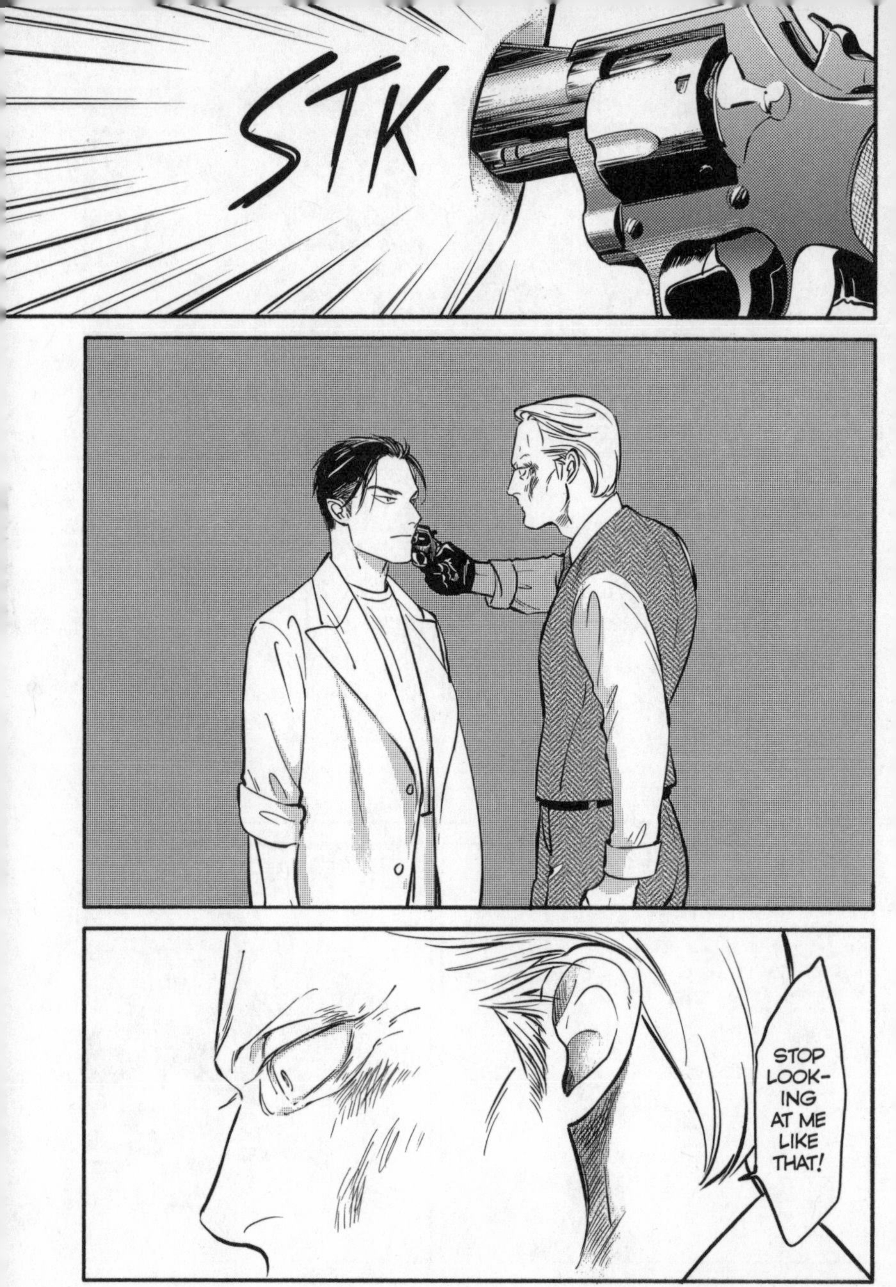
STK
STOP LOOKING AT ME LIKE THAT!

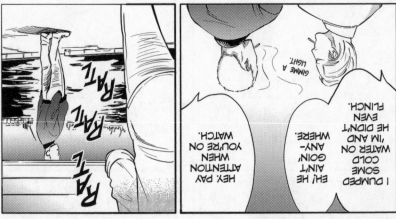

FSK
PFFF
RATL
RATL
RATL
HEY. PAY ATTENTION WHEN YOU'RE ON WATCH.
EH! HE AIN'T GOIN' ANY-WHERE.
I DUMPED SOME COLD WATER ON 'IM AND HE DIDN'T EVEN FLINCH.
GIMME A LIGHT.

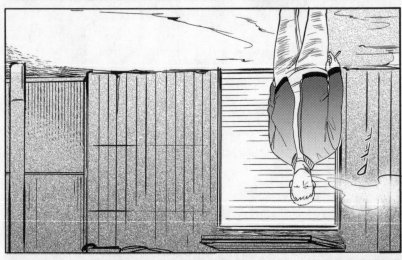

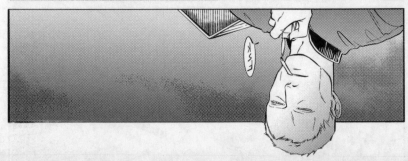

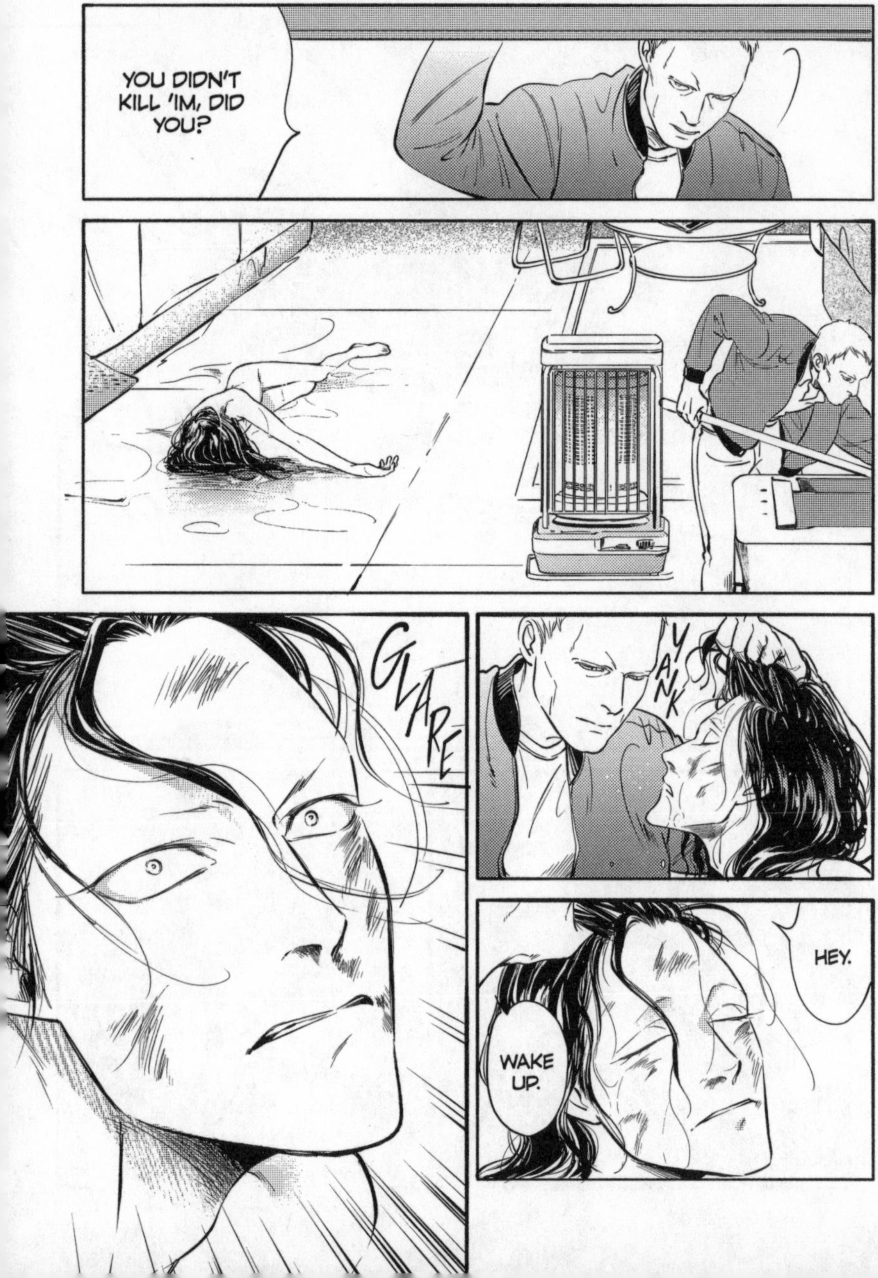
YOU DIDN'T KILL 'IM, DID YOU?
YANK
HEY.
WAKE UP.
GLARE

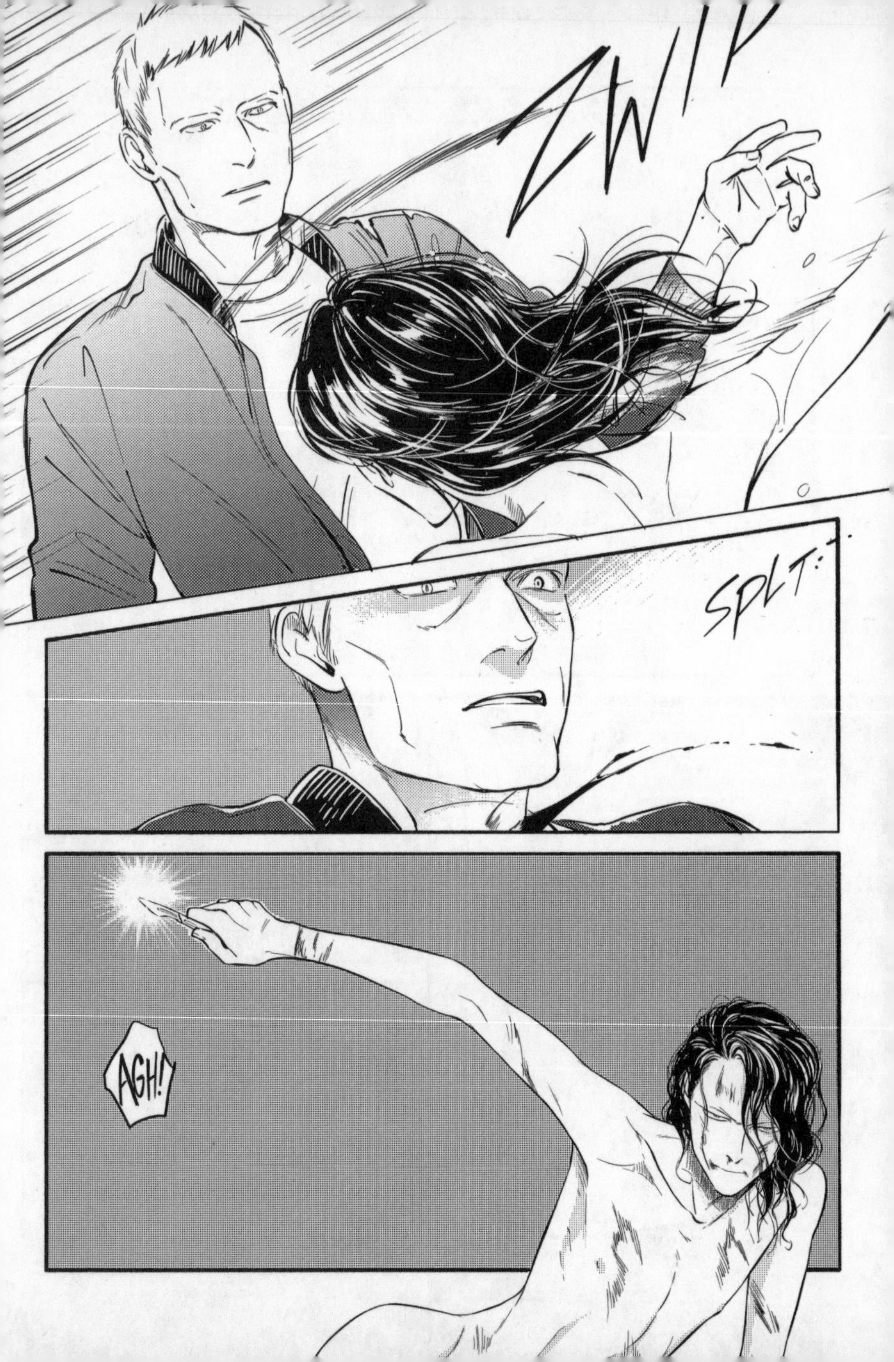
ZWIP
SPLT...
AGH!

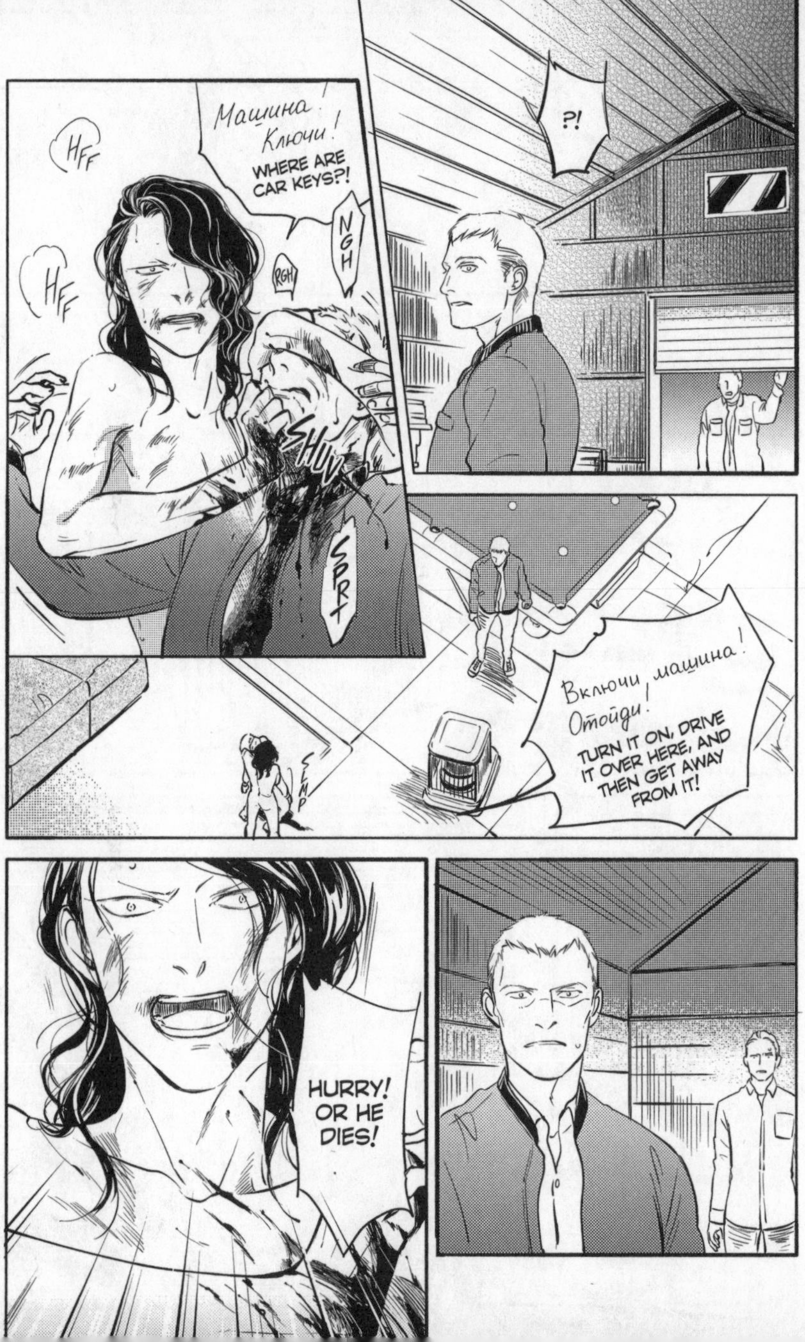
?!
Машина! Ключи!
WHERE ARE CAR KEYS?!
HFF
HFF
NGH
RGH
SHUV
SPRT
Включи машина! Отойди!
TURN IT ON, DRIVE IT OVER HERE, AND THEN GET AWAY FROM IT!
SLMP
HURRY! OR HE DIES!

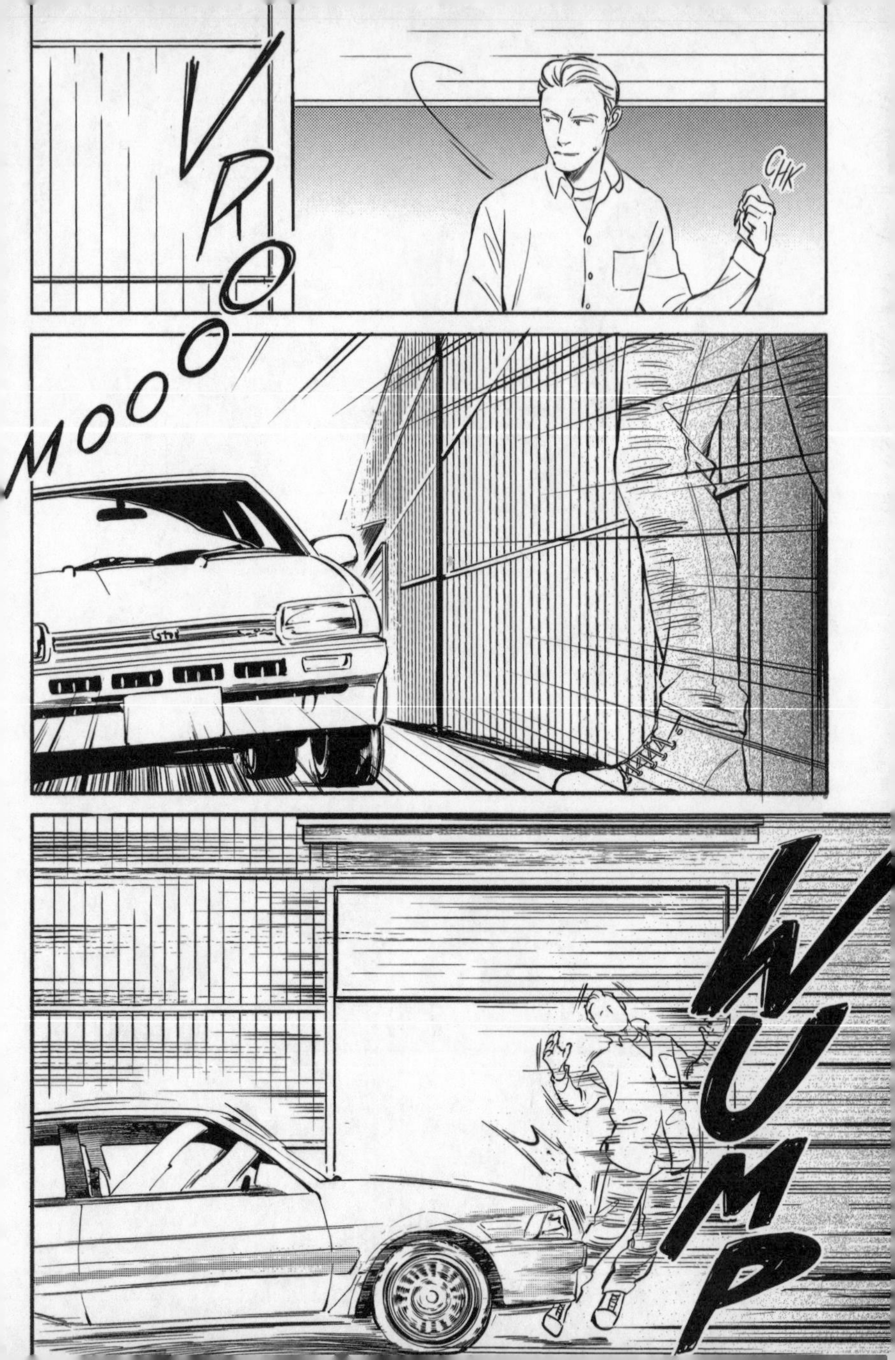
CHK
VROOOOOOM
WUMP

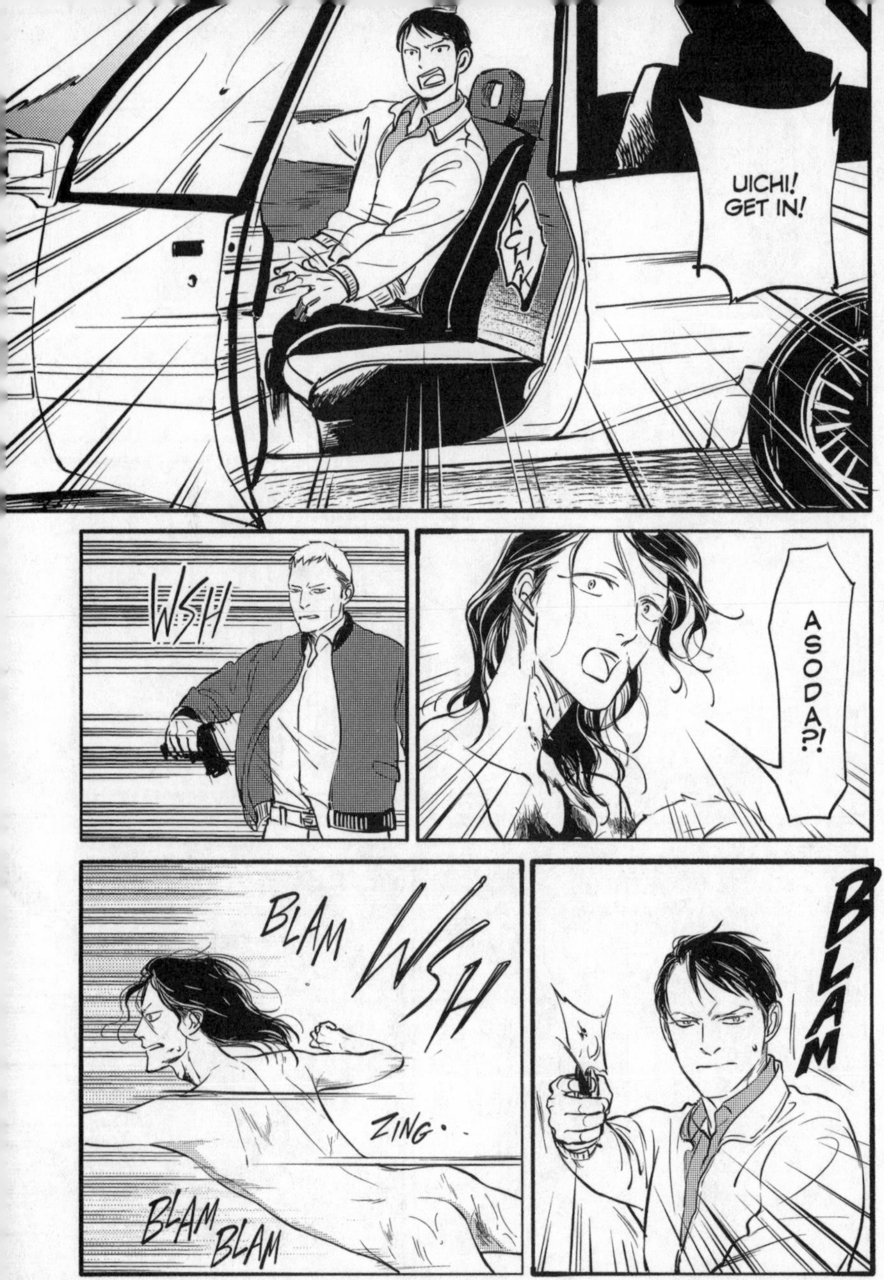
UICHI! GET IN!
KCHAK
ASODA?!
WSH
BLAM
BLAM
WSH
ZING...
BLAM BLAM

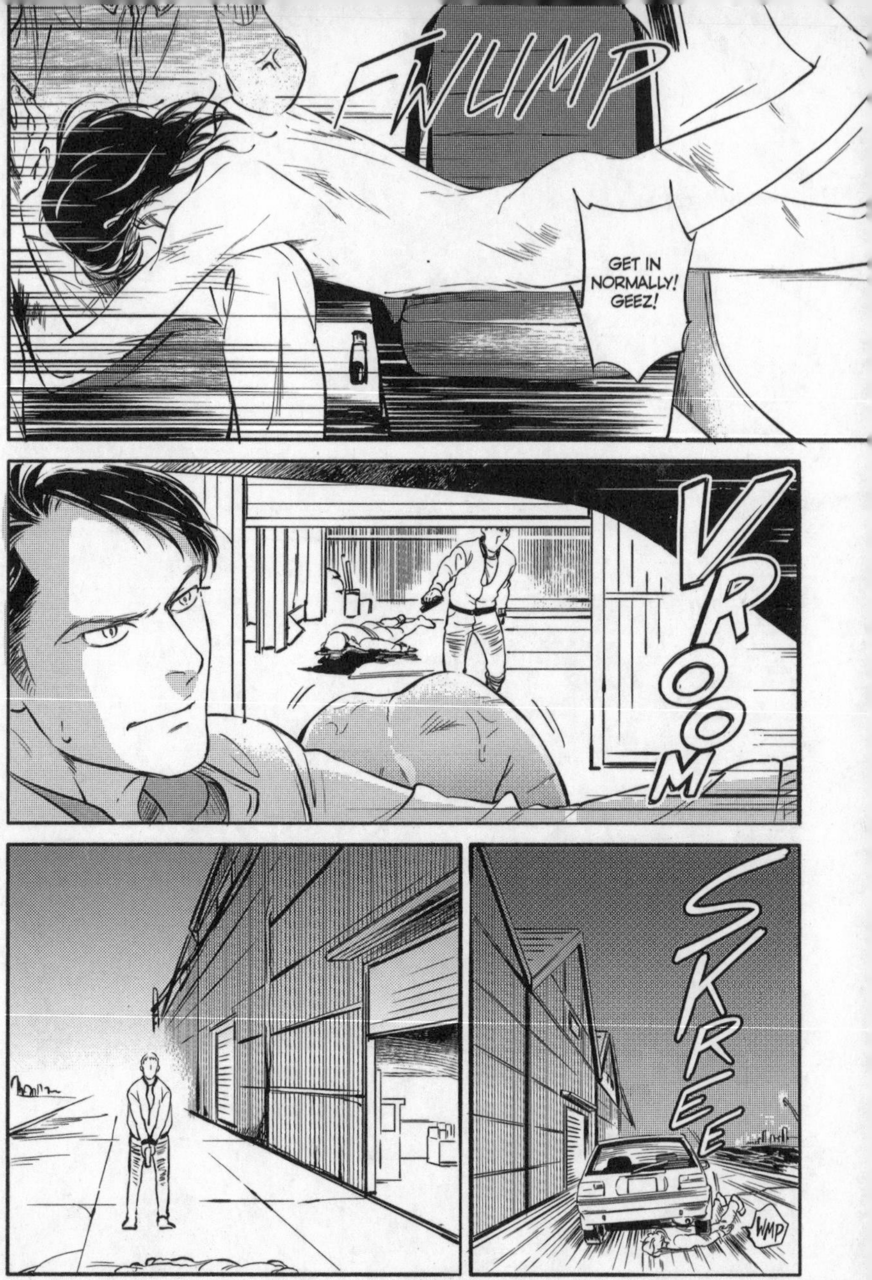
FWUMP
GET IN NORMALLY! GEEZ!
VROOOM
SKREE
WMP

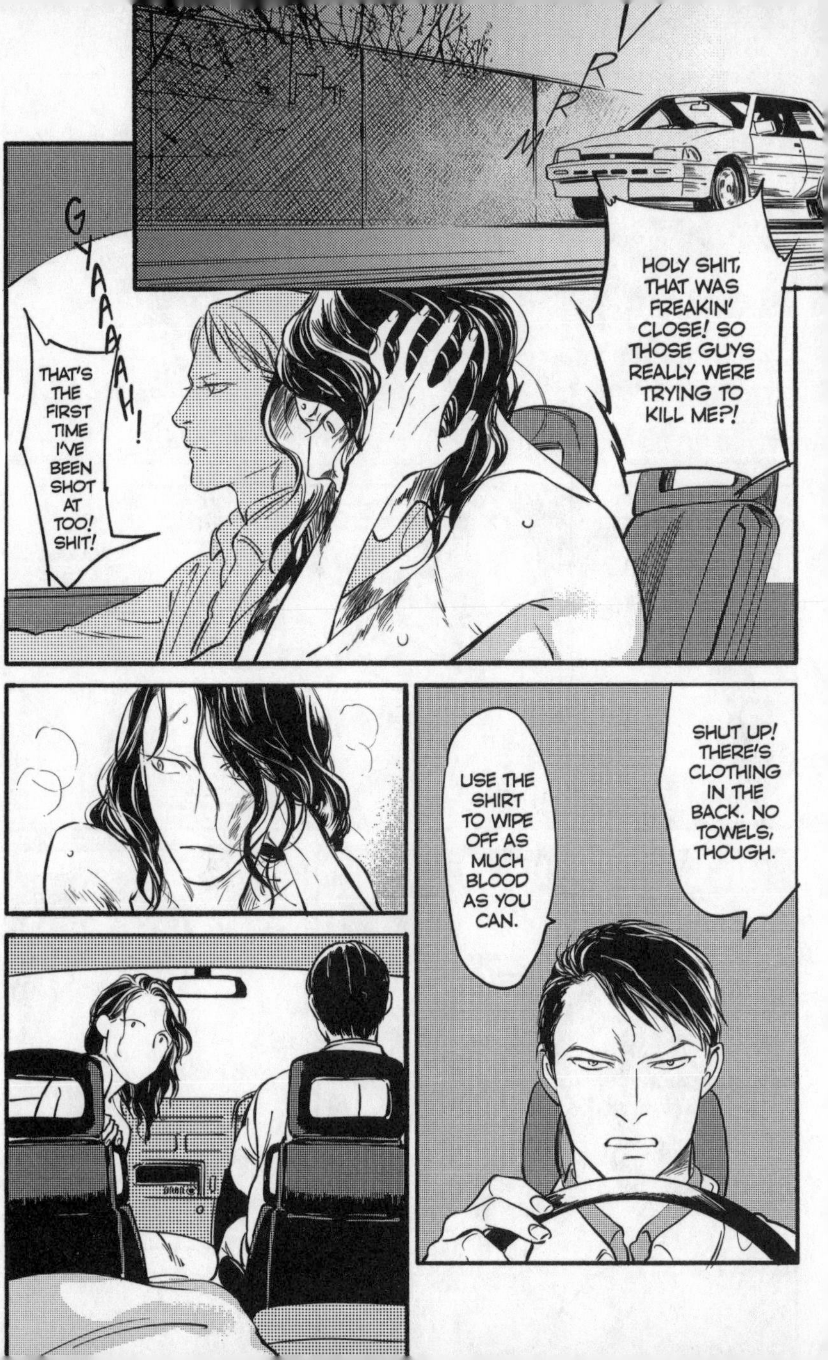
MRRR!
HOLY SHIT, THAT WAS FREAKIN' CLOSE! SO THOSE GUYS REALLY WERE TRYING TO KILL ME?!
GYAAAAH!
THAT'S THE FIRST TIME I'VE BEEN SHOT AT TOO! SHIT!
SHUT UP! THERE'S CLOTHING IN THE BACK. NO TOWELS, THOUGH.
USE THE SHIRT TO WIPE OFF AS MUCH BLOOD AS YOU CAN.

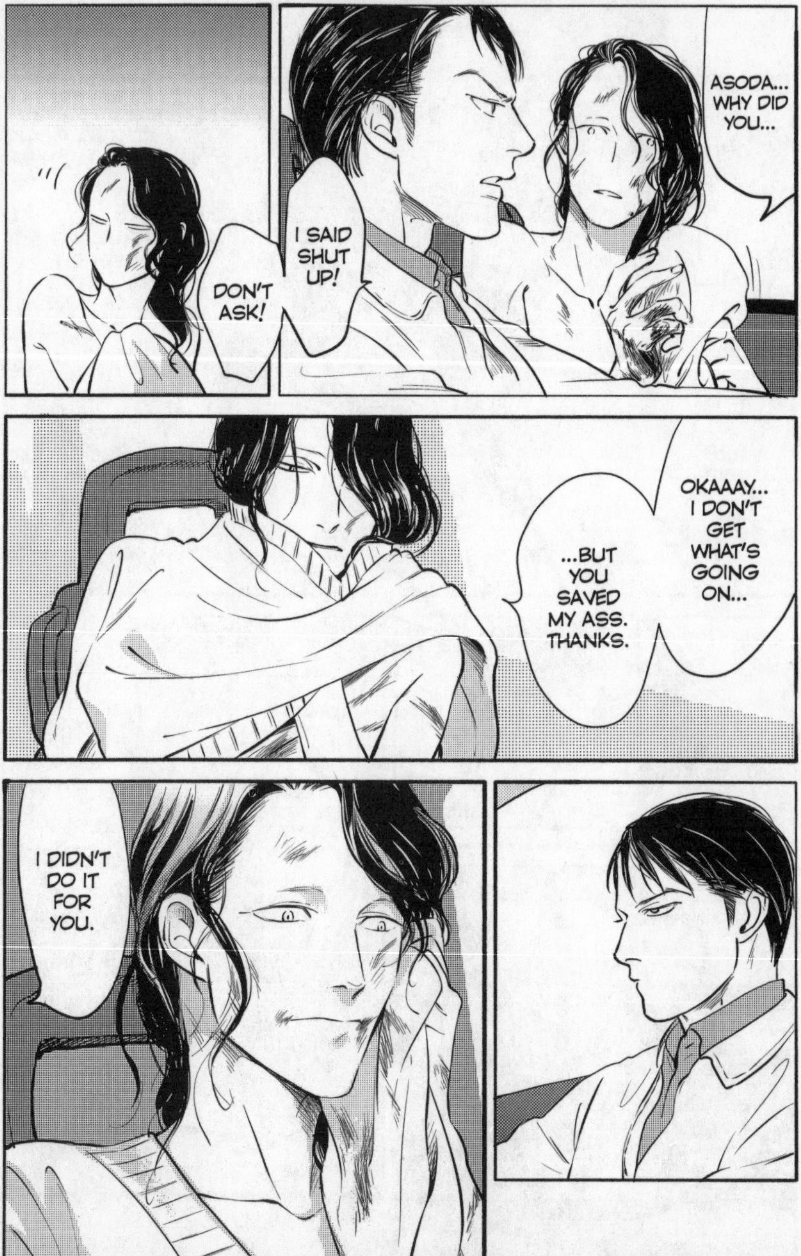
ASODA... WHY DID YOU...
I SAID SHUT UP!
DON'T ASK!
OKAAAY... I DON'T GET WHAT'S GOING ON...
...BUT YOU SAVED MY ASS. THANKS.
I DIDN'T DO IT FOR YOU.

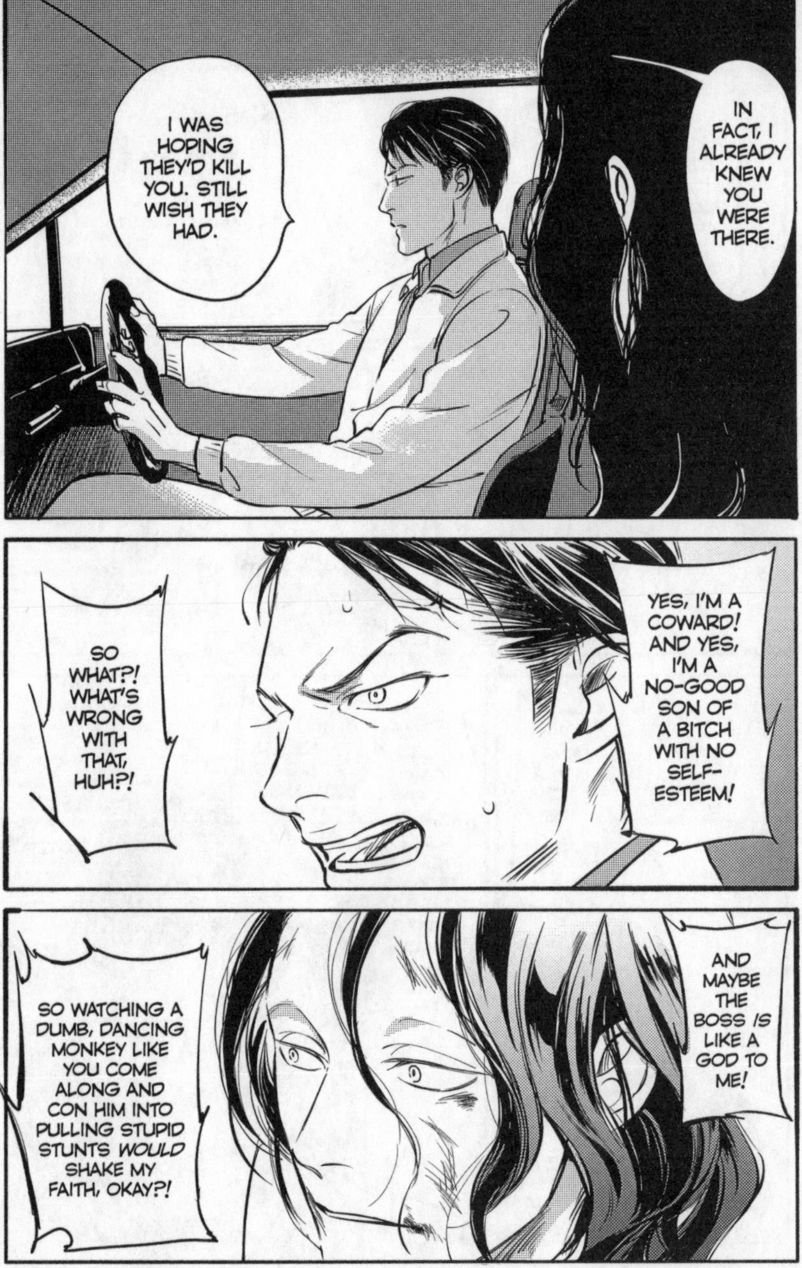
IN FACT, I ALREADY KNEW YOU WERE THERE.
I WAS HOPING THEY'D KILL YOU. STILL WISH THEY HAD.
YES, I'M A COWARD! AND YES, I'M A NO-GOOD SON OF A BITCH WITH NO SELF-ESTEEM!
SO WHAT?! WHAT'S WRONG WITH THAT, HUH?!
AND MAYBE THE BOSS *IS* LIKE A GOD TO ME!
SO WATCHING A DUMB, DANCING MONKEY LIKE YOU COME ALONG AND CON HIM INTO PULLING STUPID STUNTS *WOULD* SHAKE MY FAITH, OKAY?!

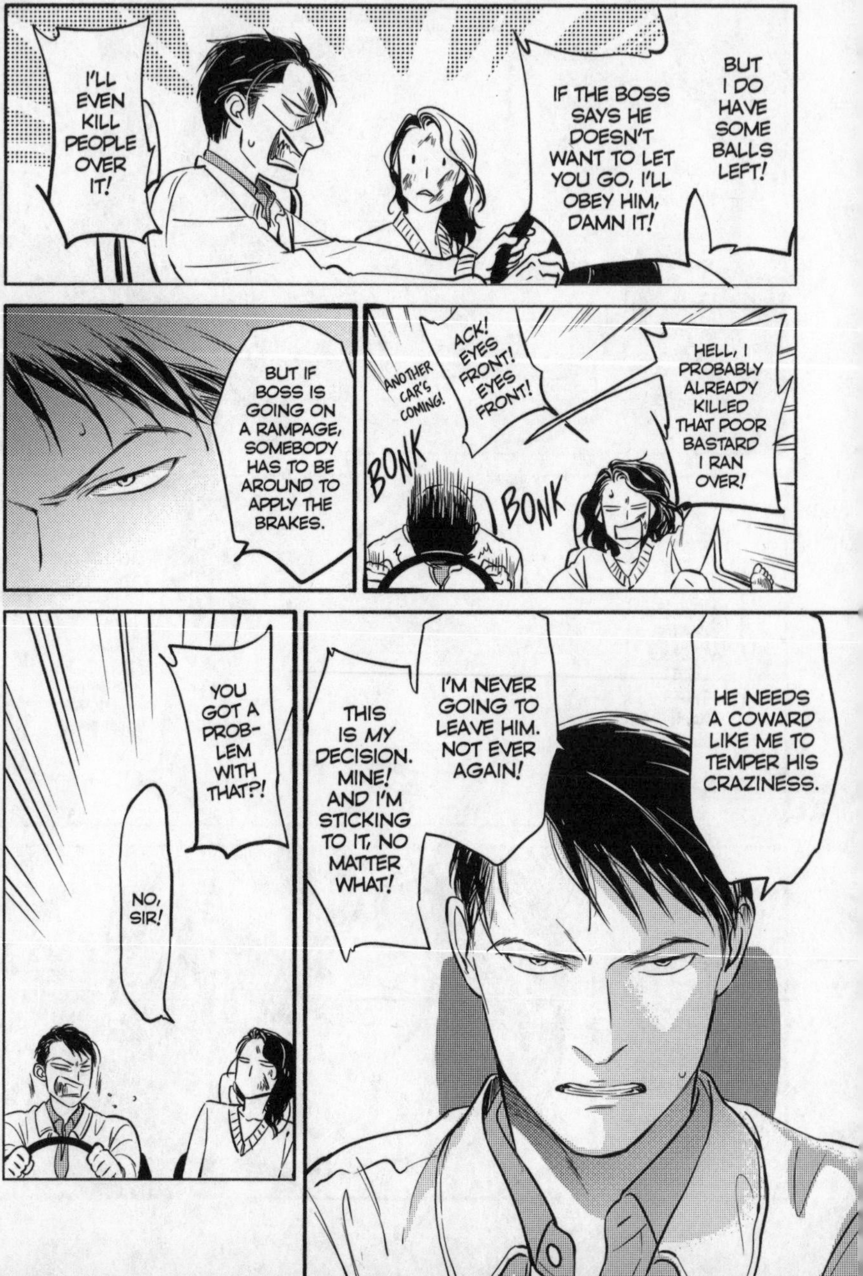
BUT I DO HAVE SOME BALLS LEFT!
IF THE BOSS SAYS HE DOESN'T WANT TO LET YOU GO, I'LL OBEY HIM, DAMN IT!
I'LL EVEN KILL PEOPLE OVER IT!
HELL, I PROBABLY ALREADY KILLED THAT POOR BASTARD I RAN OVER!
ACK! EYES FRONT! EYES FRONT!
ANOTHER CAR'S COMING!
BONK
BONK
BUT IF BOSS IS GOING ON A RAMPAGE, SOMEBODY HAS TO BE AROUND TO APPLY THE BRAKES.
HE NEEDS A COWARD LIKE ME TO TEMPER HIS CRAZINESS.
I'M NEVER GOING TO LEAVE HIM. NOT EVER AGAIN!
THIS IS MY DECISION. MINE! AND I'M STICKING TO IT, NO MATTER WHAT!
YOU GOT A PROB-LEM WITH THAT?!
NO, SIR!

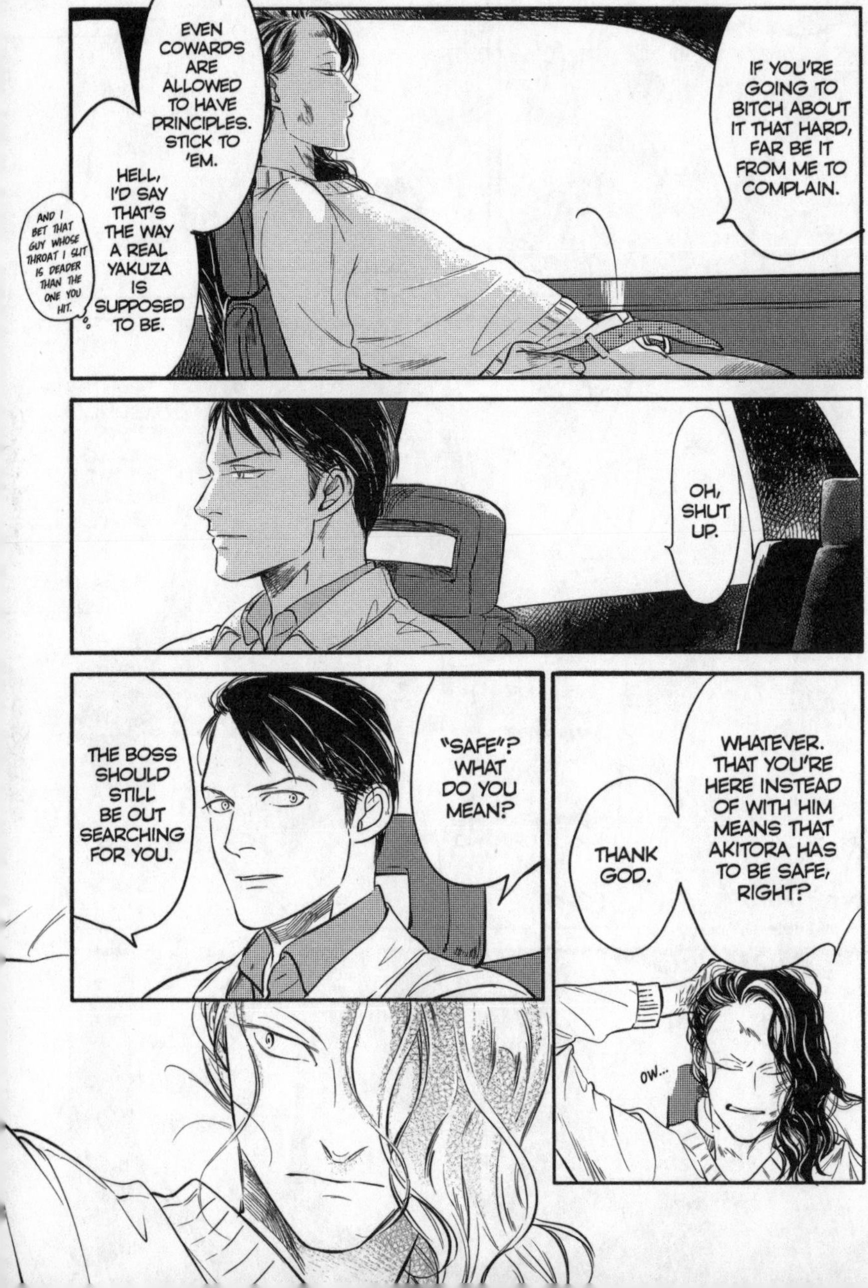
IF YOU'RE GOING TO BITCH ABOUT IT THAT HARD, FAR BE IT FROM ME TO COMPLAIN.
EVEN COWARDS ARE ALLOWED TO HAVE PRINCIPLES. STICK TO 'EM.
HELL, I'D SAY THAT'S THE WAY A REAL YAKUZA IS SUPPOSED TO BE.
AND I BET THAT GUY WHOSE THROAT I SLIT IS DEADER THAN THE ONE YOU HIT.
OH, SHUT UP.
WHATEVER. THAT YOU'RE HERE INSTEAD OF WITH HIM MEANS THAT AKITORA HAS TO BE SAFE, RIGHT?
THANK GOD.
OW...
"SAFE"? WHAT DO YOU MEAN?
THE BOSS SHOULD STILL BE OUT SEARCHING FOR YOU.

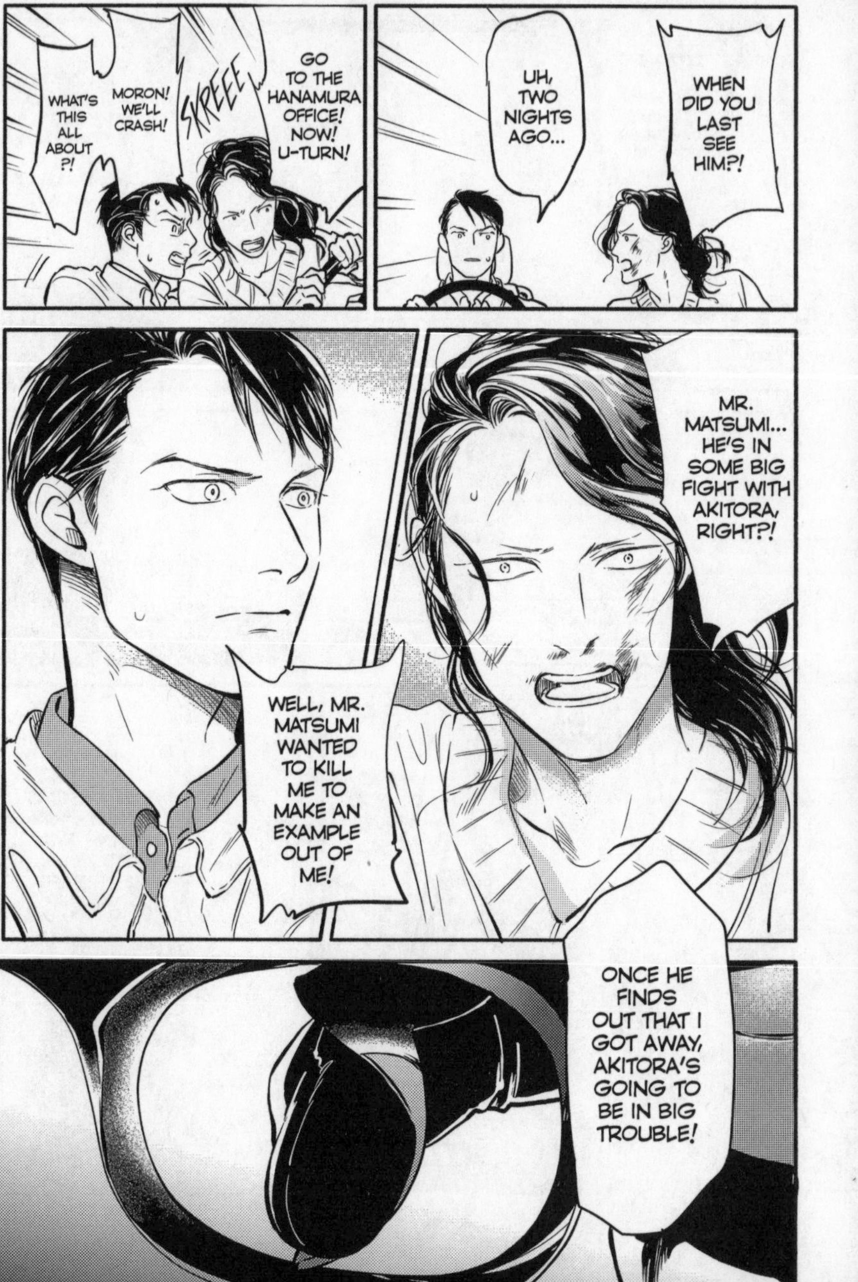
WHEN DID YOU LAST SEE HIM?!
UH, TWO NIGHTS AGO...
GO TO THE HANAMURA OFFICE! NOW! U-TURN!
SKREEE
MORON! WE'LL CRASH!
WHAT'S THIS ALL ABOUT ?!
MR. MATSUMI... HE'S IN SOME BIG FIGHT WITH AKITORA, RIGHT?!
WELL, MR. MATSUMI WANTED TO KILL ME TO MAKE AN EXAMPLE OUT OF ME!
ONCE HE FINDS OUT THAT I GOT AWAY, AKITORA'S GOING TO BE IN BIG TROUBLE!

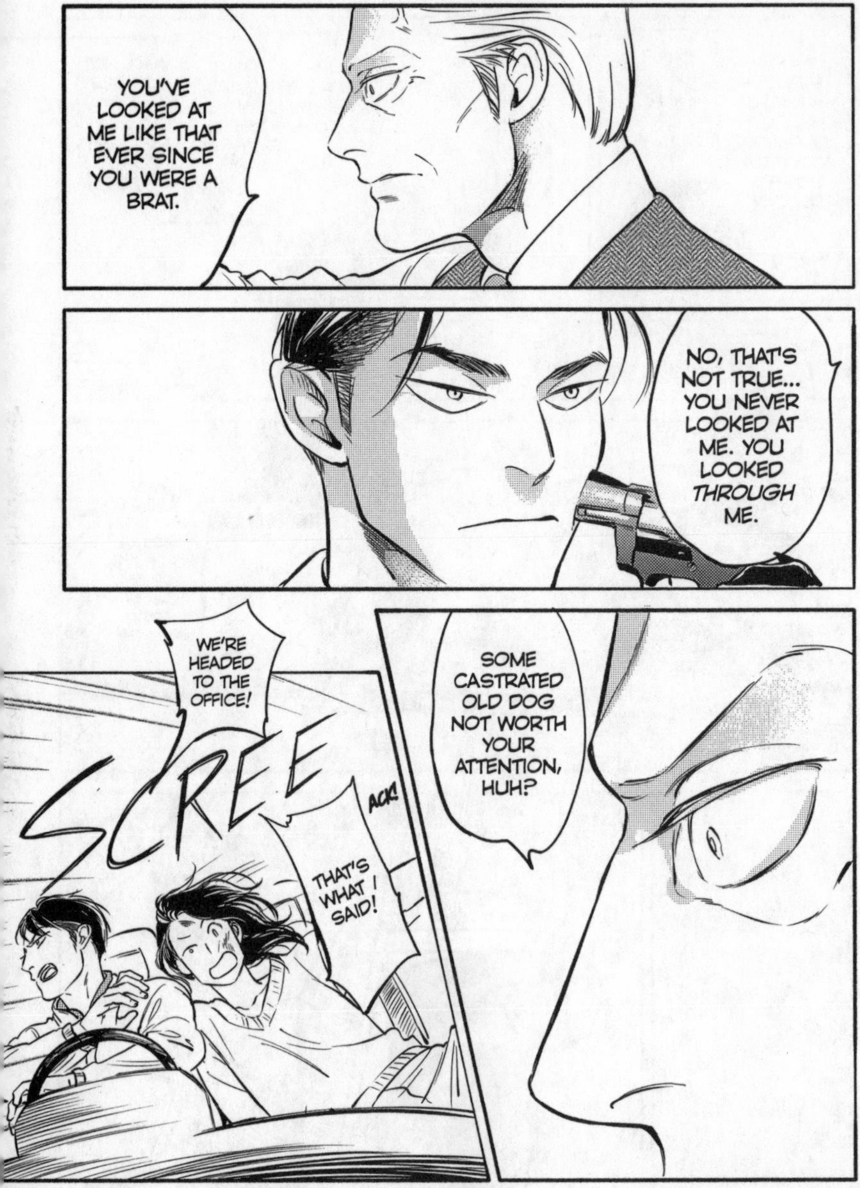
YOU'VE LOOKED AT ME LIKE THAT EVER SINCE YOU WERE A BRAT.
NO, THAT'S NOT TRUE... YOU NEVER LOOKED AT ME. YOU LOOKED *THROUGH* ME.
SOME CASTRATED OLD DOG NOT WORTH YOUR ATTENTION, HUH?
WE'RE HEADED TO THE OFFICE!
SCREE
ACK!
THAT'S WHAT I SAID!

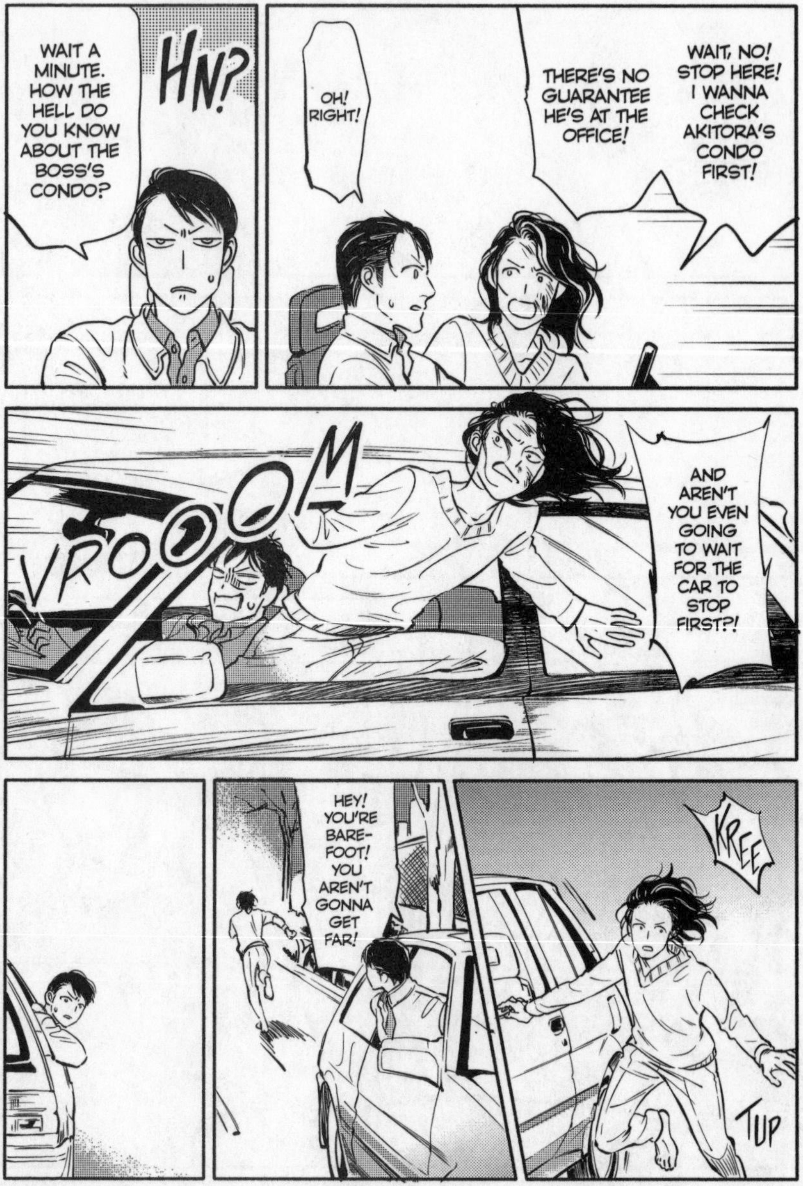
WAIT, NO! STOP HERE! I WANNA CHECK AKITORA'S CONDO FIRST!
THERE'S NO GUARANTEE HE'S AT THE OFFICE!
OH! RIGHT!
HN?
WAIT A MINUTE. HOW THE HELL DO YOU KNOW ABOUT THE BOSS'S CONDO?
AND AREN'T YOU EVEN GOING TO WAIT FOR THE CAR TO STOP FIRST?!
VROOOOM
KREE
TUP
HEY! YOU'RE BARE-FOOT! YOU AREN'T GONNA GET FAR!

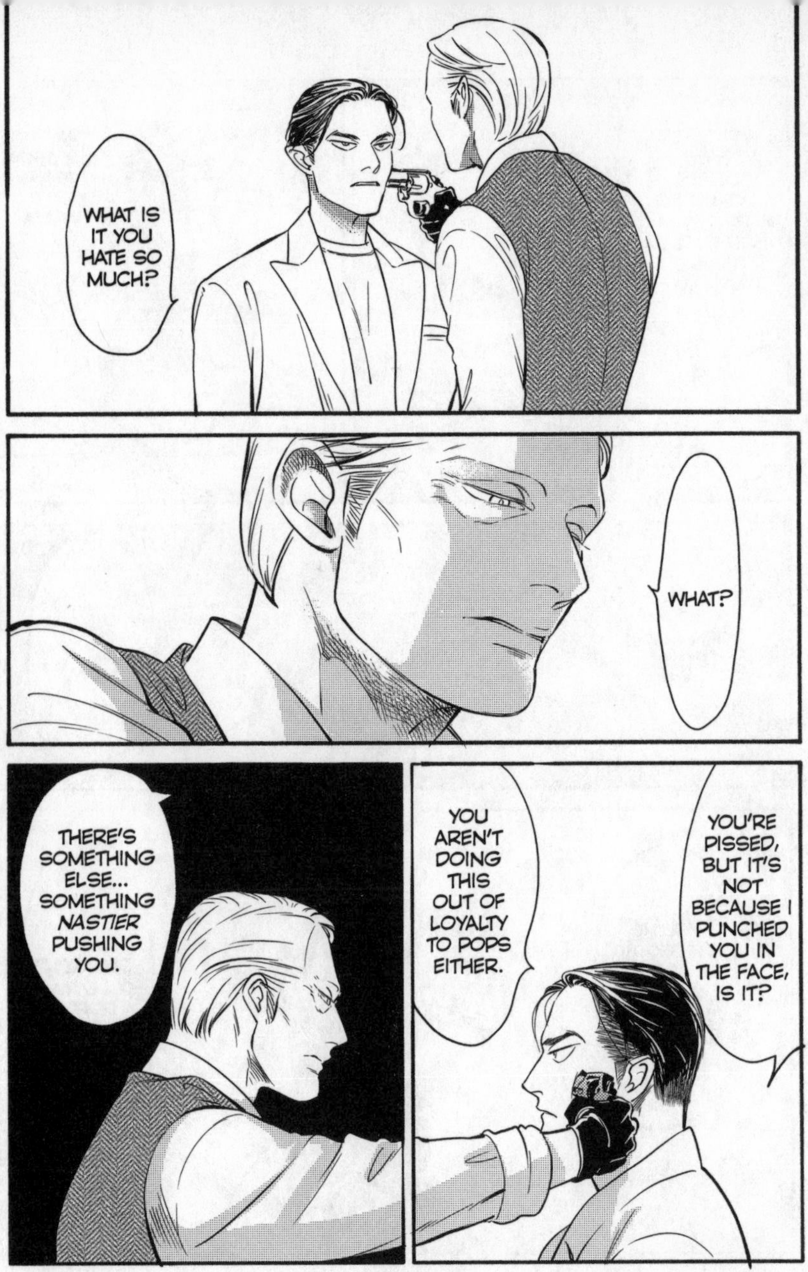
WHAT IS IT YOU HATE SO MUCH?
WHAT?
YOU'RE PISSED, BUT IT'S NOT BECAUSE I PUNCHED YOU IN THE FACE, IS IT?
YOU AREN'T DOING THIS OUT OF LOYALTY TO POPS EITHER.
THERE'S SOMETHING ELSE... SOMETHING *NASTIER* PUSHING YOU.

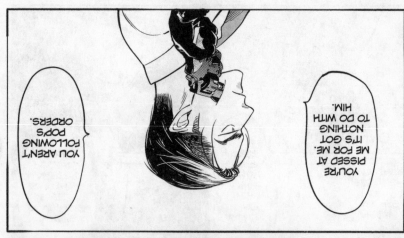

THAT'S A QUESTION I'VE HAD SINCE I WAS A KID.
I WONDERED WHY YOU ALWAYS LOOKED SO HAPPY WHEN YOU STOLE THINGS FROM ME.
BUT I GET IT NOW.
YOU FINALLY LET ME SEE.
YOU AREN'T FOLLOWING POP'S ORDERS.
YOU'RE PISSED AT ME FOR ME. IT'S GOT NOTHING TO DO WITH HIM.

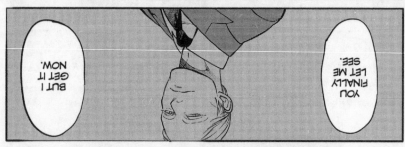

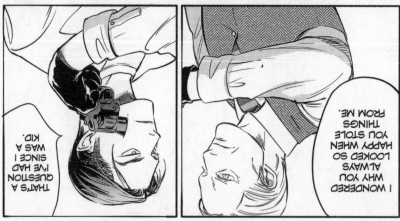

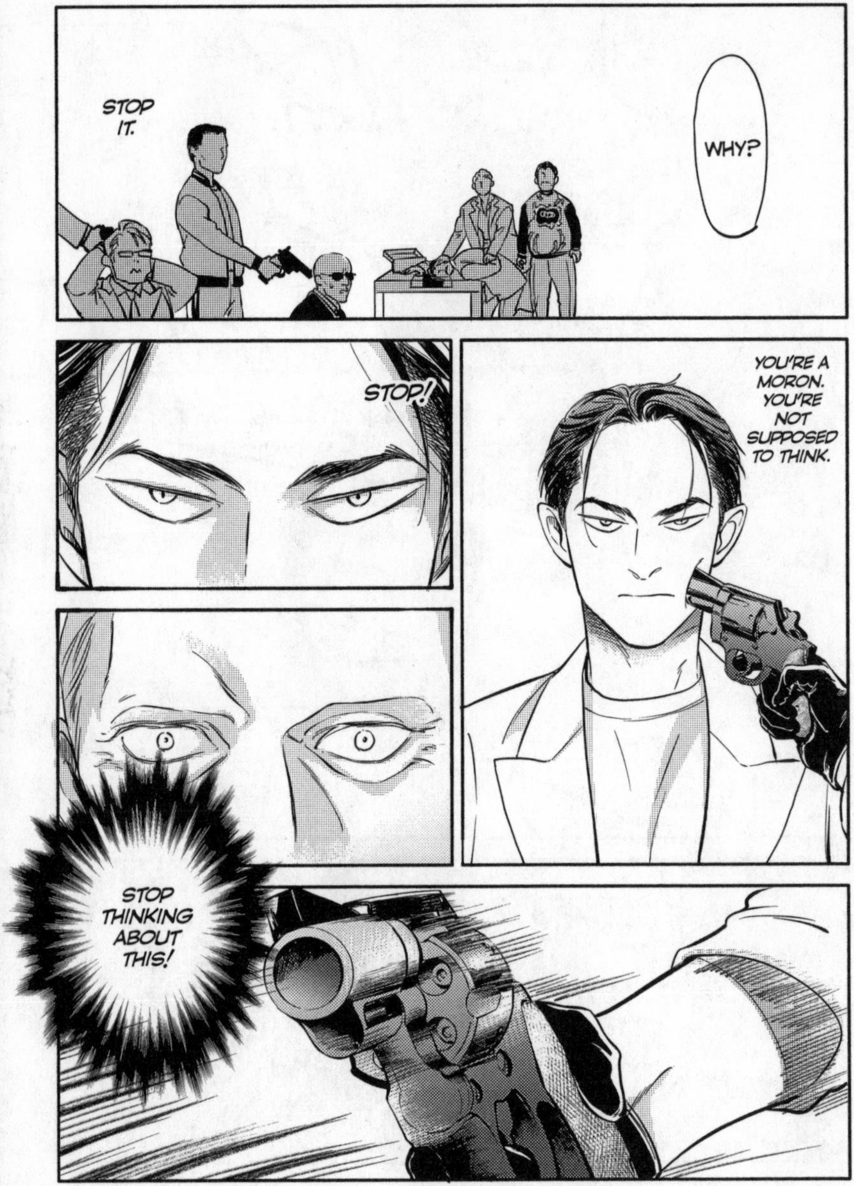
WHY?
STOP IT.
YOU'RE A MORON. YOU'RE NOT SUPPOSED TO THINK.
STOP!
STOP THINKING ABOUT THIS!

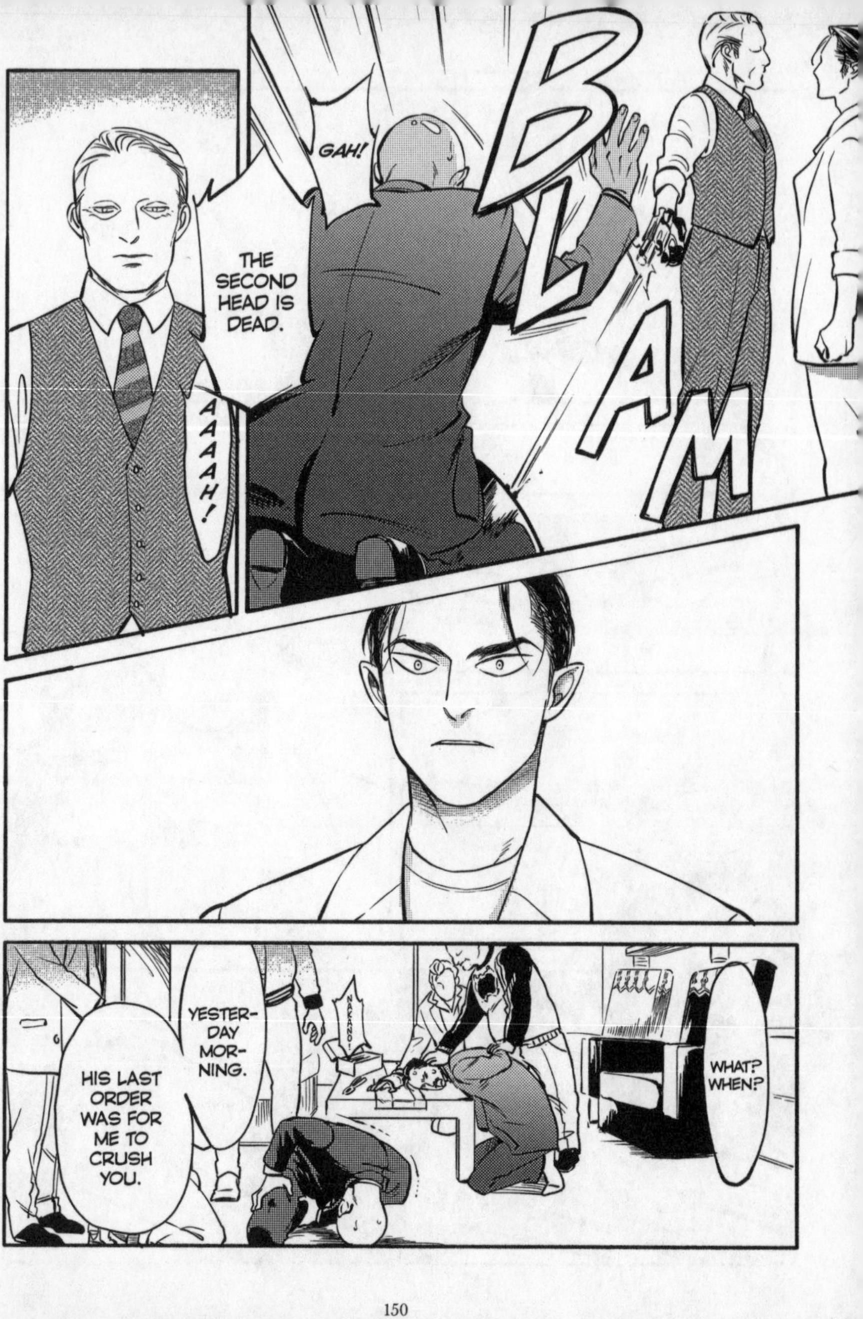
BLAM
GAH!
THE SECOND HEAD IS DEAD.
AAAAAH!
WHAT? WHEN?
NAKANO!
YESTER-DAY MOR-NING.
HIS LAST ORDER WAS FOR ME TO CRUSH YOU.

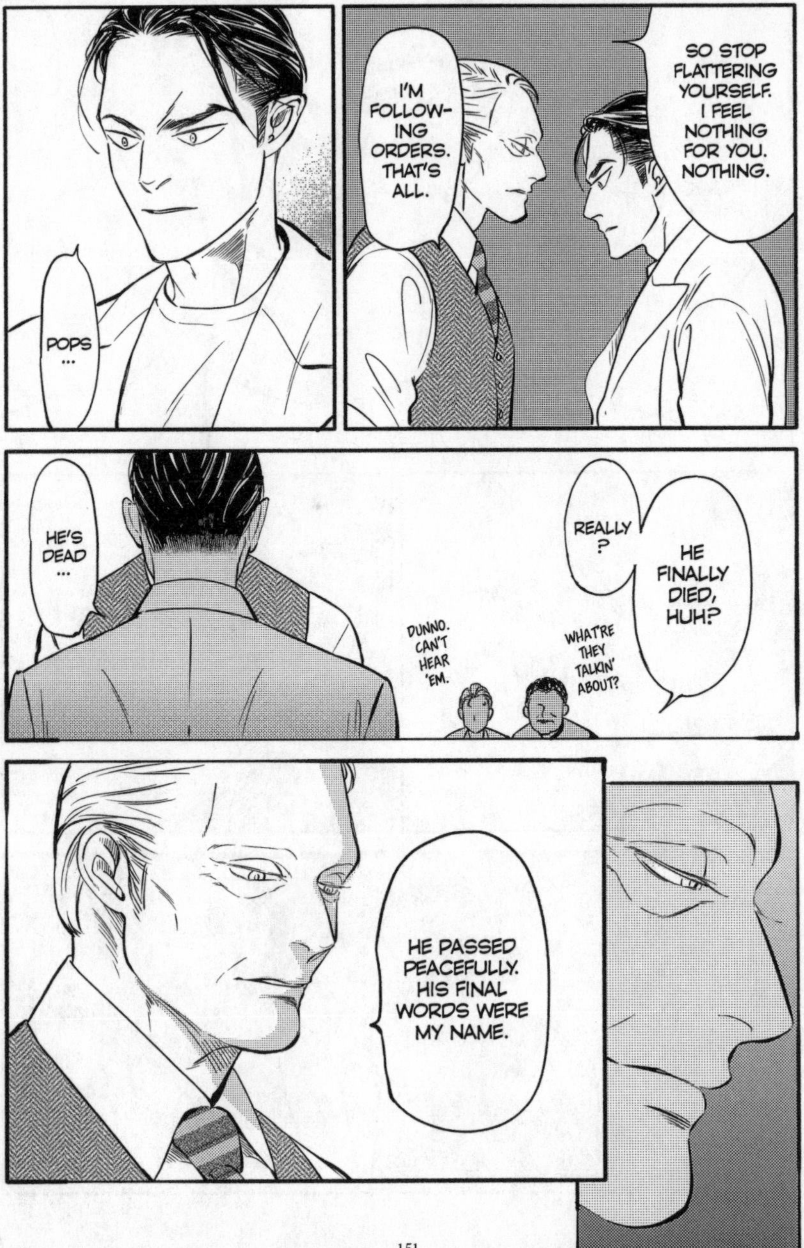
SO STOP FLATTERING YOURSELF. I FEEL NOTHING FOR YOU. NOTHING.
I'M FOLLOWING ORDERS. THAT'S ALL.
POPS...
REALLY?
HE FINALLY DIED, HUH?
WHAT'RE THEY TALKIN' ABOUT?
DUNNO. CAN'T HEAR 'EM.
HE'S DEAD...
HE PASSED PEACEFULLY. HIS FINAL WORDS WERE MY NAME.

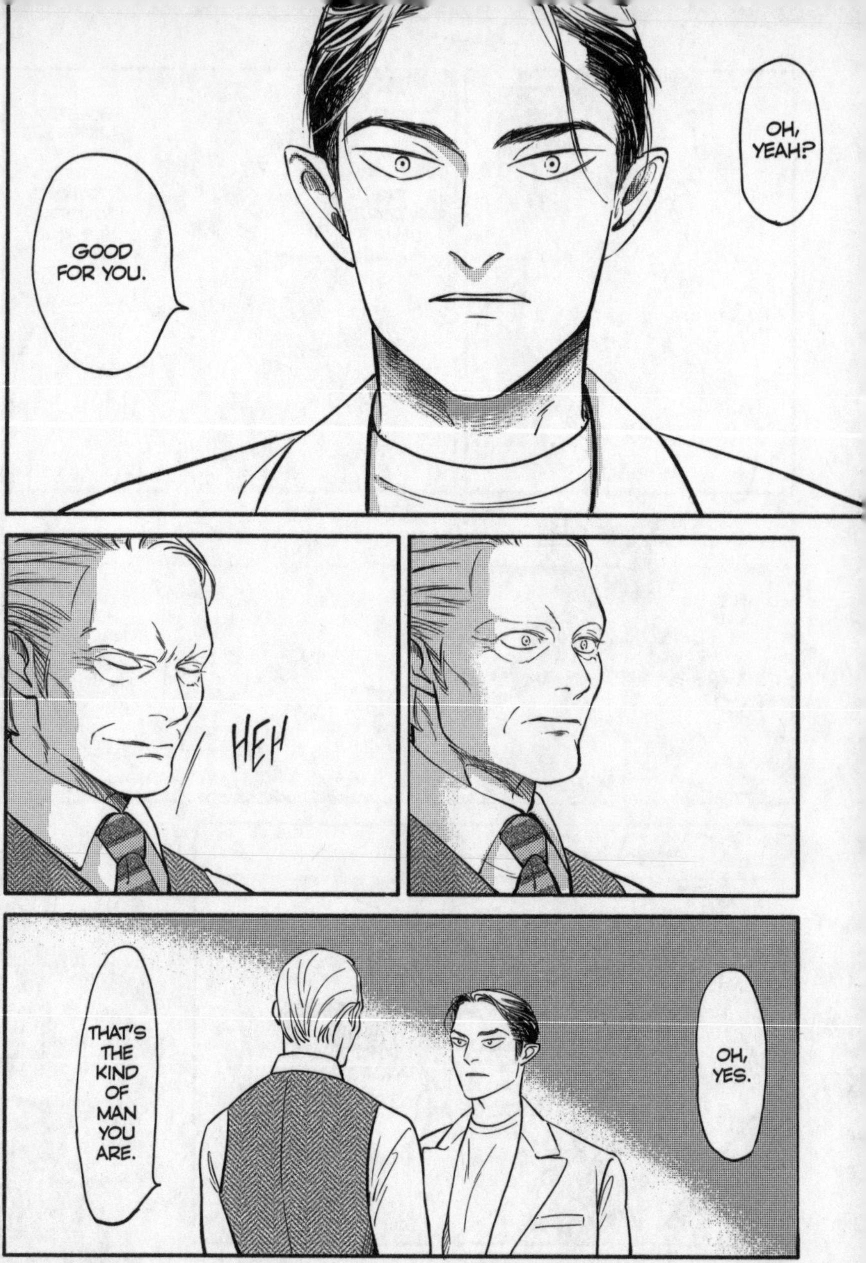
OH, YEAH?
GOOD FOR YOU.
HEH
OH, YES.
THAT'S THE KIND OF MAN YOU ARE.

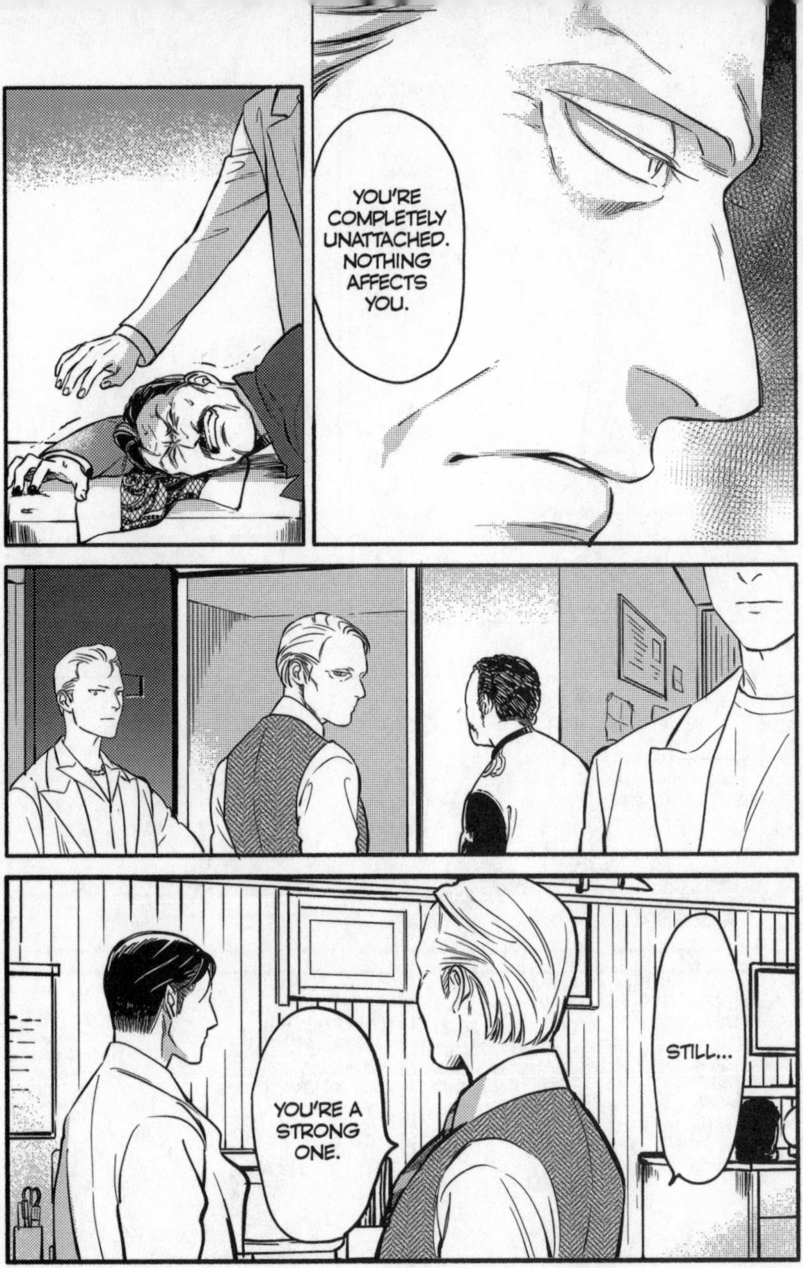
YOU'RE COMPLETELY UNATTACHED. NOTHING AFFECTS YOU.
STILL...
YOU'RE A STRONG ONE.

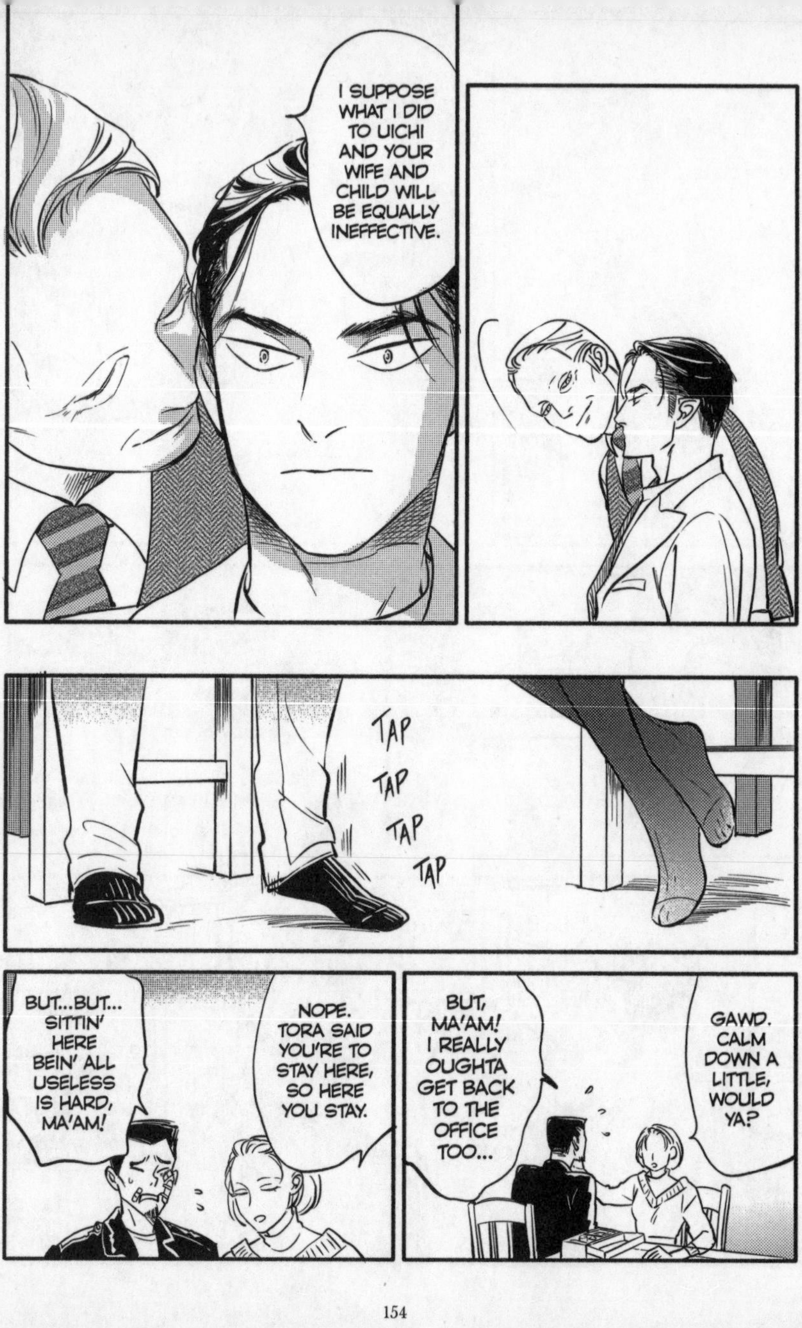
I SUPPOSE WHAT I DID TO UICHI AND YOUR WIFE AND CHILD WILL BE EQUALLY INEFFECTIVE.
TAP TAP TAP TAP
BUT...BUT... SITTIN' HERE BEIN' ALL USELESS IS HARD, MA'AM!
NOPE. TORA SAID YOU'RE TO STAY HERE, SO HERE YOU STAY.
BUT, MA'AM! I REALLY OUGHTA GET BACK TO THE OFFICE TOO...
GAWD. CALM DOWN A LITTLE, WOULD YA?

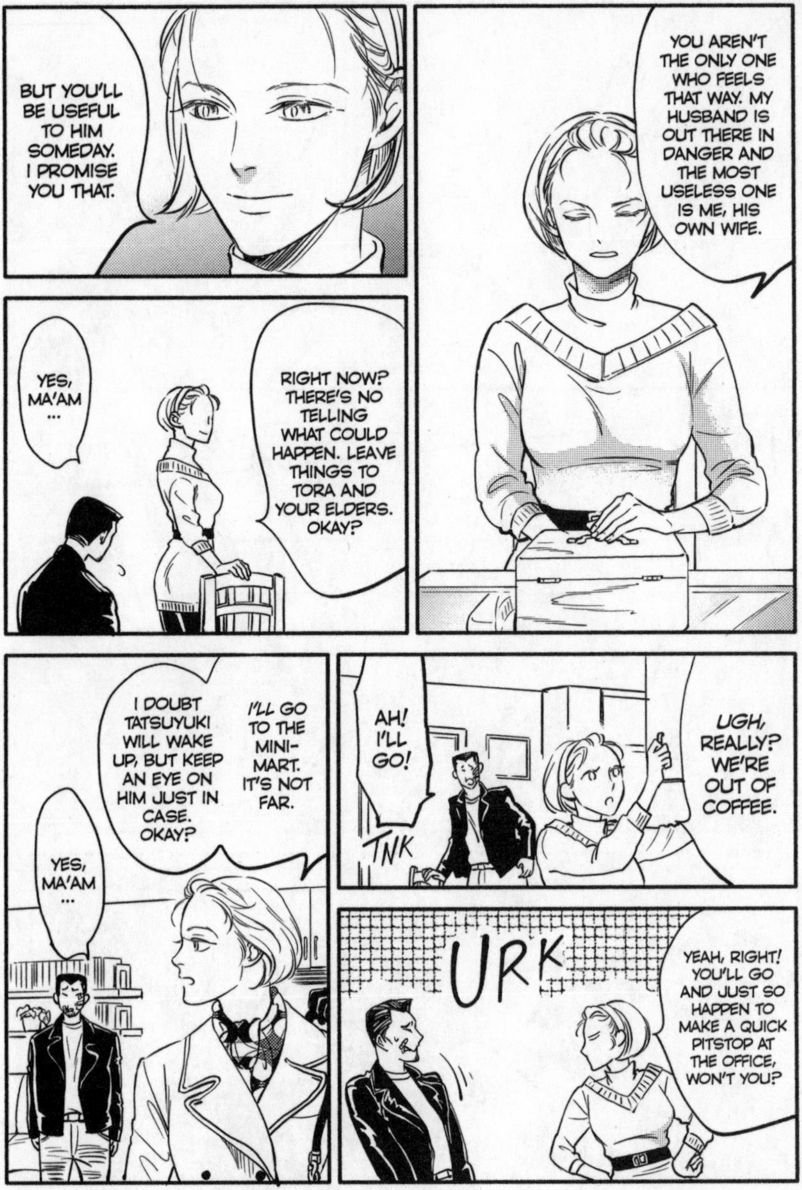
YOU AREN'T THE ONLY ONE WHO FEELS THAT WAY. MY HUSBAND IS OUT THERE IN DANGER AND THE MOST USELESS ONE IS ME, HIS OWN WIFE.
BUT YOU'LL BE USEFUL TO HIM SOMEDAY. I PROMISE YOU THAT.
RIGHT NOW? THERE'S NO TELLING WHAT COULD HAPPEN. LEAVE THINGS TO TORA AND YOUR ELDERS. OKAY?
YES, MA'AM ...
UGH, REALLY? WE'RE OUT OF COFFEE.
AH! I'LL GO!
TNK
YEAH, RIGHT! YOU'LL GO AND JUST SO HAPPEN TO MAKE A QUICK PITSTOP AT THE OFFICE, WON'T YOU?
URK
I'LL GO TO THE MINI-MART. IT'S NOT FAR.
I DOUBT TATSUYUKI WILL WAKE UP, BUT KEEP AN EYE ON HIM JUST IN CASE. OKAY?
YES, MA'AM ...

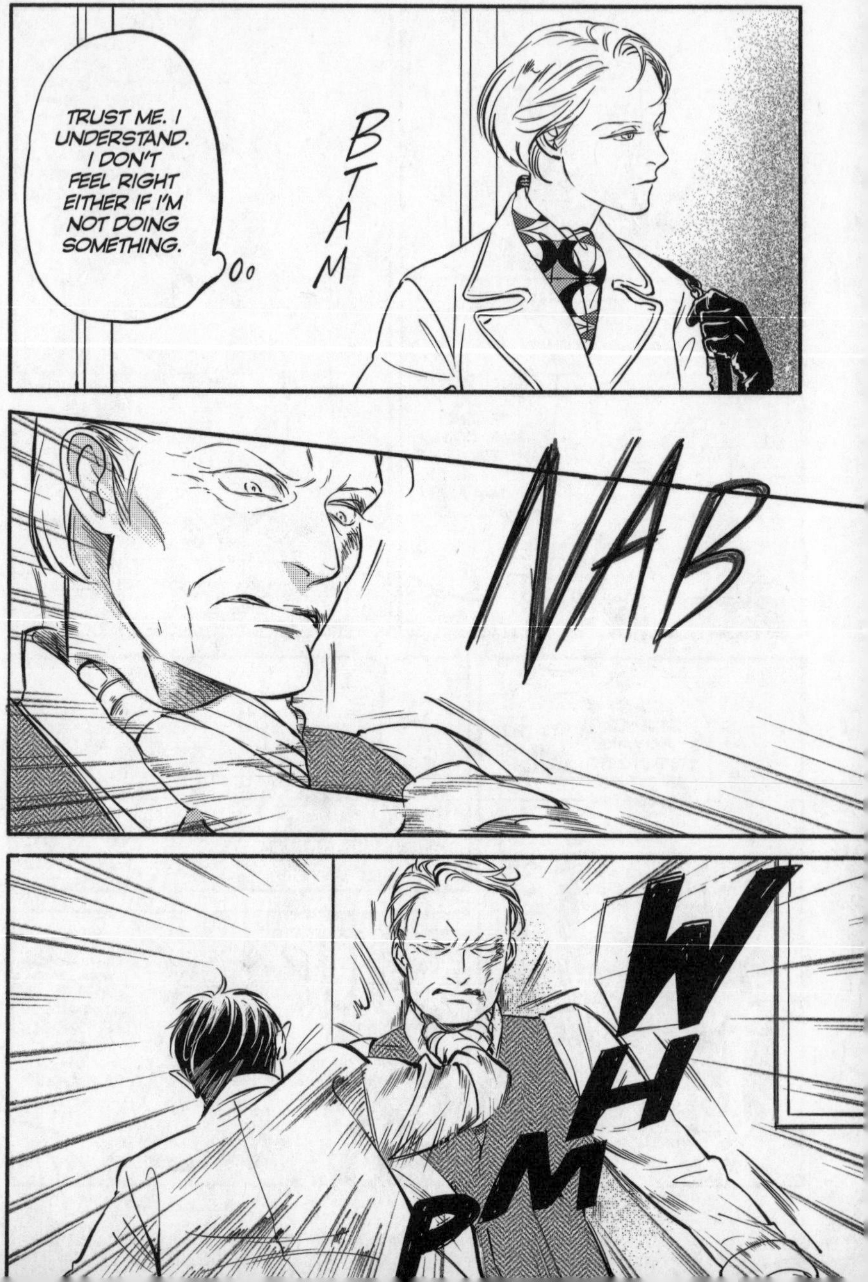
TRUST ME. I UNDERSTAND. I DON'T FEEL RIGHT EITHER IF I'M NOT DOING SOMETHING.
BTAM
NAB
WHMP

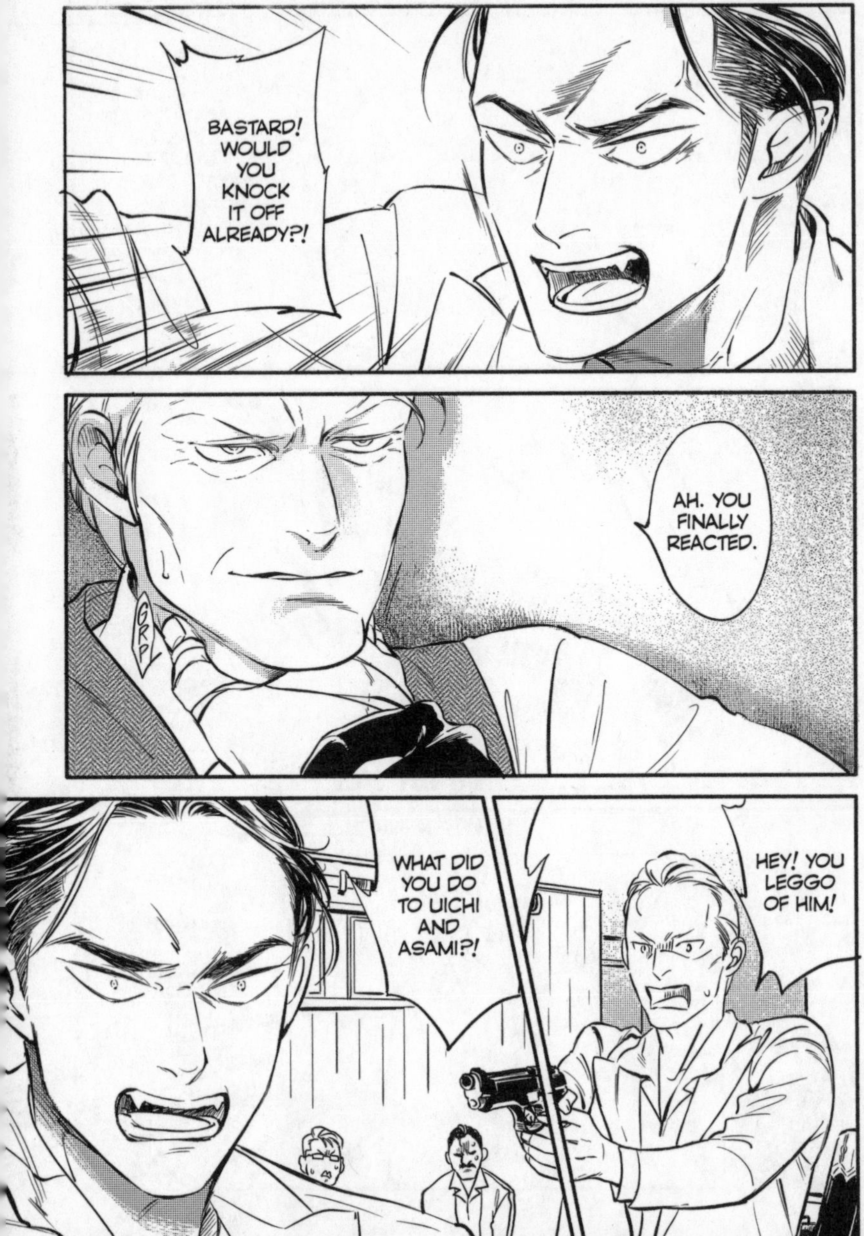
BASTARD! WOULD YOU KNOCK IT OFF ALREADY?!
AH. YOU FINALLY REACTED.
GRP
HEY! YOU LEGGO OF HIM!
WHAT DID YOU DO TO UICHI AND ASAMI?!

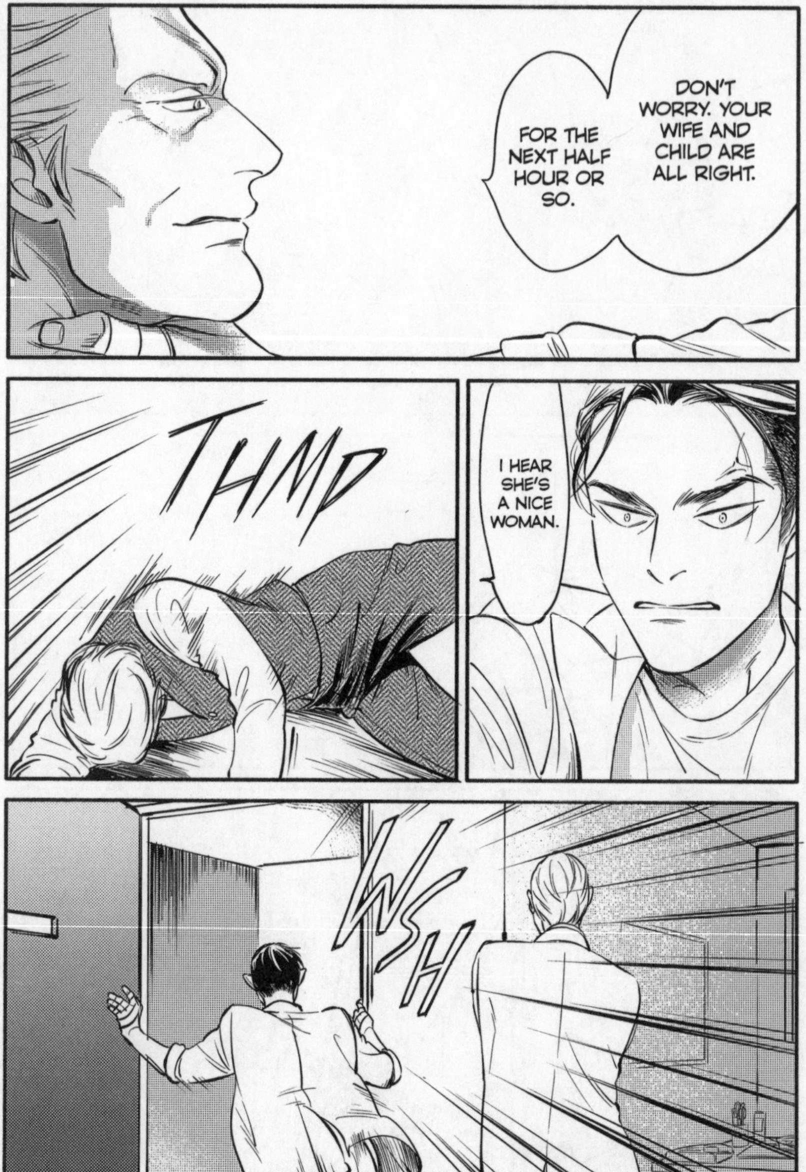
DON'T WORRY. YOUR WIFE AND CHILD ARE ALL RIGHT.
FOR THE NEXT HALF HOUR OR SO.
I HEAR SHE'S A NICE WOMAN.
THMP
WSH

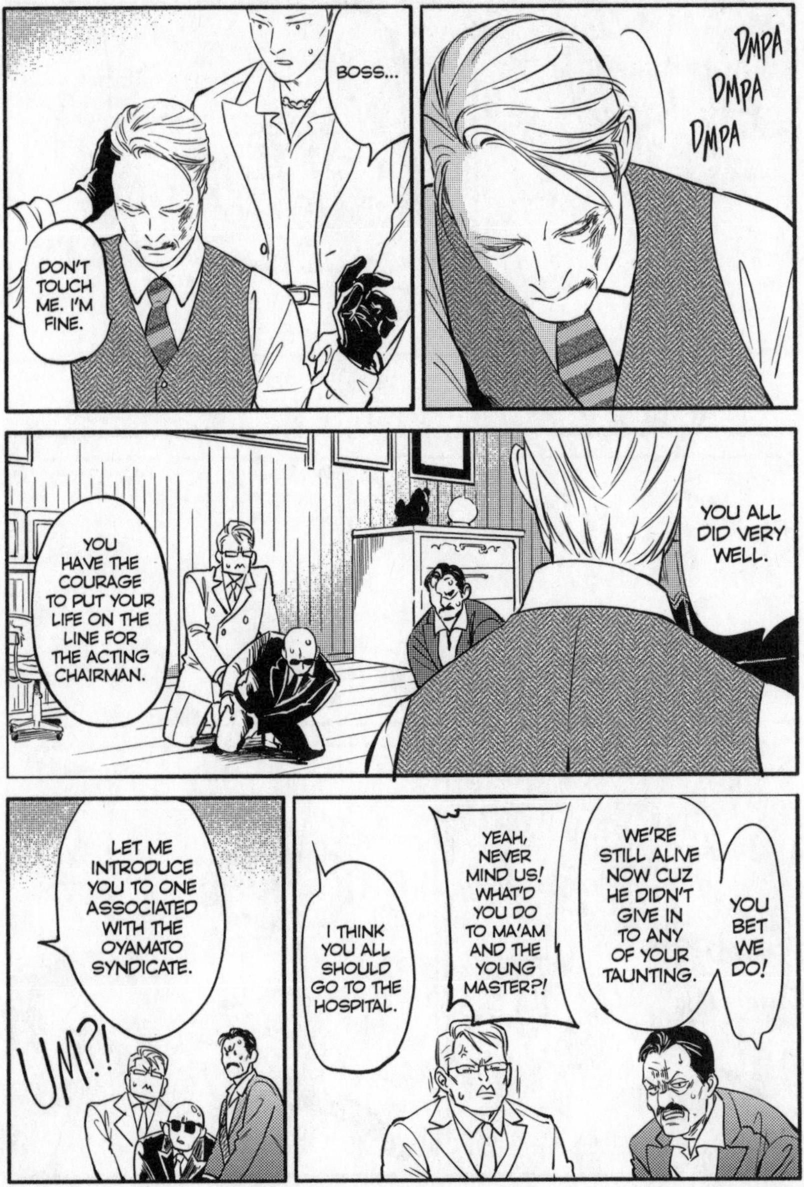
DMPA
DMPA
DMPA
BOSS...
DON'T TOUCH ME. I'M FINE.
YOU ALL DID VERY WELL.
YOU HAVE THE COURAGE TO PUT YOUR LIFE ON THE LINE FOR THE ACTING CHAIRMAN.
YOU BET WE DO!
WE'RE STILL ALIVE NOW CUZ HE DIDN'T GIVE IN TO ANY OF YOUR TAUNTING.
YEAH, NEVER MIND US! WHAT'D YOU DO TO MA'AM AND THE YOUNG MASTER?!
I THINK YOU ALL SHOULD GO TO THE HOSPITAL.
LET ME INTRODUCE YOU TO ONE ASSOCIATED WITH THE OYAMATO SYNDICATE.
UM?!

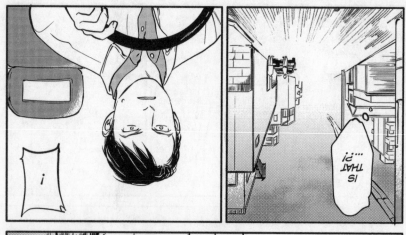

IS THAT...?!

!

VROOM

GRIN

MY APOLO-GIES FOR ALL THIS.

SHUDDER

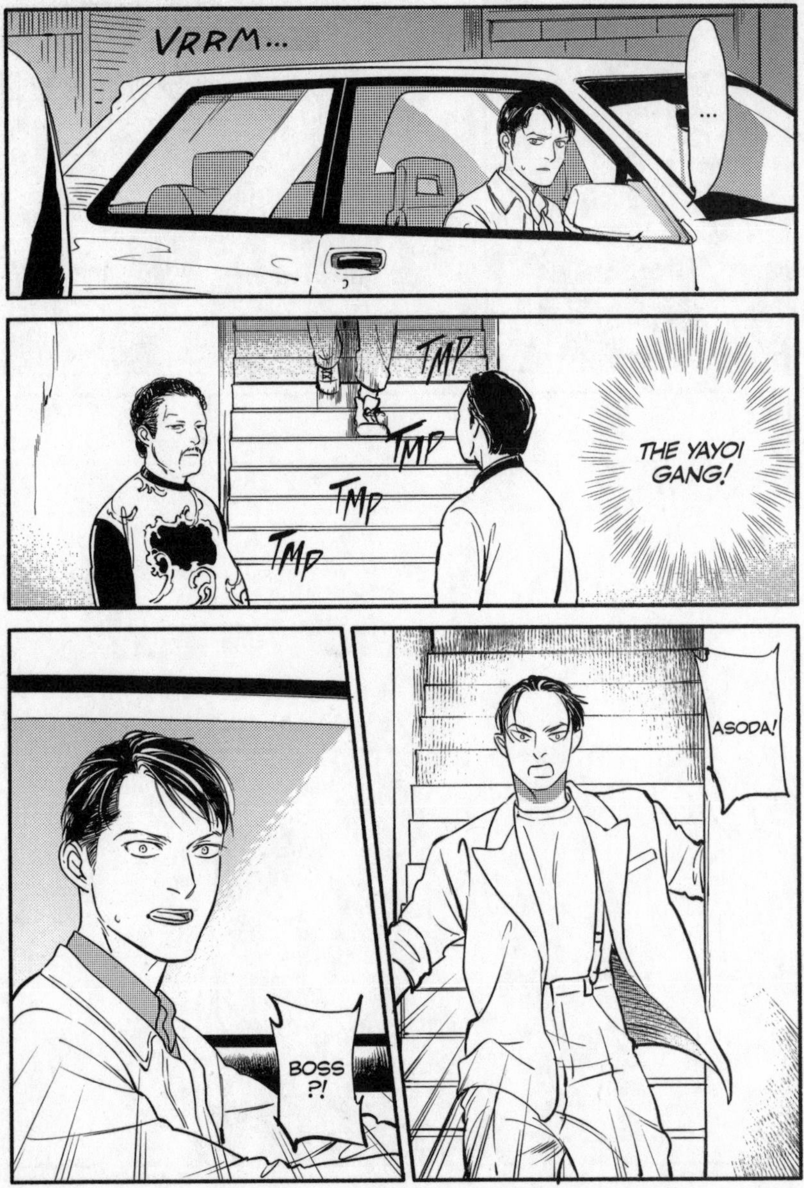
...
VRRM...
THE YAYOI GANG!
TMP
TMP
TMP
TMP
ASODA!
BOSS ?!

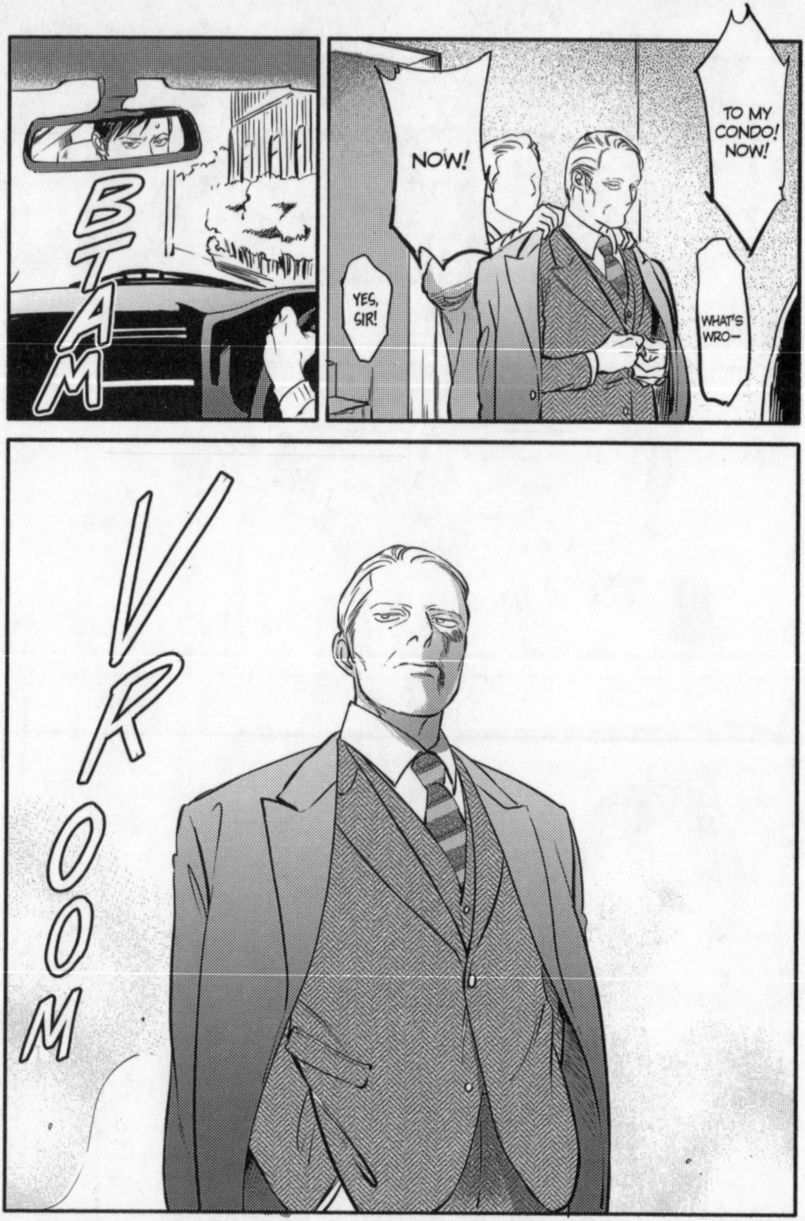
TO MY CONDO! NOW!
WHAT'S WRO—
NOW!
YES, SIR!
BTAM
VROOOM

jealousy

Chapter 20

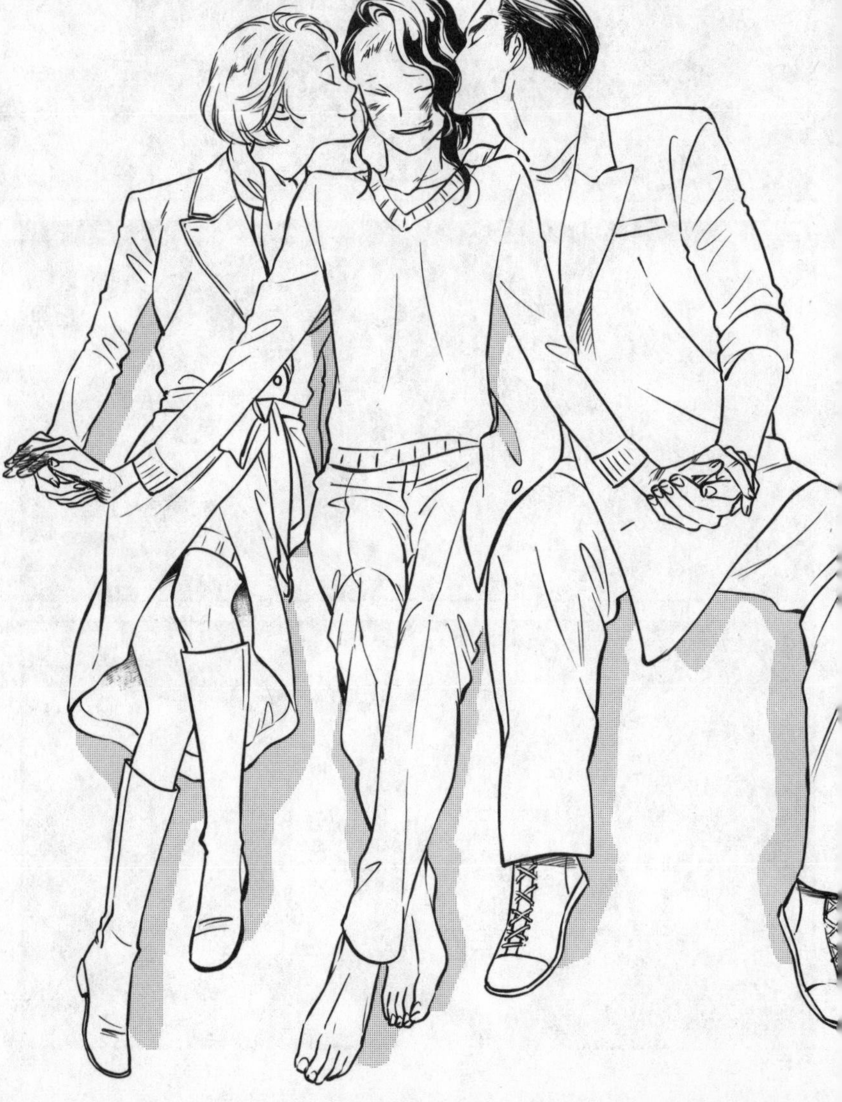

ER... WAS THAT REALLY FOR THE BEST, BOSS?

VRRM

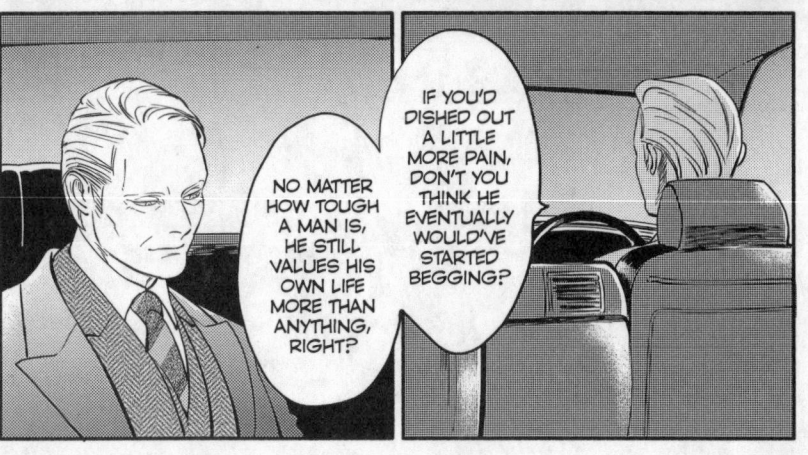

HN?

LETTING AKITORA OFF THAT EASILY, SIR.

IF YOU'D DISHED OUT A LITTLE MORE PAIN, DON'T YOU THINK HE EVENTUALLY WOULD'VE STARTED BEGGING?

NO MATTER HOW TOUGH A MAN IS, HE STILL VALUES HIS OWN LIFE MORE THAN ANYTHING, RIGHT?

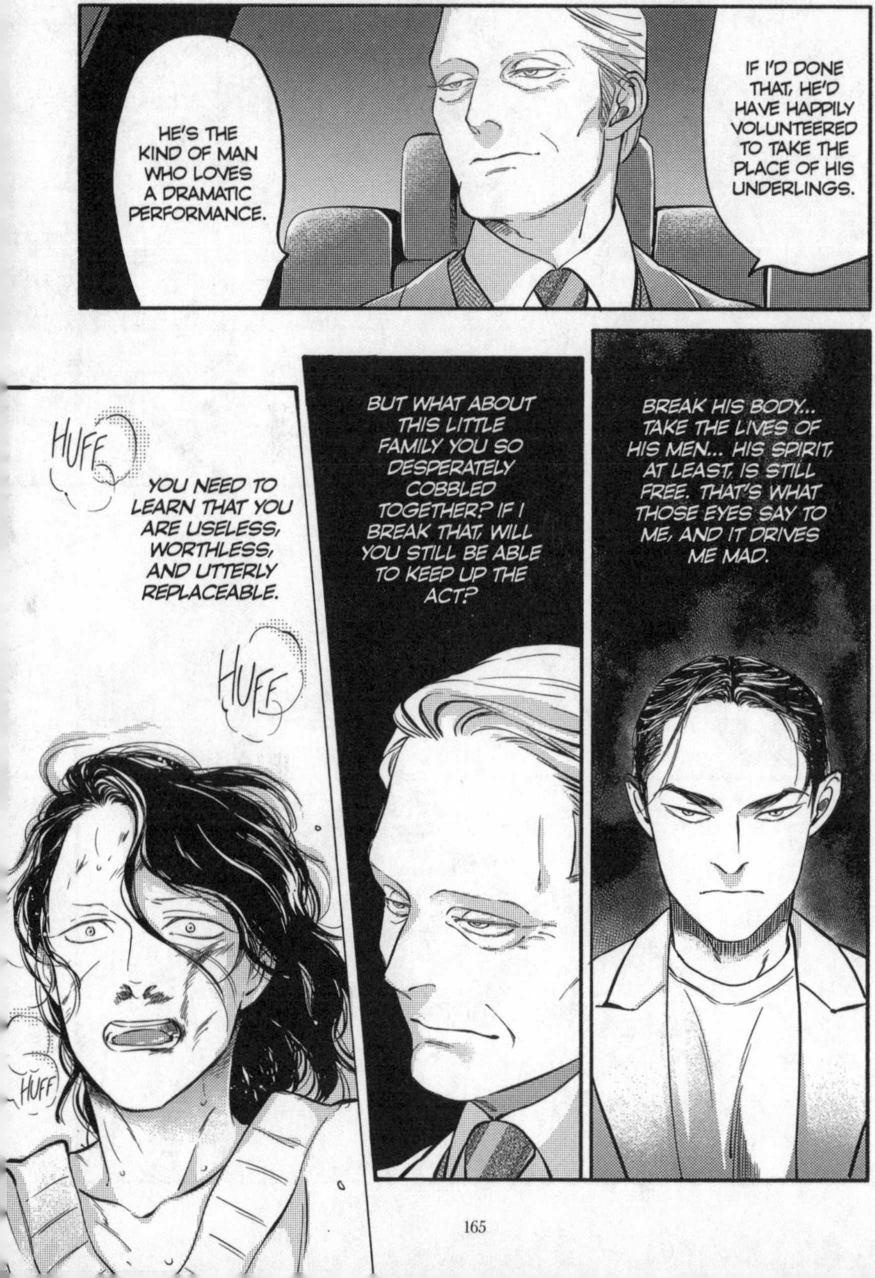
IF I'D DONE THAT, HE'D HAVE HAPPILY VOLUNTEERED TO TAKE THE PLACE OF HIS UNDERLINGS.
HE'S THE KIND OF MAN WHO LOVES A DRAMATIC PERFORMANCE.
BREAK HIS BODY... TAKE THE LIVES OF HIS MEN... HIS SPIRIT, AT LEAST, IS STILL FREE. THAT'S WHAT THOSE EYES SAY TO ME, AND IT DRIVES ME MAD.
BUT WHAT ABOUT THIS LITTLE FAMILY YOU SO DESPERATELY COBBLED TOGETHER? IF I BREAK THAT, WILL YOU STILL BE ABLE TO KEEP UP THE ACT?
HUFF
YOU NEED TO LEARN THAT YOU ARE USELESS, WORTHLESS, AND UTTERLY REPLACEABLE.
HUFF
HUFF

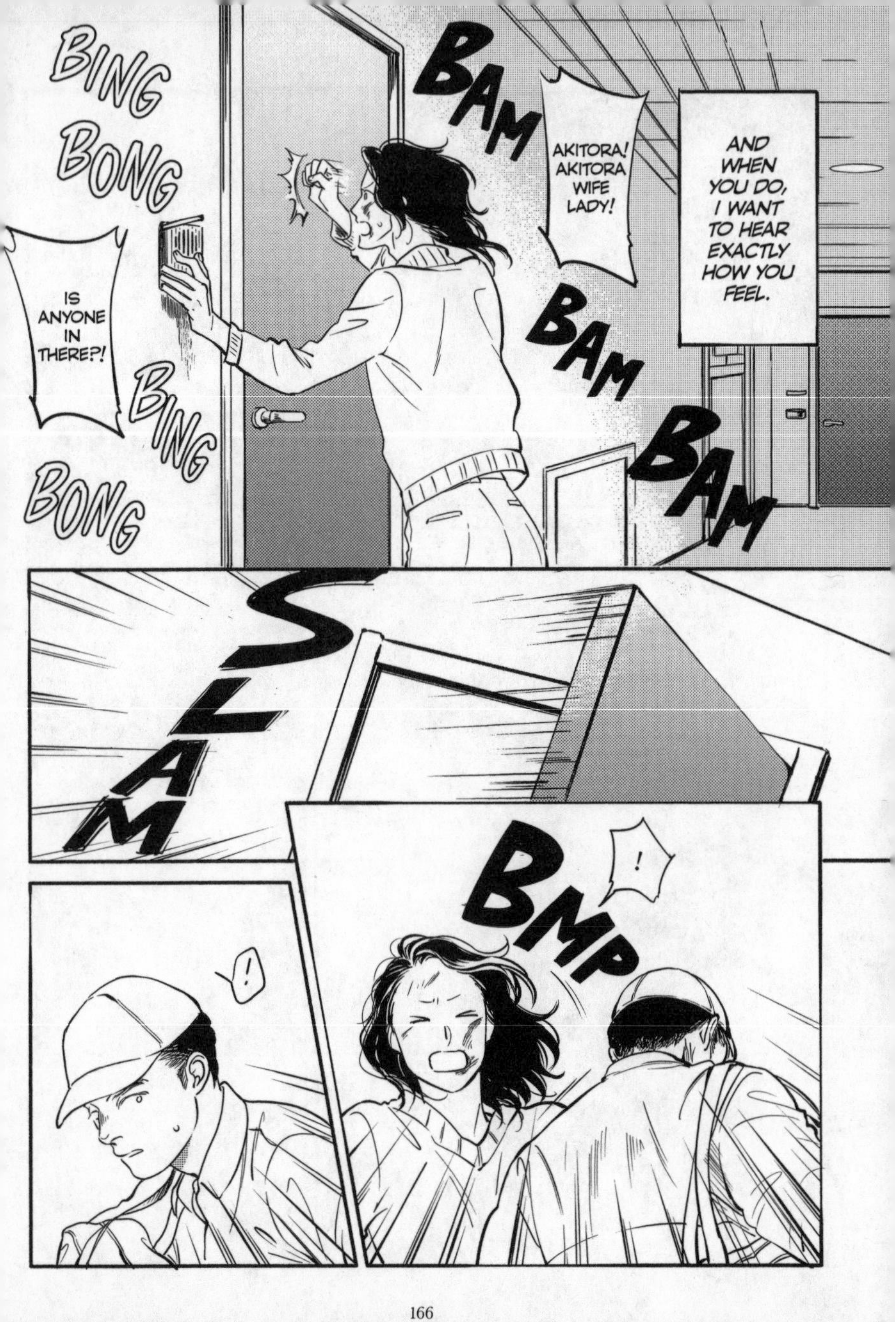
AND WHEN YOU DO, I WANT TO HEAR EXACTLY HOW YOU FEEL.
BAM
AKITORA! AKITORA WIFE LADY!
BING BONG
IS ANYONE IN THERE?!
BAM
BAM
BING BONG
SLAM
!
BMP
!

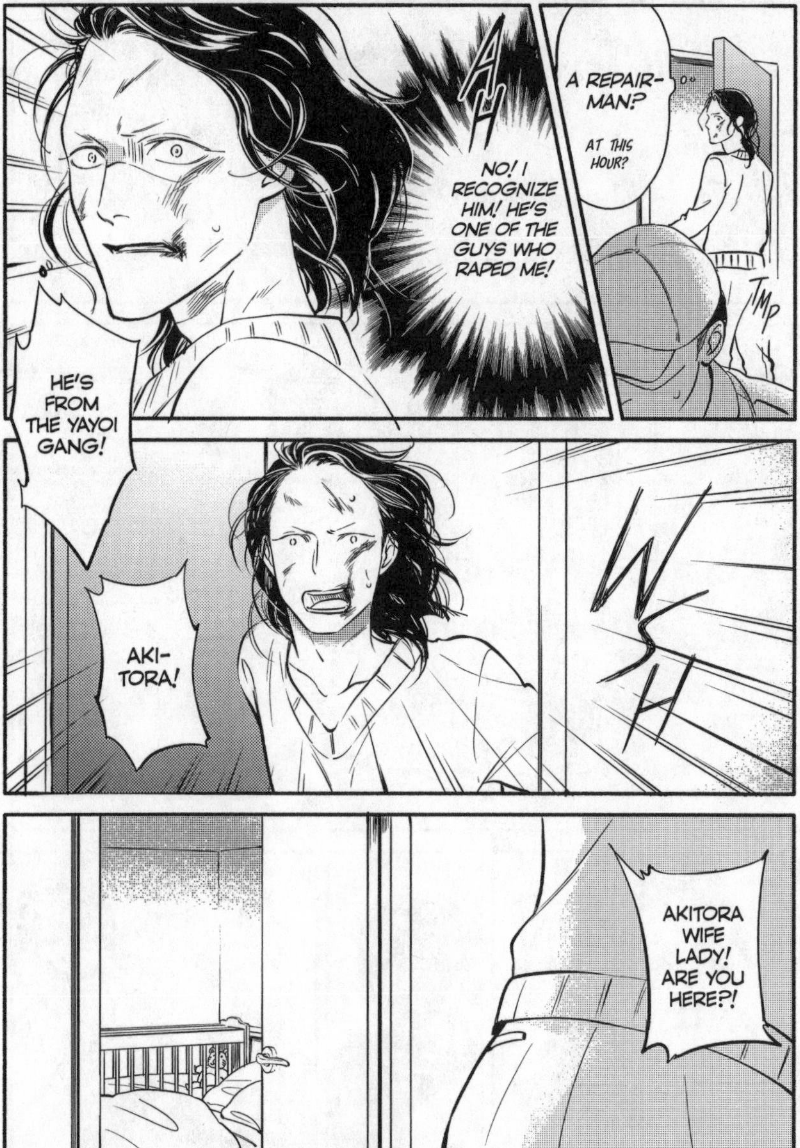
A REPAIR-MAN?
AT THIS HOUR?
TMP
AH
NO! I RECOGNIZE HIM! HE'S ONE OF THE GUYS WHO RAPED ME!
HE'S FROM THE YAYOI GANG!
WSH
AKI-TORA!
AKITORA WIFE LADY! ARE YOU HERE?!

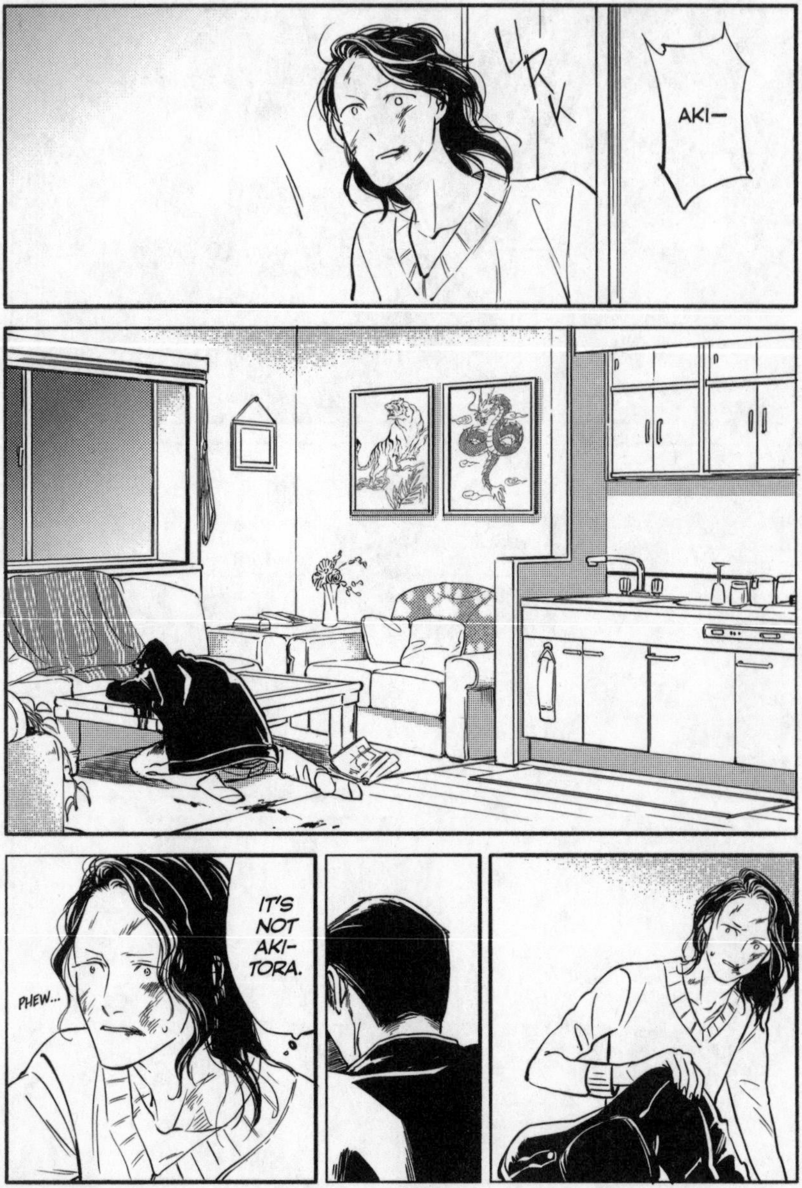
AKI—
URK
IT'S NOT AKI-TORA.
PHEW...

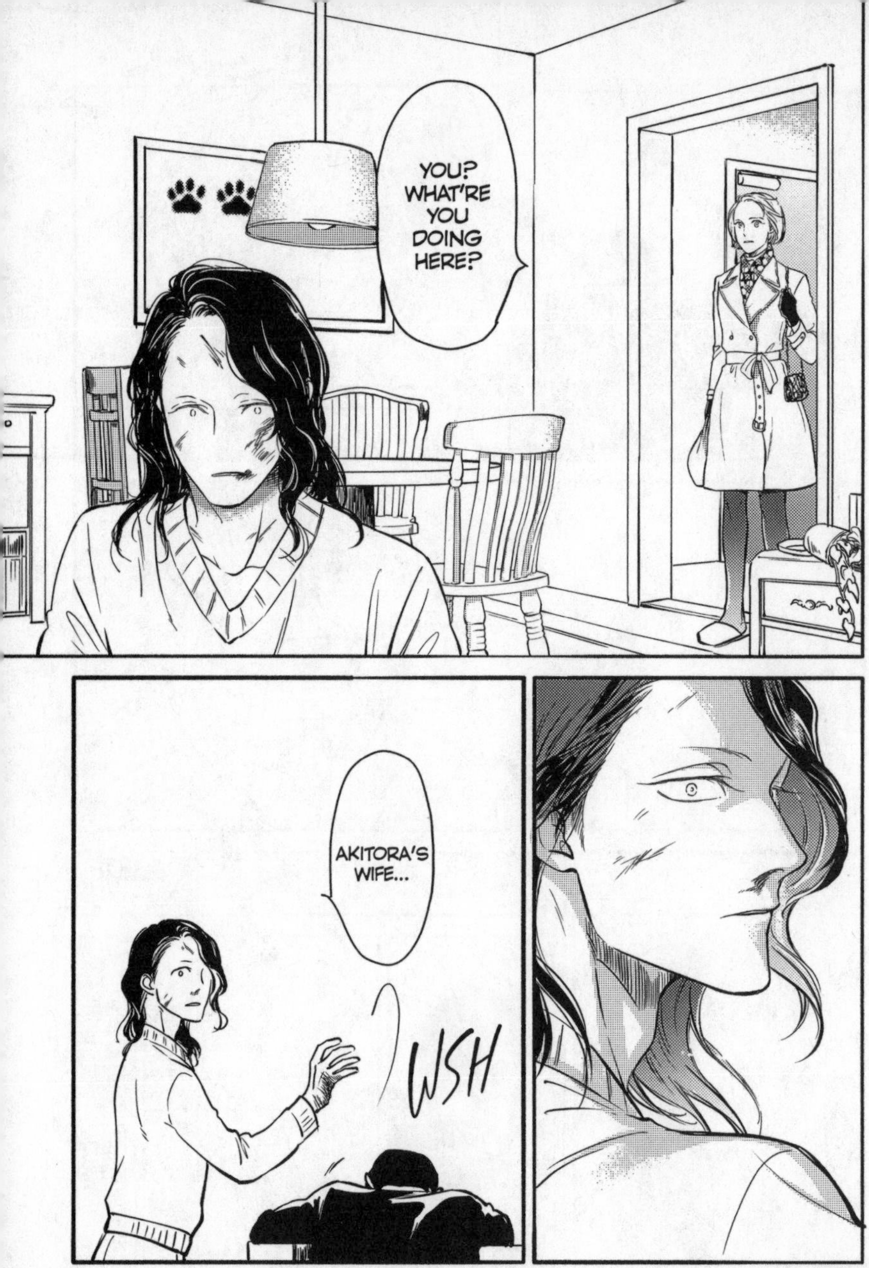
YOU? WHAT'RE YOU DOING HERE?
AKITORA'S WIFE...
WSH

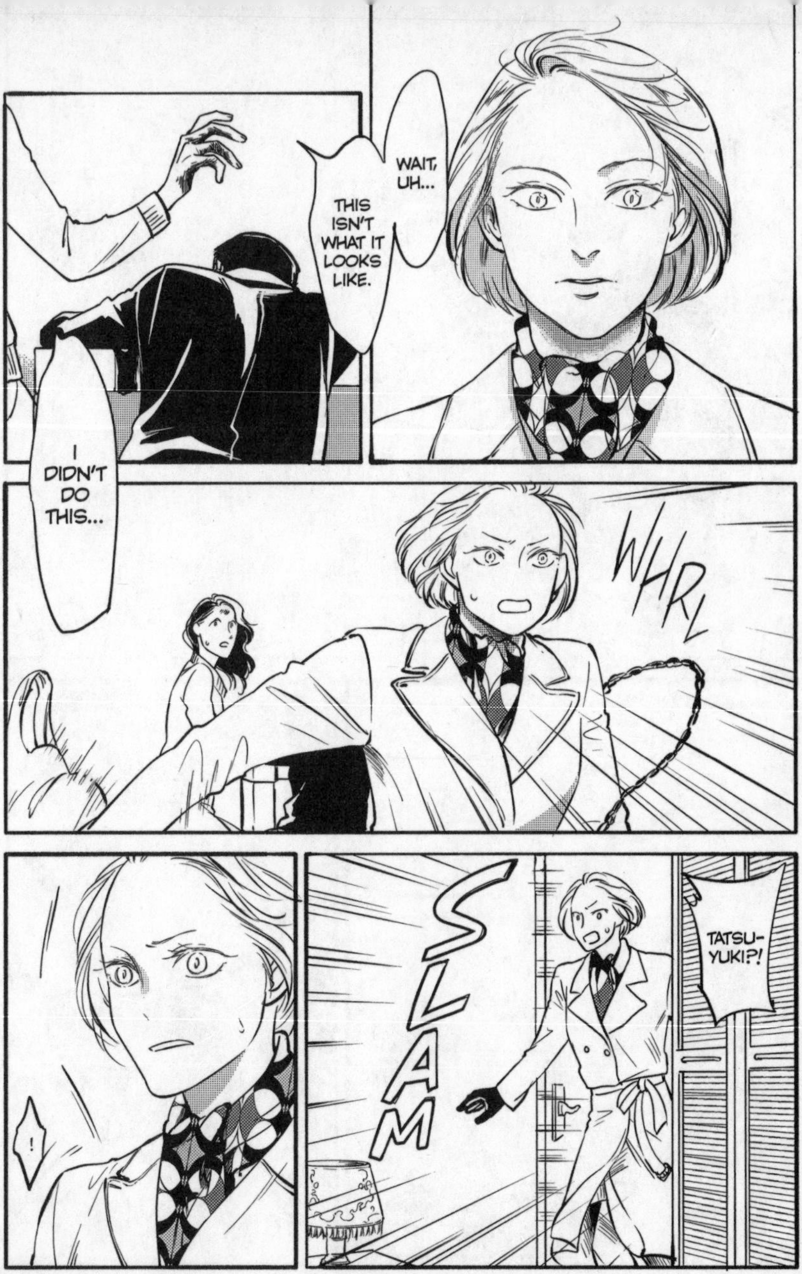
WAIT, UH...
THIS ISN'T WHAT IT LOOKS LIKE.
I DIDN'T DO THIS...
WHRL
TATSU-YUKI?!
SLAM
!

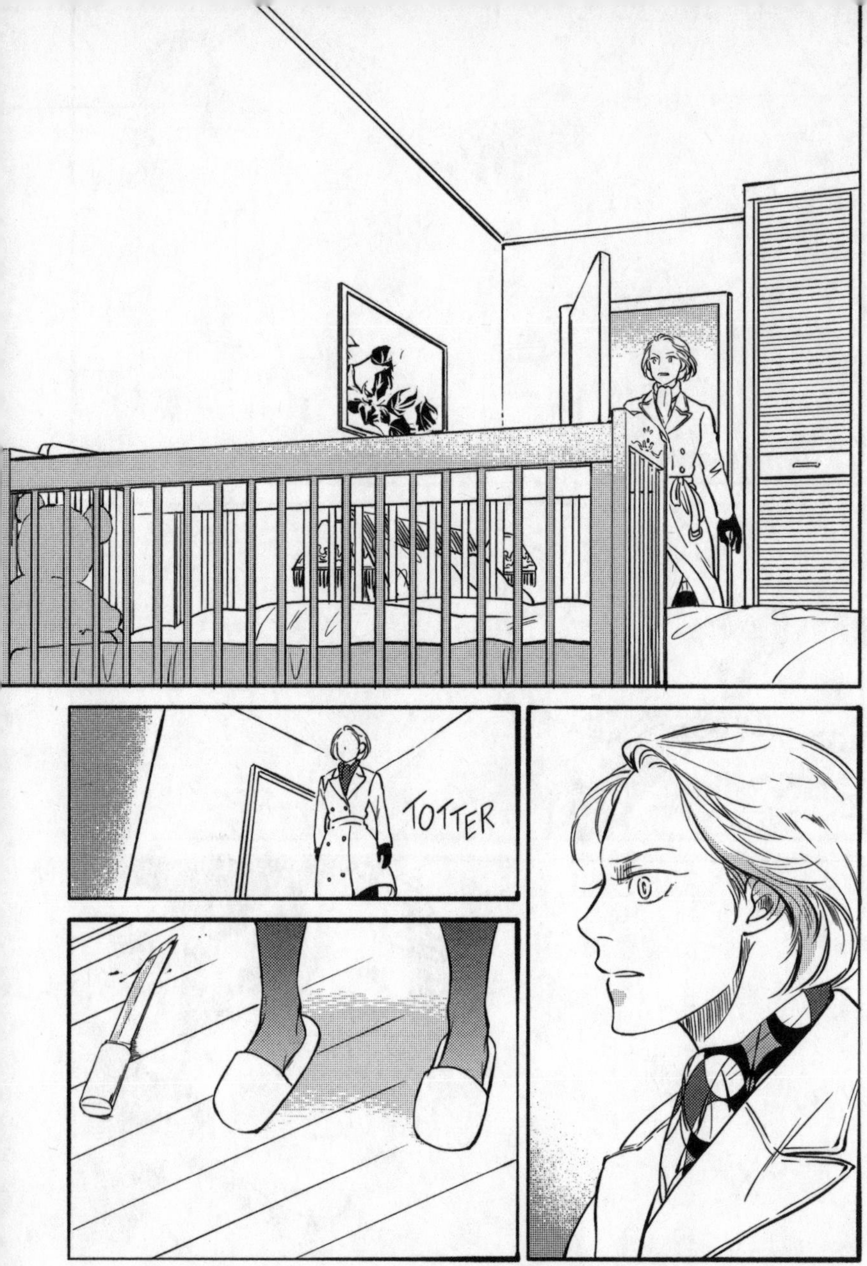
TOTTER

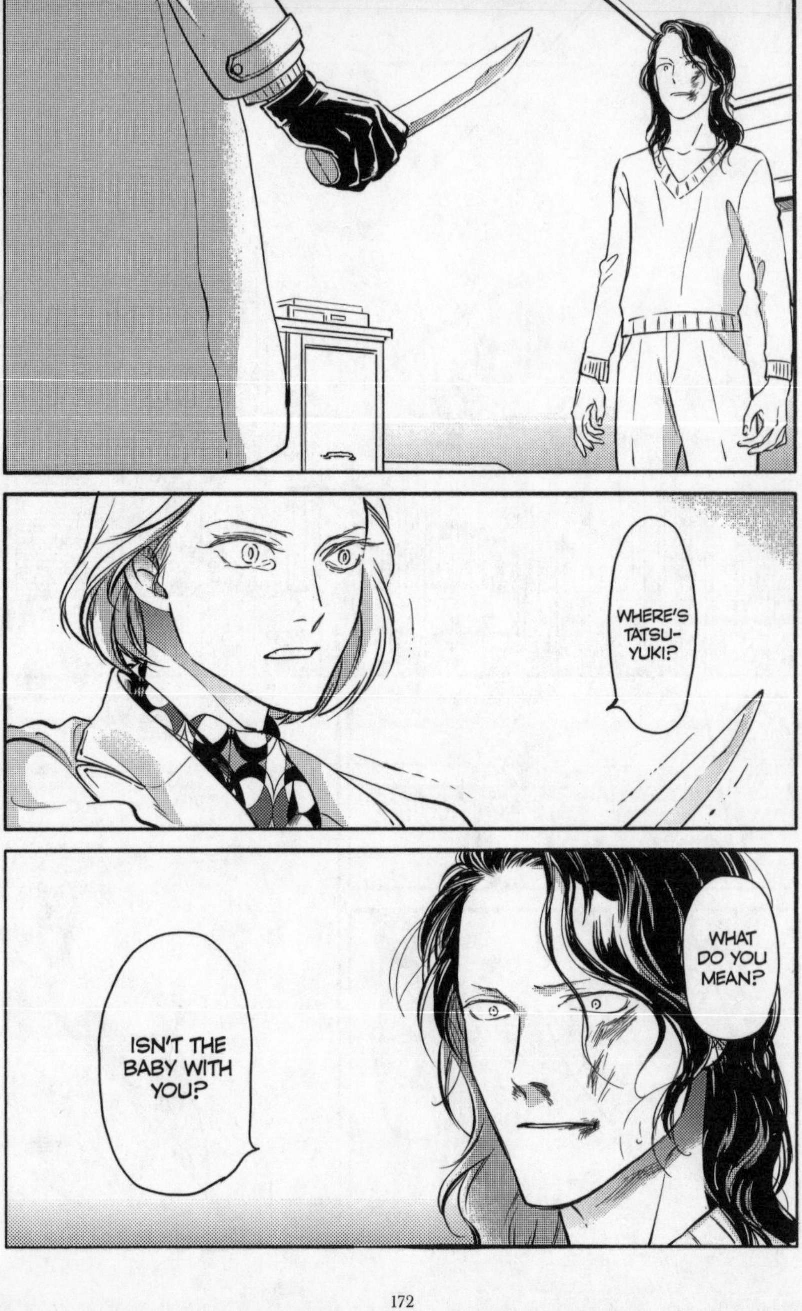
WHERE'S TATSU-YUKI?
WHAT DO YOU MEAN?
ISN'T THE BABY WITH YOU?

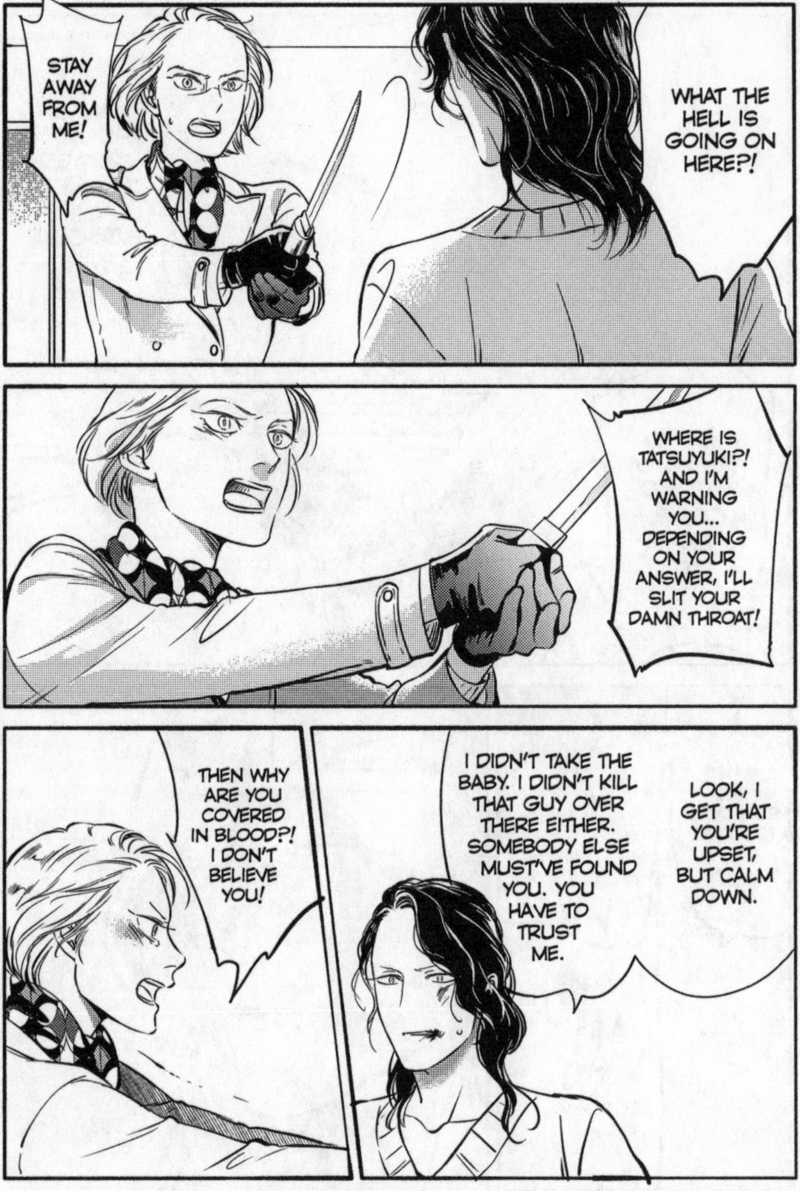
WHAT THE HELL IS GOING ON HERE?!
STAY AWAY FROM ME!
WHERE IS TATSUYUKI?! AND I'M WARNING YOU... DEPENDING ON YOUR ANSWER, I'LL SLIT YOUR DAMN THROAT!
LOOK, I GET THAT YOU'RE UPSET, BUT CALM DOWN.
I DIDN'T TAKE THE BABY. I DIDN'T KILL THAT GUY OVER THERE EITHER. SOMEBODY ELSE MUST'VE FOUND YOU. YOU HAVE TO TRUST ME.
THEN WHY ARE YOU COVERED IN BLOOD?! I DON'T BELIEVE YOU!

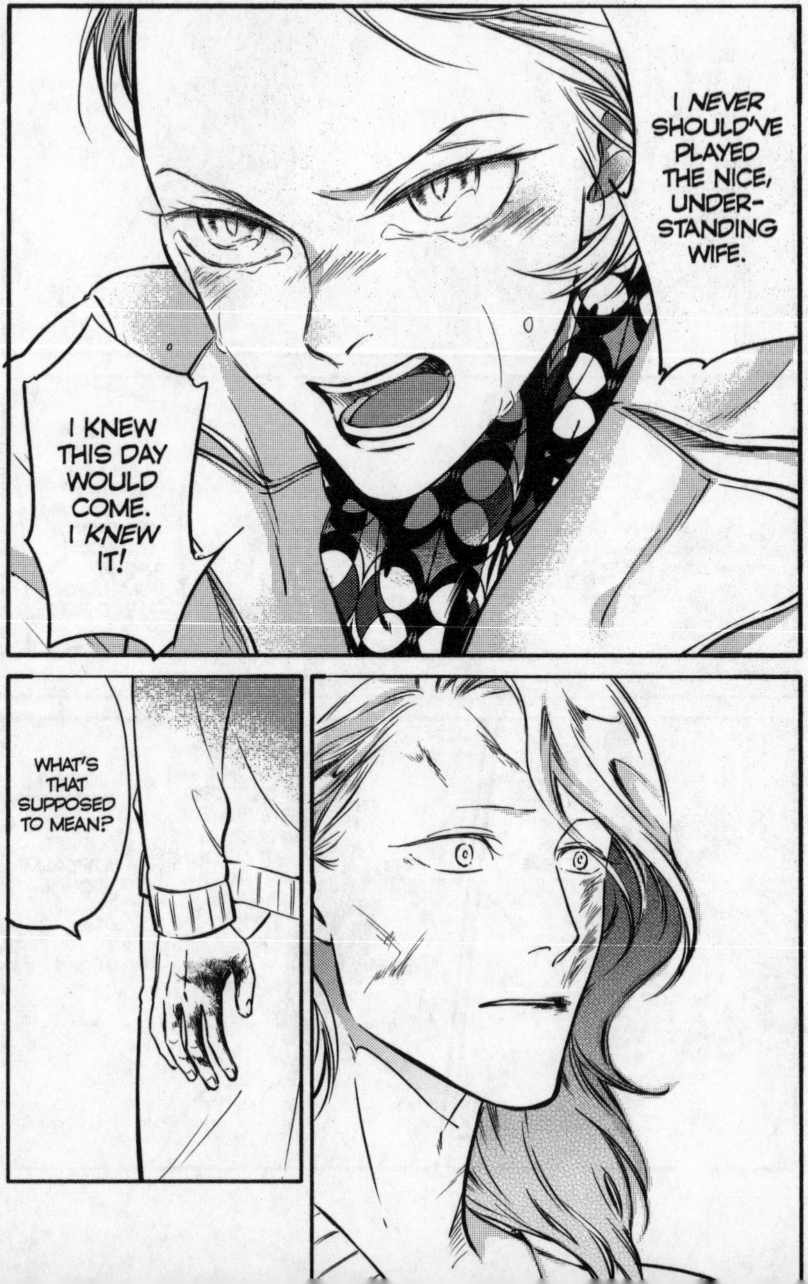
I *NEVER* SHOULD'VE PLAYED THE NICE, UNDER-STANDING WIFE.
I KNEW THIS DAY WOULD COME. I *KNEW* IT!
WHAT'S THAT SUPPOSED TO MEAN?

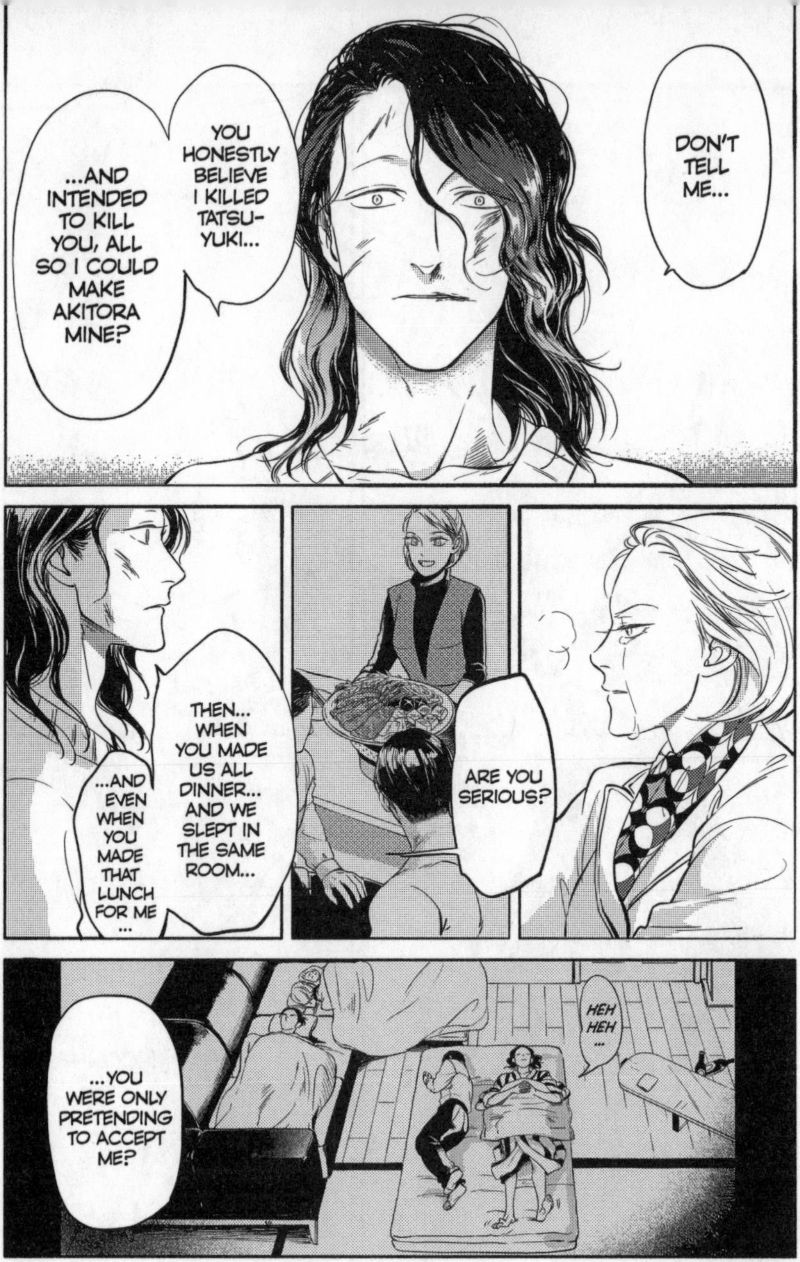
DON'T TELL ME...
YOU HONESTLY BELIEVE I KILLED TATSU-YUKI...
...AND INTENDED TO KILL YOU, ALL SO I COULD MAKE AKITORA MINE?
ARE YOU SERIOUS?
THEN... WHEN YOU MADE US ALL DINNER... AND WE SLEPT IN THE SAME ROOM...
...AND EVEN WHEN YOU MADE THAT LUNCH FOR ME ...
HEH HEH ...
...YOU WERE ONLY PRETENDING TO ACCEPT ME?

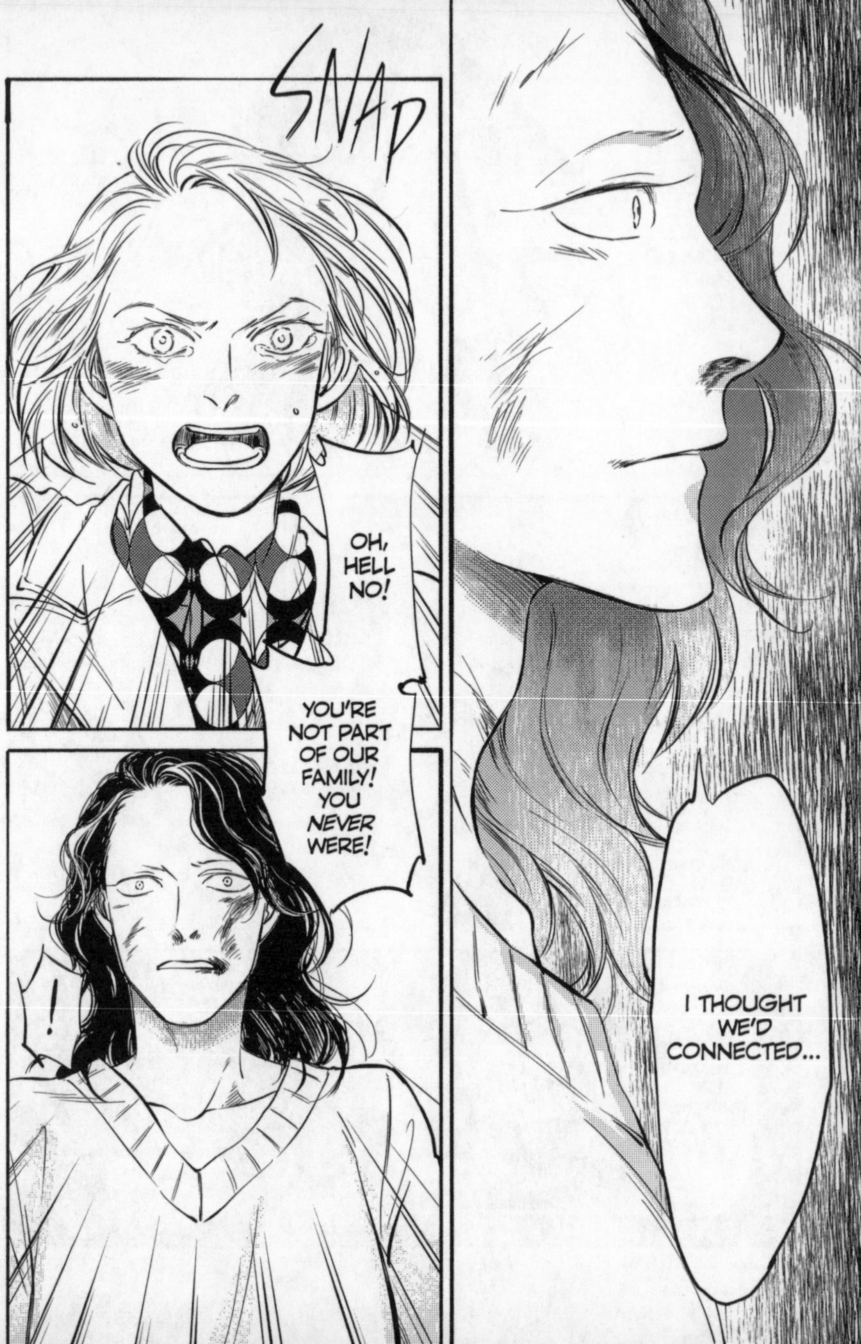
I THOUGHT WE'D CONNECTED...
SNAP
OH, HELL NO!
YOU'RE NOT PART OF OUR FAMILY! YOU *NEVER* WERE!
!

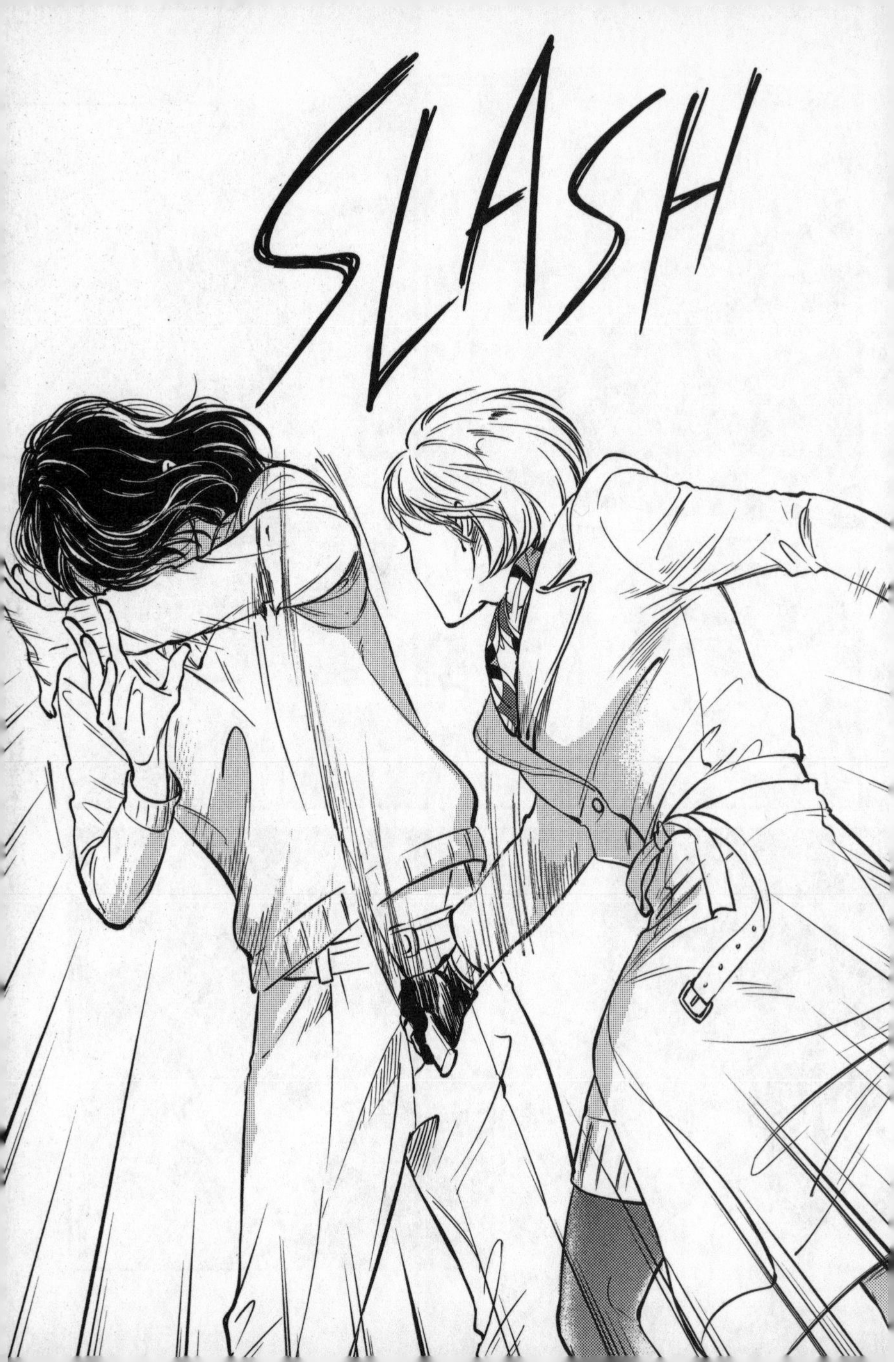
SLASH

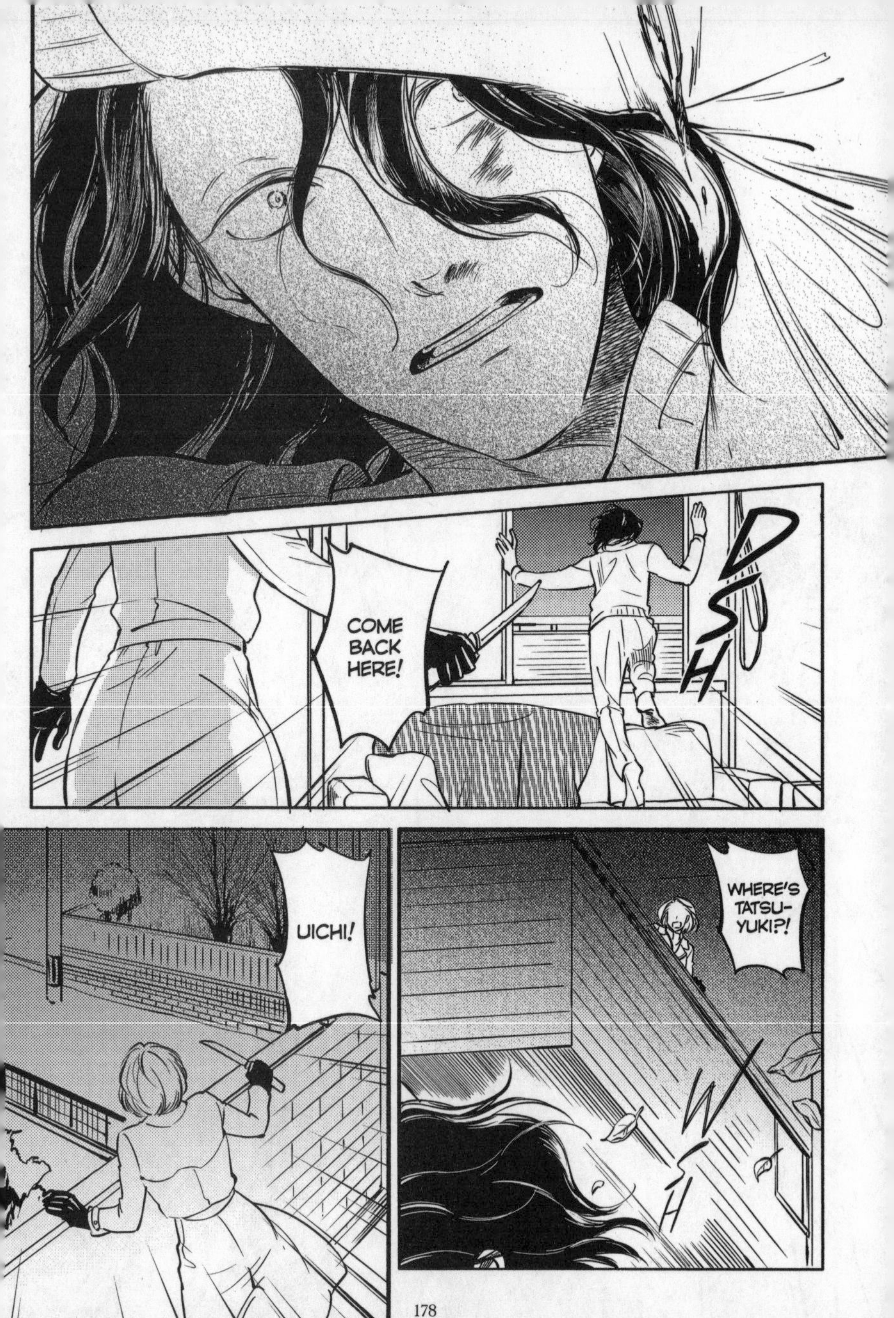
DSH
COME BACK HERE!
WHERE'S TATSU-YUKI!?!
WHSH
UICHI!

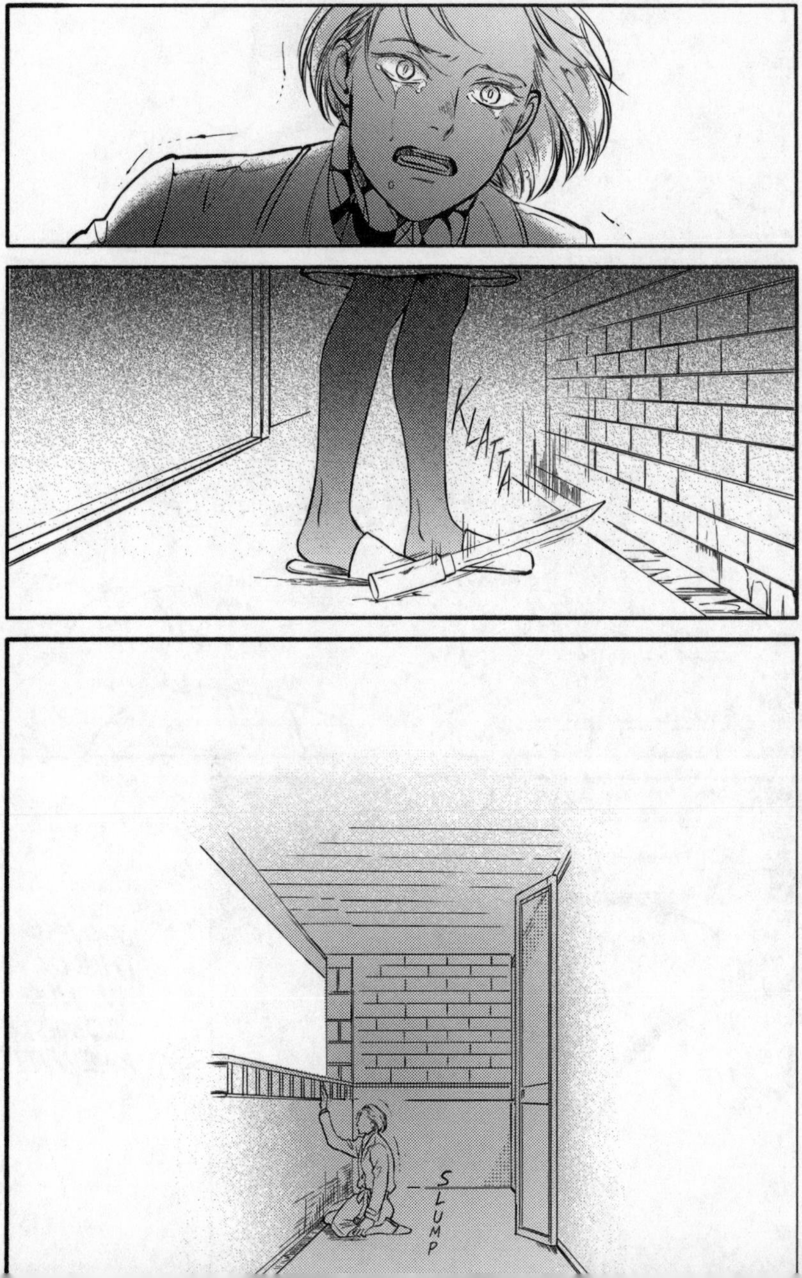
KLATTA
SLUMP

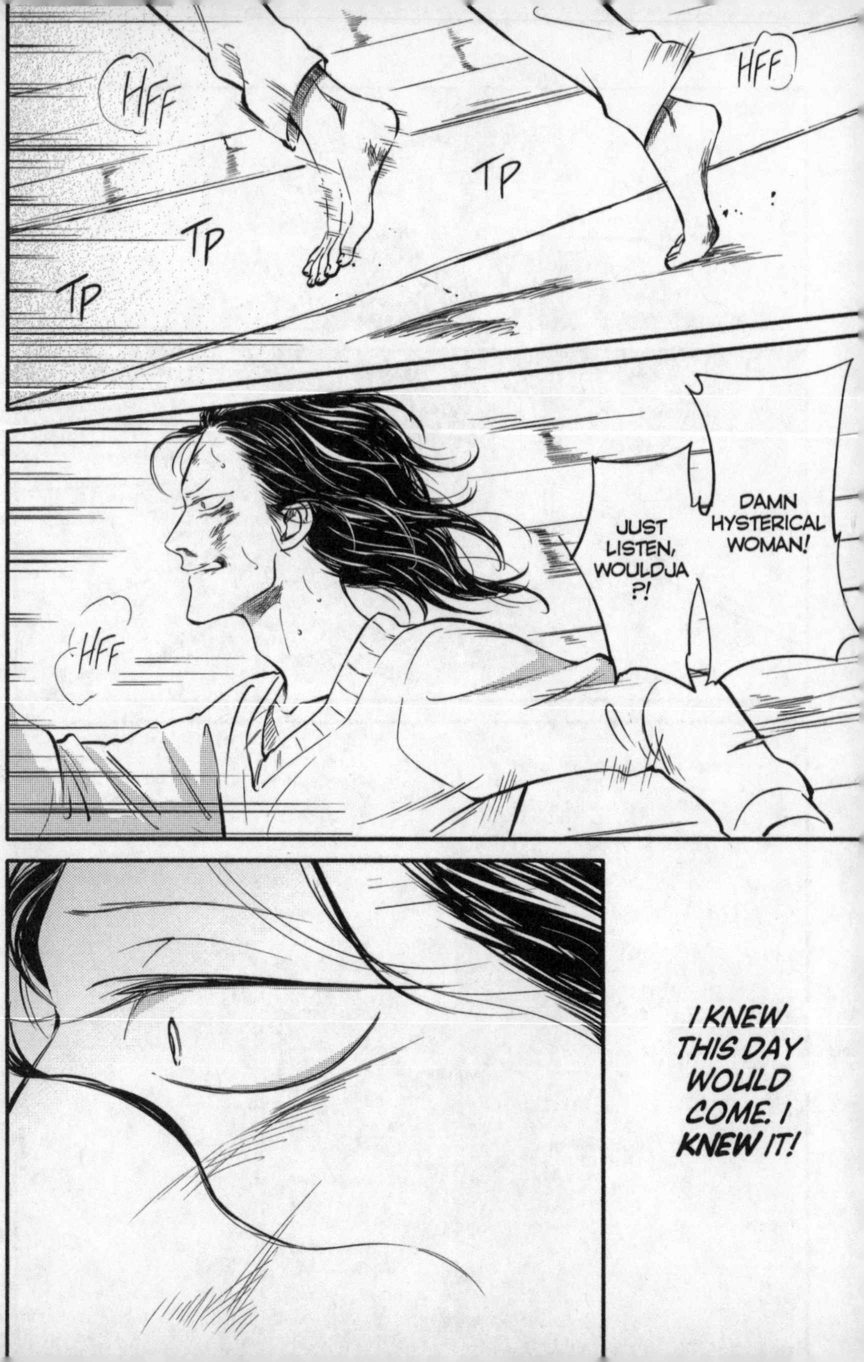
HFF
TP
HFF
TP
TP
DAMN HYSTERICAL WOMAN!
JUST LISTEN, WOULDJA ?!
HFF
I KNEW THIS DAY WOULD COME. I KNEW IT!

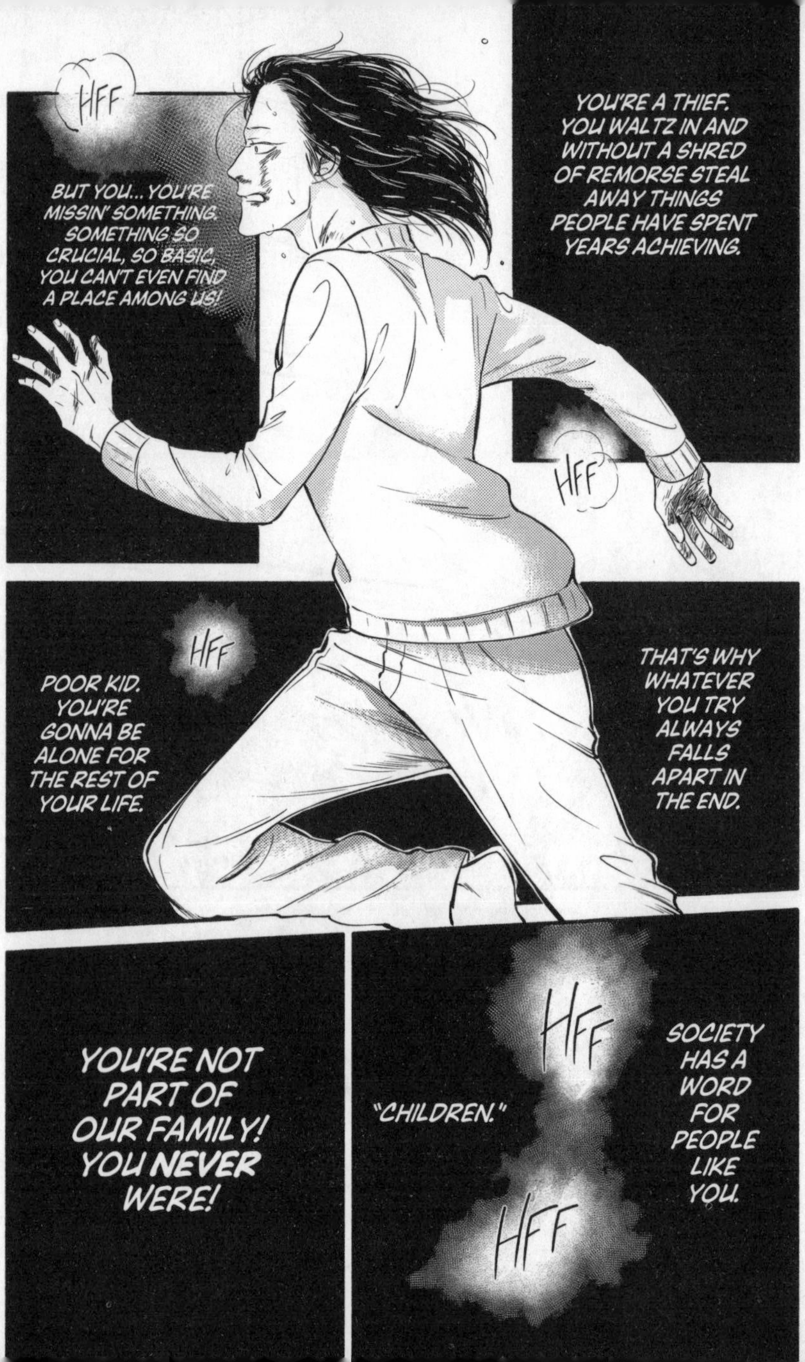
YOU'RE A THIEF. YOU WALTZ IN AND WITHOUT A SHRED OF REMORSE STEAL AWAY THINGS PEOPLE HAVE SPENT YEARS ACHIEVING.
HFF
BUT YOU... YOU'RE MISSIN' SOMETHING. SOMETHING SO CRUCIAL, SO BASIC, YOU CAN'T EVEN FIND A PLACE AMONG US!
HFF
THAT'S WHY WHATEVER YOU TRY ALWAYS FALLS APART IN THE END.
HFF
POOR KID. YOU'RE GONNA BE ALONE FOR THE REST OF YOUR LIFE.
SOCIETY HAS A WORD FOR PEOPLE LIKE YOU.
HFF
"CHILDREN."
HFF
YOU'RE NOT PART OF OUR FAMILY! YOU NEVER WERE!

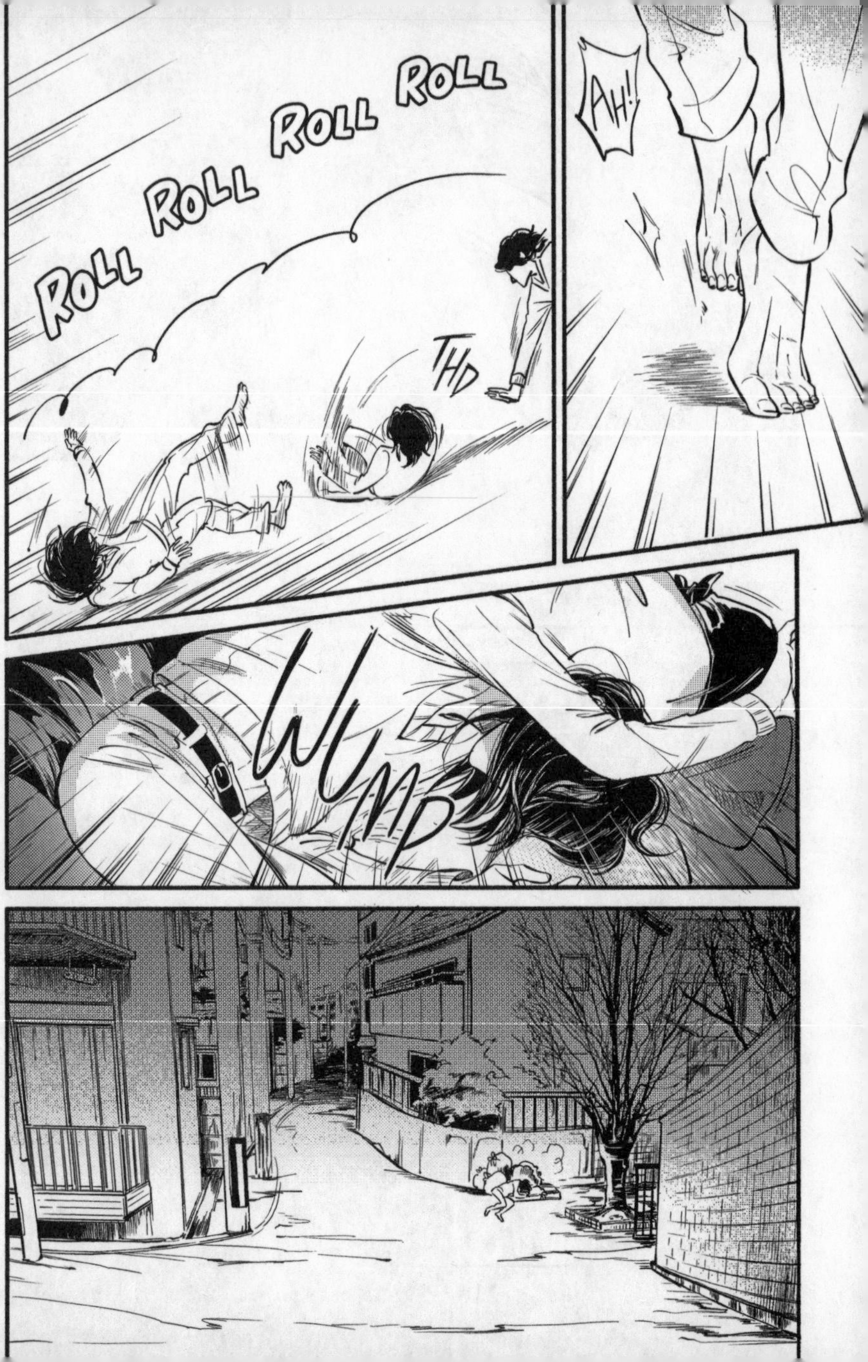
AH!
ROLL ROLL ROLL ROLL
THD
WUMP

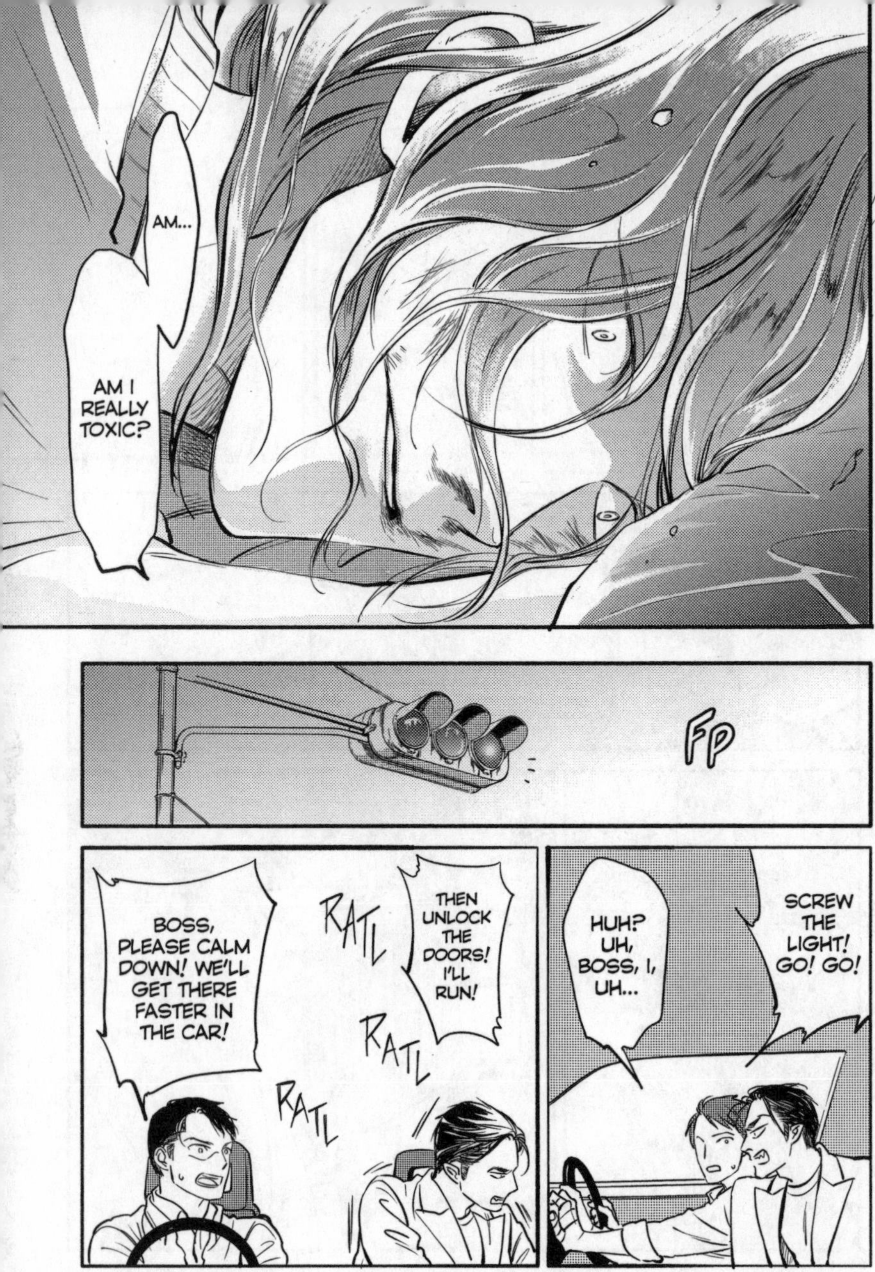
AM...
AM I REALLY TOXIC?
Fp
SCREW THE LIGHT! GO! GO!
HUH? UH, BOSS, I, UH...
THEN UNLOCK THE DOORS! I'LL RUN!
RATL
RATL
RATL
BOSS, PLEASE CALM DOWN! WE'LL GET THERE FASTER IN THE CAR!

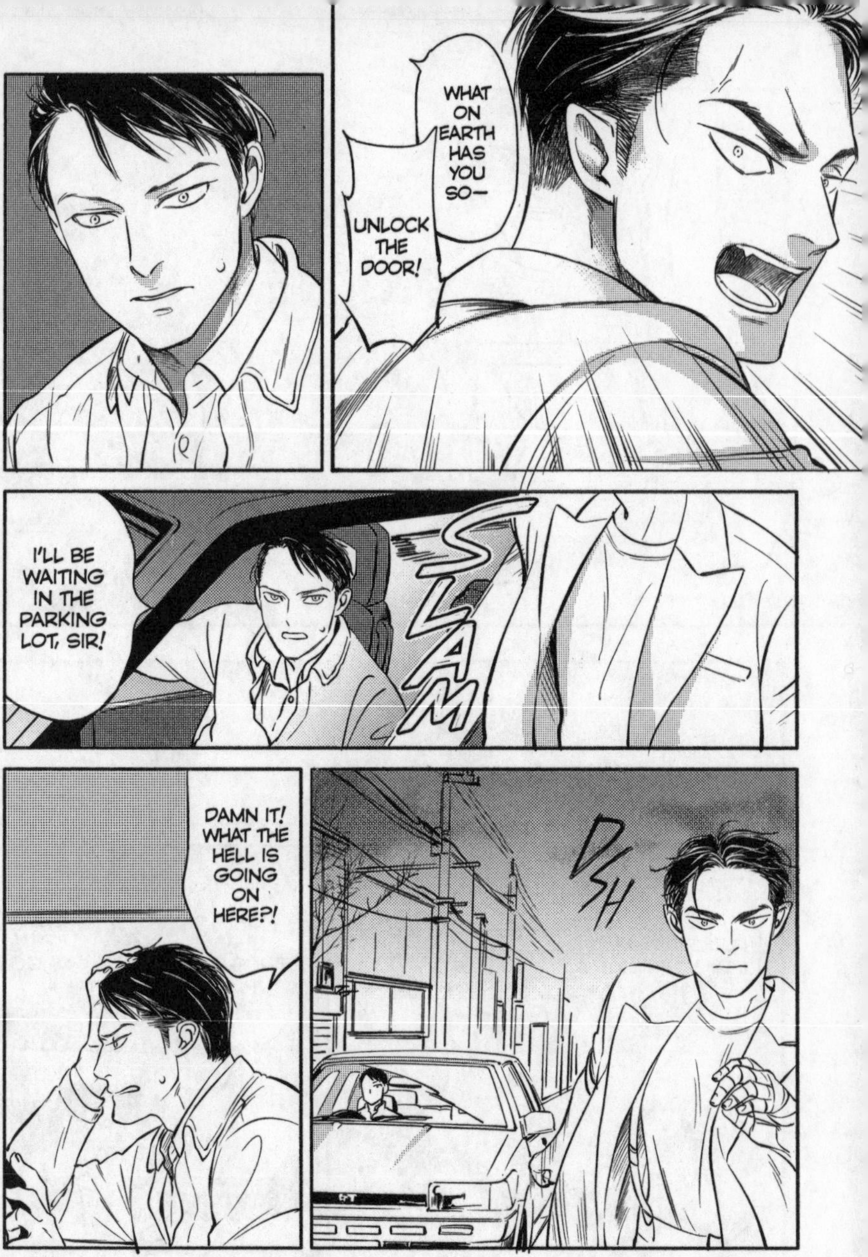
WHAT ON EARTH HAS YOU SO—
UNLOCK THE DOOR!
SLAM
I'LL BE WAITING IN THE PARKING LOT, SIR!
DSH
DAMN IT! WHAT THE HELL IS GOING ON HERE?!

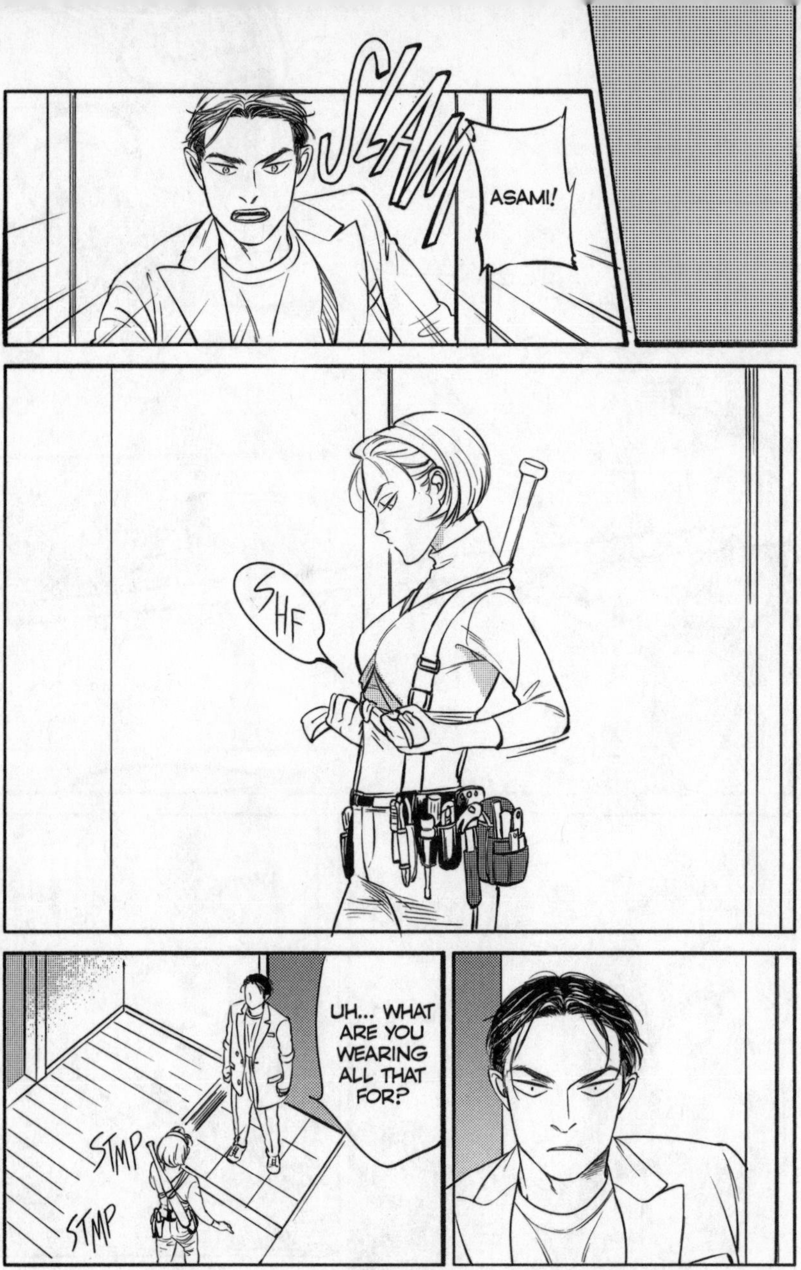
SLAM
ASAMI!
SHF
UH... WHAT ARE YOU WEARING ALL THAT FOR?
STMP
STMP

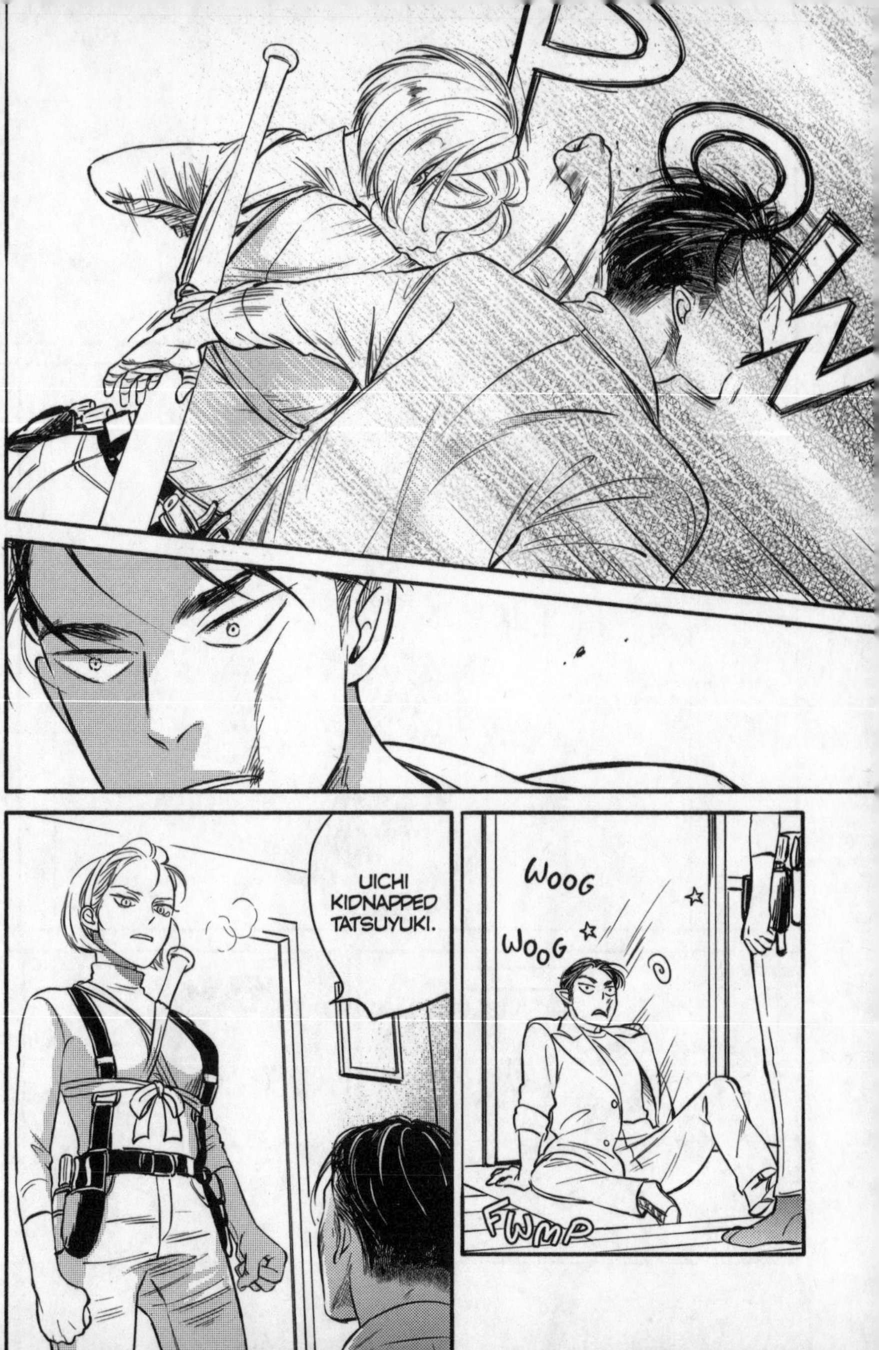
POW
WOOG
WOOG
FWMP
UICHI KIDNAPPED TATSUYUKI.

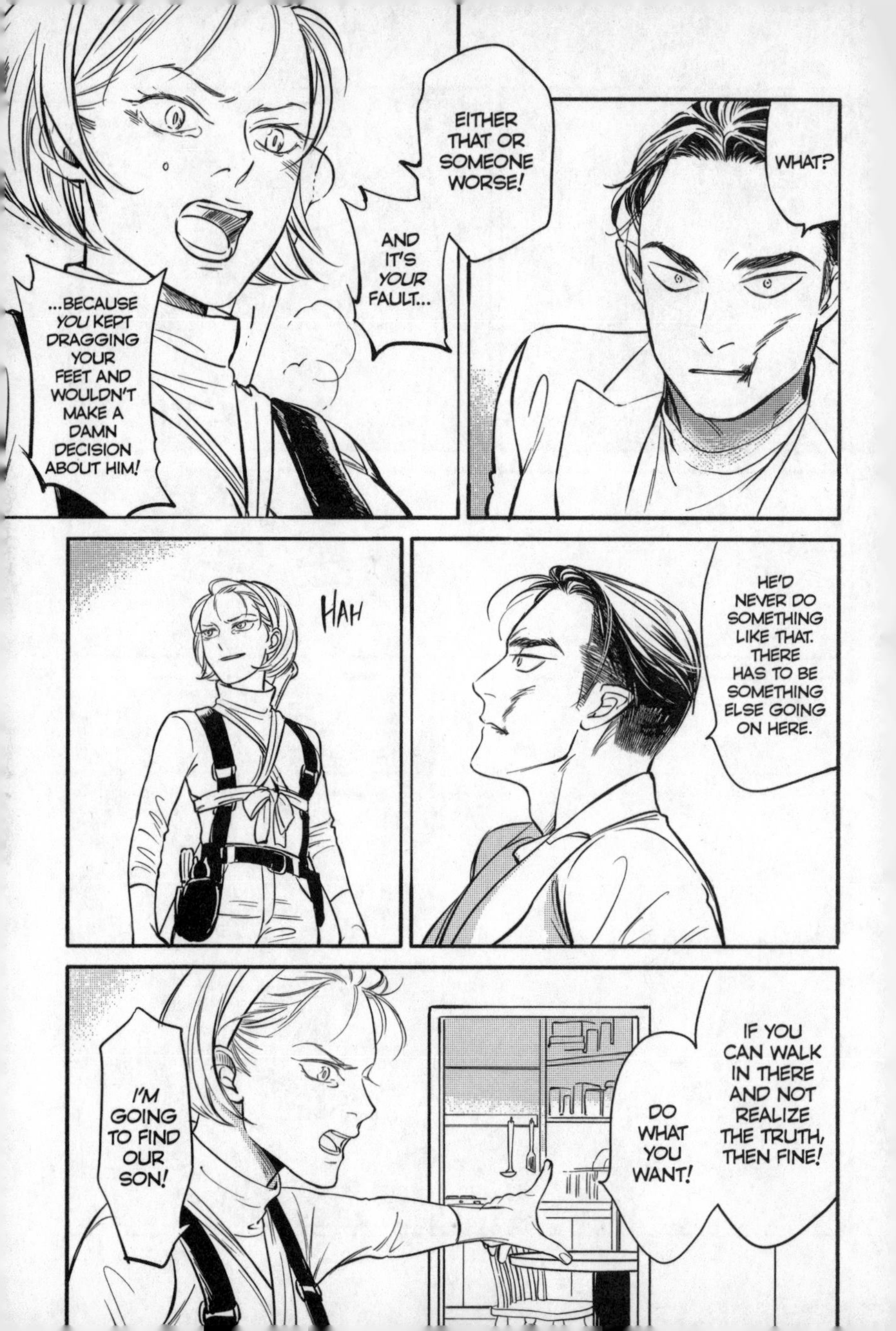
WHAT?
EITHER THAT OR SOMEONE WORSE!
AND IT'S *YOUR* FAULT...
...BECAUSE *YOU* KEPT DRAGGING YOUR FEET AND WOULDN'T MAKE A DAMN DECISION ABOUT HIM!
HE'D NEVER DO SOMETHING LIKE THAT. THERE HAS TO BE SOMETHING ELSE GOING ON HERE.
HAH
IF YOU CAN WALK IN THERE AND NOT REALIZE THE TRUTH, THEN FINE!
DO WHAT YOU WANT!
I'M GOING TO FIND OUR SON!

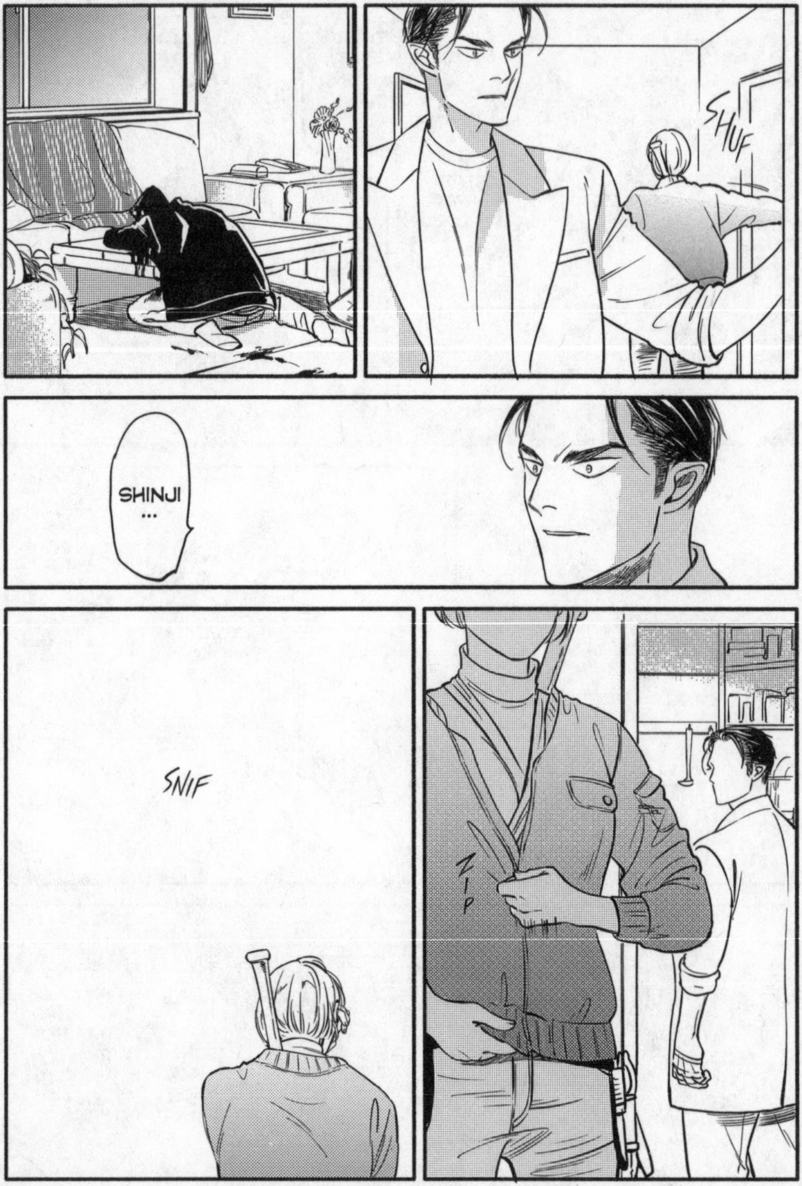
SHUF
SHINJI
...
ZIP
SNIF

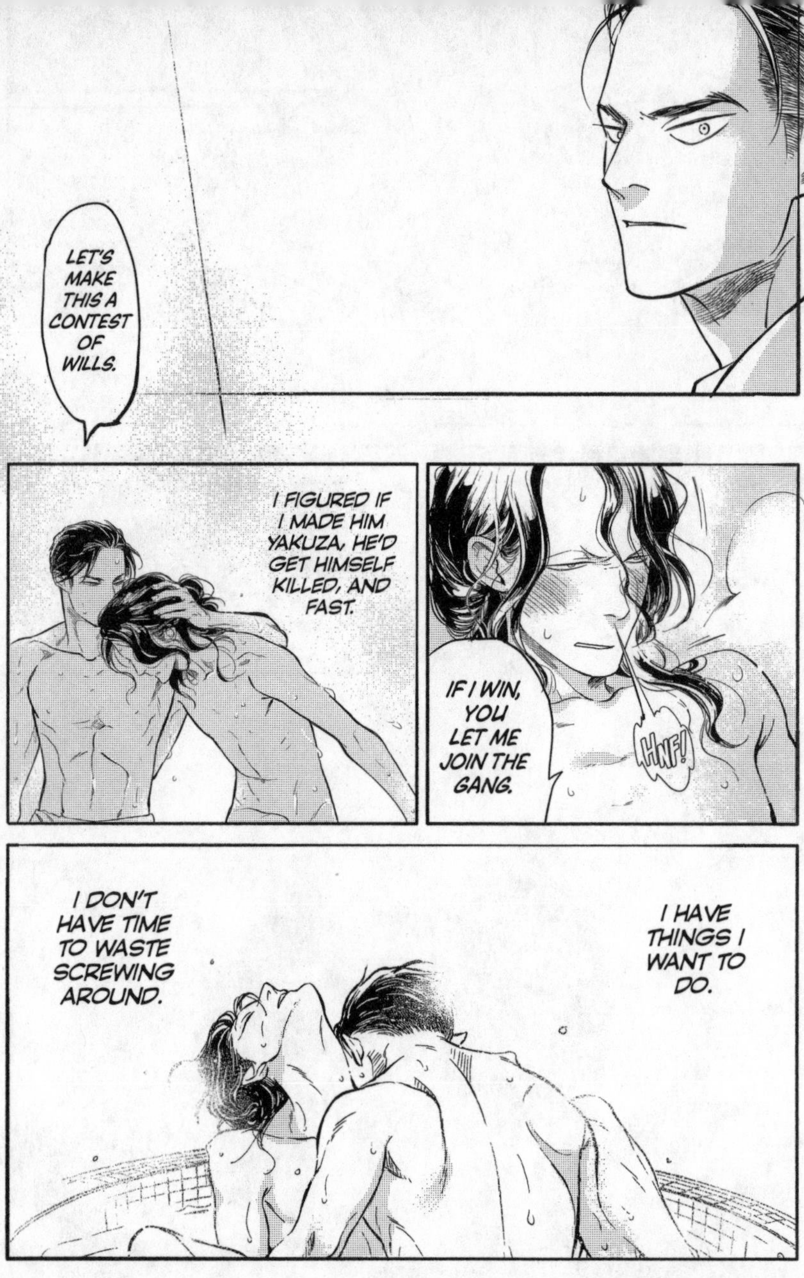
LET'S MAKE THIS A CONTEST OF WILLS.
IF I WIN, YOU LET ME JOIN THE GANG.
HNF!
I FIGURED IF I MADE HIM YAKUZA, HE'D GET HIMSELF KILLED, AND FAST.
I HAVE THINGS I WANT TO DO.
I DON'T HAVE TIME TO WASTE SCREWING AROUND.

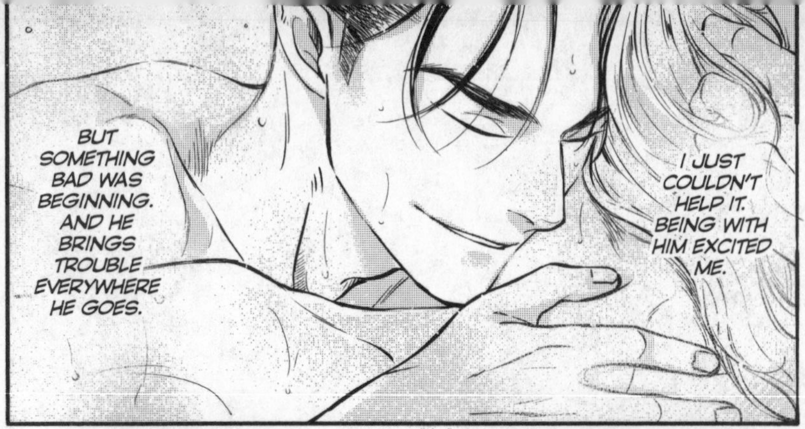
I JUST COULDN'T HELP IT. BEING WITH HIM EXCITED ME.
BUT SOMETHING BAD WAS BEGINNING. AND HE BRINGS TROUBLE EVERYWHERE HE GOES.

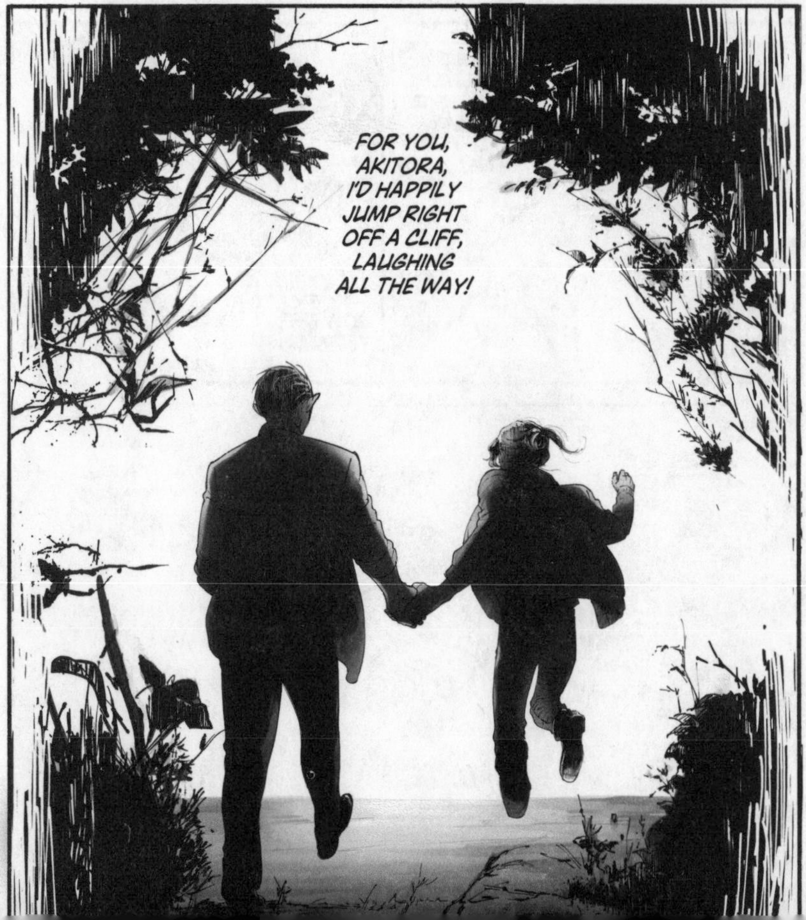
FOR YOU, AKITORA, I'D HAPPILY JUMP RIGHT OFF A CLIFF, LAUGHING ALL THE WAY!

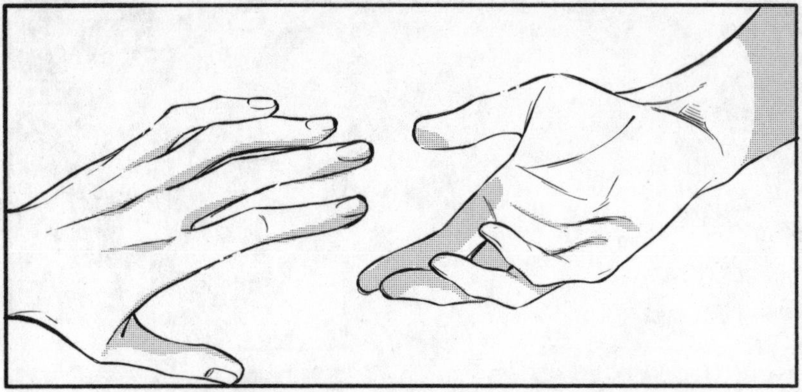
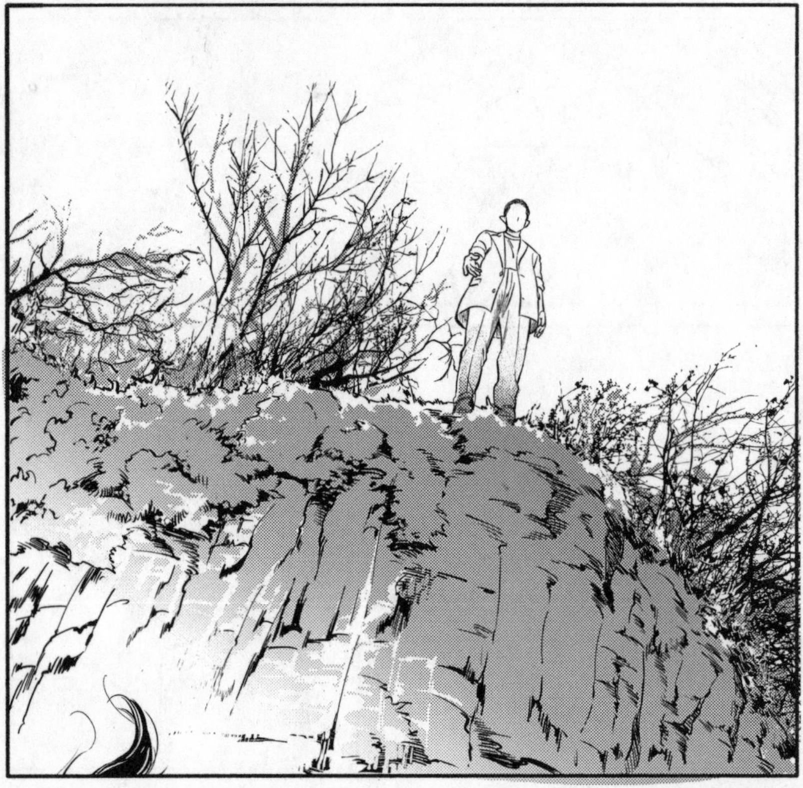

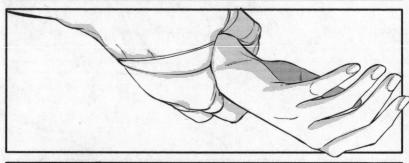

BUT NOW...

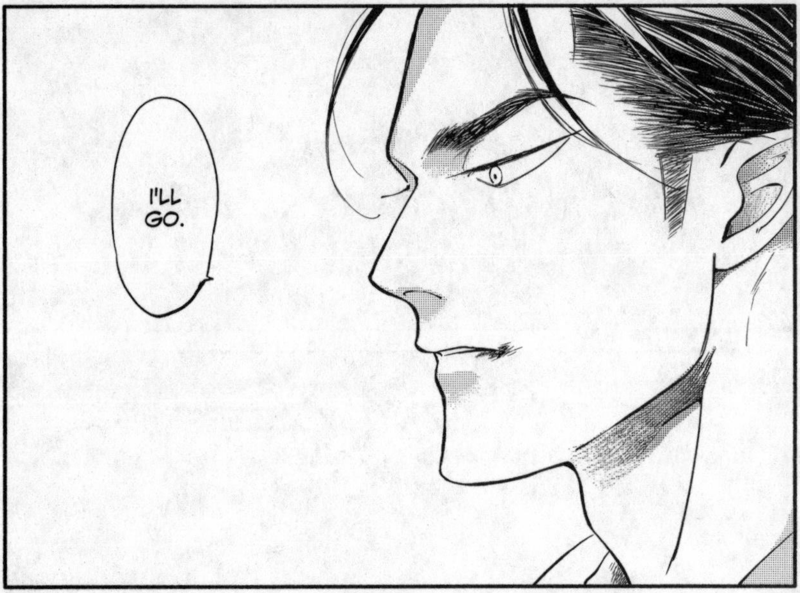
I'LL GO.
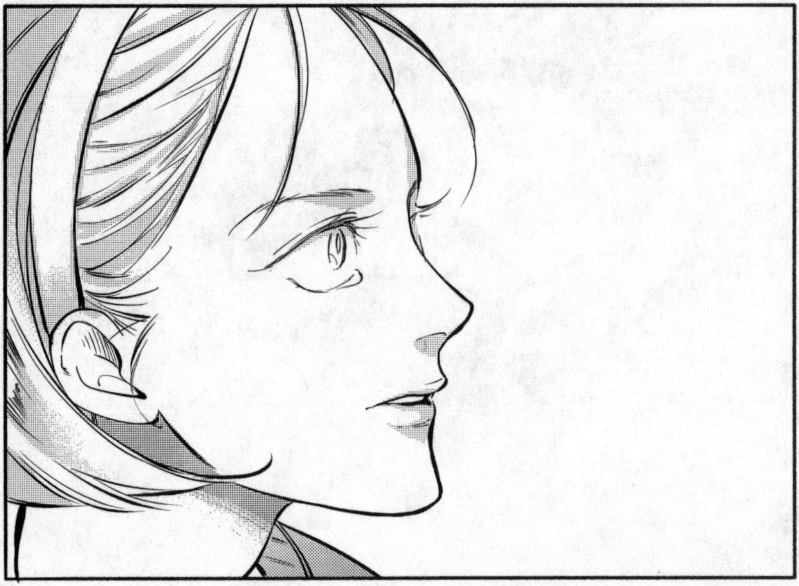

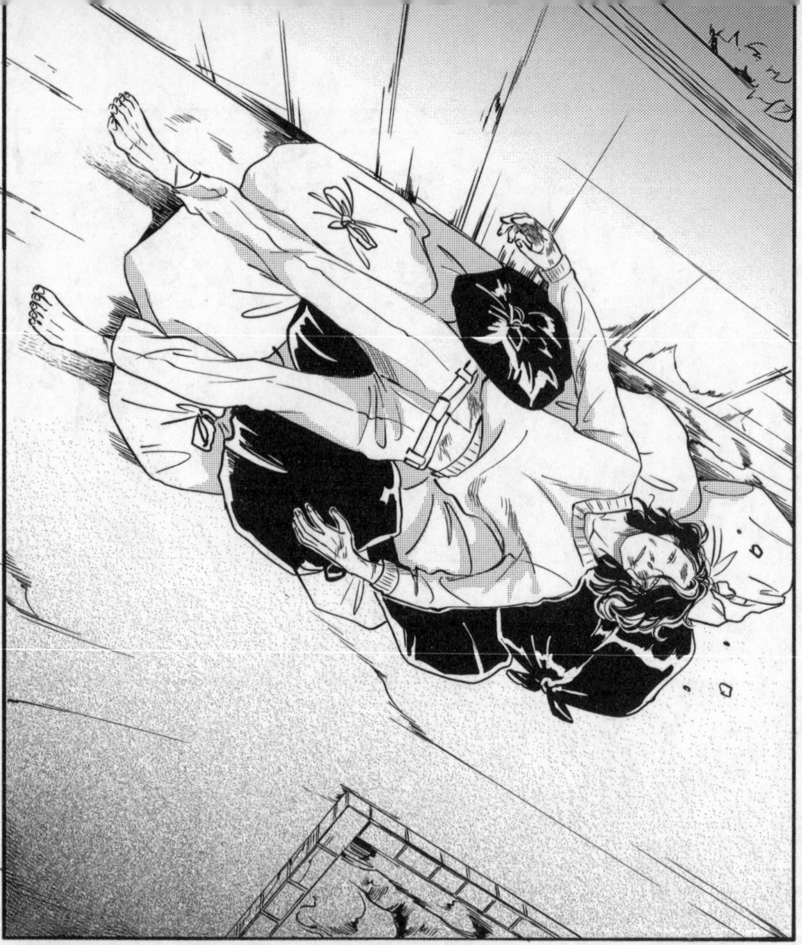
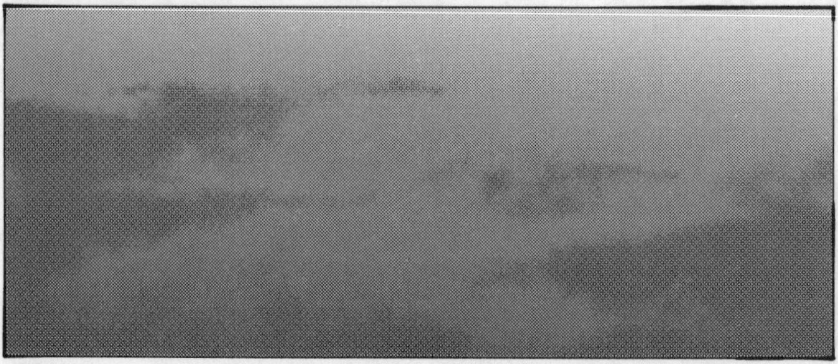

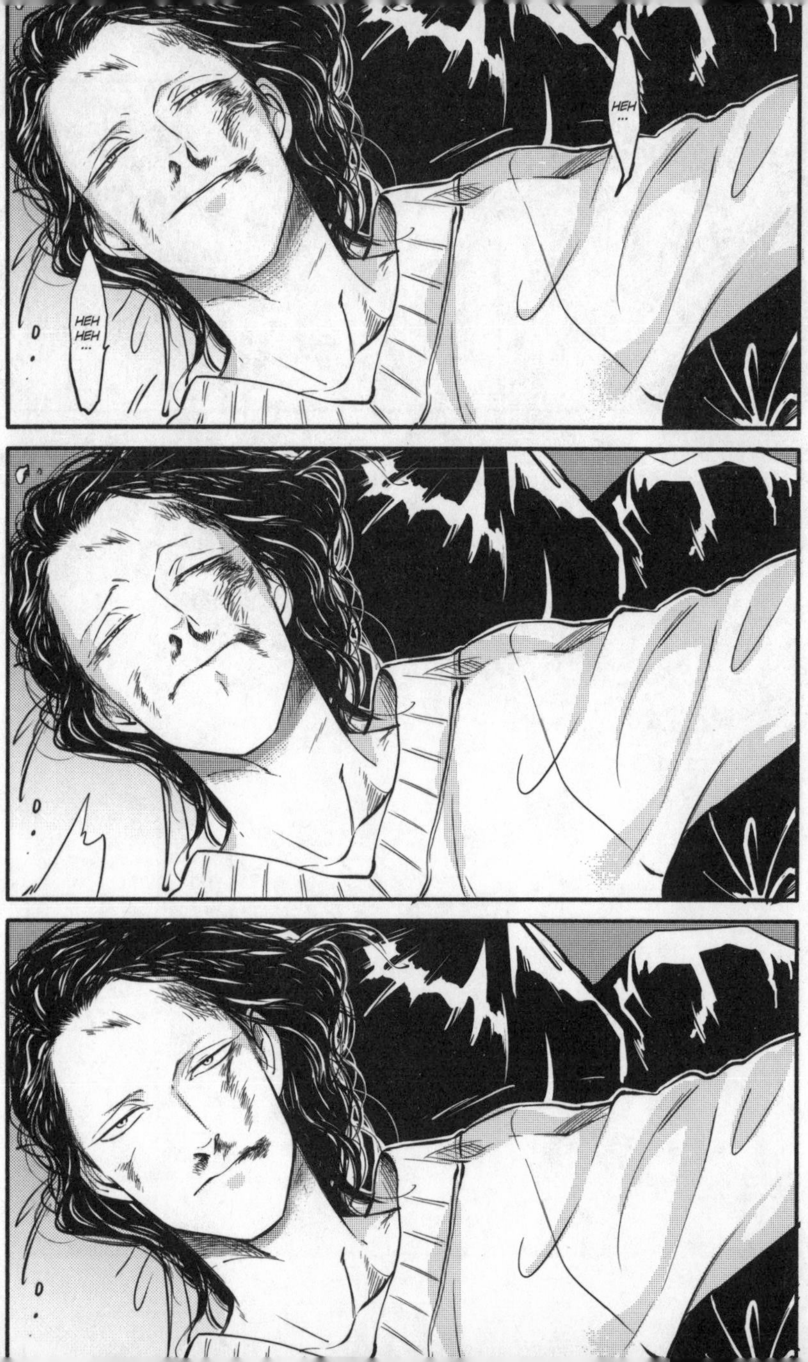
HEH...
HEH HEH...

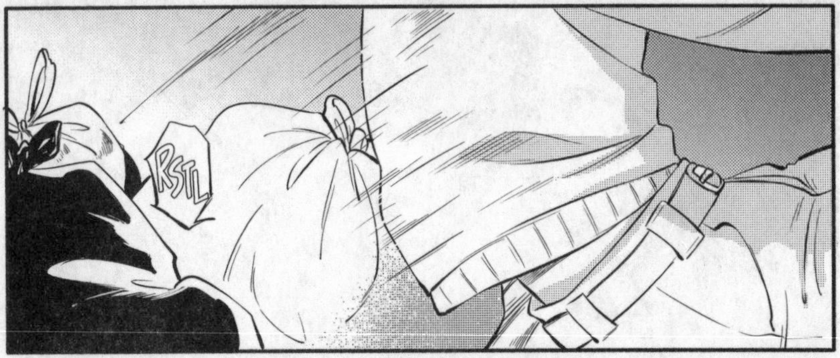
RSTL

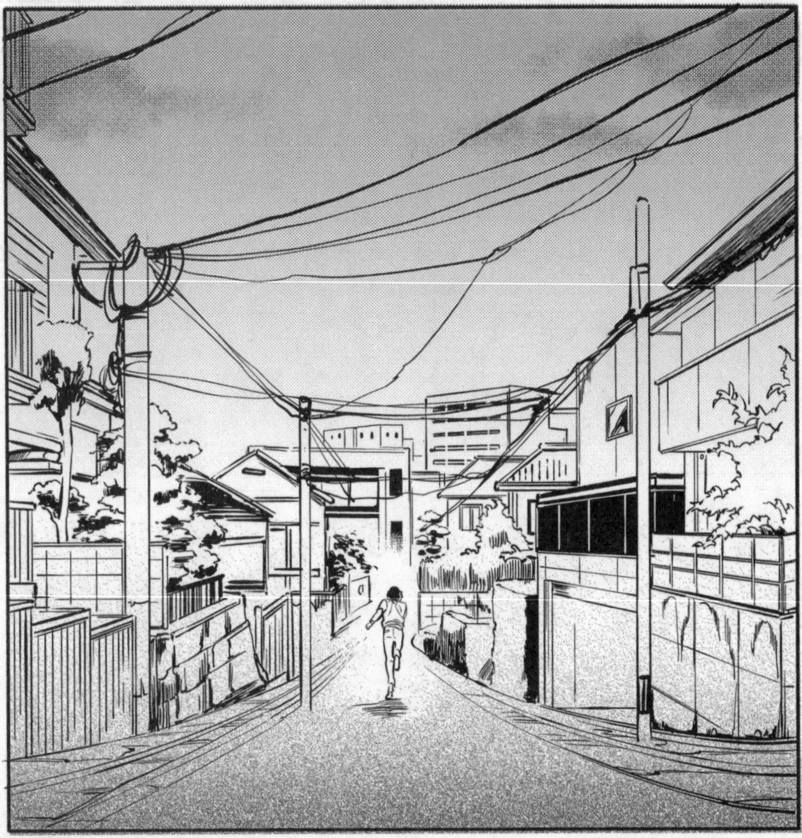

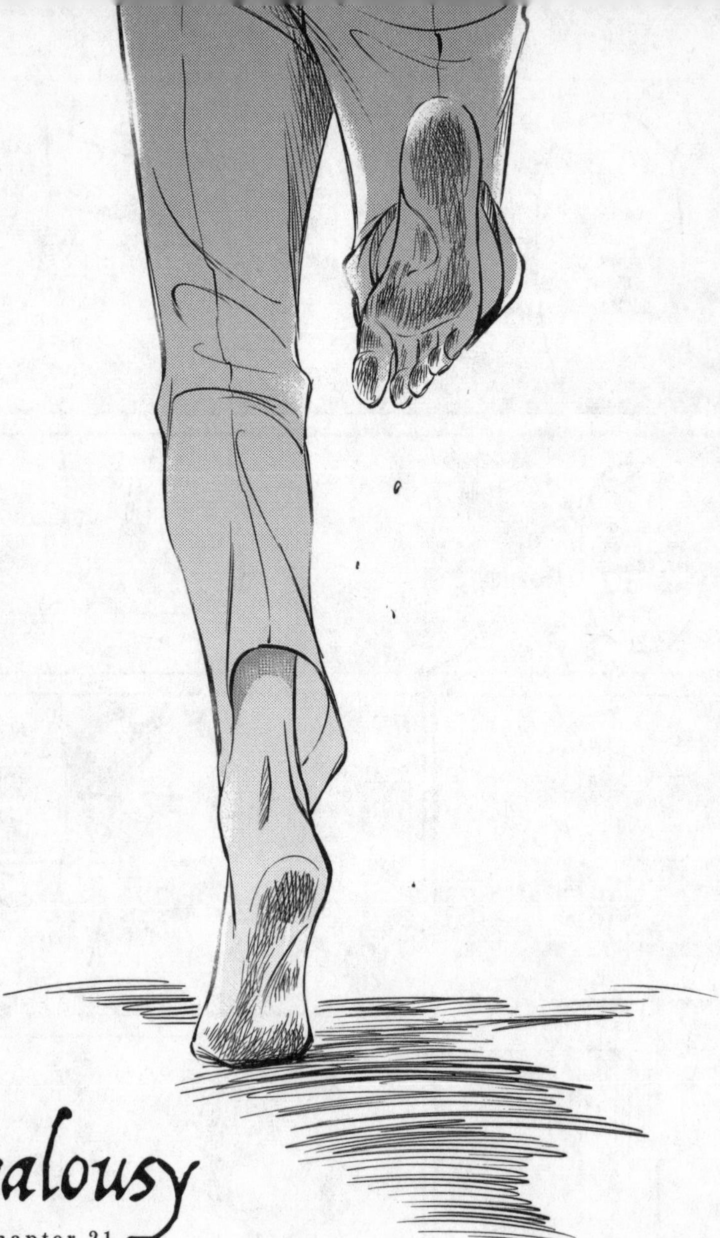

jealousy

Chapter 21

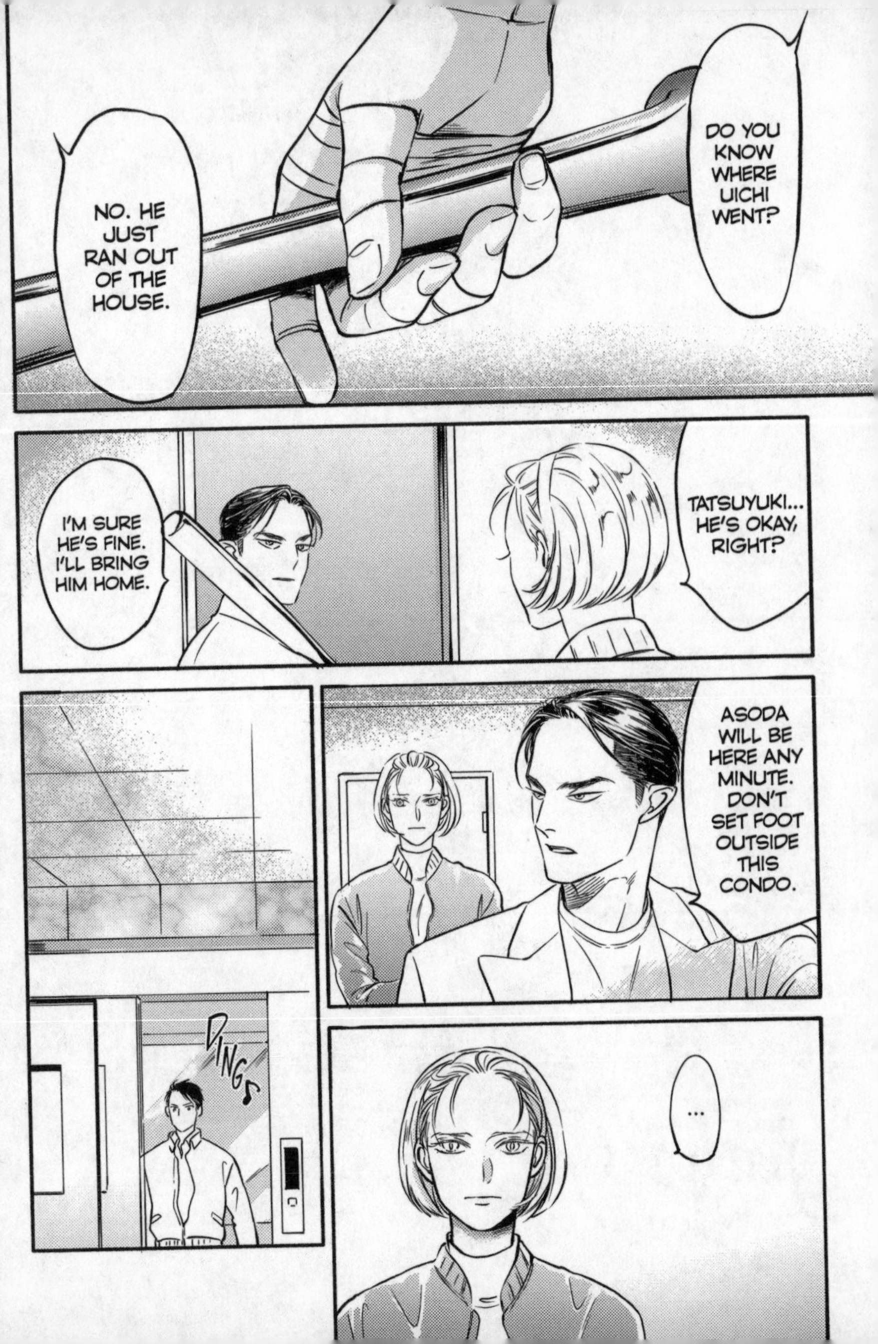
DO YOU KNOW WHERE UICHI WENT?
NO. HE JUST RAN OUT OF THE HOUSE.
TATSUYUKI... HE'S OKAY, RIGHT?
I'M SURE HE'S FINE. I'LL BRING HIM HOME.
ASODA WILL BE HERE ANY MINUTE. DON'T SET FOOT OUTSIDE THIS CONDO.
...
DINGS

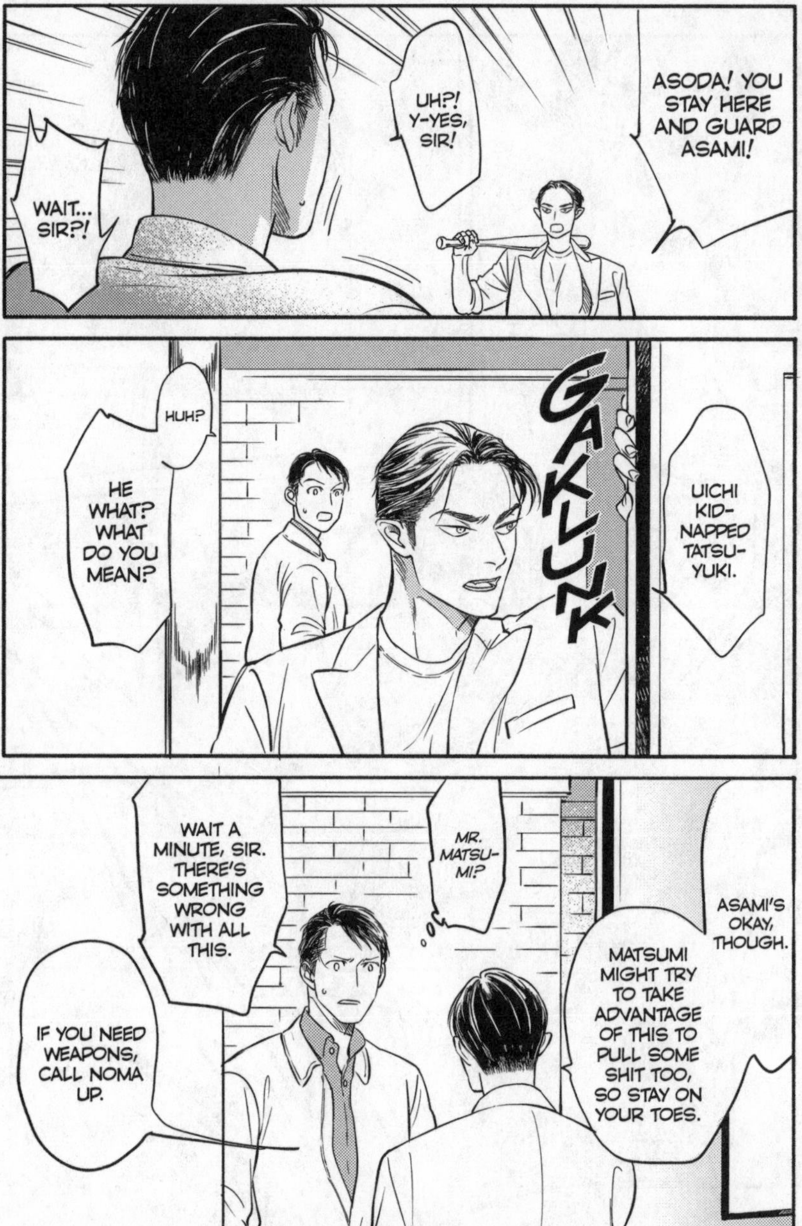
ASODA! YOU STAY HERE AND GUARD ASAMI!
UH?! Y-YES, SIR!
WAIT... SIR?!
UICHI KID-NAPPED TATSU-YUKI.
GAKLUNK
HUH?
HE WHAT? WHAT DO YOU MEAN?
ASAMI'S OKAY, THOUGH.
MATSUMI MIGHT TRY TO TAKE ADVANTAGE OF THIS TO PULL SOME SHIT TOO, SO STAY ON YOUR TOES.
MR. MATSU-MI?
WAIT A MINUTE, SIR. THERE'S SOMETHING WRONG WITH ALL THIS.
IF YOU NEED WEAPONS, CALL NOMA UP.

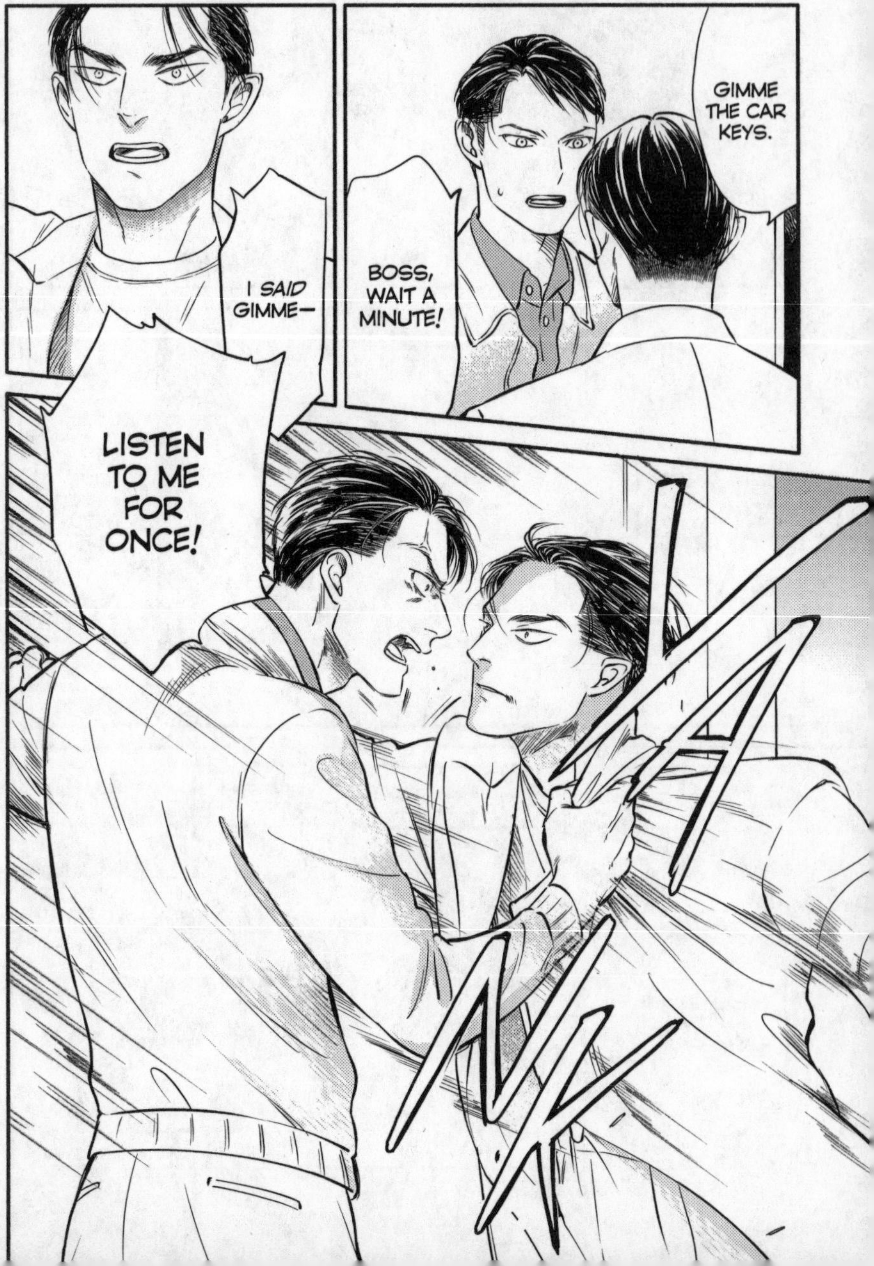
GIMME THE CAR KEYS.
BOSS, WAIT A MINUTE!
I SAID GIMME—
LISTEN TO ME FOR ONCE!

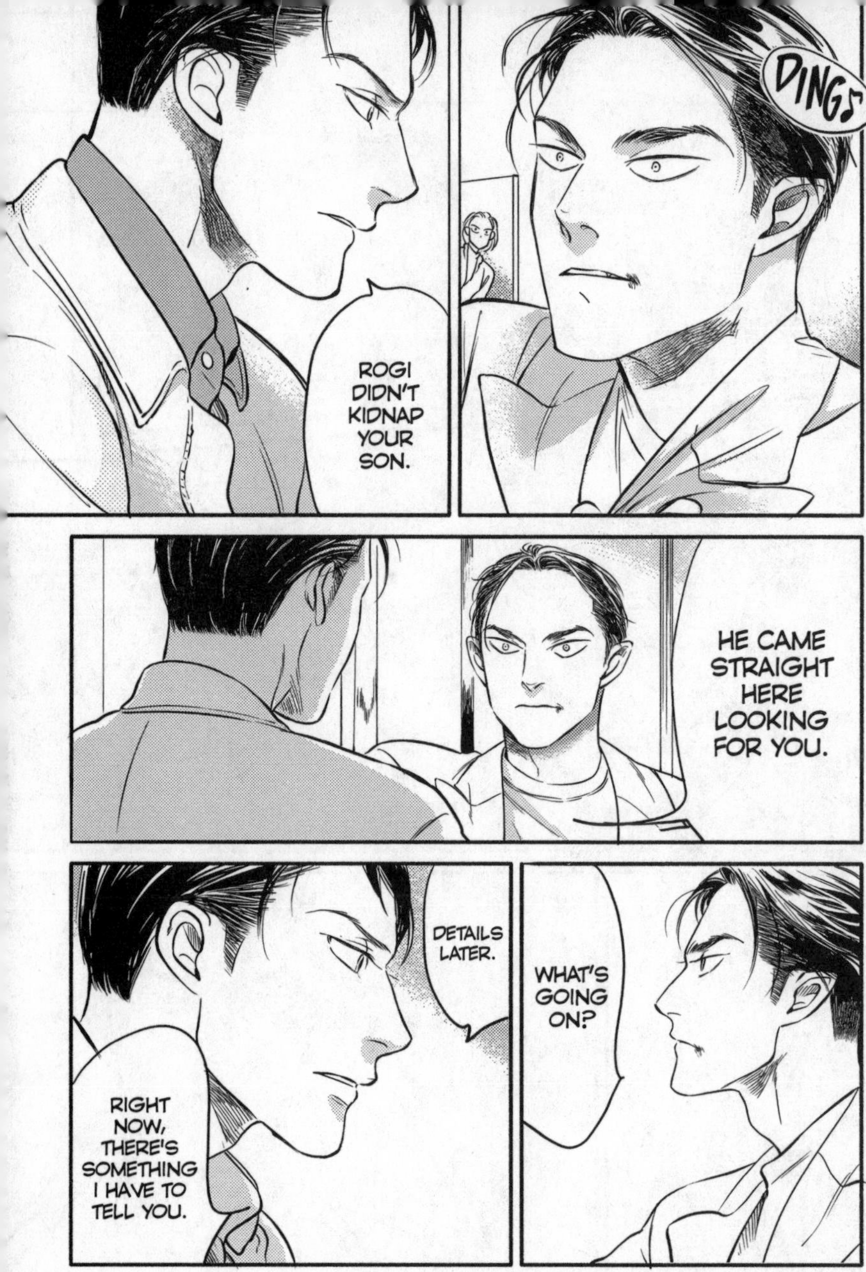
DINGS♪
ROGI DIDN'T KIDNAP YOUR SON.
HE CAME STRAIGHT HERE LOOKING FOR YOU.
WHAT'S GOING ON?
DETAILS LATER.
RIGHT NOW, THERE'S SOMETHING I HAVE TO TELL YOU.

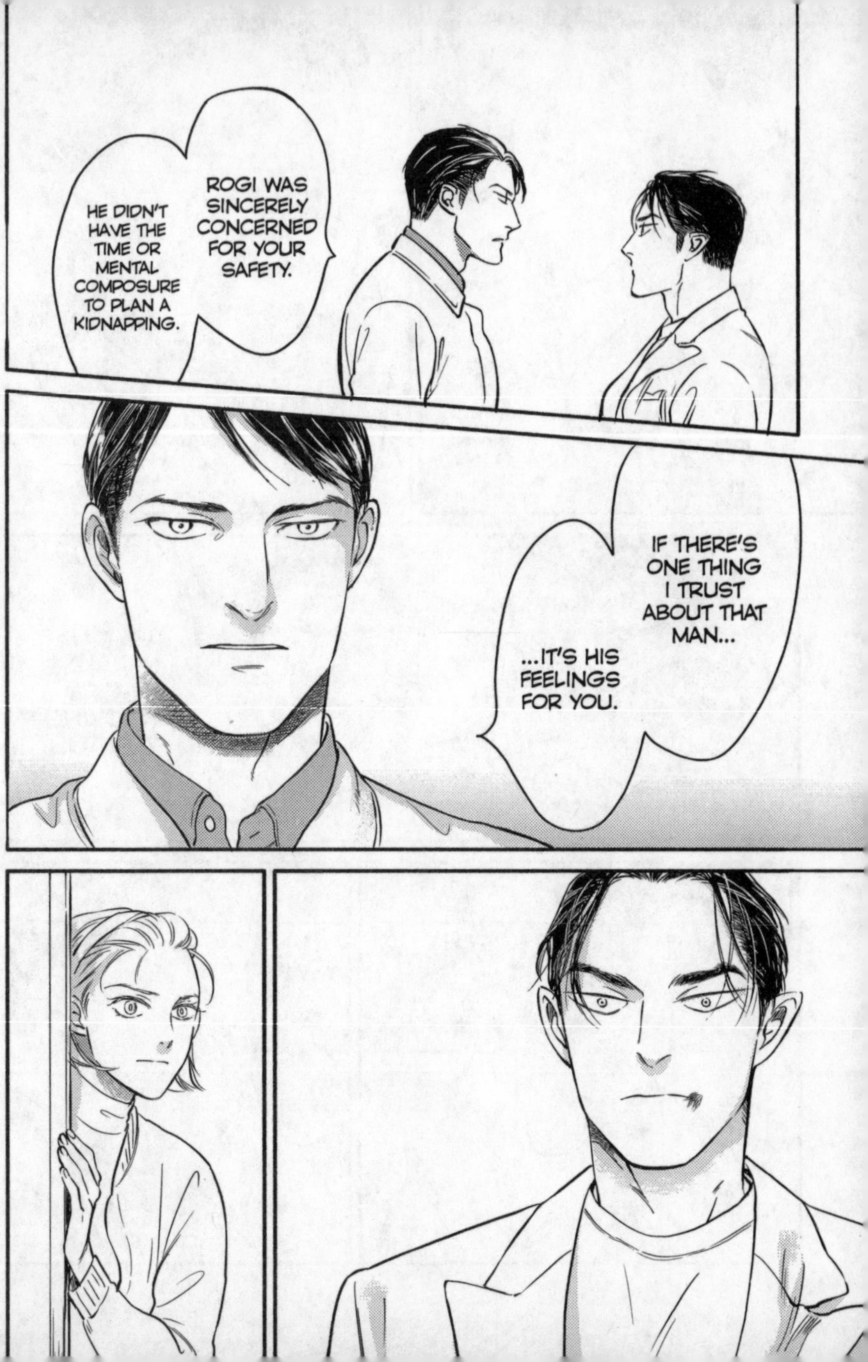
ROGI WAS SINCERELY CONCERNED FOR YOUR SAFETY.
HE DIDN'T HAVE THE TIME OR MENTAL COMPOSURE TO PLAN A KIDNAPPING.
IF THERE'S ONE THING I TRUST ABOUT THAT MAN...
...IT'S HIS FEELINGS FOR YOU.

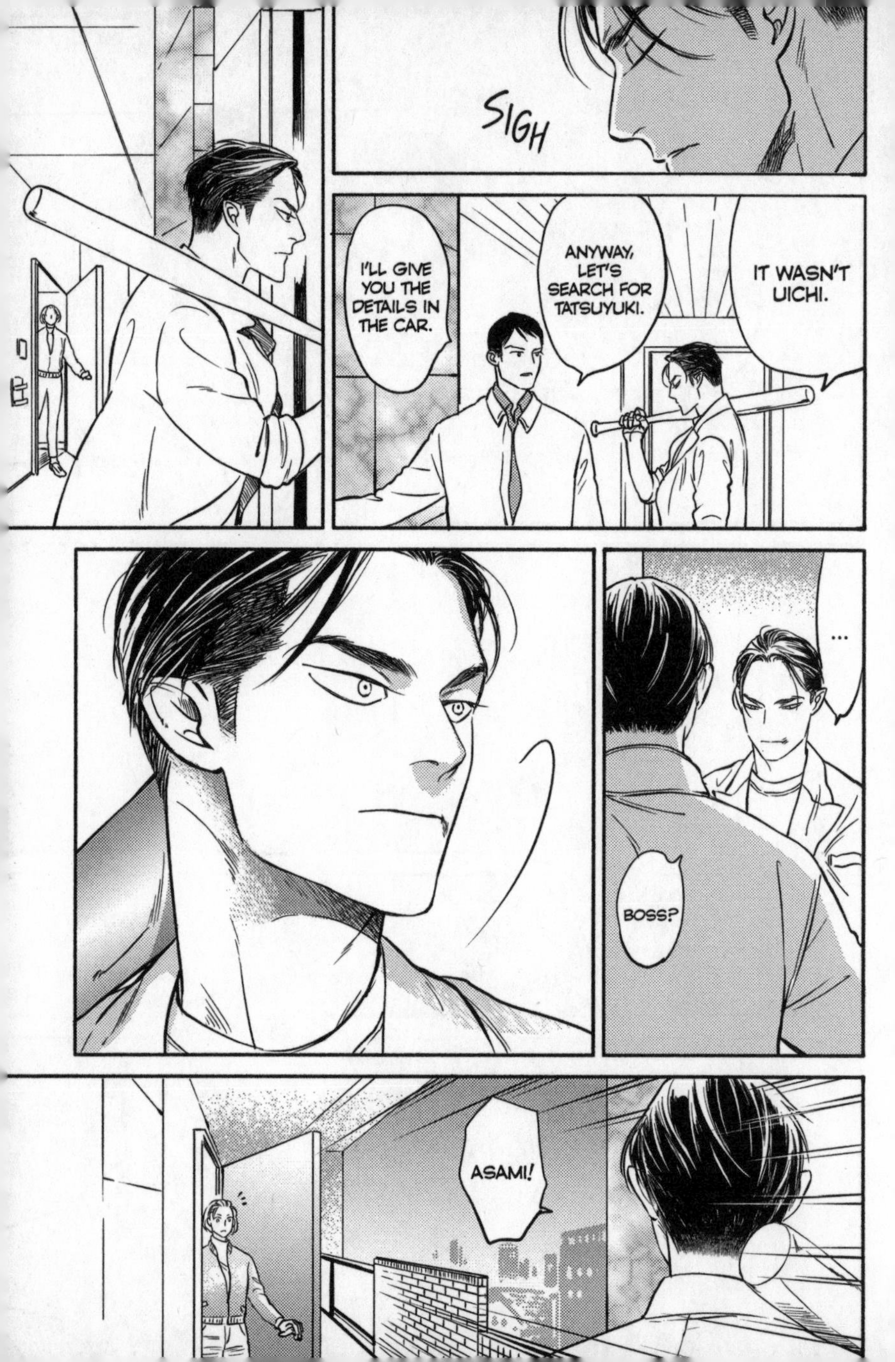
SIGH
IT WASN'T UICHI.
ANYWAY, LET'S SEARCH FOR TATSUYUKI.
I'LL GIVE YOU THE DETAILS IN THE CAR.
...
BOSS?
ASAMI!

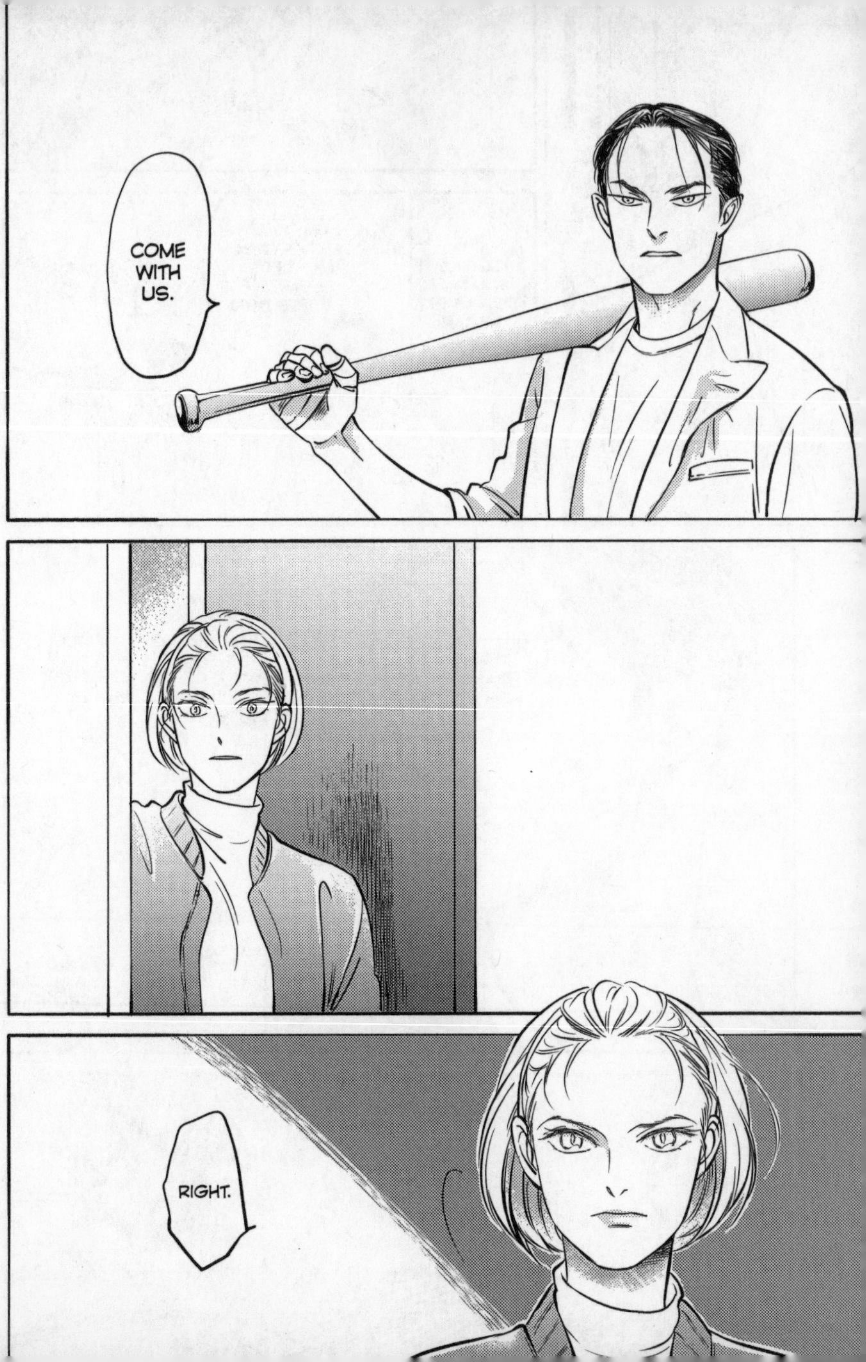
COME WITH US.
RIGHT.

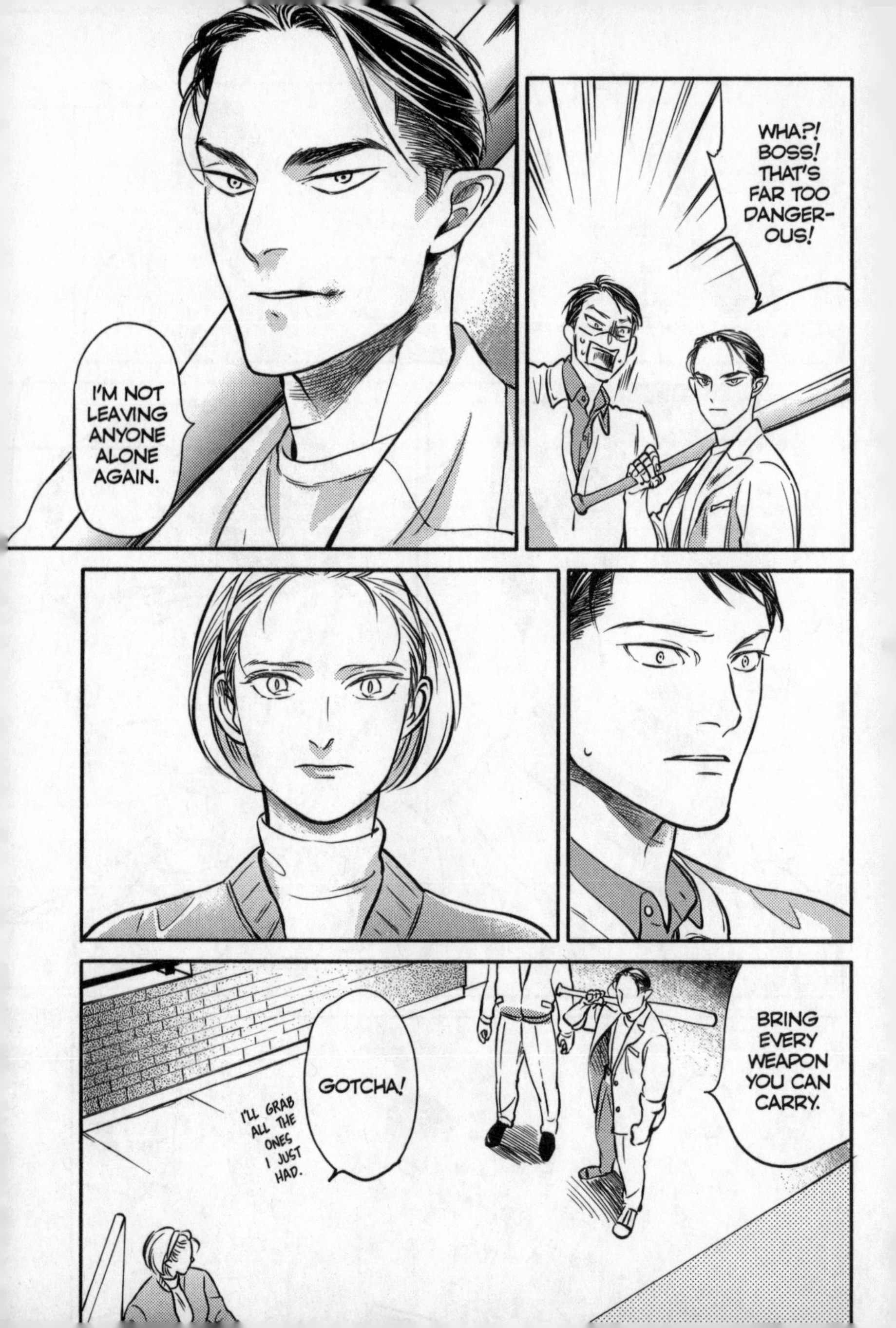
WHA?! BOSS! THAT'S FAR TOO DANGER-OUS!
I'M NOT LEAVING ANYONE ALONE AGAIN.
BRING EVERY WEAPON YOU CAN CARRY.
GOTCHA!
I'LL GRAB ALL THE ONES I JUST HAD.

SHEESH.
WHAT YOU JUST SAID.
BOSS?
ABOUT UICHI.
THANKS.
THAT'S THE FIRST AND LAST TIME I'LL EVER DO THAT, SIR!
"THANKS."
"THANKS."
"THANKS."
"THANKS."
WRINKLE PAT PAT
SURE.

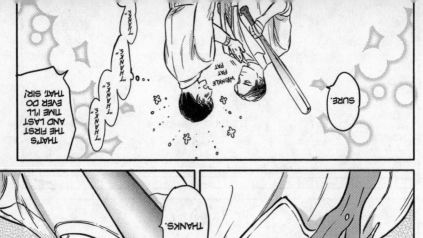

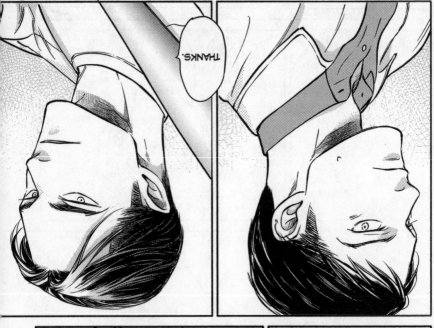

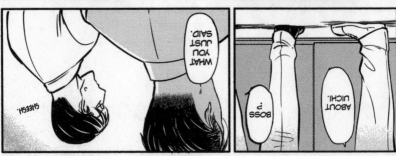

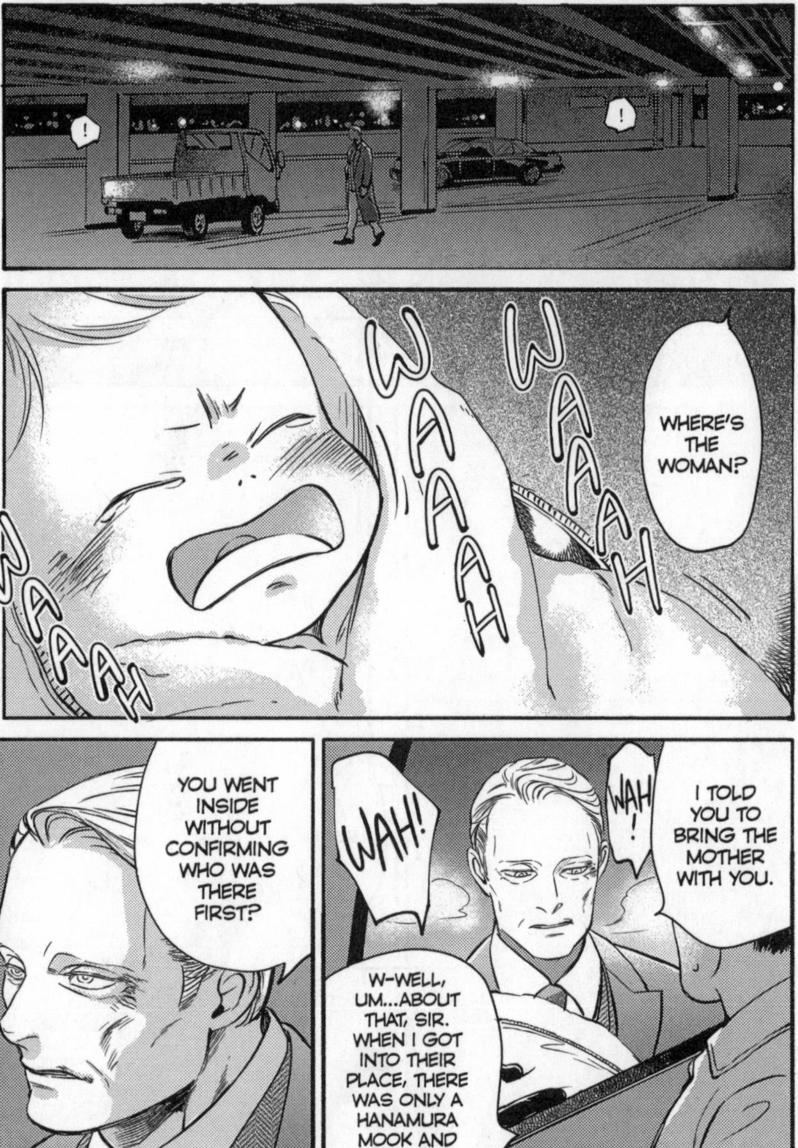
!
!
WHERE'S THE WOMAN?
WAAAAH
WAAAAH
WAAAAH
I TOLD YOU TO BRING THE MOTHER WITH YOU.
WAH!
WAH!
W-WELL, UM...ABOUT THAT, SIR. WHEN I GOT INTO THEIR PLACE, THERE WAS ONLY A HANAMURA MOOK AND THE KID...
YOU WENT INSIDE WITHOUT CONFIRMING WHO WAS THERE FIRST?

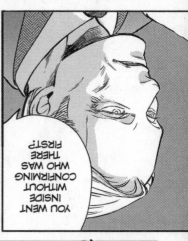

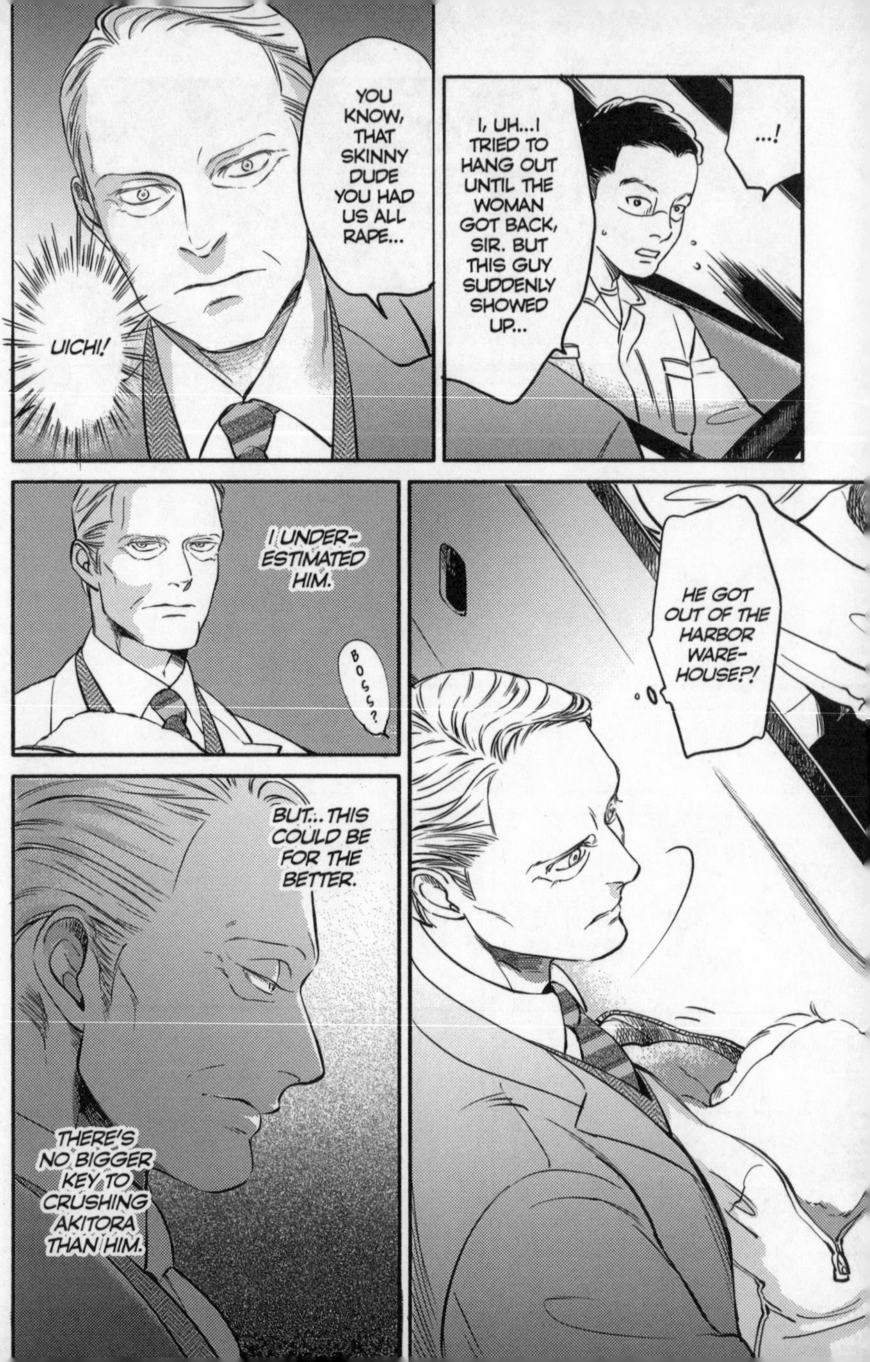
...!
I, UH...I TRIED TO HANG OUT UNTIL THE WOMAN GOT BACK, SIR. BUT THIS GUY SUDDENLY SHOWED UP...
YOU KNOW, THAT SKINNY DUDE YOU HAD US ALL RAPE...
UICHI!
HE GOT OUT OF THE HARBOR WARE-HOUSE?!
I UNDER-ESTIMATED HIM.
BOSS?
BUT...THIS COULD BE FOR THE BETTER.
THERE'S NO BIGGER KEY TO CRUSHING AKITORA THAN HIM.

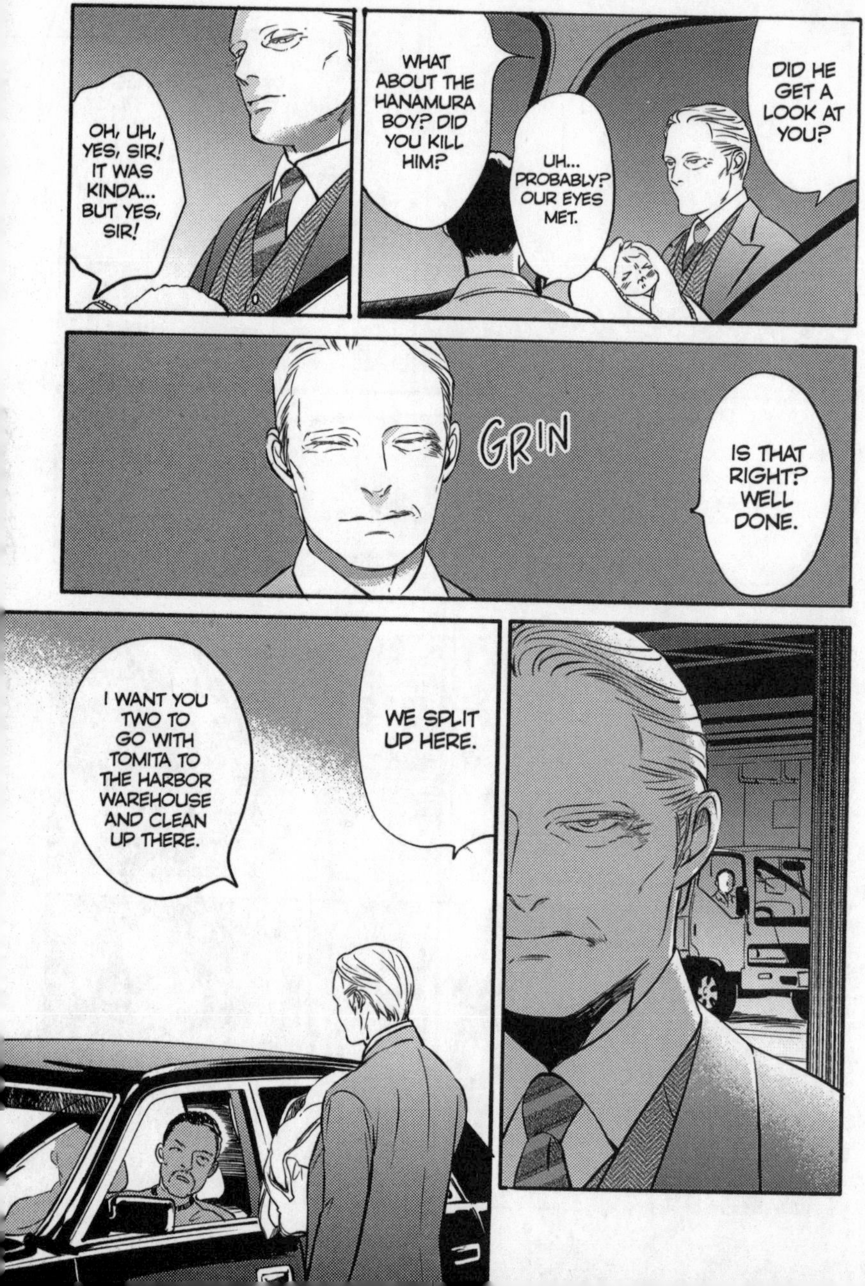
DID HE GET A LOOK AT YOU?
UH... PROBABLY? OUR EYES MET.
WHAT ABOUT THE HANAMURA BOY? DID YOU KILL HIM?
OH, UH, YES, SIR! IT WAS KINDA... BUT YES, SIR!
IS THAT RIGHT? WELL DONE.
GRIN
WE SPLIT UP HERE.
I WANT YOU TWO TO GO WITH TOMITA TO THE HARBOR WAREHOUSE AND CLEAN UP THERE.

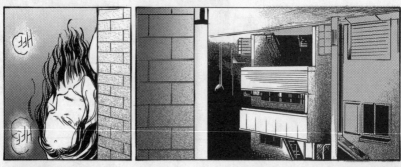

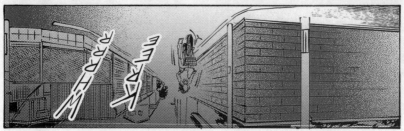

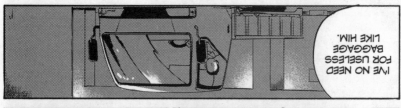

ONCE THAT MESS IS DEALT WITH... GET RID OF TOMITA TOO.
SIR ?!
NOT ONLY DID HE BUNGLE A SIMPLE JOB, HE WOUND UP KILLING A HANAMURA MEMBER.
THIS IS MERELY HIM GETTING HIS JUST DESERTS.
I'VE NO NEED FOR USELESS BAGGAGE LIKE HIM.
WHRRRR
KREE
HFF
HFF

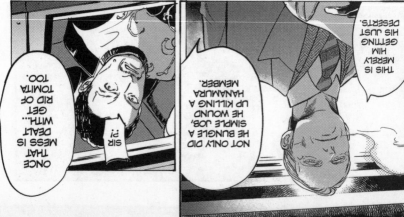

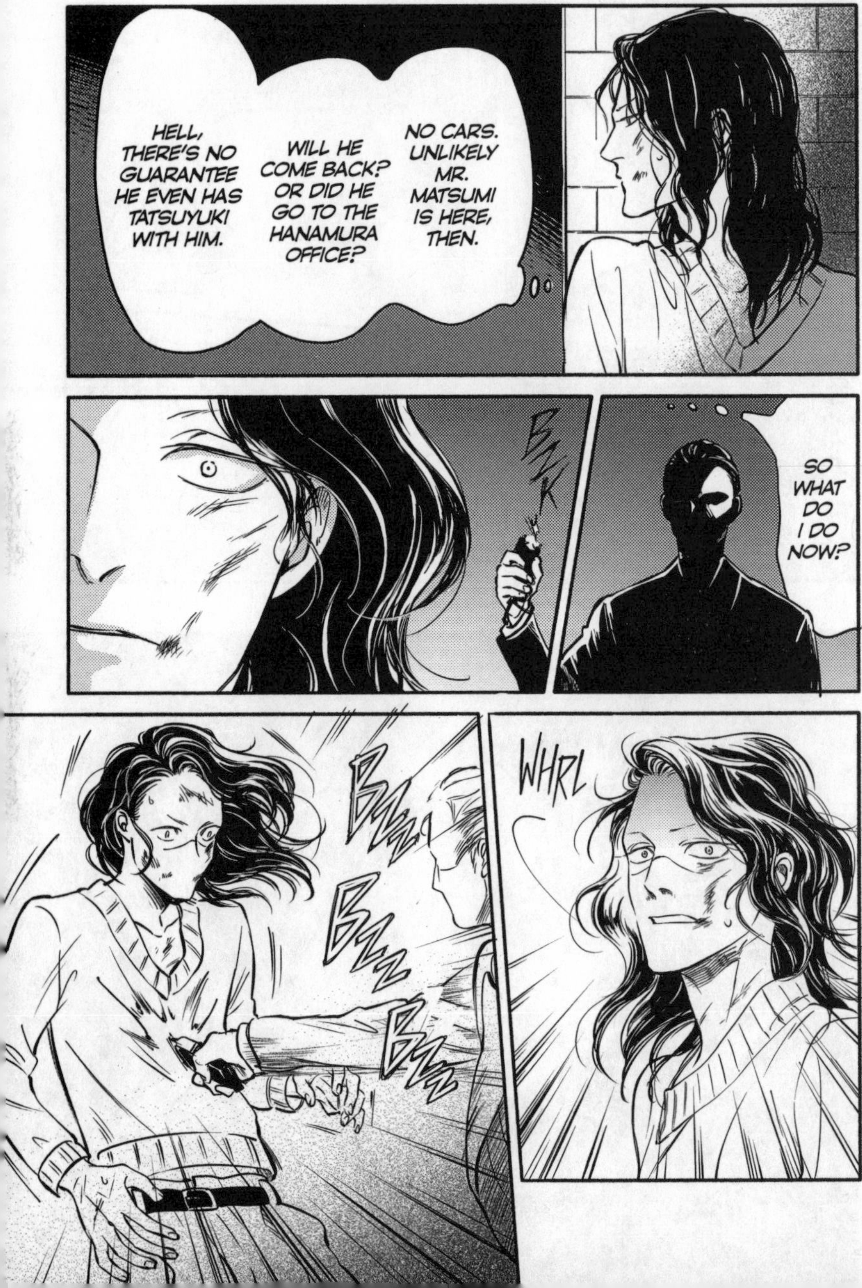
NO CARS. UNLIKELY MR. MATSUMI IS HERE, THEN.
WILL HE COME BACK? OR DID HE GO TO THE HANAMURA OFFICE?
HELL, THERE'S NO GUARANTEE HE EVEN HAS TATSUYUKI WITH HIM.
SO WHAT DO I DO NOW?
WHRL

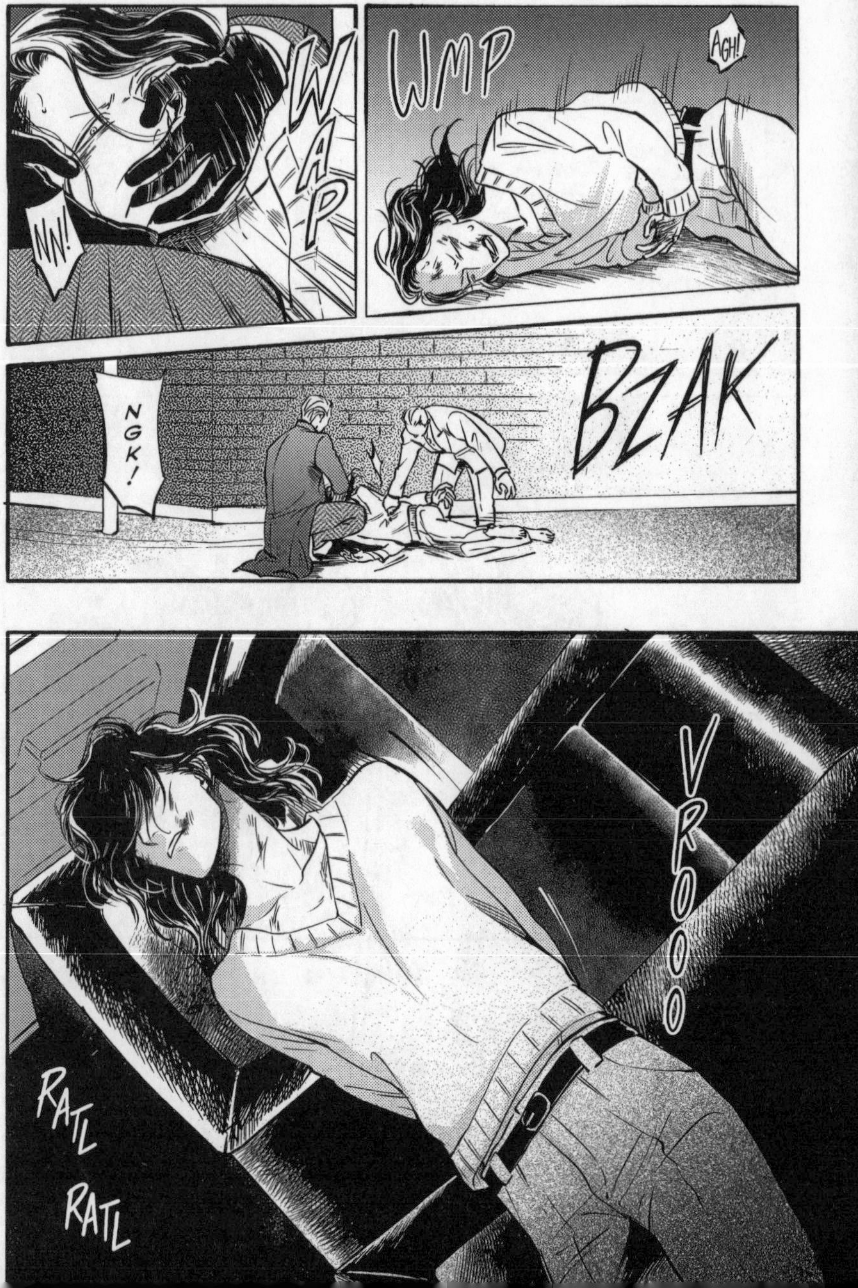
WMP
AGH!
WAP
NN!
BZAK
NGK!
VROOOO
RATL
RATL

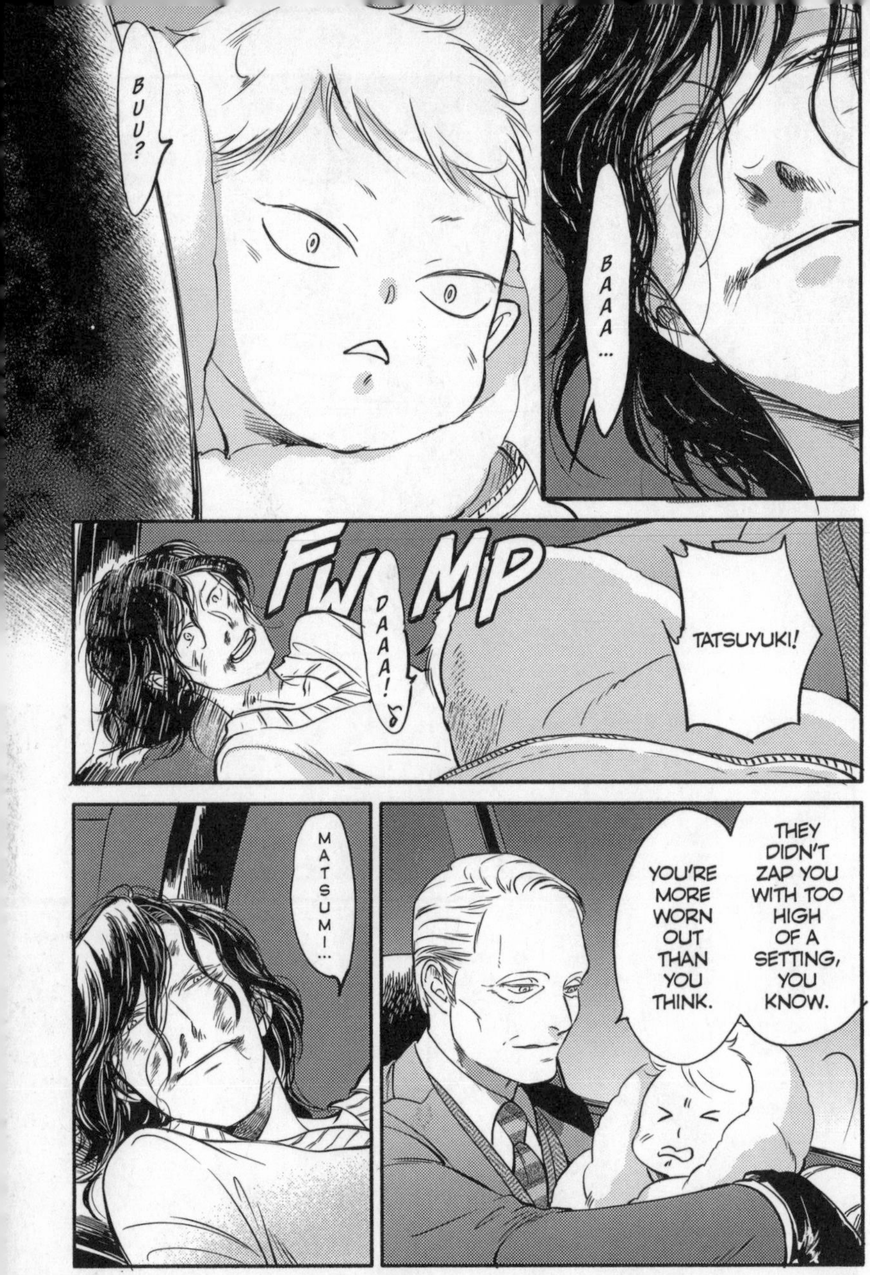
BAAAA...
BUU?
TATSUYUKI!
FWMP
DAAAA! ♪
THEY DIDN'T ZAP YOU WITH TOO HIGH OF A SETTING, YOU KNOW.
YOU'RE MORE WORN OUT THAN YOU THINK.
MATSUMI...

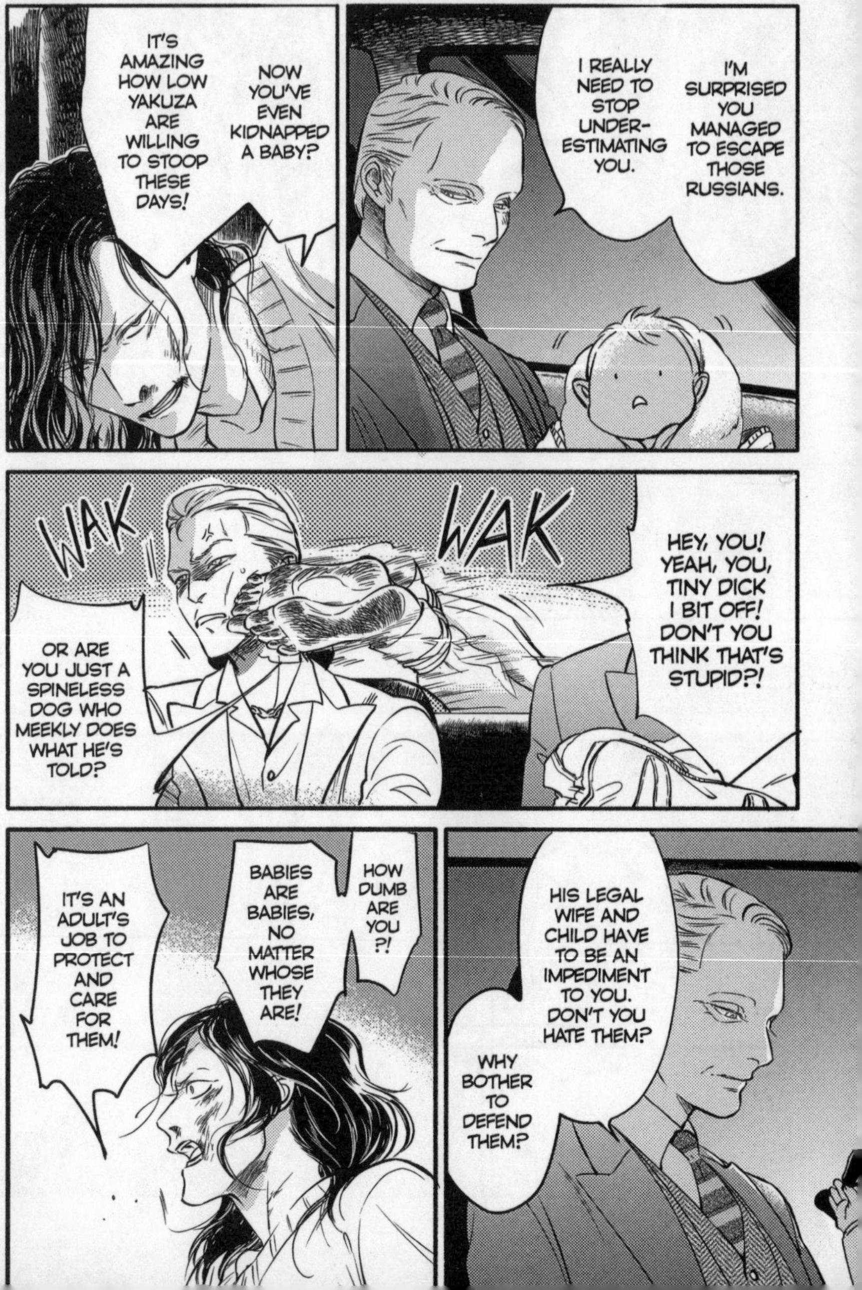
I'M SURPRISED YOU MANAGED TO ESCAPE THOSE RUSSIANS.
I REALLY NEED TO STOP UNDER-ESTIMATING YOU.
NOW YOU'VE EVEN KIDNAPPED A BABY?
IT'S AMAZING HOW LOW YAKUZA ARE WILLING TO STOOP THESE DAYS!
HEY, YOU! YEAH, YOU, TINY DICK I BIT OFF! DON'T YOU THINK THAT'S STUPID?!
WAK
WAK
OR ARE YOU JUST A SPINELESS DOG WHO MEEKLY DOES WHAT HE'S TOLD?
HIS LEGAL WIFE AND CHILD HAVE TO BE AN IMPEDIMENT TO YOU. DON'T YOU HATE THEM?
WHY BOTHER TO DEFEND THEM?
HOW DUMB ARE YOU ?!
BABIES ARE BABIES, NO MATTER WHOSE THEY ARE!
IT'S AN ADULT'S JOB TO PROTECT AND CARE FOR THEM!

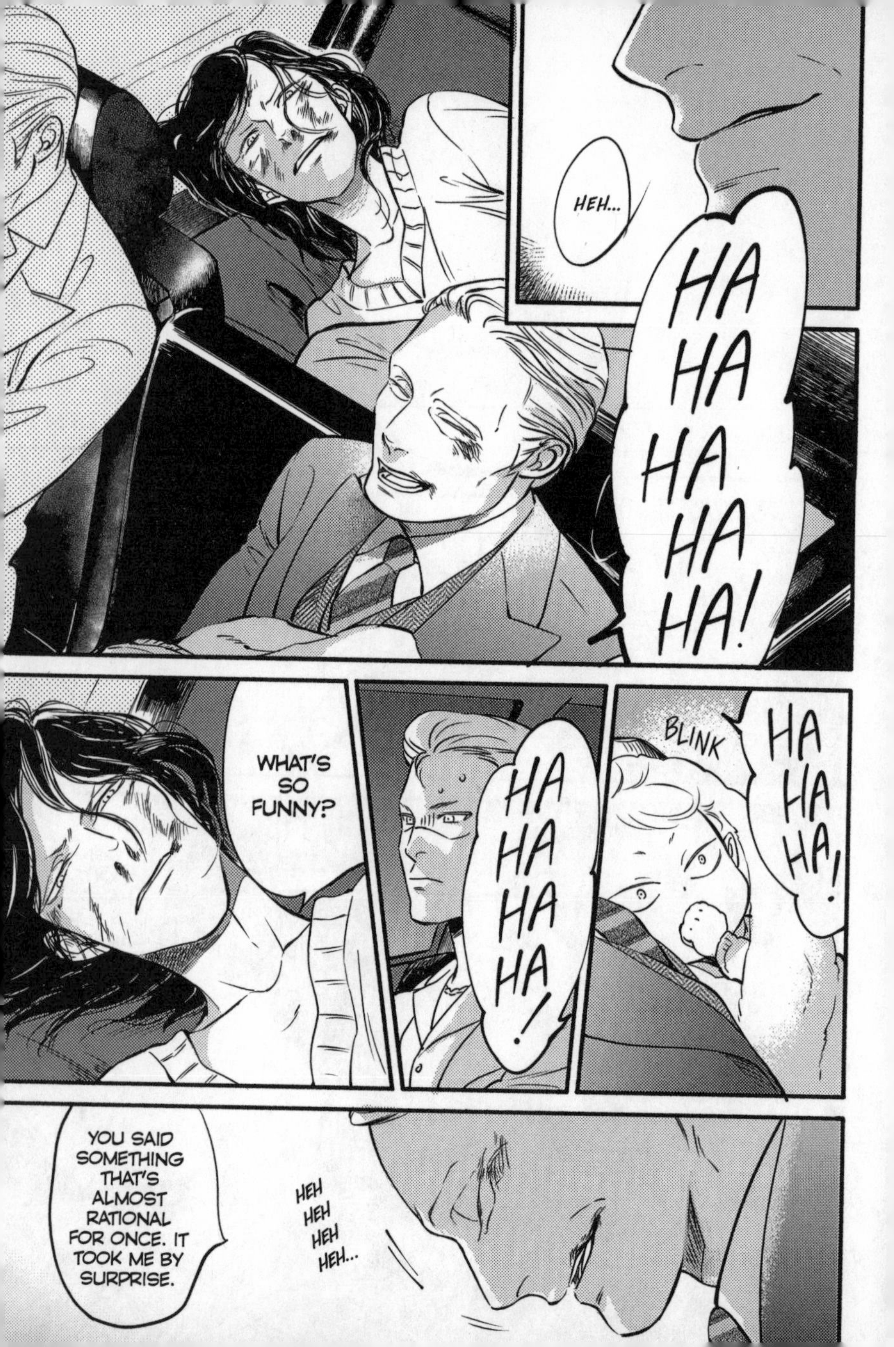
HEH...
HA HA HA HA HA HA!
HA HA HA!
BLINK
HA HA HA HA!
WHAT'S SO FUNNY?
YOU SAID SOMETHING THAT'S ALMOST RATIONAL FOR ONCE. IT TOOK ME BY SURPRISE.
HEH HEH HEH HEH...

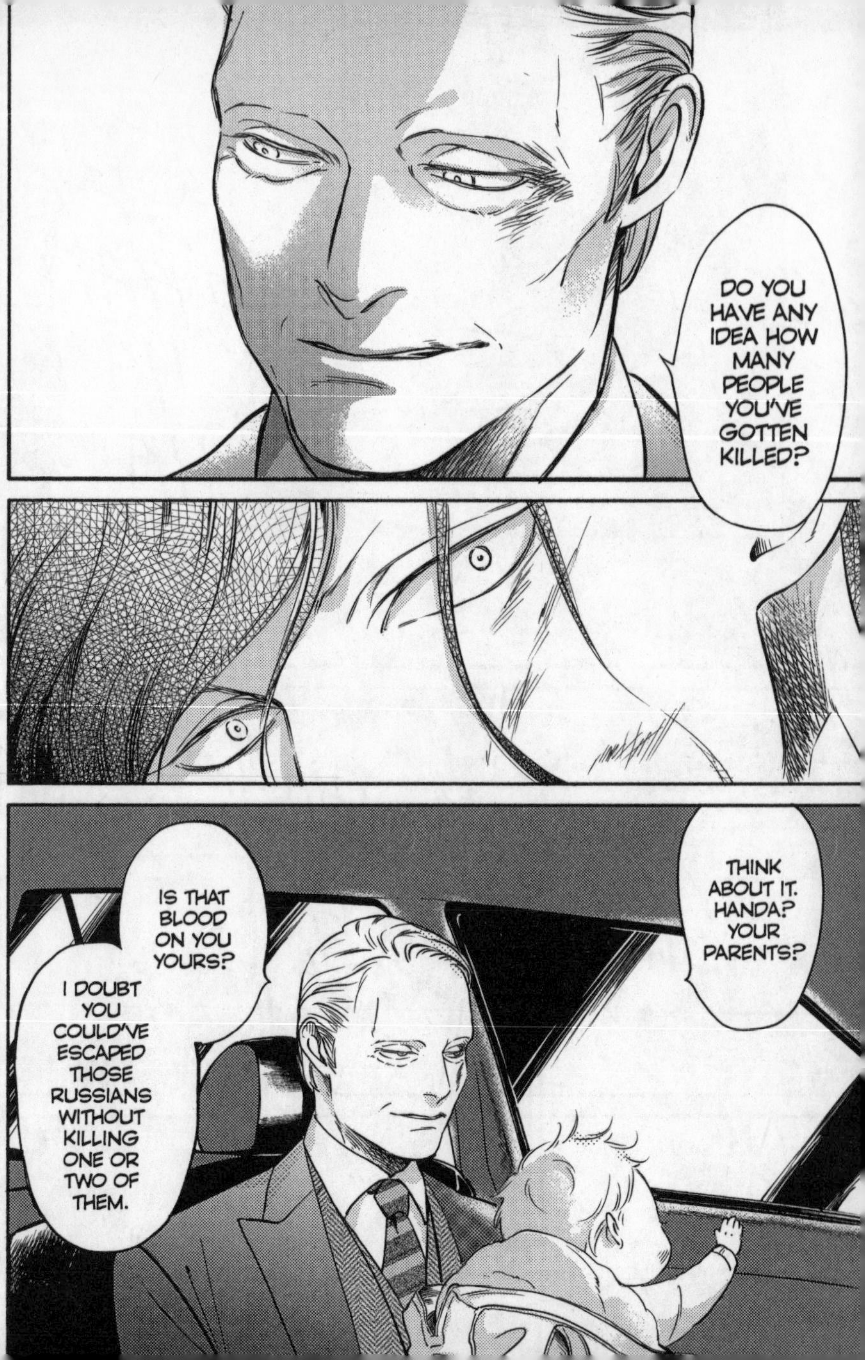
DO YOU HAVE ANY IDEA HOW MANY PEOPLE YOU'VE GOTTEN KILLED?
THINK ABOUT IT. HANDA? YOUR PARENTS?
IS THAT BLOOD ON YOU YOURS?
I DOUBT YOU COULD'VE ESCAPED THOSE RUSSIANS WITHOUT KILLING ONE OR TWO OF THEM.

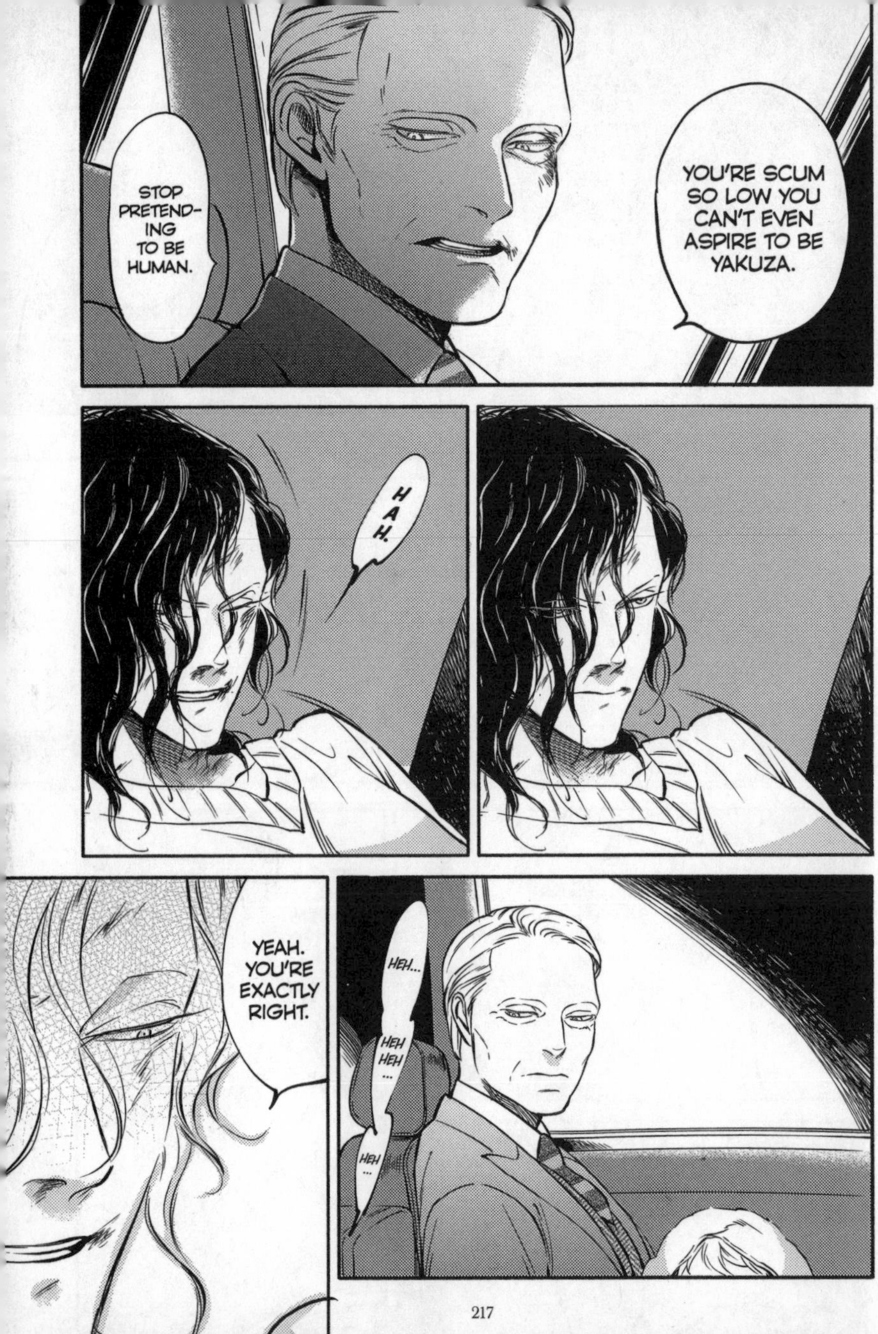
YOU'RE SCUM SO LOW YOU CAN'T EVEN ASPIRE TO BE YAKUZA.
STOP PRETEND-ING TO BE HUMAN.
HAH.
HEH...
HEH HEH ...
HEH ...
YEAH. YOU'RE EXACTLY RIGHT.

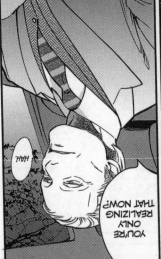

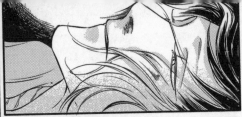

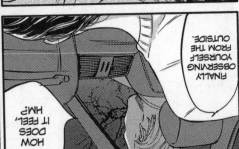

I'M STUPID. A BLIND, IGNORANT MORON.
IT'S SO HILARIOUS TOO. I MEAN, UP UNTIL NOW, I DIDN'T THINK ANY OF IT WAS MY FAULT.
YOU'RE ONLY REALIZING THAT NOW?
HAH.
HOW DOES IT FEEL, HM?
FINALLY OBSERVING YOURSELF FROM THE OUTSIDE.

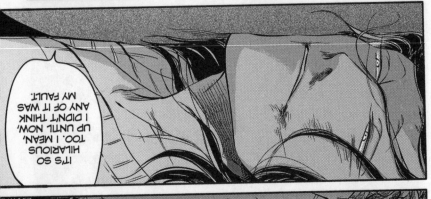

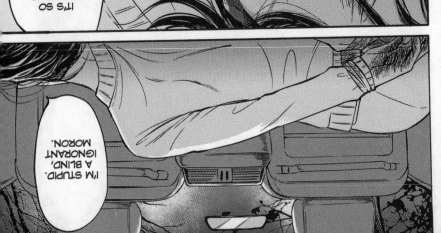

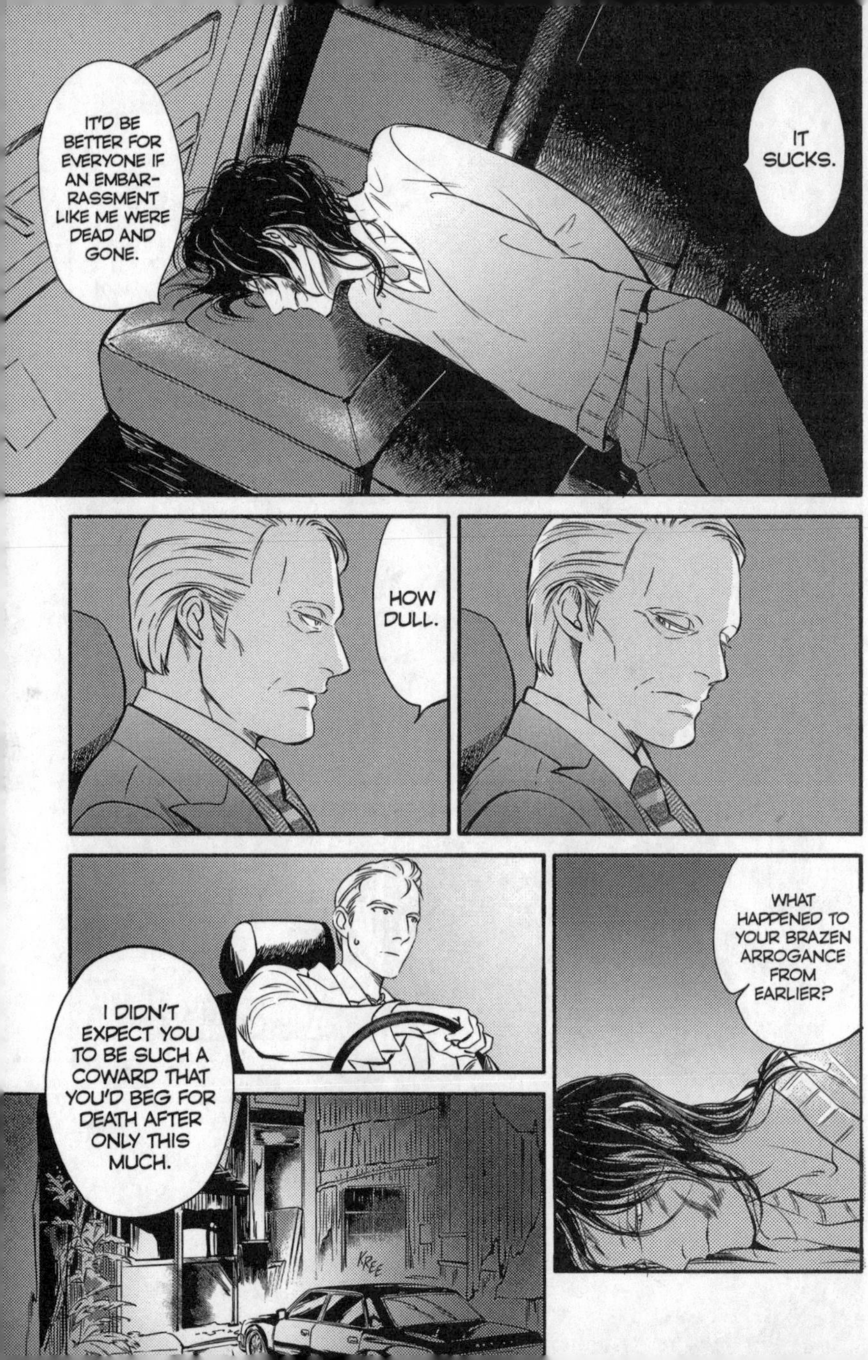
IT SUCKS.
IT'D BE BETTER FOR EVERYONE IF AN EMBAR-RASSMENT LIKE ME WERE DEAD AND GONE.
HOW DULL.
WHAT HAPPENED TO YOUR BRAZEN ARROGANCE FROM EARLIER?
I DIDN'T EXPECT YOU TO BE SUCH A COWARD THAT YOU'D BEG FOR DEATH AFTER ONLY THIS MUCH.
KREE

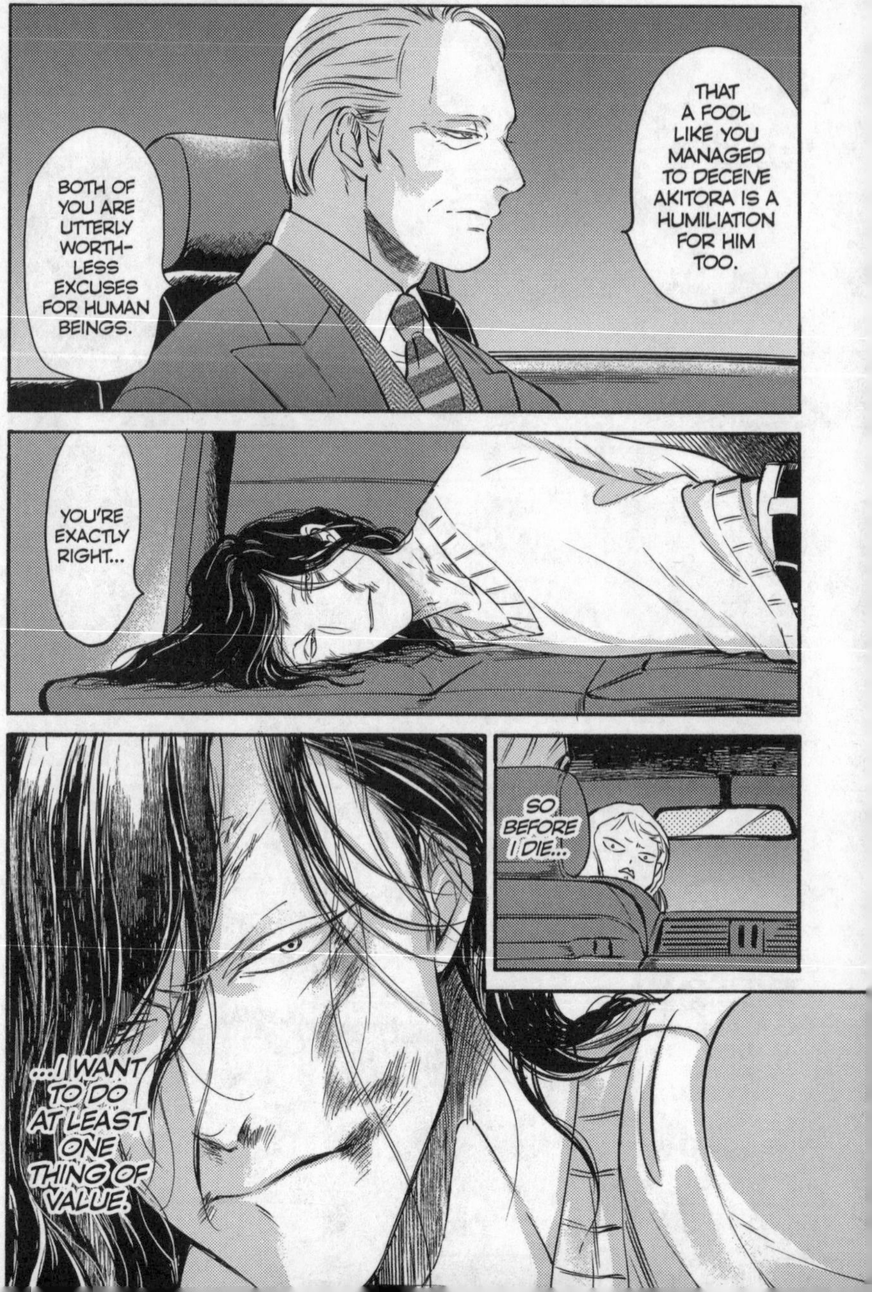
THAT A FOOL LIKE YOU MANAGED TO DECEIVE AKITORA IS A HUMILIATION FOR HIM TOO.
BOTH OF YOU ARE UTTERLY WORTHLESS EXCUSES FOR HUMAN BEINGS.
YOU'RE EXACTLY RIGHT...
SO BEFORE I DIE...
...I WANT TO DO AT LEAST ONE THING OF VALUE.

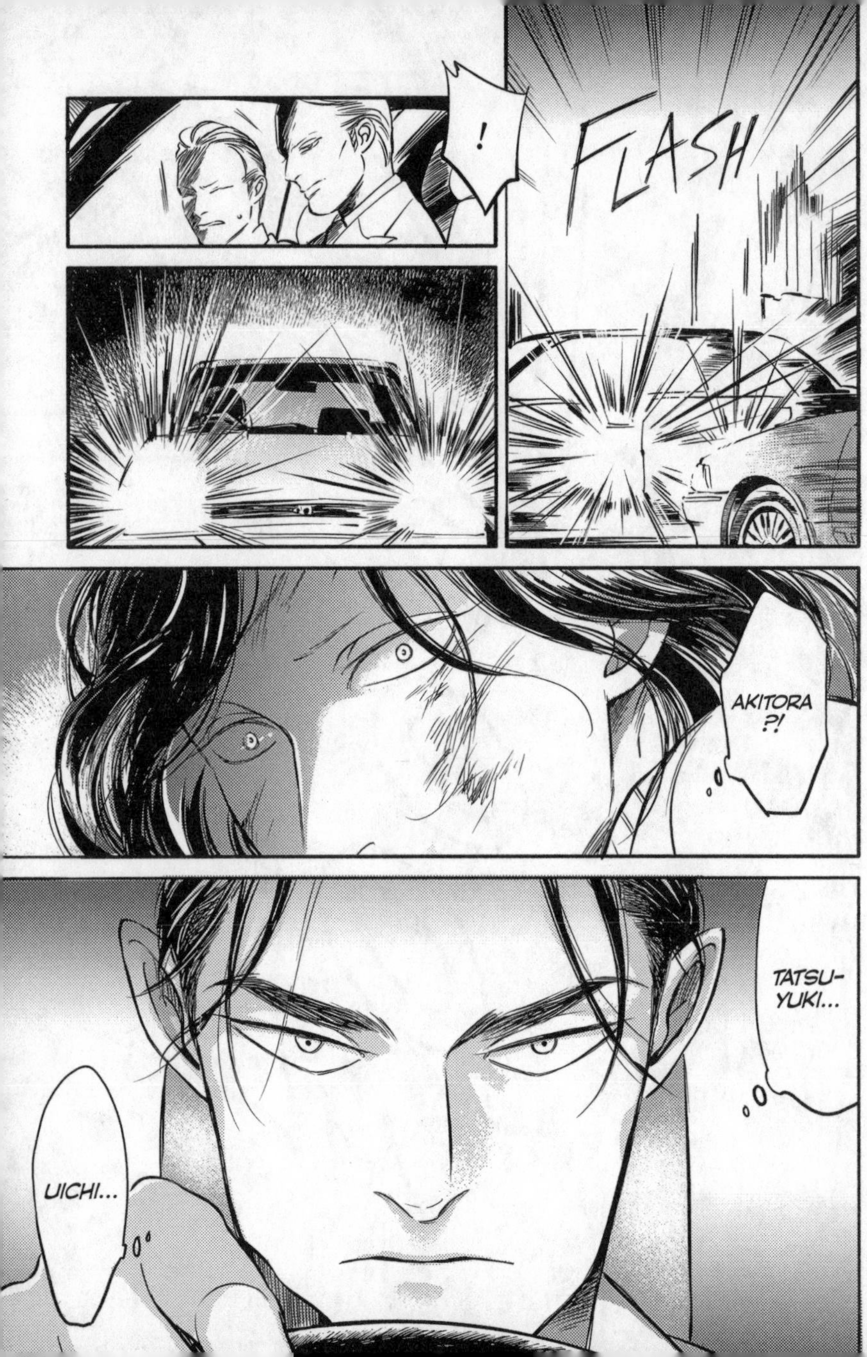
FLASH
!
AKITORA ?!
TATSU-YUKI...
UICHI...

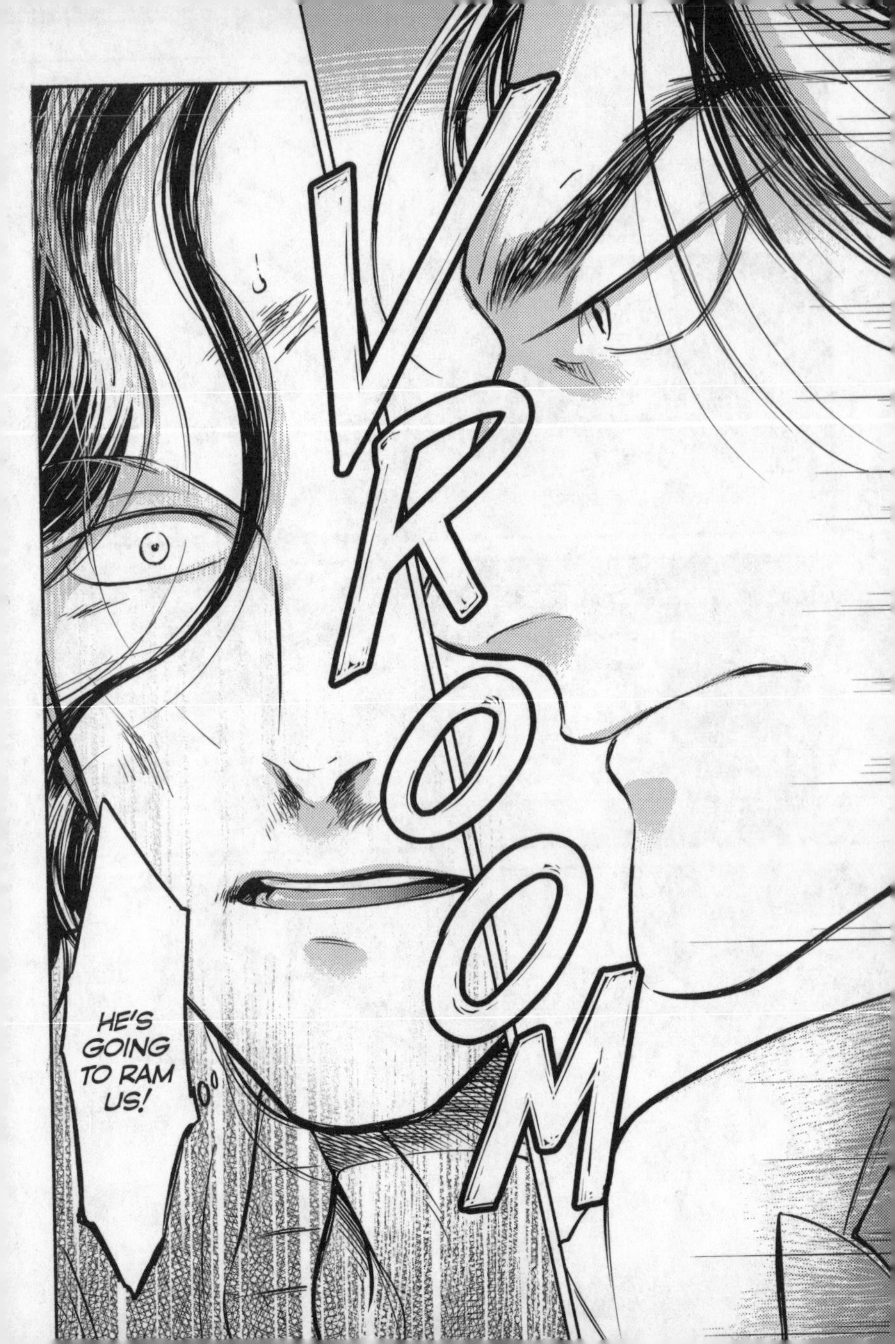
VROOM
HE'S GOING TO RAM US!

COVER BEHIND THE SCENES

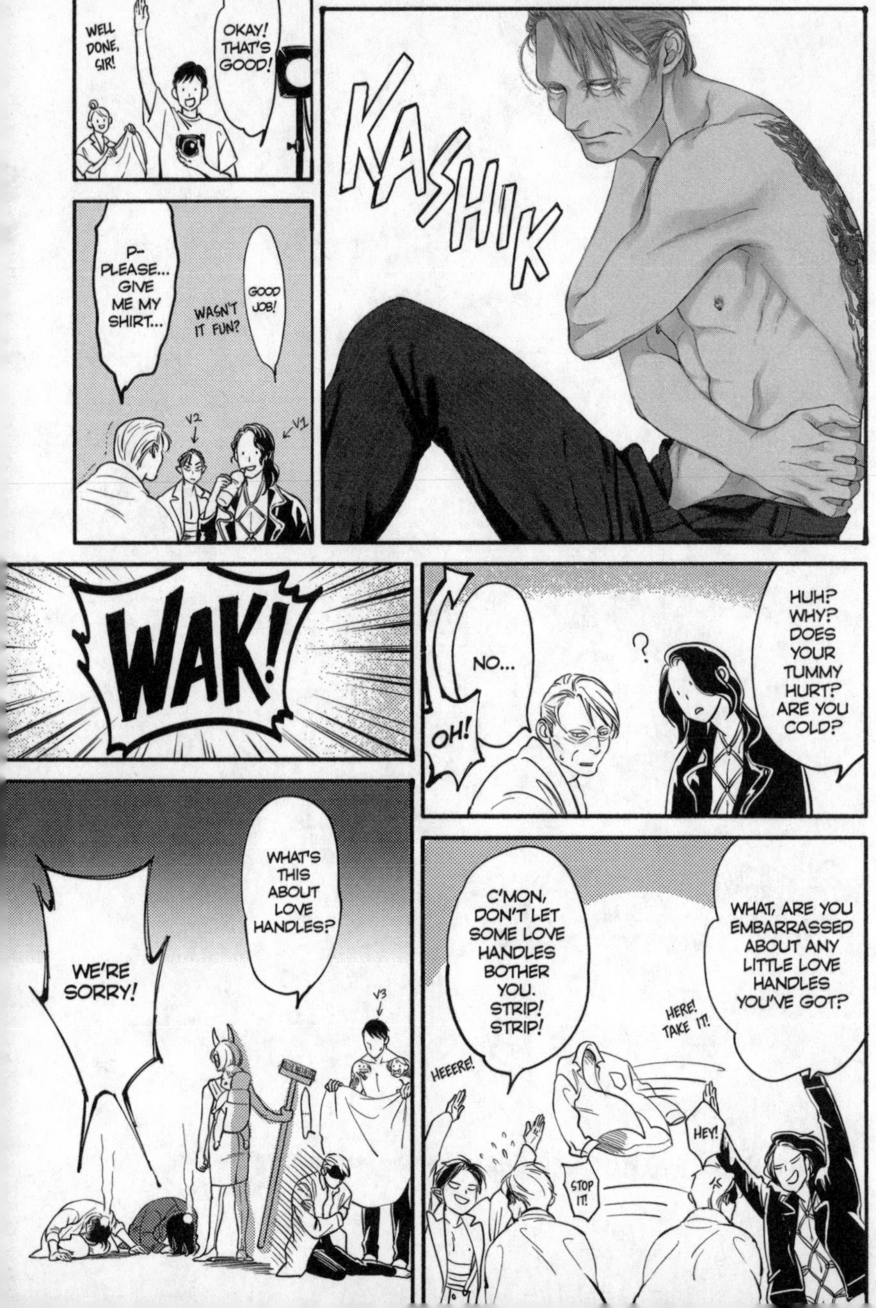
KASHIK
OKAY! THAT'S GOOD!
WELL DONE, SIR!
P-PLEASE... GIVE ME MY SHIRT...
GOOD JOB!
WASN'T IT FUN?
V2
V1
HUH? WHY? DOES YOUR TUMMY HURT? ARE YOU COLD?
NO...
OH!
?
WAK!
WHAT, ARE YOU EMBARRASSED ABOUT ANY LITTLE LOVE HANDLES YOU'VE GOT?
HERE! TAKE IT!
C'MON, DON'T LET SOME LOVE HANDLES BOTHER YOU. STRIP! STRIP!
HEEERE!
HEY!
STOP IT!
WHAT'S THIS ABOUT LOVE HANDLES?
V3
WE'RE SORRY!

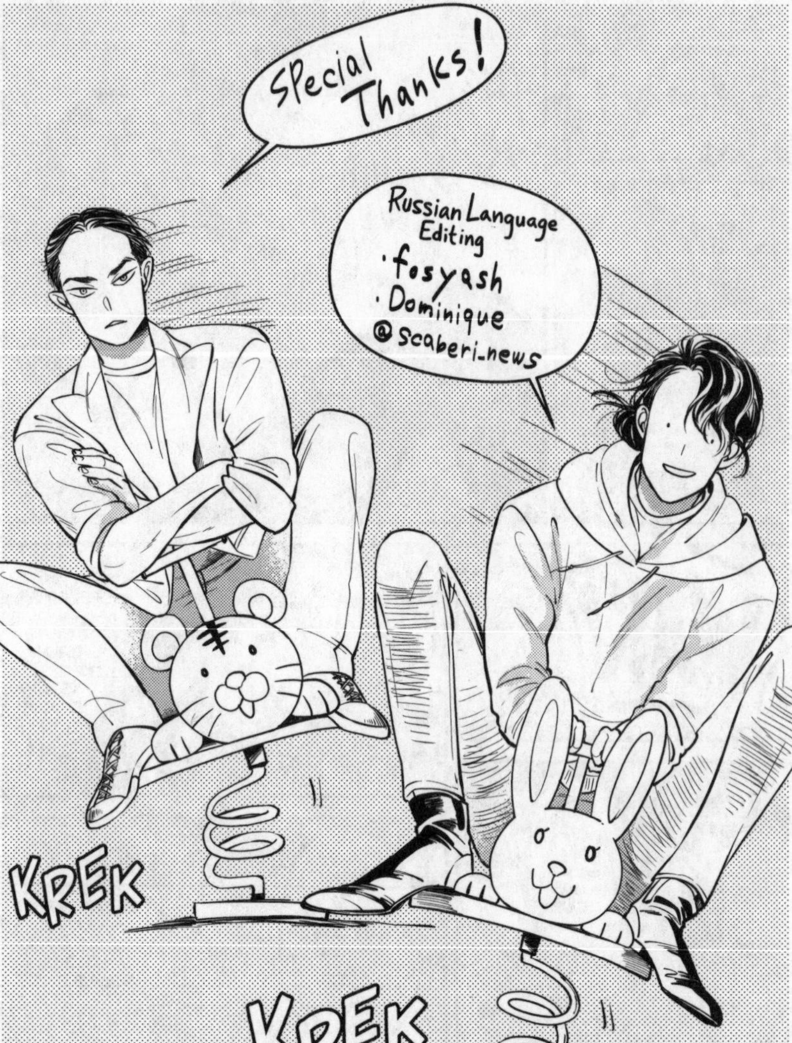
Russian Language Editing ·fosyash ·Dominique @scaberi_news
Special Thanks!
KREK
KREK
Kanzaki Masato and KumaG.